THE FANTASTIC ART OF
RON TURNER

A 1990 original Ron Turner painting inspired by *The Interloper* by Vargo Statten (Scion, 1953); first used as the cover for *The Ghost World* by John Russell Fearn (Gryphon Books, 2005).

THE FANTASTIC ART OF
RON TURNER

JOHN LAWRENCE

First published in England in 2025 by:
Telos Publishing Ltd, 139 Whitstable Road, Canterbury, Kent CT2 8EQ
www.telos.co.uk

Telos Publishing Ltd values feedback. Please e-mail any comments you might have about this book to: feedback@telos.co.uk.

ISBN: 978-1-84583-255-1

The Fantastic Art of Ron Turner © 2025 The Estate of John Lawrence
My Inspiration © 2025 Rod Turner
The Ron Turner I Knew © 2025 Clive Turner
Ron Turner, My Dad © 2025 Dianne Turner
Like Father, Like Son © 2025 Mark Turner
Envoi © 2025 Philip Harbottle
Photographs on pages 8, 16, 22, 24, 25, 26 (top), 28, 29, 218 and 327 © Dianne Turner
Photographs on pages 17 and 18 © Rod Turner
All other photographs © The Estate of John Lawrence
All original Ron Turner artwork © The Estate of Ron Turner
All Fleetway and IPC comics material © Rebellion Publishing Ltd
All copyright contents used with kind permission.

The moral right of the author has been asserted.

Edited by Stephen James Walker.

Design, typesetting and layout by Stephen James Walker.

British Library Cataloguing in Publication Data.
A catalogue record for this book is available from the British Library.

This book is sold subject to the condition that it shall not, by way of trade or otherwise, be lent, resold, hired out or otherwise circulated without the publisher's prior written consent in any form of binding or cover other than that in which it is published and without a similar condition including this condition being imposed on the subsequent purchaser.

PUBLISHERS' NOTE

Shortly after completing his manuscript for this book, the author John Lawrence sadly passed away. Although he never got to see the finished product of all his hard work, we like to think he would have been happy with how it has turned out. We are certainly very pleased and proud to have been able to publish *The Fantastic Art of Ron Turner*, and hope it stands as a fitting tribute to John's memory.

David J Howe and Stephen James Walker, Telos Publishing Ltd

DEDICATION

To Rita, Julie and Angie
and to the memory of Ron Turner

ACKNOWLEDGEMENTS

I would like to thank the following for the help and information they have provided in putting this book together: Clive Turner, Dianne Turner, Rod Turner, Joan Hall, Michael Keenan, Frances Keemer, Philip Harbottle, Edward Holmes, Kevin O'Neill, Bob Paynter, David Hunt, Barrie Tomlinson, Dez Skinn, Angus Allen, Steve Holland and the staff of the British Library. **John Lawrence, 2023**

The publishers would like to record their sincere thanks to John Lawrence's good friend and agent Philip Harbottle; to Rod, Clive, Dianne and Mark Turner; and to John Lawrence's family. Without their generous help and contributions, this book would not have come to fruition. Thanks also to the British Library, and to Martin Baines for suggesting we pursue this idea in the first place. **Telos Publishing Ltd, 2025**

CONTENTS

INTRODUCTION: THE FANTASTIC ART OF RON TURNER 9
    50 YEARS OF FANTASTIC ART by John Lawrence 11
FOREWORD: A FATHER REMEMBERED 15
    MY INSPIRATION by Rod Turner 17
    THE RON TURNER I KNEW by Clive Turner 19
    RON TURNER, MY DAD by Dianne Turner 23
    LIKE FATHER, LIKE SON by Mark Turner 25
PART 1: 1922-1984 27
    CHAPTER 1   SKETCHES OF EARLY LIFE 29
    CHAPTER 2   NEW BEGINNINGS 39
    CHAPTER 3   FROM COVER TO COVER 43
    CHAPTER 4   ODD STRIPS AND TIT-BITS 69
    CHAPTER 5   FURTHER 'ACE' ASSIGNMENTS 85
    CHAPTER 6   RANDOM ELEMENTS 109
    CHAPTER 7   WAR IS HELL! 133
    CHAPTER 8   THE NUMBERS GAME 141
    CHAPTER 9   A YEAR ON SKARO 151
    CHAPTER 10   HIGHS AND LOWS 161
    CHAPTER 11   KIDS' STUFF 165
    CHAPTER 12   BACK TO THE FUTURE 179
    CHAPTER 13   A QUICK BURST OF *SPEED* 191
    CHAPTER 14   A SPORTING CHANCE 197
    CHAPTER 15   NO FORCED ACTION! 205
PART 2: 1984-1998 211
    CHAPTER 16   A QUEST BEGINS 213
    CHAPTER 17   A DREAM IS REALISED 217
    CHAPTER 18   A RETURN TO SF 221
    CHAPTER 19   HAZARDS AHEAD 227
    CHAPTER 20   A GOLDEN OPPORTUNITY 247
    CHAPTER 21   CUT-OUTS AND SETBACKS 257
    CHAPTER 22   ALL THAT GLITTERS 265
    CHAPTER 23   A DALIANCE WITH THE DALEKS 275
    CHAPTER 24   THJUNDERBIRDS ARE GO, AGAIN? 285
    CHAPTER 25   BACK ON FAMILIAR GROUND 297
    CHAPTER 26   CRIME DOES PAY! 305
    CHAPTER 27   A RETURN TO SKARO 319
    CHAPTER 28   CARVING OUT NEW INTERESTS 327
    CHAPTER 29   FAREWELL TO THE MASTER 337
    CHAPTER 30   INTO THE FUTURE 343
CONCLUSION 349
    TRIBUTES 351
    AFTERWORD by John Lawrence 355
BIBLIOGRAPHY 359
    ENVOI by Philip Harbottle 383
    ABOUT THE AUTHOR 384

Ron Turner (3 August 1922 – 19 December 1998)

INTRODUCTION:
THE FANTASTIC ART OF RON TURNER

A 1985 unlettered recreation by Turner of his cover for *The Renegade Star* by Vargo Statten (Scion, 1952).

INTRODUCTION

50 YEARS OF FANTASTIC ART
by John Lawrence

When Ron Turner died in 1998, British SF illustration lost one of its guiding lights, for Ron was one of a rare breed that included Frank Hampson, Frank Bellamy and Ron Embleton – artists who had made an incredible impact on post-war comic-strip illustration and whose comic-strip and book cover artwork has inspired and continues to influence many others today. But, for me, as a collector and admirer of his work for more than 65 years, Ron Turner was the finest. When lesser artists were drawing spacecraft that looked like cigar tubes with fins, Ron's were of the most complex designs, yet amazingly detailed and realistically rendered. And when the limits of others extended to nothing more than antennae-waggling Martians, Ron was eagerly introducing us to some really bizarre, yet totally believable, alien beings from the other side of the galaxy. Truly, two words sum up his work: 'creative' and 'realistic'. Most artists might be capable of one or the other of these qualities, but Ron could achieve both, and in abundance.

My interest in Ron Turner – some might call it an obsession – really began in 1957, when I discovered one of his now legendary *Rick Random* comic books. I remember well, as a 12-year old schoolboy, browsing through the latest comics in my local newsagent on a Saturday morning, coming across one called *The Time Travellers*. But as I looked inside, I was completely blown away, for the quality of the artwork was far superior to that of the cover (by another hand), not only for the convincing detail, but for the incredible imagination behind it. Having been a *Dan Dare* fan for many years, I'd believed that only Frank Hampson could achieve work of this standard in delivering both of these qualities to an SF strip, yet here was someone who could produce, in my opinion, something equally as good. Then I also recognised from the style that I had seen this artist's work before, in an earlier publication called *Lone Star Magazine*; but at that time it had been not as detailed or as polished. Whoever the artist was, his work had since improved immensely.

Above: the title page of the Ron Turner-illustrated *Rick Random* strip story *The Time Travellers* (aka *The Mystery of the Time Travellers*), which formed Number 97 in the Amalgamated Press's Super-Detective Library, published on 7 February 1957.

From then on, I was totally hooked and sought out every copy of *Rick Random* as it was published by the Amalgamated Press in their series of 64-page Super-Detective Library publications. I soon realised that here was another of the few British comic artists, like Frank Hampson, to adopt a 'designer' look, creating not only spacecraft and aliens, but architecture, machines, uniforms and everything else to present a convincing impression of futuristic worlds. To my younger self, it was almost as if the artist had the ability to see into the future or view a parallel universe where these things might actually exist! I was also impressed by the clean, uncluttered style; there was no confusion in the presentation, and a thoughtful emphasis on perspective gave each scene an effective depth of vision. Also, the method of juxtaposing large areas of white against deep shadow to produce a high contrast effect (known as *chiaroscuro*) was quite unique in comic strips, and the lack of virtually any tonal qualities, such as cross-hatching (which I always felt spoilt the illusion, no matter how accomplished the art), gave his work a realistic, almost three-dimensional appearance.

He then seemed to drop out of sight for a few years, and I assumed that he must have retired. But then, in 1966, there he was again, illustrating *The Daleks* for *TV Century 21* in full colour, where I relished his beautifully-rendered treatment of incredible machines, fantastic monsters and sleekly-designed spacecraft in his inimitable style. The high-contrast effect of his black-and-white work was now replaced by vibrant, carefully chosen colours that perfectly contrasted with or complemented one another, both within each frame and within the page as a whole. I also loved the way he had abandoned the old idea of standard box-like frames in favour of a more open style, where panels merged and borders were eliminated – the subjects forming their own frames, from which beautifully-designed spacecraft fairly leapt off the page.

Next, he was producing strips based on all the Gerry Anderson shows, particularly *Thunderbirds* and *Captain Scarlet* for annuals and specials, and later, a short period on *Star Trek*. But then I lost track of him again, until, in 1977, *2000 AD* appeared.

In *2000 AD*'s ninth issue, there he was again, illustrating *Judge Dredd*. Where had he been in the meantime? At that point, I was still unaware of the artist's identity, but it was the time when comic marts were in full swing, and through meetings with various collectors, dealers and other aficionados, I was finally able to confirm his name. I was also able to discover other examples of Ron's work of which previously I had been unaware, such as the 64-page *Tit-Bits* Science Fiction Comics series that had preceded *Rick Random* in 1953/54. There was also *Space Ace*, a more dynamic version of *Rick Random*, which I realised was the strip I had recalled, hidden away in the Western-themed *Lone Star Magazine* some years before. Attending these marts enabled me eventually to acquire copies of all these 'lost' gems, and being so impressed with them, I felt that amongst all the praise being heaped upon others of his calibre, such as Hampson and Bellamy, this artist had been overlooked. His work fascinated me, but it still left me curious as to who he was and how he could create such incredibly imaginative art. I wanted to know more about the man himself.

In 1978, following his *Judge Dredd* work, *2000 AD* had reprinted a couple of Ron's original *Rick Random* stories and, spurred by their interest, I contacted the staff for more information about the artist. Ironically, as far as background details were concerned, they were equally in the dark. Ron Turner appeared to be a very mysterious character whom no-one had ever met, spoken to or knew anything about. All dealings with him were conducted via his equally mysterious agent, a Mr Hall, who was reluctant to discuss his client, and all attempts at communicating with him direct brought nothing. All this mystery served only to intrigue me further, and I asked to be put in touch with Hall. I was told I'd be wasting my time; and this proved to be correct, as Hall initially snubbed my requests for any information about Ron, citing that he was a very private person and had no inclination to meet fans, not even the most dedicated, like me.

But although many attempts made over the years to contact Ron, both by editors and by fans, had been met by Hall's seemingly impenetrable wall of silence, I nevertheless, against all the odds, finally managed to break through that wall. How I achieved it and was able to track Ron down, become his friend, colleague and eventual working partner, is related in Part 2 of this book. During those years, I got to know Ron very well, and despite him being a very private person, he revealed to me a great deal about his life and work, which is detailed in Part 1.

Ron Turner has left behind a marvellous legacy of unique and inspirational comic-strip and book cover artwork. The majority of this is probably already known to the general collector. However, in order to present a fuller account of his life and work, I have spent the years since his death, researching some of his more obscure yet nonetheless significant contributions and gaining a deeper insight into the man himself, provided by family members and others. I'm therefore now pleased to be able to pay Ron Turner the tribute he so truly deserves, with this volume – a book that clearly shows *50 Years of Fantastic Art*.

John Lawrence, Dunstable, 2023

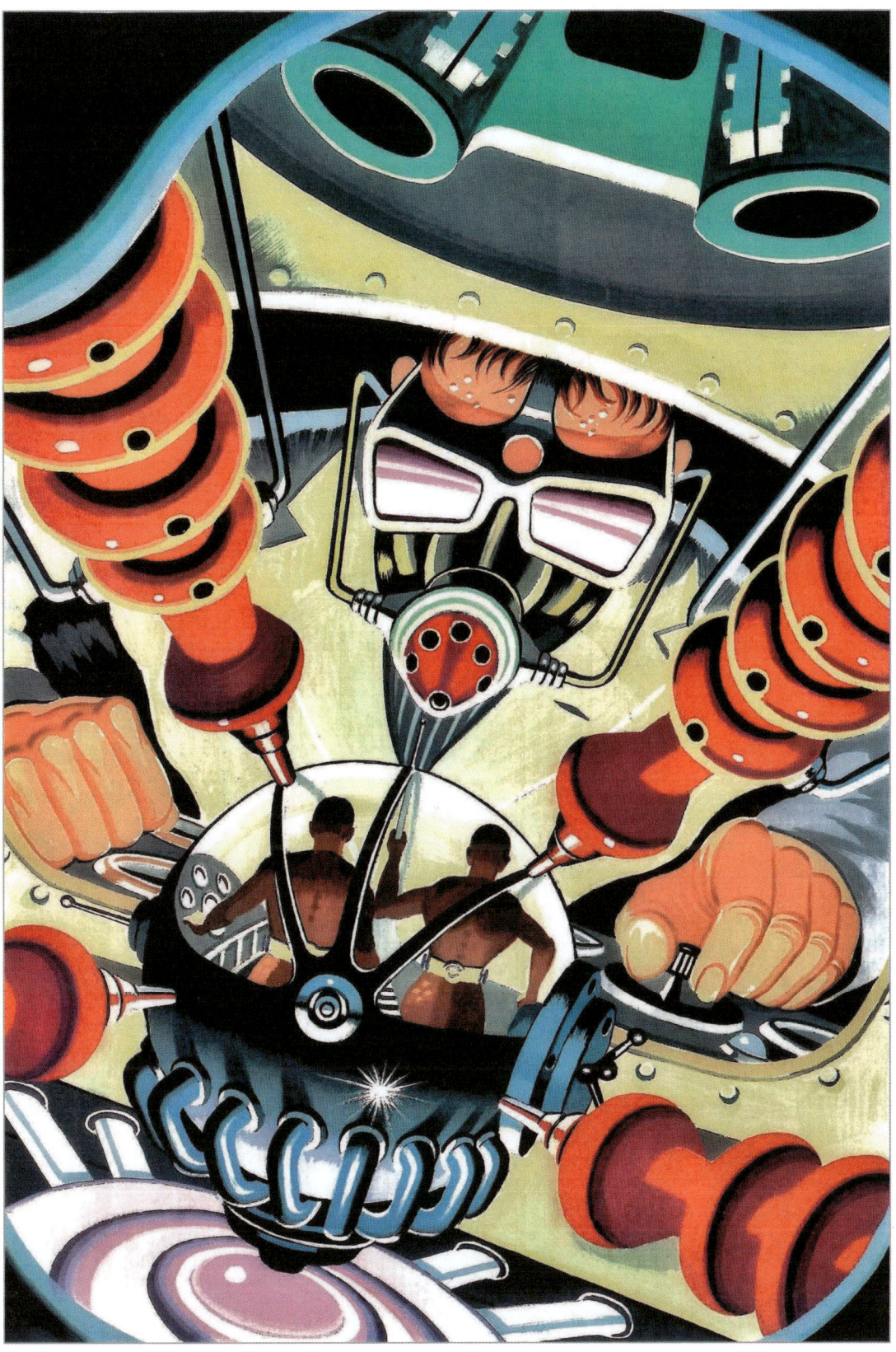

A 1994 unlettered recreation by Turner of his cover for *The Micro Men* by Vargo Statten (Scion, 1950).

A 1985 recreation by Turner of his cover for *The Petrified Planet* by Vargo Statten (Scion, 1951).

FOREWORD:
A FATHER REMEMBERED

Ron Turner, the family man, pictured in 1966 with his daughter Dianne and sons Rodney, Clive and – held in the arms of his then wife Ruby – baby Mark.

MY INSPIRATION
by Rod Turner

Dad inspired me to design.

I have photos of him in my office and workshop along with some of his prolific artwork hanging on the walls as a daily reminder of him and how much I miss him.

When I was a rebellious teenager creating show-winning custom motorcycles, he added his artwork to the petrol tanks. When I started my own company, designing, building and installing television studios around the world, he produced the artwork for the covers of the product catalogues. When I built my first sports car, it took him back to when he built his. And now I sense him looking on while I design drones.

Amongst his effects was an artist's folder, full of sketches, that now sits in my office. The desk-light that illuminated every piece of art he produced, sits in the workshop, along with his trays of inks, airbrushes and pencils, as he must have tidied them up for the last time. They are as he left them.

He missed my birthday one year, and hurriedly made a birthday card out of a scrap piece of fashion board. On it he drew a picture of me on one of my motorbikes, and under it he wrote, 'Present to Follow!' No present followed, but that card is another cherished object that sits in a drawer of a tool cabinet I bought with the money he left us when he died. I've had that card 51 years. That is what Dad means to me.

So many stories about him, you could fill a book.

Diving into the Thames to save a child he knew couldn't swim.

Bringing one of my motorbikes into the downstairs bedroom to help me repair it, then starting it up.

Then there was the time Mother asked him to

Below left: the petrol tank of Rod Turner's 'Resurrection' motorbike is adorned with his father's artwork. Below right: a tray of the artist's materials, exactly as he left it; and the 'Present to Follow!' birthday card that Rod received from him one year.

This page: Ron Turner's artwork used on advertising materials for his son Rod's former company R & R, and (bottom left) current company, drone manufacturers Red Tail.

wallpaper the lounge while she was at work. Having taken the old wallpaper down to reveal a dark blue painted wall beneath, he trotted off to the garage, came back with a pot of white paint and spent an hour or so creating a huge mural of a ski resort, with skiers, cable cars, mountains and falling snow. He stood back, took a look at it, then wallpapered over it. Mother never had any idea what was under that newly-applied wallpaper.

Mother would knit a new jumper for Dad, and within a day of him wearing it, he would appear at the dining-room table with a multicoloured crust starting to appear under the left armpit. Over the next few days, this crust would grow to the stage where it was very noticeable, and Mother would comment on it. You see, when Dad was working with watercolours, he would mix up a colour on a sheet of glass, apply the paint to the artwork, rinse his brush in a large jar of water, and finally wipe the brush under the armpit of his jumper!

Growing up around him in the '60s and '70s, long before the internet, none of us realised his volume of work, and it's been a real eye-opener since his death to see the sheer amount one very talented artist produced. Such imagination, such ability.

He was a master of understatement, he was a gentleman, and he was, and still is, Dad.

Rod Turner, 2024

THE RON TURNER I KNEW
by Clive Turner

Although it may seem hard to believe, I have to confess that it was not until my father became unwell that I came to appreciate fully the magnitude and extent of his work, and specifically the outstanding contribution that he'd made to the world of science-fiction publications. In fact, it was due solely to the contact that I had on occasion with his biographer, John Lawrence, during Dad's confinement in hospital, that the true scale of it all became apparent to me, for John revealed just how acclaimed and revered his artistic talent had become over the years.

I don't know if the reader can relate to this, but throughout my childhood and adolescent years at home, Dad's work was, I suppose, something of a closed book. Since he was working from home during this time, the opportunity was ever there to see a piece of his artwork in progress. But – and this probably sounds a little complacent – to me, this was Dad doing his job, Dad earning a living. How does the child of a clerical worker view his father's briefcase, or the child of a long-distance lorry driver view his father's truck, if he happens to see it from time to time?

I am ashamed to admit it now, but I remember that, during my school years, I felt more than a little embarrassed at telling my peers that my father was an artist. I guess I just felt awkward when so-and-so's dad ran a coach business or someone else's was an electrician. Silly, really; but that's kids.

In addition to growing up with my father's work always being there, was the fact that he was extremely private where his artwork was concerned and was never one to volunteer information relating to it. I guess that, as he worked from home, he felt the need to keep this side of his life detached from his domestic one. So, for all this time, Dad's work was Dad's work, and even in his later years and my adult life, it was never something we discussed at length. He would much prefer to chat about more everyday things, such as a little problem with his car or a current affairs topic, for instance. He would maybe make some remark about a particular assignment now and again, but this was not commonplace.

Looking back, the most amazing thing to me is the 'make do' conditions that Dad worked under during certain periods. I have already mentioned his working from home, and my earliest recollection is of the semi-detached house in Middlesex where I was born. It was here that Dad's 'studio' doubled as the bathroom – or should that be the other way round! His main work-surface was a wooden board covering the bath, and I can visualise it now with its spattering of different coloured flecks of paint and inks. I am pretty sure that when we moved to our next address near Hersham, he likewise made do with that bathroom in which to work! Our subsequent move to Sandhurst, however, must have fulfilled a dream for him. A room, albeit a modest-size box room, finally provided a dedicated place from which he could work, and must truly have been a welcome change from the previously less-than-ideal surroundings.

The most extraordinary workplace, however, has to be the houseboat Dad lived on after he got divorced. He obviously had a yearning actually to live on the river like this; and, despite certain setbacks, he loved the time he spent there. Once again, Dad was having to work in a fairly confined space, but now with the added challenge of coping with the wash from passing river craft, for this was on the Thames at Windsor. Unfortunately, the decision to give up this idyllic lifestyle was made for him due to the deterioration of the boat's ageing wooden hull. It was twice lifted completely out of the water for essential maintenance, but in the end, despite Dad's best efforts to keep it afloat, it finally succumbed to the elements. This then was when Dad had reluctantly to rely on the authorities to house him and he ended up in a maisonette near Sunningdale. I say 'reluctantly', because he was never one who

Above: Ron Turner in his home studio; and the ageing houseboat on which he lived and worked for some years.

wished to be a burden on the state – or anyone else, for that matter – and had there been any other option open to him, he would have chosen it.

Dad always had a passion for all things mechanical, and this must have rubbed off on my elder brother and me, playing a significant part in the direction of our respective careers. We were little older than four or five when Dad built a motorised buggy for us to trundle around the garden on. This was powered by the engine from a 1950s Velocette LE motorcycle – better known as the 'Noddy' bike, which served our boys in blue for a number of years. From the point of view of good neighbourliness, this was a very considerate choice for use in a moderately-sized suburban garden, for being water-cooled, it was extremely quiet!

Indeed, Dad spent a great deal of his spare time in the garage, either tinkering with the car or making something or other, and for us it was a fascinating place to be. In fact, it still brings to mind all manner of childhood memories, even now. All the various tools and the assortment of bits and pieces that I suppose would have appeared to many as little more than mere scrap metal, were to him, useful and useable material for some future project and not to be discarded. The aroma – a subtle blend of roll-up tobacco, motor oil and all the other various elements of a garage-cum-workshop – is still an intense recollection of mine. This, then, was the creative side of Dad that I was familiar with – the toy farmhouse, the medieval forts with working, wind-up drawbridges, my sister's dolls' house and all manner of other creations.

Running parallel to a fascination and love for the mechanical world was my father's immense interest and understanding of the natural world around him. This encompassed everything from microscopic organisms to the largest animal life – including the extinct – and all manner of plant life. I feel this is very much in evidence in a great deal of his work, particularly if one examines the characteristics of the various alien life-forms that manifest in so many of his commissions. Most striking are the reptilian and insect-like creations, which demonstrate an enormous insight into and knowledge of the structure of the real-life creatures from which their component features presumably originated.

Dad would often spend hours with us on seaside holidays in and around rockpools, with net and bucket ready to hand. He would always reveal some enlightening fact or detail about the latest find, whether its habitat, its feeding behaviour or maybe some little-known peculiarity that it had. In this way, I suppose he instilled in us the desire to look at things in more depth and attempt to glean a little more knowledge about the subject. This was also true in relation to mechanical items, and I have to say that my own passion for the mechanical owes much to this childhood experience.

Dad was an extremely inventive man, and very adept at turning a basic concept into an end result. I can't recall a time in his life when he was ever not mulling over some idea that had occurred to him, considering perhaps the best way in which to tackle the problem. I can honestly say, without exaggeration, that up until the time when John Lawrence began to show me some of his vast collection of Dad's work, I had seen a great deal more of his small sketches and doodlings, relevant to some small project or other, than I had ever seen of his artwork proper.

There is much more that I could relate of my late father's life, but overall he was an exceptionally private person, almost reclusive some might say, preferring total anonymity to fame. There were things he told me in his last days that I was certainly not aware of; and, upon reflection, I do not consider it my place to betray his memory by divulging any more than I feel appropriate. I have, however, furnished John with some background details, some of which were at one point unknown to me and could be gained only by contacting distant relatives.

Finally, I would like to take this opportunity to thank John personally for all his hard work and efforts in researching and writing this book, and for providing a magnificent insight into my father's career. It has been, and continues to be, of immense comfort to learn of the tremendous following and interest that has grown around his life's work.

Clive Turner, 2020

Ron Turner pictured in 1960 holding his new baby daughter Dianne at her birthplace, Bridge Gardens in Ashford, Middlesex.

RON TURNER, MY DAD
by Dianne Turner

Meeting John Lawrence for the first time at my Dad's funeral opened up a whole new realm of knowledge for me about the many years of his outstanding art and magnificently detailed science-fiction work.

Growing up, I knew Dad was an artist but was oblivious to exactly what was being produced in his tiny box-room 'studio' – which was temporarily vacated on the birth of my younger brother Mark and transformed into a nursery with Donald Duck design wallpaper, while the artwork was relocated to the marital bedroom.

Dad was unassuming and modest about his work. When asked that usual question, 'What does your Dad do?', I'd answer, 'He's a commercial artist and works at home.' Sounded good enough to me, even though as a kid I didn't know exactly what he drew or painted. Not much was shared with us back then.

Saturday teatime had to be punctual so that afterwards Dad could retire to the lounge, draw his armchair up close to the television set and watch *Doctor Who*. Other unmissable programmes were *Thunderbirds*, *Star Trek* and war films. Now it all makes sense.

Dad enjoyed his late-night viewing, too, after we children had gone off to bed. Cheese and biscuits, a glass of Martini Rosso, *The Sky at Night* and sketching inventions on his daily newspaper. He was full of ideas.

Mornings we were awakened by the smell of cremated toast, the way Dad liked it. Then, when he opened the door to retreat back to his work, out would waft a smell of stale tobacco, paint – and singeing. Dad would stand hours on end with a heater almost touching the back of his legs, scorching his trousers.

Tins of Old Holborn and green Rizla papers were on hand for him to make his own roll-up cigarettes. The numerous tins got recycled: stacked in his garage and used to store nuts and bolts. On occasions when Dad went out to post work or to meet up with his agent, Mum and I, armed with buckets of soapy water, would sponge down the acrid brown walls of his now reclaimed box-room, once again revealing Donald Duck and friends.

On one of Dad's trips out, I remember, he was driving to collect a new pair of glasses and managed to have an unfortunate encounter with a milk float on a roundabout!

Dad's creativity was endless. Disappearing into his garage and using his own designs, he would construct a fort with working drawbridge; a garage with wind-up car lift; or a dolls' house with lights, bed and wardrobe. I always thought how clever Father Christmas was!

Dad's garage was his 'man cave'. He dug out a six-foot-deep inspection pit and, with the aid of a manual and a spotlamp, carried out his own car mechanics. Swarfega was another familiar smell, as he cleaned up his greasy hands to get back to the artwork.

Amidst his many deadlines he found time to lay paving slabs round our entire huge garden, and we children then whizzed round them on our bikes. He also built a Wendy house, and put up a metal-rimmed swimming pool of which our ducks were very appreciative – until their wings got clipped!

Like most families, we had short holidays, and ours were expeditions. The eve before we left, Dad would sit with a map and a small wheeled gadget checking the distance we had to travel. In his fine block lettering, he would write out the route on a piece of card, which would then be displayed on his car dashboard. Up early the next morning, he would dress in his best beige suit and cravat, and after breakfast would go out and sit in the car while Mum packed up our old caravan with provisions. Tins of baked beans, ravioli, spam, peaches, evaporated milk, and anything else edible in a tin.

Our route would take us via scenic B roads, so that a journey that could have been completed in a couple of hours saw us arrive at our destination in the late afternoon. Feeling extremely car sick and tired, we would follow Dad onto the beach. Sitting on the travel rug in his best suit, he'd say, 'Isn't anyone going in the sea for a swim? That's appreciation for you! Driven all this bloody way!' Then we would march off into the cold sea and, shivering, come back to an almost deserted beach, as most other holidaymakers had by that time gone to tea. But we did have our tins of food and our cosy old caravan. The following days, we would enjoy spending time with Dad, building the best creative sandcastles and rock-pooling, something he really loved. Only now, with the knowledge of Dad's intensive workload, can I fully appreciate the time taken out for these memorable trips to the coast.

Leaving our family home many years later, Dad went on to live in a houseboat on the Thames, just downstream from Windsor Castle. He loved the idyllic views and the peace and quiet. Swans and ducks would come by, and soon learned that if they tapped on the end of his houseboat, he would feed them. During my summer visits to him, we'd chug down the Thames in his small boat with a smoking outboard motor, taking in the beauty of the countryside he so loved. We could now catch up on conversations covering a broad spectrum of topics. Dad was a learned, widely-travelled man with a good sense of humour. He had turned a few heads back in the day, driving his sports car proudly down Mum's street in the East End of London. Neighbours had stood on their doorsteps as he, attired in his best suit, swept Mum off to the dancehall where they both regularly enjoyed ballroom dancing.

Through an unexpected visit to the houseboat by John Lawrence, a good, long-lasting friendship was formed, and new work flowed as John became Dad's agent. John having been an ardent fan of Dad's work since boyhood, this fulfilled a lifelong dream for him. He dedicated years of research to writing this extensive, authentic biography, filled with fantastic artwork. I thank everyone involved for their hard work in bringing it all so wonderfully together, including John's agent Philip Harbottle and editor Stephen James Walker. Through this book I have gained a new insight into my Dad's life and work, finding out more than I could ever have

Above: Dianne Turner pays a visit to her father Ron on his houseboat.

known before. Discovering that he used Mum as a model for 1950s Scion covers such as those for *Magnetic Brain* and *The Purple Wizard* (reproduced on pages 68 and 87 respectively), I would love to think I was also one of his characters.

Words cannot describe how proud I am for Dad to receive, finally, the recognition he so richly deserves for his work on *The Daleks*, *Thunderbirds*, *Stingray*, *Judge Dredd*, *Dan Dare* and *Nick Hazard*, to name just a few.

This is a true tribute to Dad. Thank you, John Lawrence!

Dianne Turner, 2024

LIKE FATHER, LIKE SON
by Mark Turner

When I was a young child, Mum would roll out wallpaper on the reverse side along our eight-foot dining table. I would draw on it for hours on end.

I overheard Greg Hall, then Dad's agent, say on one of his visits to our house, 'You'd better watch out, Ron – he's good!' Greg took an interest in my early artwork and would spend some time talking to me.

I always thought the character Joe 90 was based on me, as I also wore glasses.

My love of art was put on hold when, after attending Eagle House and Wellington College, I went on to Oxford University to read Medieval French and German. After graduating, I studied Fine Art at art colleges in Bournemouth and Taunton, Somerset.

Some of my father's artistic talent must have rubbed off on me, as I have always enjoyed painting, especially landscapes.

My father was a great artist who made outstanding achievements in his artform that will be admired for many years to come.

He saw the World of the Future, and brought it to life for all of us.

Mark Turner, 2024

Below left: Mark Turner at work on one of his own paintings. Below right: young Mark pictured with his father Ron in the late 1960s.

Above, left to right: Rodney, Mark, Dianne and Clive (known to the family as Cliff), the four Turner siblings, pictured together in 1985. Below: Ron Turner with a piece of his celebrated Dalek artwork.

PART 1:
1922-1984

Ron Turner pictured circa 1965 with his parents Ellen and Herbert, and children (left to right) Clive, Dianne and Rodney.

1: SKETCHES OF EARLY LIFE

Despite having been wounded in both legs, gassed on the Somme and taken prisoner, Private Herbert Edward Turner of the Norfolk regiment had survived the horrors of the First World War to return home to his wife Ellen and their two young daughters Evelyn, born 1910, and Doris, born 1912. 'Home' was married quarters at Britannia Barracks in Norwich, and it would remain so for several more years, with Herbert signing on as a quartermaster's clerk, his recent injuries for the time being restricting him from securing any other peacetime employment. It was here, following the birth of an elder brother, also Herbert, in 1920, that Ron Turner was born on 3 August 1922. Three years later, having sufficiently recovered from his injuries, Herbert senior was discharged from the Army, and with Ron's sisters now teenagers, circumstances dictated that he would need to find his family other accommodation. In receipt of disablement benefit, he was able to move the family back to Southend-on-Sea, their home town, where he resumed his pre-war employment as a tram driver. With his family, he then settled down again to a relatively routine life.

Born in 1892, Herbert came from a family of Essex farmers. He was small, quiet and serious – characteristics that Ron inherited. Ron's mother Ellen, born 1893, was by contrast a large lady, warm and friendly – traits passed on more to Ron's elder brother, who was the 'life and soul of the party'. It was also Ellen's family who were the more artistic. Her father and grandfather were skilled in marquetry (creating pictures in wood), fret cutting and French polishing, and Ellen herself was known for her needlework. With Ron's sister Evelyn achieving the heights of being a court dressmaker who could knit, crochet, quilt and embroider, artistic traits certainly ran in the family.

Growing up in Southend-on Sea, Ron displayed at school an aptitude for art and an interest in science, but it was after discovering during these formative years the scientific romance novels of H G Wells, Jules Verne and Edgar Rice Burroughs that he quickly developed an interest in science-fiction.

It was during his pre-teen years, in schoolyard swapping sessions, that Ron came across the British

Below: still standing today, largely unchanged, the site of Ron Turner's birth, the Britannia Barracks in Britannia Road, Norwich.

SF magazine *Scoops*, which introduced him to the work of John Russell Fearn, an author with whom his career would become closely linked, though not until some years later. *Scoops* lasted only twenty issues, but it whetted Ron's appetite for contemporary SF and led to his discovery of American 'pulp' magazines such as *Amazing Stories* and *Astounding Stories*, which had found their way to British shores as ballast in the holds of cargo ships, later to be sold off cheaply as remainders in stores such as Woolworth's.

But although Ron's interest was captivated by the incredible stories in these magazines, it was the vividly imaginative covers by the likes of Hans Wesso and Frank R Paul that made more of an impression on his young mind and stimulated his interest sufficiently to prompt him to grab a pencil and copy what he saw. To Ron, these drawings were no more than a pleasant pastime; but it was when he began not only to copy, but also to embellish his

Right: the cover of Issue 14 of *Scoops*. Below: printed inside the magazine, the John Russell Fearn story 'Invaders from Time', with a fantastical illustration of the type that fired young Ron Turner's imagination.

sketches with ideas of his own, that his mother recognised a creative talent emerging. It was one that she actively encouraged him to develop: when he left school at age 14, he found himself lined up for an interview for the position of trainee artist at Odhams Press's art studios in London, arranged by Ellen on the strength of his drawings. Though these sketches were fairly basic, the company's art editor could see they showed a great deal of promise, and so Ron was taken on.

Initially, Ron's work involved such menial tasks as making tea, sweeping the floor and running errands, all of which helped to acquaint him with other artists and the general running of the studio. Later, he was given a bike on which to deliver proofs to clients, and this was an errand he always enjoyed, as it took him on a route through Covent Garden, with the wonderful atmosphere of fruit and flowers, crushed underfoot. But soon after, he began to establish himself in the studio proper and was given to lettering crossword grids, retouching photographic plates and inking in large areas of other artists' work (a task too labour-intensive for them to perform themselves).

As time went by, being in the company of skilled artists, Ron was soon picking up tips and techniques for himself. As Odhams offered no formal training scheme, this was the manner in which his tuition progressed, until eventually he began producing work of his own: mostly spot illustrations for Odhams' various books and magazines. But it was during his lunch breaks that he was able to pursue his passion for SF, transported to other worlds via the serialised big-screen adventures of *Flash Gordon*, then showing in many of the ubiquitous News Theatres of the time. It was a passion later intensified by screenings of the 1936 Alexander Korda-produced movie adaptation of H G Wells' *Things To Come* and of Fritz Lang's 1927 silent cinematic masterpiece *Metropolis*. Ron was mesmerised by the special effects of the day, but more so by the design of the hardware and settings; their striking scientific imagery was subsequently to have a profound influence on his own creative talents. Later movies, such as *Destination Moon*, *War*

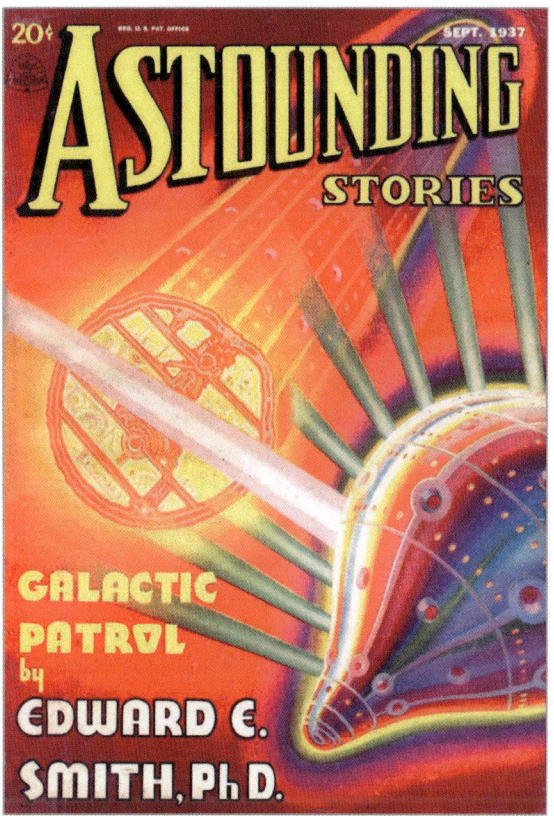

Right: imported mid-1930s issues of the US pulp magazines *Amazing Stories* and *Astounding Stories*, the former stickered as a 'British edition'.

of the Worlds and *Forbidden Planet*, would have a similar effect.

In 1938, Ron began contributing spot illustrations to *Modern Wonder*, Odhams' science and technology weekly. Another artist contributing to this publication, albeit only via the syndicated American comic strip *Flash Gordon*, was Alex Raymond, and Ron's attention was immediately drawn to his superb draughtsmanship. Raymond's grasp of atmospheric detail, together with his mastery of action and movement, were characteristics that greatly impressed Ron, and again would later play an integral role in the development of his own style.

With the onset of war in 1939, *Modern Wonder* became *Modern World* and began documenting the day-to-day events as the conflict progressed. With an interest in the technical aspects of warfare, Ron decided, purely as an exercise, to try his hand at producing one of the double-page illustrations that featured regularly within the magazine pages, usually drawn by L Ashwell-Wood, later to work on the *Eagle* comic. Ron's attempt featured the planes of the Russian Air Force, presented from a variety of different angles; and, relatively pleased with his efforts, he showed the results to his editor. To Ron's delight, his work met with approval, and this encouraged him to produce another, similar piece, this one depicting the Italian Air Force. This was also commended, and led to an official commission for him to paint the planes of the German Air Force. But although this work was duly carried out, it was never to see print, for ironically, on the night of 15 April 1941, one of the many planes that Ron had depicted put in a real-life appearance: Odhams received a direct hit, courtesy of the Luftwaffe, demolishing the whole building. Work eventually continued from another location in High Holborn, but Ron himself was soon experiencing the nature of war from a much closer perspective: in 1942, his brush was replaced with a rifle as he was conscripted into the Army to take an active part in the conflict itself.

Ron received his basic training in Ireland with the Royal Ulster Rifles (RUR) or, as Ron liked to think of them, Rossum's Universal Robots – a reference to Czech playwright Karel Čapek's classic 1920s stage play of that title, concerning subservient androids.

Above: the covers of the May 1938 issue of *Modern Wonder* and the March 1940 issue of the retitled *Modern World*, two of the Odhams titles on which Turner began his professional career.

In the 1990s, Turner produced a fictionalised account of his war years in an eight-page strip called 'Autobiography of an Artist', published by Cosmos in their *Fantasy Annual No 2* in 1998. This first page tells of the bombing of Odhams' premises.

In October 1942, he embarked for North Africa, before moving on to the Med and finally ending up in Italy, where he saw a great deal of action. His commanding officer during the Italian campaign was one Captain Kirk, and although to SF fans this name now evokes memories of a classic TV series, to Ron it always brought forth recollections of a more personal and traumatic nature: specifically, seeing Kirk get blown apart by an exploding mortar during the Battle of Monte Cassino.

Ron's artistic abilities weren't dormant for too long, however, for as his part in the conflict progressed, he took every opportunity to capture the details of battle on paper. On one occasion, his artistic interests almost certainly saved his life, when he was struck by a piece of shrapnel, and the art board he was carrying in his backpack shielded him from the full force of the impact.

Ron survived a number of other close shaves during this period. On one occasion, out on company manoeuvres, his group had stopped in the shadow of a ridge for a brew-up. As he bent down to pick up a kettle, a bullet suddenly whistled over his head. Turning, he instinctively grabbed his pistol and fired at three figures retreating down the other side of the ridge. They were German soldiers, and one of them was hit with what Ron soon discovered was a fatal shot. Despite all being fair in love and war, this was something Ron bitterly regretted, particularly as the soldier had been only about 18 years old. However, he consoled himself with the thought that, had he not retaliated immediately, a second shot from the attacking trio could have been disastrous for him, or for any of his company.

In May 1944, heading for Rome after having survived the Battle of Monte Cassino, his company came under heavy fire while going to the assistance of another regiment. The air was so thick with smoke and dust that Ron could see the trails of the bullets as they whistled past. It was during this operation that he was shot and wounded in the leg. Initially, the impact was surprisingly painless, like receiving a heavy punch, but then he succumbed to it and keeled over. In retrospect, no doubt he had been lucky – a shot higher up his body could have been fatal, and in being invalided out, he was spared the fate that befell thousands of others who died during one of the bitterest and bloodiest campaigns of the Second World War. After spending a couple of weeks viewing the world from a three-foot perspective in a Naples hospital bed, he was sent back to England to recover. A period of convalescence followed at Bedford infirmary before he was finally able to return home. He later received two medals: the Star of Italy and a General Service Medal (GSM).

By now, Ron's father Herbert had been forced by ill health to retire from his former job as a tram driver and had found more conducive employment working at the local post office in Romford, Essex, the town to which the family had relocated under a war housing scheme for disabled ex-servicemen. Hitler having temporarily turned his attentions away from Great Britain, the family must have felt relatively safe; but they had reckoned without a second onslaught later in 1944. This brought into sharp focus the fact that Ron's part in the ongoing conflict was still not over, as one of the Nazis' dreaded V2 flying bombs landed only a few streets away, rocking his home and blowing out the windows. However, although physically he was shaken by this incident, mentally it bolstered his growing conviction that rocketry, far from being just science fantasy, was the beginnings of a future with much wider implications.

By December 1944, Ron had almost recovered from his injuries, but he was now considered only a reservist and, 'excused boots', was given an Army desk job. When the war in Europe was over, however, he had no wish to continue as a home-based pen-pusher: he was young and wanted to see the world. So, when the opportunity arose in 1945, he continued his service in India, on a mopping-up operation. While there, something occurred that further reinforced his conviction that dramatic technological change was in the air, though this particular development was one that gave him serious concern for the future: the dropping of the atomic bombs on Hiroshima and Nagasaki.

Ron's subsequent tour of duty in the Far East took in Malaya, Singapore, Burma and the Philippines. Finally he found himself in Java, Indonesia, which was experiencing a certain amount of civil unrest. It was here that his company again went to the aid of another that was under attack, successfully relieving them before the rebels

SKETCHES OF EARLY LIFE

In the second and third pages of his 1990s 'Autobiography of an Artist' strip, Turner recalled incidents from his military training. This fourth page recounts his lucky escape in the Battle of Monte Cassino.

The fifth page of Turner's 1990s 'Autobiography of an Artist' strip recounts his wartime injury, hospitalisation and return to Britain.

closed in. For his part in the rescue mission, Ron was awarded two further medals: the bar of SE Asia and a second GSM. He was then demobbed, his obligations to the British Army finally concluded.

In 1947, Ron returned to Odhams Press to continue his career as an artist. He picked up almost where he'd left off, providing spot illustrations, maps and diagrams for various publications. One of these was *Kinematograph Weekly*, on which he assisted other artists in producing poster-like illustrations to promote films that were about to be released. A little rusty after six years serving King and country, he needed some time to re-hone his skills, although most of the work he was required to do was rather tedious and uninspiring. It wasn't until a while later, when he began to be tasked with producing cutaways of cars, aircraft and other machines for Odhams' series of technical hardbacks, that the job became more enjoyable. This aspect of his work ultimately helped him to gain a greater understanding of technology; something he would later put to good use in the devising of his own futuristic machines and hardware.

At this stage in his career, Ron had no particular direction in mind, and having had a pre-war interest in biology – particularly aquatic life, surrounding himself with fishtanks, microscopes and cameras – he was seriously nurturing the possibility of changing direction and studying to become a marine biologist. However, post-war needs were such that he decided he would have to stay at his drawing board for a few more years yet. Things didn't really change until he came across the work of a writer who was to have such a profound influence on him that it would help to determine the future course of his career.

Left: the issues of *Kinematograph Weekly* for 18 December 1947, trailing the forthcoming British re-release of the classic *Gone With the Wind*, and 23 December 1948, wishing readers a Merry Christmas and alerting them to the cinematic highlights expected to 'Shine in '49'. It is unknown exactly which issues of *Kinematograph Weekly* Ron Turner worked on after resuming his employment with Odhams in 1947, but they could possibly have included these festive numbers.

In the sixth page of his 1990s 'Autobiography of an Artist' strip, Turner uses the development of the Nazis' V2 weapon as a lead-in to an SF-flavoured speculation on the future of rocketry; and in doing so, points toward his own future.

2: NEW BEGINNINGS

In the late 1940s, numerous small independent publishing houses began to spring up, seemingly overnight, taking advantage of post-war paper-rationing regulations that constrained the larger, well-established companies but presented opportunities for fledgeling ones to get a foothold in the market. One of these 'mushroom' publishers was Scion Ltd of Kensington, London, founded by a Latvian businessman, Binyamin Z Immanuel, and his wife Esther Benjamin. Together with his editor Maurice Read, Immanuel proceeded to launch a 3d-priced comic series. A legal loophole in the rationing regulations meant that if they changed the title slightly each time, they were entitled to receive the full quota of paper usually allowed for a one-off publication. Consequently, each issue of their comic appeared under a different title, made identifiable as part of the same series by the use of the generic word 'Big', such as in *Big Chuckle* or *Big Win*.

Below: a 1948 example of one of Scion's 'Big' comics, this one with cover art by S K Perkins.

Scion were ever on the lookout for artists to contribute to this new line of comics, and some of that demand was met by Odhams employees keen to supplement their income by freelancing in their spare time. Most of this extracurricular activity was handled by an artists' agent named Charles Montague Hall, known to family and friends as Greg Hall. During the Second World War, Hall had been stationed at Biggin Hill, Britain's key RAF Fighter Command base; and in early 1940 he had met and married Lily Maud Davis, a fashion painter for Norman Hartnell. After the war, having developed a good relationship with his wife's agent William Partridge, Hall joined Partridge's agency, managing his wife along with many of their other clients. However, with the burgeoning of the 'mushroom' publishers, all of them requiring artists, Hall quickly realised the lucrative potential. He felt there was a gap that could be cornered in this niche market … except that most of the artists he represented weren't cut out for that type of work, or the rates they charged were prohibitive. Fortunately, he was on good terms with Odhams' art editor Arthur Gould, having provided him with the occasional artist 'undercover' from Partridge's agency if a particular skill was suddenly required or if one of their regular artists was unavailable or indisposed. Now he felt it was time to call in the favour.

In this way, Hall became a frequent visitor to Odhams' studios in the late '40s, not only to discuss supplying artists, as and when they were needed, but also sometimes to see if he could recruit them, knowing that he would always find willing candidates eager to boost their income. As a result, the services of several young Odhams artists, such as Ron Embleton, Jim Holdaway, Norman Light and George Radcliffe, were acquired for outside commissions.

Hall soon built up a reputation for never turning work away, knowing that if Partridge's regular artists were too busy, he could invariably find an appropriate alternative from within the array of Odhams talent; a practice to which Odhams turned a blind eye in view of the reciprocal service he offered them. It was an arrangement that benefited all parties; especially Hall himself, as he saw his own income increase significantly. Soon, having acquired a reasonable retinue he could call upon, and with the 'indie' publishers requiring ever more cover work, Hall left Partridge's agency and, with his wife, set up his own in West Hampstead.

Despite having already supplied various types of illustration for Odhams, Ron had no experience of comic-strip work. This changed around 1948, when he was called upon to 'ghost' on a strip that an indisposed colleague was unable to complete for one of Odhams' publications. This was observed by Hall on one of his customary visits, and seeing another financial opportunity in the making, he asked Ron if he would be interested in boosting his income by contributing a strip of his own to Scion's line of comics. Ron knew that some of his colleagues were already producing this type of work for Scion and receiving £1 per page for their efforts – a not inconsiderable sum by early '50s standards – and so, ever-willing to accept a challenge and add another string to his artistic bow, he agreed. Hall offered to represent him, but explained that unlike some of the larger publishing houses such as the Amalgamated Press, Scion didn't provide scripts: artists who were prepared to undertake this type of work had to produce the stories themselves, and these needed to be action-based adventures. But this didn't deter Ron. Quite the opposite, in fact, for it gave him a golden opportunity to create and present the work in his own fashion. The result was a three-page strip story that he entitled 'The Atomic Mole'.

Clearly drawing on Ron's childhood influences such as the 'inner space' sagas of Verne and Burroughs, with overtones of Conan Doyles' *The Lost World*, 'The Atomic Mole' concerns a huge earth-burrowing machine powered by 'atomic destructor tubes' and piloted by one Rip Rivers who, together with his son Jim and friend Professor Jeans, proceeds to venture down 75 miles below the Earth's crust. There they find themselves battling prehistoric creatures in a series of vast, subterranean caverns.

Feeling reasonably satisfied with Ron's efforts, Hall submitted them to Scion's editor Maurice Read for approval. Read was impressed: simple line drawings they may have been, but crude as they were, they displayed a great deal of creativity, both in subject matter and in presentation. Ron's flair for scientific machinery and cinematic perspectives indicated a highly individual approach (one that would typify his style for years to come), but most of all the strip included action; the one ingredient guaranteed to capture a schoolboy's imagination. In that respect, Read felt the story would have made good front cover material. Unfortunately, however, Ron had presented it as a series of small, regimented frames more suited to the interior pages and lacking the necessary 'splash' panel. Agreeing to publish 'The Atomic Mole' in the next issue, Read asked Hall if Ron would be prepared to draw another three-page strip for its cover story, this time opening with a large action frame that would grab the attention. Read didn't want more SF, so he suggested a contemporary tale concerning black market racketeers, which might open with a car chase. Ron had treated 'The Atomic Mole' as little more than a one-off exercise, not expecting a great deal of interest, so he was both surprised and delighted that not only had it been accepted but more was wanted.

Fuelled with enthusiasm and keen to establish himself with a publisher that was actually interested in his work, Ron quickly set about attempting to realise Read's ideas. The result was *Big Scoop*, with a dynamic, eye-catching, action-packed opening sequence depicting a group of crooks fleeing in a getaway van, almost swerving out of the frame with a police car in hot pursuit. Ron's clever use of varying cinematic angles and perspectives produced a fast-moving story, with one particularly effective frame showing the van speeding along flanked by motor-cycle outriders, viewed unconventionally from overhead; a most innovative approach for a comic strip at that time. Read was more than delighted with the results and realised that, in Ron, he had an artist he couldn't afford to lose. He knew there would be many more occasions when Ron's abilities would prove an invaluable asset to Scion and be of great benefit to their publishing ventures.

With the company now prepared to accept whatever he could produce, Ron was soon submitting many more strips. In order to show his versatility, he agreed to produce a story involving the Canadian Mounties for *Big Mounty*, and one about speedway racing for *Big Combat*. Read however, quickly realised that SF was Ron's real forte. Consequently more Atomic Mole adventures followed, for comics such as *Big Atlantis* and *Big Ranch*.

In early 1949, however, just as Ron had begun to develop and exploit his newfound talent for strip work, Scion suddenly announced that they were going to be terminating their comic-book series and branching out into the paperback market. Ron was initially very disappointed by this development; he had just begun to hit his stride, and the extra income had been more than welcome. However, he soon discovered that his abilities weren't about to be overlooked: Hall quickly secured for him the opportunity to provide a series of two-colour covers for Scion's new range of 16-, 32- and 64-page paperback romance novelettes.

Although the very nature of romantic fiction precluded the kind of action scenes characteristic of other genres, Ron nevertheless remained keen to establish himself with work that at least offered a challenge to his imagination, in contrast to some of the more tedious projects he was required to tackle for Odhams. Therefore, although his first covers for the romance range were rather flat and little more than line drawings with added colour and wash, as he progressed, both his technique and his general presentation improved immeasurably. With more brushwork and little outline, his scenes now began to rely more on a heavy contrast of colour, rather than any actual separation lines – a technique that would later become synonymous with his working style. Posture and facial expressions were also given more thought and attention, with scenes moving away from the traditional image of couples embracing to include some background elements from the story itself.

Ron eventually produced eight of these romance covers, and also began to provide full colour covers for some of Scion's new crime novels series, which he found more inspirational. Then, in early 1950, events took a turn that would finally enable him to achieve his full potential.

Right: Ron Turner's two-colour covers for the romance novelettes *Heartbreak* and *Take Your Happiness*, both written pseudonymously by John Russell Fearn and published by Scion as paperbacks in 1950.

Above: three further examples of Turner's two-colour covers for Scion's paperback romance novelettes, all published in 1950: *Dance to Heaven*, *Poison Ivy* and *Forget Me Not*. Although credited to Vivienne Carne, these books – like those shown on the previous page – were actually authored by John Russell Fearn, who preferred to use pseudonyms for his contributions to this genre.

Below: two of Turner's first full-colour paperback covers, for early Scion crime novels: L G Horsfield's *Mystery at Vellum*, published in 1949, and Norman Lazenby's *Death in the Stars*, published the following year.

 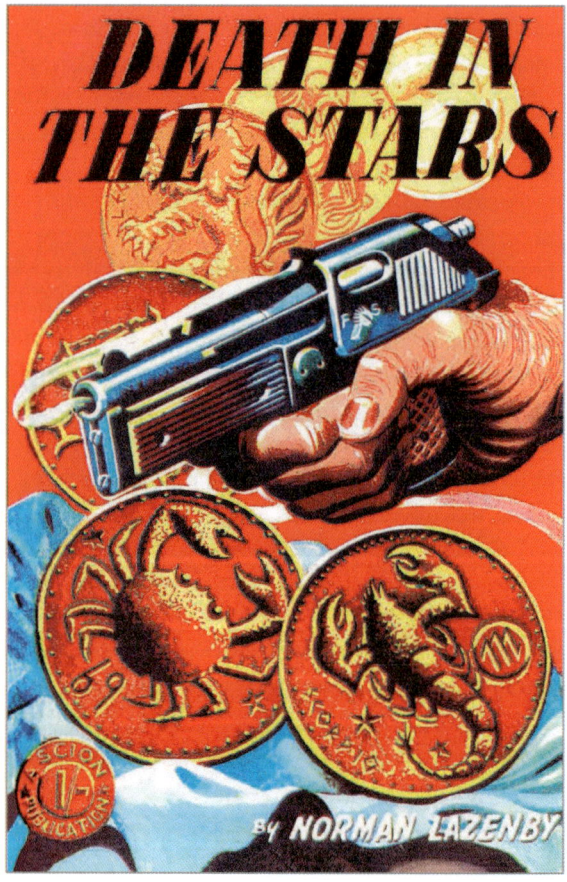

3: FROM COVER TO COVER

One of the many authors employed by Scion in 1950 was John Russell Fearn. Prolific in output, he had already contributed many pseudonymous novelettes to their romance series, and was now providing them with Western novels under his own name. Primarily, however, he was an SF writer; in fact, he was at that time the *only* British author to make a living writing SF.

Born in Worsley near Manchester in 1908, Fearn was gifted with a vivid imagination. Influenced by the likes of H G Wells and Jules Verne, he began writing stories from the age of ten. Having discovered the American pulps in 1931, he later submitted a story, 'The Intelligence Gigantic', to *Amazing Stories*, who published it in 1933. Throughout the rest of the '30s and the '40s, Fearn supplied a steady stream of SF stories to similar American titles, and in 1934 he also began providing occasional stories to British SF publications such as *Scoops* and magazine fiction to Odhams' science weekly *Modern Wonder*. However, his regular contributions to the American market came to a halt in 1943, when he fell out with his agent over 'misappropriated funds'. He was then forced to concentrate on the British market. Initially he focused on Westerns and crime and thrillers. In 1944, however, he created the Golden Amazon, a superheroine who preceded Wonder Woman by two years, though in literary rather than in comic-strip form. The character's eponymous debut novel was first published as an SF hardback in the UK, but this resulted in Fearn receiving an invitation to write follow-up stories for serialisation in the Toronto-based Canadian magazine *Star Weekly*. The Golden Amazon became the most successful and enduring character he ever conceived, her adventures later being collected in a series of 26 novels by him.

But Fearn hankered to return to writing more magazine SF, and as he became more financially solvent, he began submitting again to US pulps such as *Startling Stories* and *Thrilling Wonder Stories*, this time representing himself. Two full-length novels were also amongst his output, and were actually optioned by American publishers; however, the companies involved then ran into financial difficulties, and the books never appeared. Consequently, when in November 1949 Fearn received an invitation to write Westerns for Scion, he gladly accepted, knowing that this company was at least financially secure and could thus be relied upon. But still he felt aggravated that SF, his favourite genre and the one at which he was most adept, was not being catered for in the UK. On impulse, he decided to submit two of his unsold SF novels, *Queen of Venus* and *Fool's Paradise*, to Scion for Maurice Read's approval, with an offer to provide more if required. Read was familiar with SF, knew a good tale when he saw one, and realised that these two stories were far better than those being produced by Scion's rivals John Spencer & Co, who had only recently begun an SF series of their own. In fact, the John Spencer offerings were quite possibly the worst SF stories *ever* written. But how could Read publish and find a market for Fearn's novels, without potential buyers wrongly assuming they would be just more of the same? Noting Ron Turner's natural flair for futuristic imagery, and his ability to produce attractive covers, Read felt it was only natural to combine his talents with Fearn's, to promote a far superior quality of SF.

Through his agent, Hall, Ron was given the manuscript of *Queen of Venus* – later to be retitled *Operation Venus* – and briefed to come up with a cover showing two men at the controls of a spaceship as it heads out toward the titular planet. But first Read wanted Ron to produce three different pencil roughs of the scene, to allow him to choose the one he considered the most effective. The specified composition precluded Ron from showing the overall design of the spaceship, which he felt would be preferable to depicting the pilots, but nevertheless he stuck closely to the brief for two of the roughs. For the third, however, by a clever use of perspective to show a second ship flying parallel to the first, he managed to depict both the pilots *and* the ship, creating the more dynamic effect he'd been after. Approving of Ron's innovative presentation, Read gave him the go-ahead to produce the full-colour cover; and when Hall later delivered the finished piece, he was delighted with the results.

Ron had again thought this commission to be only a one-off. Read, though, had other ideas: the *Operation Venus* piece had more than satisfied his requirements, and confirmed to him that if Ron could provide equally good covers for other Fearn stories, the way was now open for Scion to publish a whole new line of SF novels. But first he had to get Ron on board. The last thing he wanted was for *Operation Venus* to be published, only for Ron to be immediately poached by a rival like John Spencer!

Up until this point, all of Ron's work for Scion had been handled through Hall's agency. Now, though, Read felt it necessary to discuss his ideas with Ron personally, to guarantee his interest in becoming the main cover artist for the proposed SF series. Through Hall, Ron was introduced to Read, whom he found immediately likeable. He listened with mounting interest and a certain degree of surprise as the editor unveiled his plans. Ron had been thrilled to be asked to produce the *Operation Venus* cover, but now to be invited to contribute to a whole series of SF books, he felt extremely honoured. With the recent publication of the John Spencer books, but more significantly the launch of the *Eagle* comic with Frank Hampson's *Dan Dare* strip still fresh in his mind, Ron felt that he was on the cusp of a pivotal moment in British SF; that something huge and exciting was about to break, and he was being given the chance to be a part of it. He immediately agreed to Read's proposal, delighted to have the opportunity to produce regular full-colour SF illustration; and with the offer of £12 to £15 per cover, each of which would take him only three to four days to complete, it would earn him a nice little bonus by 1950s standards.

With Ron on board, the last piece of the plan was in place, and Read gave him the second Fearn manuscript, *Fool's Paradise*, now retitled *Annihilation!*, again asking to see some pencil roughs first, based on scenes from the story. Ron couldn't wait to get started; at last he felt he had something he could get his teeth into, and on the train home, he began eagerly reading the manuscript. By the time he arrived back in Romford, a few ideas had already formed in his mind, and that evening in his bedroom-cum-studio, he began to sketch them out.

Inspired, Ron now knew the direction he wanted his career to take, and had ideas about how he would like to present his work. He'd recently come across a book by Willy Ley about the solar system, *The Conquest of Space*, which had included some amazing colour plates by Chesley Bonestell, an American astronomical artist. Bonestell's photorealistic technique, developed in order to depict remarkably detailed other-worldly landscapes, was incredibly effective in a time before space probes would reveal the true appearance of other planets, and Ron was impressed enough to see this 'camera-like' method of presentation as an admirable standard for which to aim. Therefore, when he came to paint his own SF covers, Bonestell's influence would be evident in the way

Below: Turner's outstanding cover for John Russell Fearn's novel *Operation Venus* (Scion, May 1950).

they were also realistically expressed; except that instead of mere planetary landscapes, Ron would depict imaginative scenes also involving incredible spacecraft, weird aliens and fantastic machines.

After Ron produced his three *Annihilation!* roughs, which were actually quite detailed pencil drawings, Hall delivered them to Read. Read then asked to see Ron again, and Ron wondered if there was a problem; maybe Read wasn't happy with his ideas, or had even changed his mind about using him. In fact, quite the opposite was the case: Read wanted to tell Ron personally how pleased he was with the work. If Ron had any lingering doubts as to his own capabilities, these were now dispelled. The three roughs were all superb, and Read was spoilt for choice when deciding on the one to be used – as Ron discovered later, on seeing the other two framed and hanging in his office!

Read realised that Ron's covers alone would be strong enough to sell the SF series, so he decided to dispense with Fearn's cover byline in favour of a newly-devised pseudonym; for, although *Operation Venus* had been published under Fearn's own name, Read wasn't entirely happy with that, as Fearn was being established as a writer of Scion's Westerns. A pseudonym would give the new series a fresh, distinctive identity that would stick in readers' minds and become quickly associated with the type of stories he intended to publish. More particularly, he wanted a name that would be exclusive to Scion!

Read asked Ron if he had any suggestions for a suitably strong and vibrant-sounding name. For Ron, SF immediately brought to mind H G Wells, and 'Wells' led Read to think of 'Wells Fargo' – a byline he'd already considered using for Fearn's Westerns. Although that would obviously be totally inappropriate here, he liked the sound of 'Fargo', and hit upon the idea of changing it slightly to 'Vargo', to give it the tougher, almost Teutonic edge he was seeking. It was perfect for the first part of the pseudonym – but that still left the matter of the surname. Read wanted the stories to be startling and electrifying, and this prompted Ron to think of 'Static', which then led them jointly to 'Statten'. An appropriate choice, as Staten Island, New York, had been the birthplace in 1926 of the very first SF magazine, Hugo Gernsback's *Amazing Stories*. Thus, from this freewheeling stream of

Above: Turner's final cover for *Annihilation!* (Scion, 1950), published under the newly-coined Vargo Statten pseudonym.

word associations, the pseudonym 'Vargo Statten' was finally coined and decided upon.

The matching of Ron Turner with John Russell Fearn proved to be a winning combination; Fearn's highly-charged, descriptive narratives fired Ron's imagination to stunning effect. The covers were colourful, vibrant, dynamic, inventive, superbly composed and realistically rendered, the cinematic presentation of Alex Raymond and the realism of Chesley Bonestell being fully reflected to enhance Ron's own ideas.

But, above all, in each of his covers, Ron accurately portrayed a scene from the story – unlike most cover artists of the period, who took the easy option of a generic 'rockets and ray-guns' approach. In order to do each story justice, Ron would always read the manuscript from cover to cover so he could choose a key scene to illustrate. He would spend many hours, sometimes working late into the night, to achieve results to his satisfaction, especially if a story presented a wealth of good cover ideas from which to choose. A huge amount of creative energy and enthusiasm was poured into this work, to produce a series of covers of unsurpassed quality and originality, each in itself a mini-masterpiece.

In 1950 alone, Ron's cover illustrations graced eight tremendous Vargo Statten novels that helped to revive the jaded spirits of a book-hungry public still recovering from the effects of a terrible war. For many readers, this was their first exposure to SF, and the combination of story and cover made a lasting impression.

Annihilation! showed a rocket blasting away from a cratered world while an electrical storm raged in the background. *2,000 Years On!* featured an aerial view of a futuristic city with elevated highways radiating out from a central tower and aero-cars speeding by. *Inferno!* again featured a spacecraft taking off, but this time the composition was an improvement on the last, as the angle was increased to take in the launching pit, showing the blast thrusting the ship upward. But it was for *Nebula X* that Ron felt most inspired, being immediately taken by Fearn's opening paragraph: 'In the great physical laboratory of Transmutations Limited, twenty million volts of man-made lightning writhed and crackled between anode and cathode spheres as base elements were changed into commercial products.' Ron didn't need to read any further (although of course he did), for a scene sprang almost fully-formed into his mind. His subsequent painting dramatically showed scientists operating an incredible atom-smashing machine; but this was presented from an almost surreal angle, thereby emphasising the unusual nature of the subject matter. Ron considered this his best cover yet, managing to include all the elements and compositional techniques he'd been steadily working toward: hardware design, dramatic action and unusual perspectives. His overall satisfaction with the piece was evidenced by his decision to sign it – albeit as 'Roland Turner', as at the time he felt that 'Roland' sounded more impressive than 'Ronald'. This practice was quickly discouraged by his agent, Hall, out of deference to Odhams, whose

Right: Turner's covers for the Vargo Statten novels *2,000 Years On!* and *Inferno!*, both published by Scion in 1950.

Nebula X by Vargo Statten (Scion, 1950)

Turner's covers for *The Micro Men, Wanderer of Space, The Cosmic Flame* and *The Sun Makers*, all written by John Russell Fearn under his Vargo Statten pseudonym and all published by Scion in 1950.

other artists had never been allowed to sign their work. Aside from a few other covers, some signed as 'RT', the rest of Ron's work was produced anonymously, although by now it really spoke for itself. Certainly no-one could mistake the artist responsible for *The Sun Makers*, Ron's last cover for 1950: another piece of brilliance in both its composition and its execution. In essence, it showed two men in protective gear, operating a control panel while observing an element being subjected to a powerful ray to create an artificial sun. But Ron's interpretation was inspired, from the dramatic pose of the two men, the layout of the control panel jam-packed with complex instrumentation, and the perceptive angle of the scene, all painted using a virtual spectrum of glowing yet beautifully-balanced colours, to stunning effect.

The only cover Ron produced during this period that failed to live up to the standard of the others was that for *Wanderer of Space*, where the main focus of the scene was on a character as opposed to a spacecraft or a machine – an unusual choice, probably dictated by Read, and one that clearly proved problematic, as the resultant figure was ungainly and ill-proportioned. Ron would have been the first to admit that the human figure work was not his strongest point; but his previous covers for Scion's romance series proved that he could do better than this. In fact, the figure's Adonis-like torso and small, heavily-delineated head perched awkwardly on top are so uncharacteristic of his work that it is safe to conclude the painting was altered by another artist – maybe even by Read himself – prior to publication. Even background details behind the figure are inconsistent with Ron's usual style – particularly the moon, which has clearly been put in freehand, whereas Ron typically drew circles using a pair of compasses.

A notable attribute of Ron's covers was their accurate portrayal of elements from the novel itself, and in this case, the lead character, according to Fearn's description, should have been wearing a tight-fitting tunic and a silver mask. Read, however, obviously favoured a more powerfully heroic 'muscleman' type instead. This was just the first of many occasions over the years when Ron would suffer his work being altered by an editor who, for whatever reason, disagreed with his interpretation.

Nevertheless, Read would be the most agreeable editor he would ever work for; and Ron's income by the end of the year was such that it was worth any minor aggravations he might have to endure. A few days' work producing a single cover could earn him almost double the £5 average weekly wage for the period, and this was in addition to the salary he was receiving from Odhams. Plus, there was the added benefit of the enjoyment he gained from doing the work itself.

One of Ron's dreams was to be able to buy a car, but for the time being he felt that was still a little over-ambitious, so he settled instead on getting a motorbike: a Sunbeam S7. This was a very classy, high-end machine, much revered in biking circles and something of a luxury for its day. Shaft driven, with wide tyres, a fully sprung saddle and front forks, it was a big departure from pre-war bike design. As such, it was promoted as 'The Bike of the Future' – a tag that appealed to Ron's sensibilities – and justified this by providing an extremely smooth, comfortable ride. It was therefore an ideal 'tourer', and as Ron also longed to travel, this gave him the opportunity during his weekend breaks to exploit the freedom of the open road.

By now, Scion's novels were successfully covering all the main genres, but the company looked to expand even further. In 1951, after a two-year hiatus, they began publishing comics again on a grand scale, and their output soared with such diverse titles as *Crime Fighter*, *Five Star Western*, *Space Hero*, *Electroman*, *High Speed Comics* and others. Much of the artwork was provided by the King-Ganteaume studios, managed by two Americans, Kenneth King and Malcolm 'Mac' Ganteaume, ex-GIs who had stayed in England after the war and set up the business on their war gratuity. With America currently leading the way in popular culture, particularly pop music and pulp literature, any publisher planning to bring out new paperbacks or comics knew that it paid to have heavy US overtones. Consequently the pair had no trouble supplying plenty of Americanised action/adventure strips to a variety of the smaller publishers of the time, and they were extremely successful. Scion by now had its own little group of artists, including Ron Embleton, Jim Holdaway, Norman Light and Terry Patrick (also managed by Ron's agent Greg Hall) and they were now required

to adopt this US-influenced style in the their own material. Ron was already carving out a good career for himself as a cover artist, but the resurgence of Scion's comics line also gave him the chance to promote his own strip work. This led to him gaining an assignment on one of their new titles, *Commando Craig*, which required him to produce four black-and-white pages per month. Read would provide the brief for the story, whereupon Ron would write, pencil, ink and letter the strip. It was challenging work, and meant that although he was able to complete seven further Vargo Statten covers in 1951, and an additional science-fiction one for a novel credited to Franz Harkon, he missed out on tackling three others, *The Red Insects*, *Cataclysm* and *Born of Luna*. However, he valued the experience, and it did at least give him a break from continuous cover illustration.

The launch issue of *Commando Craig* actually contained two Turner strips. The first was 'Jack Hawkins – Powder Monkey', the very basic linework of which clearly suggests that it was a leftover, intended for the earlier 'Big' series but unpublished then due to the latter's sudden termination. The story, doubtless at Read's suggestion, was a historical one set at the time of Drake and the Spanish Armada – another example of Ron demonstrating his versatility. The second, doubtless newer offering, 'Valley of Death', showed considerable improvement in Ron's technique, with harder lines, more detail and interesting perspectives. In this case, the story concerned two adventurers searching for a missing professor in the Amazon jungle, and although not SF, it did contain scientific elements.

'Valley of Death' was followed up in the next two issues by 'Sons of Darkness' and 'The Red Devil', and over the course of this trilogy Ron had his heroes battling giant insects, a lost tribe and a gang of oil thieves before successfully completing their mission.

Although these strip projects allowed Ron to tell a story in addition to providing the art, the demand for his cover work was steadily growing. Having witnessed his skill at visualising the 'sense of wonder' element of the Vargo Statten stories, other publishers such as John Spencer and Edwin Self were now eager for his art to grace their books too. He agreed, supplying the former with a cover for the third issue of their *Tales of Tomorrow* periodical and the latter with a cover for the George Sheldon Brown novel *Destination Mars*.

Left: Ron's covers for *Tales of Tomorrow* No 3 (John Spencer, 1951) and *Destination Mars* by George Sheldon Brown (Edwin Self, 1951).

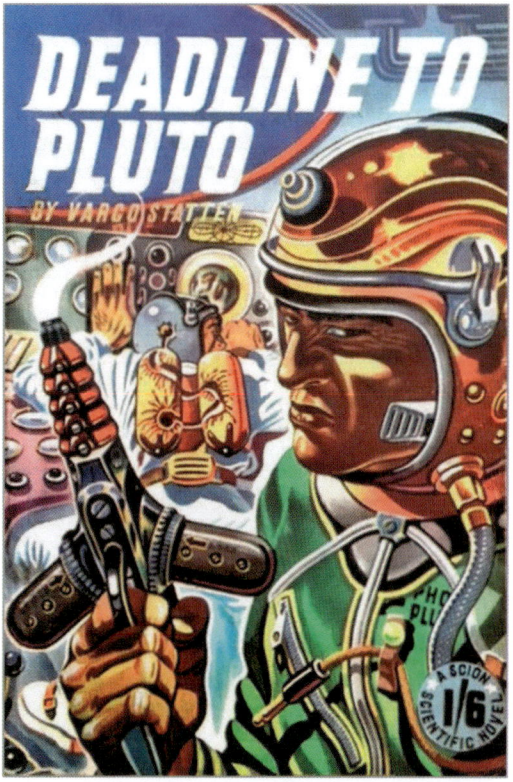

Turner's covers for *The Avenging Martian*, *Deadline to Pluto*, *The Petrified Planet* and *The Devouring Fire*, all written by John Russell Fearn under his Vargo Statten pseudonym and all published by Scion in 1951.

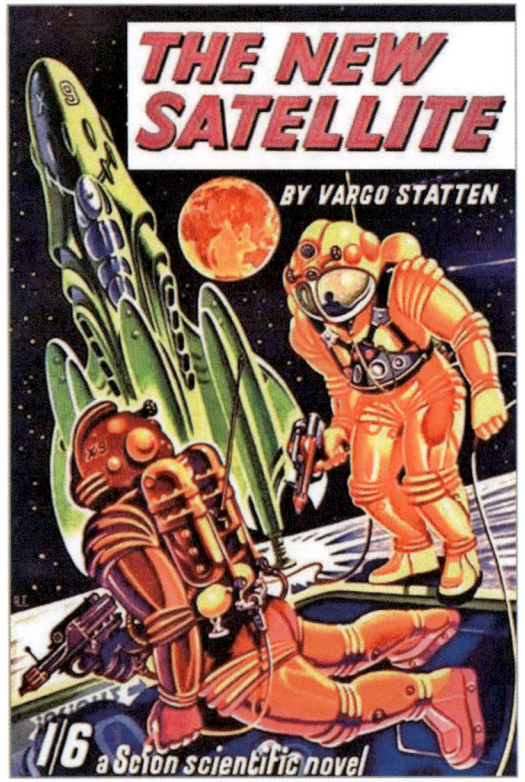

Turner's covers for *The New Satellite*, *The Renegade Star* and *The Catalyst*, written by John Russell Fearn under his Vargo Statten pseudonym, and *Spawn of Space* credited to Franz Harkon, all published by Scion in 1951.

In July 1951, Scion decided to add a new jungle novel series to their output. Edgar Rice Burroughs' Tarzan stories being hugely popular at the time, many publishers were keen to jump on the bandwagon, and Scion were no exception. Read commissioned John Russell Fearn to launch the new series under the house name 'Earl Titan', with Ron again providing the covers. However, although Fearn completed the first two stories, *The Gold of Akada* and *Anjani the Mighty*, he wasn't keen to write any more. Realising that it was far more important to keep him on the SF line, Read then brought in another stalwart Scion author, Victor Norwood, to continue the jungle series. Norwood was a good choice: a much travelled man with his own experiences up the Amazon, which added a note of authenticity to the tales. Consequently his series entries were published under his own name. Although Ron turned out fine covers for the next four titles, *The Untamed*, *Caves of Death*, *Temple of the Dead* and *The Skull of Kanaima*, he found the limited subject matter of natives and wild animals increasingly tedious; and so, like Fearn, he was only too pleased then to return to the more stimulating theme of the SF work he loved best.

1952 saw Ron supply Scion with the covers for a further seven Vargo Statten novels, including *The Inner Cosmos*, *The Man from Tomorrow* and *The G-Bomb*; and, as awareness of his abilities became increasingly widespread within the industry, other similar publishers of the time such as Kaye and Cherry Tree also commissioned him to provide covers.

In short, Ron's career was now riding high, with an income that had increased exponentially since the start of his involvement with Scion; and finally he felt financially secure enough to be able to treat himself to something a little sturdier and more exciting even than the Sunbeam S7: his dream car, a Jowett Jupiter Sports. The Jupiter's look was quite unlike the traditional design of previous British sports cars, and Ron was unable to resist the curvy lines of this lovely red roadster. He proceeded to make full use of it on his trips away; and, having bought a passport, he now planned to extend his travels to take in the sights of Europe as well.

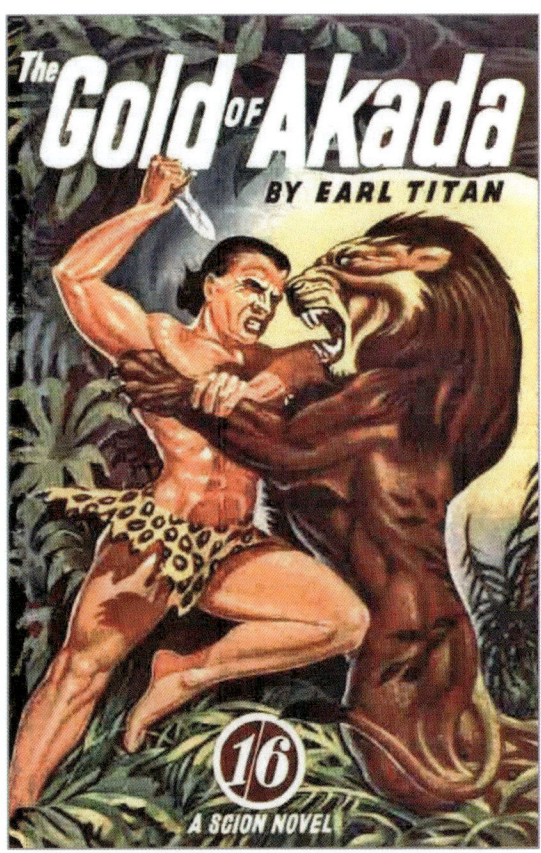

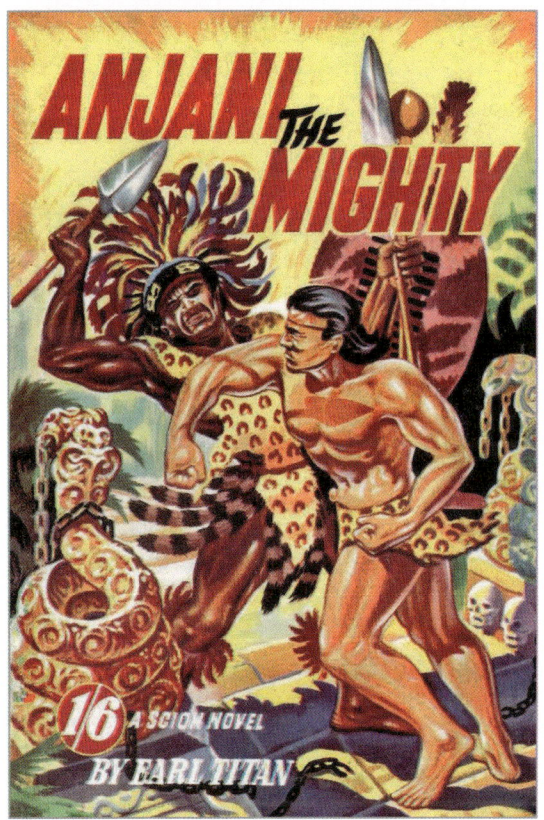

Right: Turner's covers for *The Gold of Akada* and *Anjani the Mighty*, both written by John Russell Fearn under the Earl Titan pseudonym and published in 1951 as the first titles in Scion's new jungle series.

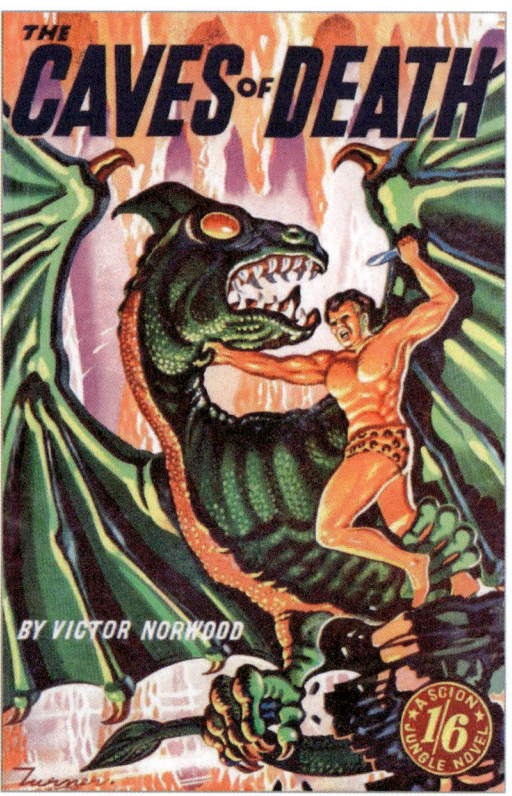

Turner's covers for the Scion jungle series novels *The Untamed*, *The Caves of Death* (signed, unusually, with the artist's surname), *The Temple of the Dead* and *The Skull of Kanaima*, all written by Victor Norwood and published in 1951.

FROM COVER TO COVER

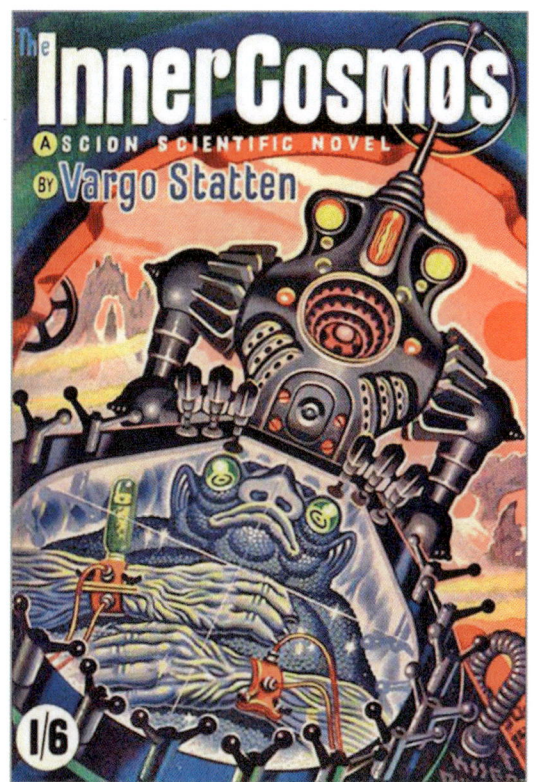
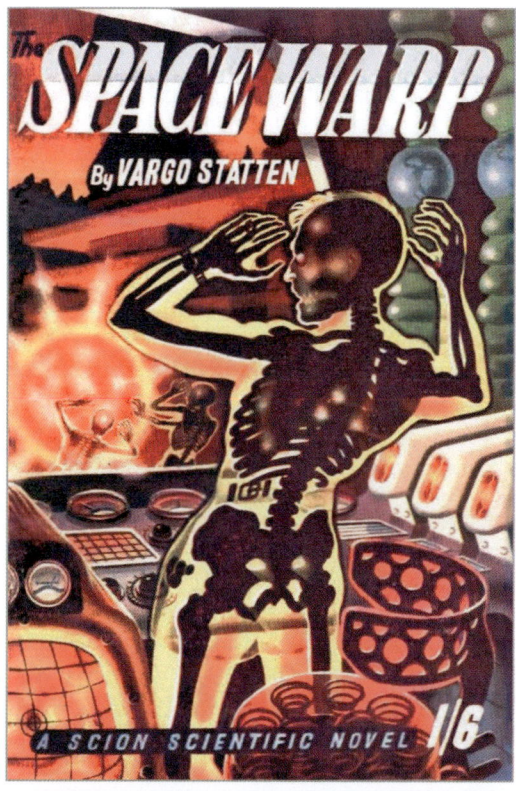

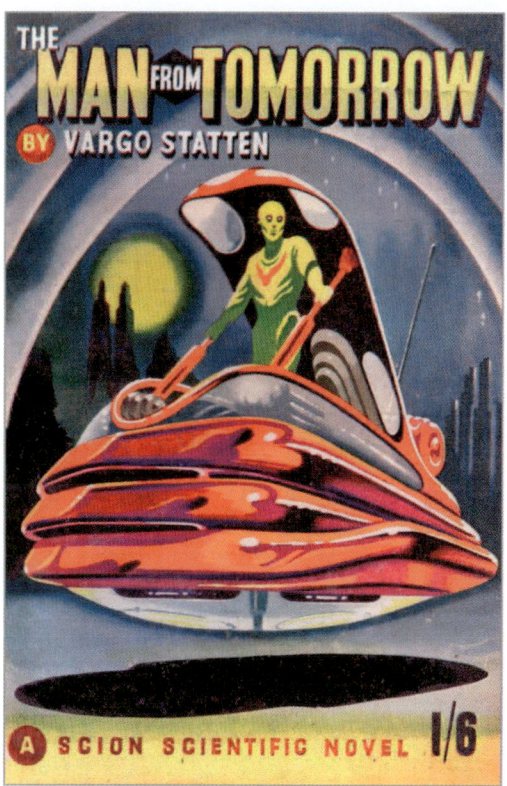

Turner's covers for the Vargo Statten novels *The Inner Cosmos*, *The Space Warp*, *The Time Bridge* and *The Man from Tomorrow*, all published by Scion in 1952.

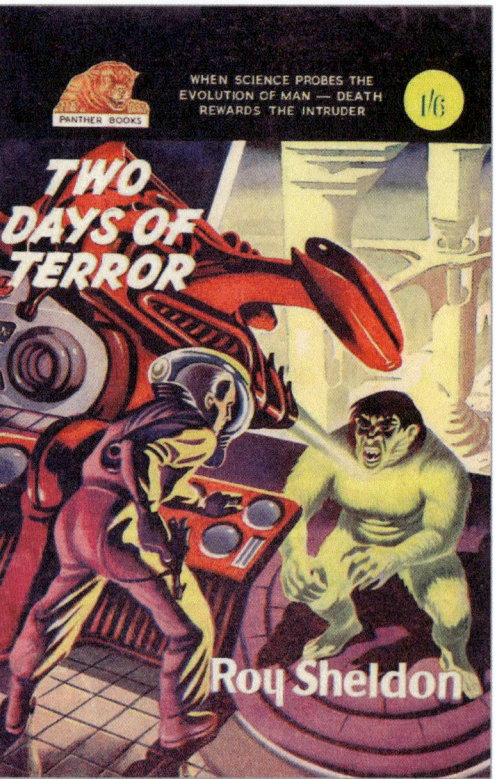

Turner's covers for the Scion-published Vargo Statten novels *The Eclipse Express* (another rare case where he added a 'Roland Turner' signature), *Laughter in Space* and *The G-Bomb*, and the Panther-published *Two Days of Terror* by Roy Sheldon, all from 1952.

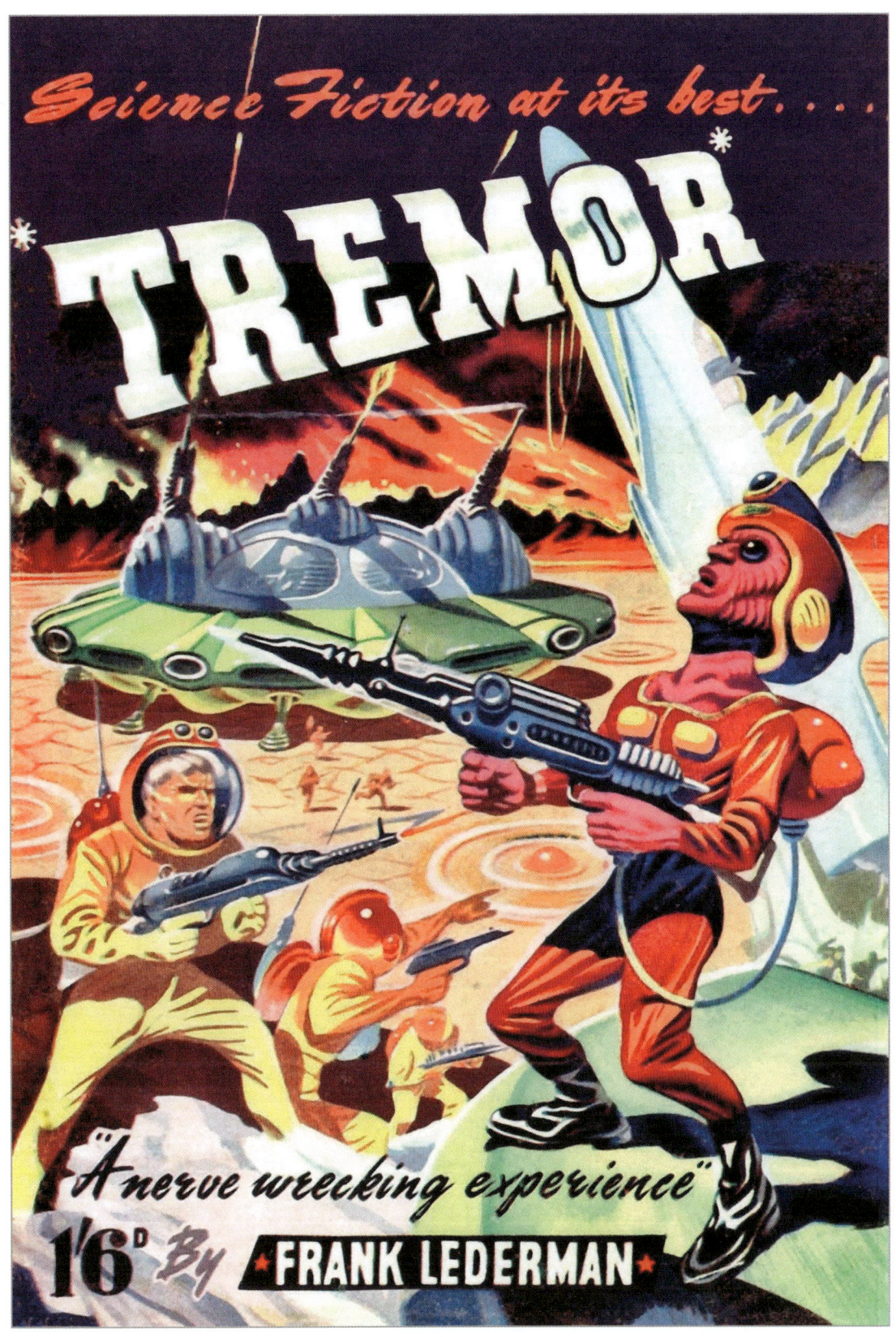

Tremor by Frank Lederman (Kaye, 1952)

Turner's covers for the Cherry Tree-published paperback *Vanguard to Neptune* by J M Walsh and for the John Spencer-published periodicals *Tales of Tomorrow* No. 4, *Wonders of the Spaceways* No. 3 and *Worlds of Fantasy* No. 7, all from 1952.

It was in early 1952 that Ron's eldest sister Evelyn, now widowed, came to live with him and his family in Romford, bringing along her 8-year-old son Michael. Ron soon became Michael's favourite uncle, being effectively a father figure to him, treating him very generously, not only to sweets and comics and Dinky toys but sometimes to more elaborate gifts like Meccano sets, train sets and on one occasion a fully-working model steam engine.

When he wasn't painting, Ron was often found tinkering with his new car, the Jupiter, always carrying out his own repairs and often enlisting Michael to hand him tools and watch him work. Consequently, Michael learnt a lot about the car, and loved to see Ron driving in it. On one very warm summer's day, Michael was taken for a walk by Ron's father, and they stopped at a local pub for a drink. While they were sitting outside, Ron happened to pull up at some nearby traffic lights in the Jupiter, whereupon a couple of fellow drinkers remarked on 'the Yank in the car'. Ron's father retorted that this was no 'Yank', but his son Ron Turner, who was well-known in the local community. When the drinkers expressed scepticism, the landlord confirmed that Ron was a famous painter. Even the landlord, though, was unaware that Ron's income, being exceptional for the period, had enabled him to buy that car outright for cash.

This was only one of many times that Ron, driving such a flashy car, was mistaken for a 'Yank'. With US culture influencing British attitudes so much in those post-war times, he felt quite 'the guy'. Unfortunately, his enthusiasm sometimes got the better of him. Having such a powerful car made it easy for him to break the speed limit, which he did often, leading to many a brush with the law!

Although Ron was always quite private about the work he did, on occasion he would invite his young nephew into his studio/bedroom if there was a piece he was particularly pleased with, and Michael would marvel at some of his covers for the Vargo Statten paperbacks. To Ron, these were no more than forays into his imagination, but to young Michael, it seemed that his uncle had the uncanny gift of making scenes come to life. So realistic were some of the weird alien creatures depicted on the covers of novels such as *The Inner Cosmos* and *The G-Bomb* that Michael actually found them quite frightening. This was particularly so of a piece that Ron would produce a couple of years later for the cover of *The Scourge of the Carbon Belt*, one of the *Tit-Bits* Science Fiction Comics series, where an alien warrior charging out on his equally alien steed would fairly scare the youngster out of his wits!

But just as life was going very nicely for Ron, a drastic change occurred around the middle of 1952, when Scion were dealt a crushing blow that nearly put them out of business. Since the early '50s, Scion's line of gangster novels, in competition with many others, had flirted with themes of sex and violence; but the steady increase in these elements had not gone unnoticed. Having attracted the attention of the various Watch Committees set up as unelected moral guardians, the publishers now found themselves landed with a massive fine for obscenity, resulting in all payments to authors and artists being immediately suspended. This was a tremendous shock for Ron, and although his agent, Hall, managed to secure him a few further commissions from John Spencer for their SF series,

Below: *The Scourge of the Carbon Belt* (C Arthur Pearson, 1954).

Futuristic Science Stories No. 7 (John Spencer, 1952)

Ron would get no further freelance work that year.

Faced with the possibility that his 'golden days' might now be over, and with his thirtieth birthday fast approaching, Ron decided that he should nevertheless get some benefit from all his efforts, and have one 'last hurrah'. So, in the August of 1952, he set out on a journey across Europe, heading for Italy. It was a trip he had been contemplating for some time, more as a pilgrimage than as a holiday: a return to the Second World War battlefields of nearly 18 years earlier. Ron's part in the Battle of Monte Cassino had been a traumatic experience for him, and with memories still haunting him, there were a few ghosts to be laid.

When Ron returned to England several weeks later, there was no positive news from Hall regarding Scion, so he still felt fairly uncertain about his future. The past two years had been the best of his life, working for a company that really appreciated his efforts and gave him free rein to interpret scenes in his own particular way. And having the opportunity to read all those great SF stories as they were written had been the icing on the cake. But, if his involvement with Scion was now to end, what next? He was still employed by Odhams, of course, but they offered him none of the type of work he so enjoyed. Should he consider going freelance in the hope that Hall could secure for him sufficient commissions from established, professional companies such as the Amalgamated Press, who did publish that type of material? In some doubt, Ron bided his time, and as the New Year dawned, he discovered that the situation wasn't as dire as he had first feared.

In January 1953, Scion rallied and, with financial backing, re-established themselves at smaller premises. They were still heavily in debt, however, and some of their team, including editor Maurice Read, left to form their own company, Milestone Publications. On credit extended via connections with a paper supplier, Milestone were able to start up almost immediately, and quickly became a direct rival to Scion. One of the authors they recruited was E C Tubb, known generally as Ted Tubb, who had already written two SF stories for Scion under the pseudonym 'Volsted Gridban'. Tubb's first novel for Milestone, under the same pseudonym, was *Planetoid Disposals Ltd.*, and Ron was commissioned to provide the cover.

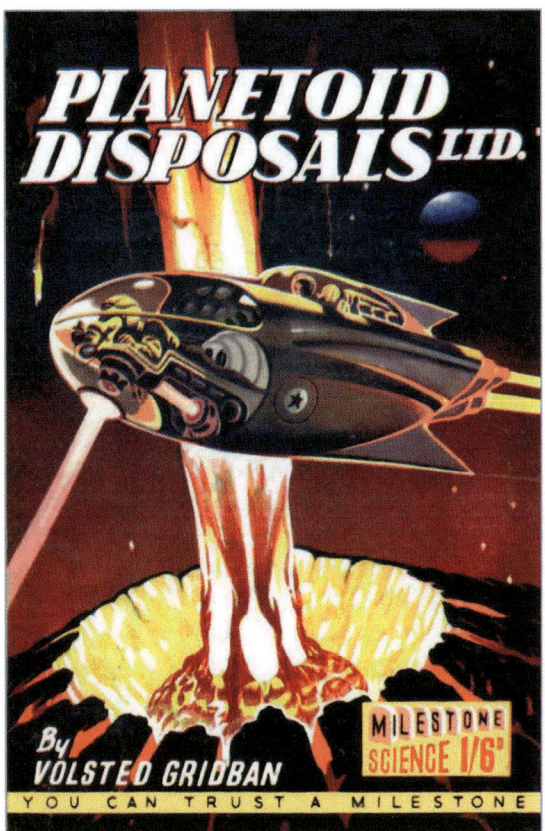

Above: *Planetoid Disposals Ltd.* by E C Tubb writing as Volsted Gridban, published by Milestone in January 1953.

John Russell Fearn's exclusive five-year contract to provide SF novels for Scion having been effectively broken by the company's failure to pay him, he also began offering stories to Milestone. One of these, *Fugitive of Time*, was immediately accepted, and again Ron was asked to supply the cover. Fuelled by enthusiasm and the promise of his SF career returning, Ron took key elements from the story to produce a superb painting: one of his best ever symbolic pieces. In the meantime, though, Scion, having realised they were in danger of losing their strongest literary asset, had quickly settled their debt to Fearn and tempted him back to them with the promise of payment in advance for all future stories; something quite unheard of at the time. Fearn accepted, and as part of the agreement, withdrew his *Fugitive of Time* from Milestone. This left Milestone with a completed cover and title – but no book!

Milestone's solution to this problem was to reassign the cover and title to a second submission they had accepted from Ted Tubb, who was fast emerging as one of the most popular SF authors of the day. Consequently Tubb's novel – the original title of which remains unknown – appeared as *Fugitive of Time* by Volsted Gridban; and although on this occasion Ron's stunning cover bore no relation to the events of the story, it certainly ensured that sales didn't suffer.

The *Fugitive of Time* that Fearn had withdrawn from Milestone was subsequently published by Scion under the new title *Zero Hour*, and Ron was again asked to provide the cover – his second for this novel. Once again he produced a symbolic interpretation, this time depicting a giant eye. Symbolic pieces like this were increasingly becoming a distinctive part of his repertoire. Occasionally, if a story was too cerebral for him to be able to select a specific incident to interpret literally, he would choose to combine certain elements in order to set the scene in a more figurative manner. Though this was a more challenging prospect creatively, Ron felt that when it was successful it was sometimes more rewarding than conventional illustration. The giant eye was a motif he would revisit to particularly impressive effect on subsequent covers, such as that for the 1954 Vargo Statten novel *I Spy*. An image of giant, disembodied hands was another highly effective device he used to denote an unseen power, as shown on innovative SF covers he produced in the spring of 1953 for the Milestone-published *The Wall* by Ted Tubb writing as Charles Grey and the Panther-published *The Great Ones* by Jon J Deegan, and later in the year for the Vargo Statten title *Black Bargain*. The latter cover was impressive on another account, too, for not only did it present a strong symbolic image of space itself curving round the Earth to form a giant hand, it also gave an accurate depiction of the planet as seen from orbit, years before NASA photos would confirm Ron's vision.

Turner's symbolic covers for the novels eventually published as *Fugitive of Time* by Volsted Gridban (Milestone, 1953) and *Zero Hour* by Vargo Statten (Scion, 1953).

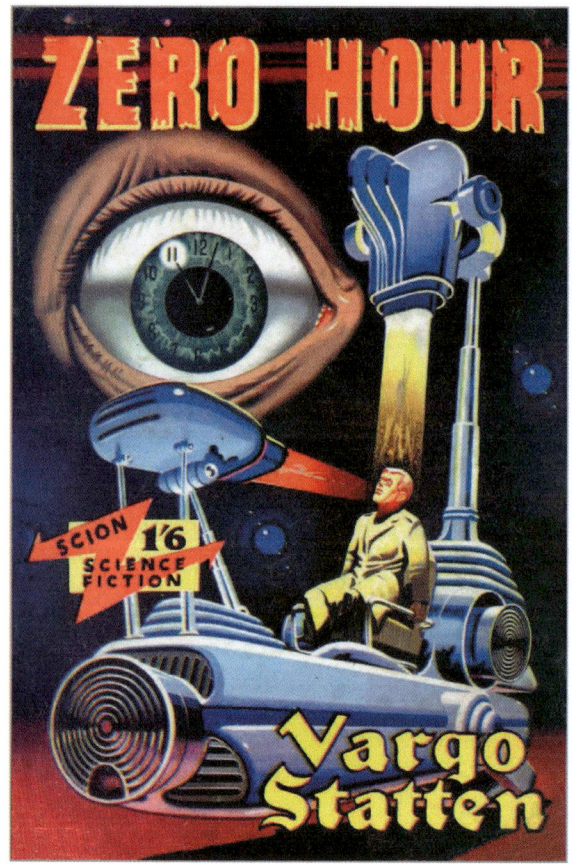

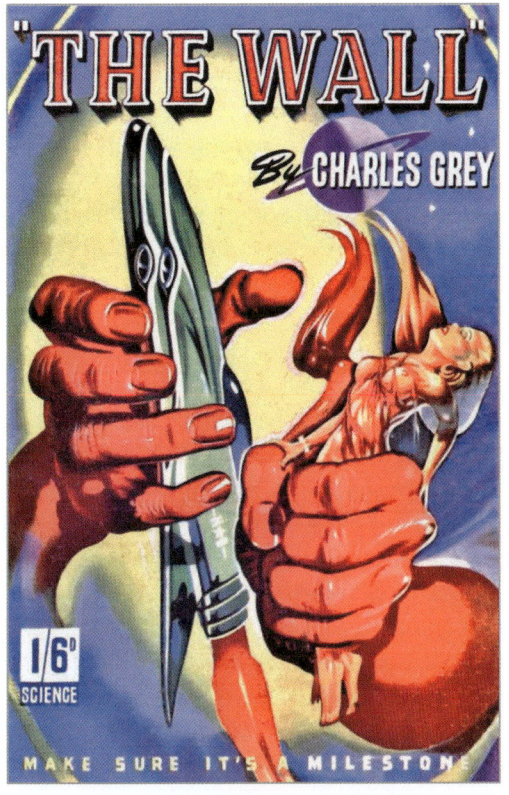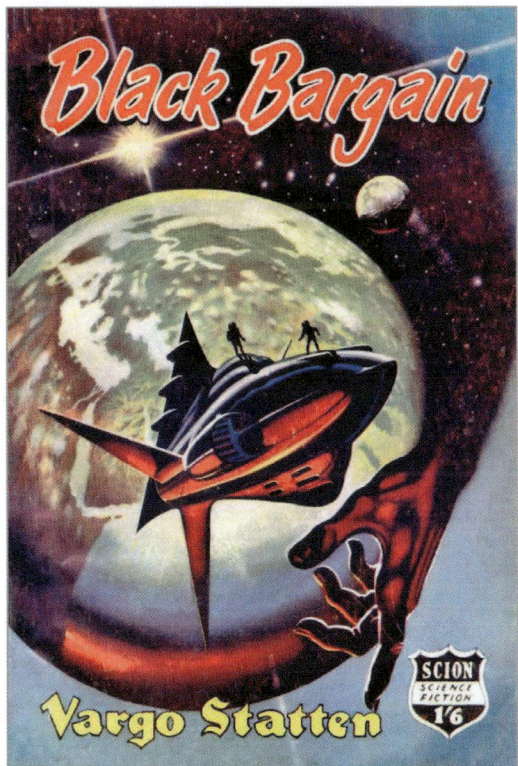

Turner's impressive symbolic covers for *The Wall* by Charles Grey (Milestone, 1953), *The Great Ones* by Jon J Deegan (Panther, 1953), *Black Bargain* by Vargo Statten (Scion, 1953) and *I Spy* by Vargo Statten IScion, 1954)..

Mindful of how book cover work had suddenly disappeared in the latter half of 1952, Ron was keen to keep his hand in with comic strip assignments, and his ever-industrious agent Greg Hall managed to find him one: a back-up story called 'The Caverns of Doom' for Issue 14 of the Anglo-American *Masterman* comic, published in February 1953. The story tells of a professor going missing on Jupiter after discovering a vast diamond deposit there, and the Planetary Bureau of Investigation despatching their operatives Captain Universe and Sergeant 'Dozer' Dunkley to investigate. The titular caverns hold a weird pterodactyl-like creature that vaporises its victims between the 'electrostatic barbs of its twin tentacles'; something that saves the spacemen twice: once when they are attacked by another strange creature, and again when they are menaced by the villain of the piece, who is holding the professor hostage in the hope of learning the location of the diamond deposits. When the creature finally turns on the trio themselves for dessert, the professor returns the favour by protecting the spacemen with a device that reverses the beast's charge, thereby inducing a violent short-circuit that kills it!

Captain Universe would have been an unlikely name for Ron to choose for one of his characters, so it was probably suggested by the publishers in the expectation that they would be getting a superhero-type strip – especially as it was to appear alongside the superhero-themed main 'Masterman' story. Ron's agent agreed to the brief simply to secure the commission, despite Ron disliking anything to do with the superhero genre, but the artist was then left to his own devices as to how to present the story. Therefore it's not surprising that he drew Captain Universe and Sergeant Dunkley simply as two spacemen, virtually indistinguishable from one another, with the former hardly referred to by name at all. It's possible that this would initially have come as something of an annoyance to the publishers, although when they saw the results and realised that the story would fill the pages satisfactorily, no doubt they found it more than acceptable. Ron took inspiration for his work from various sources, and in this particular case he clearly based the story in part upon Victor Norwood's *The Caves of Death*, one of the Scion jungle series novels for which he had previously provided the covers.

The cavern in Norwood's story holds a similar creature likewise encountered by two explorers. There, though, the similarity ends: in Ron's tale, the explorers become spacemen, and all the scientific and technical aspects are pure Turner. Unlike Norwood's story, Ron's is also tongue-in-cheek, with a certain amount of humorous and witty dialogue to counterbalance the more dramatic elements; an aspect of storytelling that Ron would continue to develop in much of his later strip work.

Meantime, any fears Ron might have had about a lack of cover work in 1953 proved to be unfounded. John Russell Fearn's return to Scion generated a steady stream of further SF novels, with the Vargo Statten and Volsted Gridban pseudonyms being used interchangeably, and Ron was in constant demand to provide the covers. The succession of superb pieces he painted for Fearn novels such as *Moons for Sale*, *The Dyno-Depressant* and *Scourge of the Atom* were exactly what the publishers needed, and all helped to secure Ron a

Below: *Moons for Sale*, written by John Russell Fearn as Volsted Gridban and published by Scion in 1953.

reputation as the top British SF cover artist of the day. Indeed, Ron was now in the extremely advantageous position of having two regular customers for his covers, as Milestone also secured his services to work on a new line of Ted Tubb SF novels written under the Charles Grey pseudonym. Just as his striking visualisations of Fearn's novels had done for Scion, his vivid interpretations of Tubb's stories such as *The Wall* and *Dynasty of Doom* soon helped establish Milestone as another of the country's leading SF publishers.

However, while Ron was producing all these marvellous covers, he was still employed by Odhams, and he found his work for them tedious by comparison. Able to indulge his passion for SF illustration with publishers prepared to accept his own interpretations, and high in confidence due to the positive reaction his work was getting, he felt constricted by Odhams' more disciplined attitude, and found himself increasingly in disagreement with the art editor, Arthur Gould. Ron had his own ideas on presentation, but they just didn't meet with approval, and he failed to see why he wasn't getting the same appreciation from Gould as he was from Read. Ron fell out with his editor on several occasions – and even at times with some of his colleagues who agreed with Gould that he was playing fast and loose with Odhams' 'house style'. To Ron, Odhams were simply getting in his way. He knew now where his future lay; and, with far more exciting projects on offer from other publishers, he was sorely tempted to quit and turn freelance. This was encouraged by Greg Hall; and when Hall mentioned to Gould that Ron was considering leaving Odhams and joining his agency, Gould's reply gave Ron further pause for thought, being to the effect that if he didn't change his attitude soon, he would be fired! However, caught between the choice of a guaranteed salary and the irregular income that freelance work would bring, Ron was still undecided. June 1953 would prove the turning point.

Odhams published a film magazine called *Picturegoer*, and Ron was tasked with producing two illustrations for their special Queen's Coronation issue, one being of the interior of Westminster

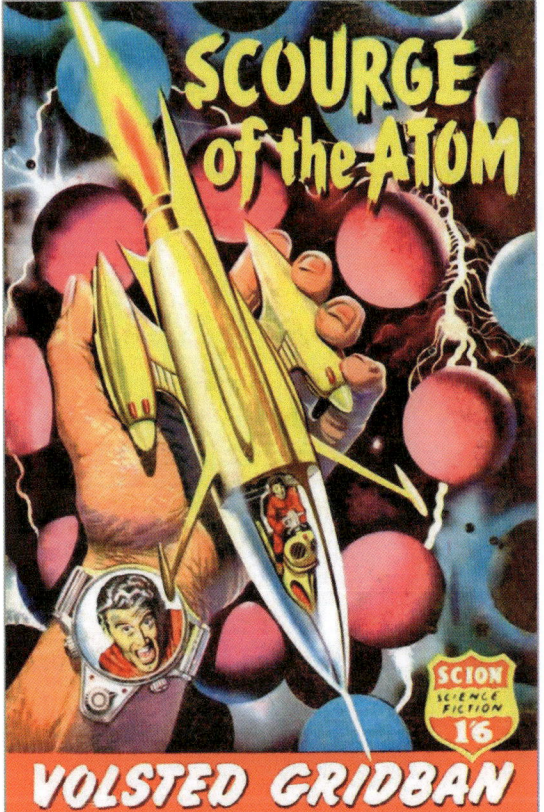

Left: Turner's covers for *The Dyno-Depressant* and *Scourge of the Atom*, both written by John Russell Fearn as Volsted Gridban and published by Scion in 1953.

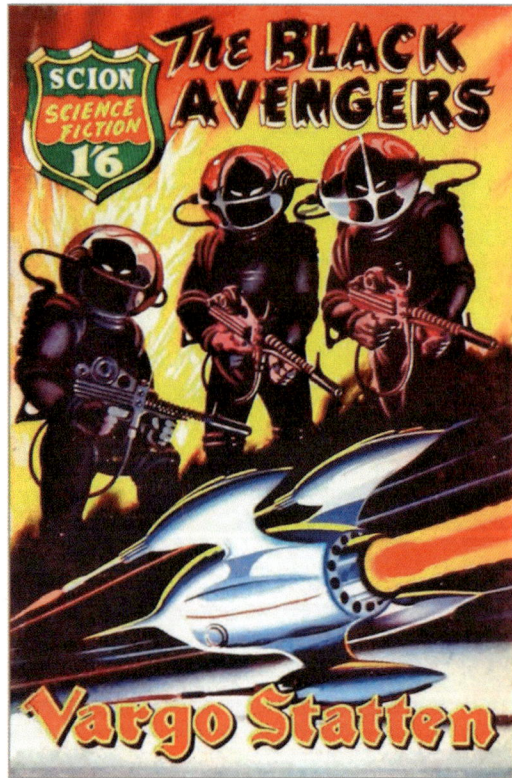
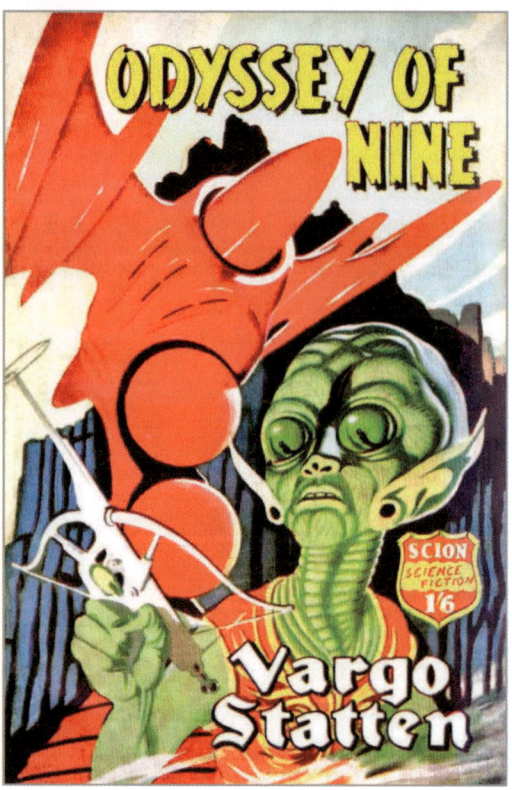

Turner's covers for the Milestone-published *Dynasty of Doom* by E C Tubb writing as Charles Grey, and the Scion-published *Ultra Spectrum*, *The Black Avengers* and *Odyssey of Nine* by John Russell Fearn writing as Vargo Statten, all from early 1953.

FROM COVER TO COVER

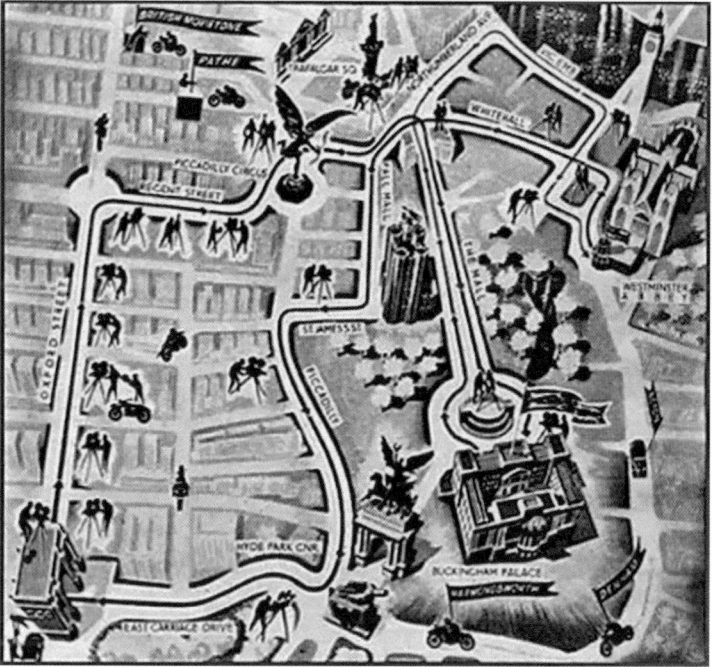

Abbey, showing how the TV cameras would be positioned over the aisle, and the other a map of the route the procession would take. The problem was the deadline. Ron was given the brief on a Friday afternoon, and was expected to have the two pieces ready for the following Monday morning. This meant that he would have to work throughout the weekend in order to complete the task. The Abbey scene itself proved particularly long and tedious to do, with the need to present row upon row of small figures, but Ron persevered and eventually delivered on time; a remarkable piece of work.

But, for all his efforts, Ron received only Odhams' standard overtime payment, which overall compared poorly to what he could expect for a piece of his SF cover art. Ron now began seriously to re-evaluate the situation. If weekend work was to become a regular and accepted practice at Odhams, then it could well impact on the time he had available to produce the type of work he found financially and creatively more rewarding. He discussed the situation again with Hall, and when the agent assured him that he could find him more cover work than he could handle, he finally decided to take the plunge and leave Odhams. Afterwards, although now free of restrictions, Ron was still a little concerned as to whether or not he'd made the right decision; but as some of the companies for whom he would be providing covers would also be publishing comics, that was an encouraging prospect, as he still harboured the desire to create further strip stories of his own.

Left: Turner's contributions to the *Picturegoer* issue marking the Coronation of Queen Elizabeth II (Odhams, 2 May 1953).

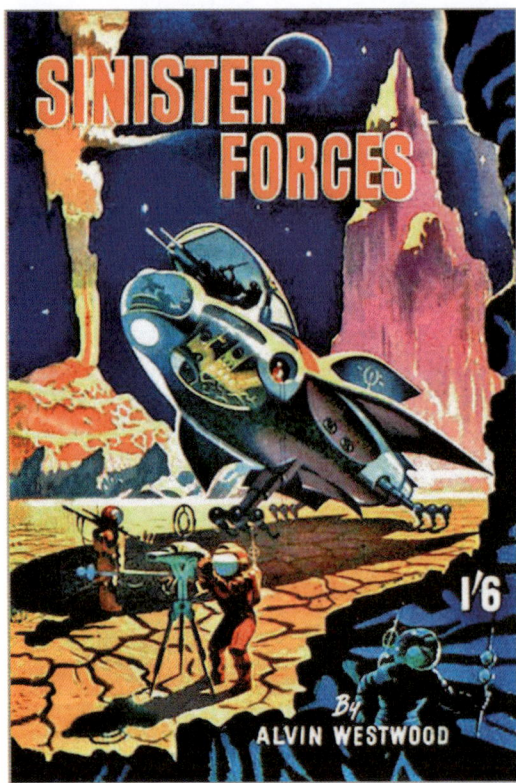
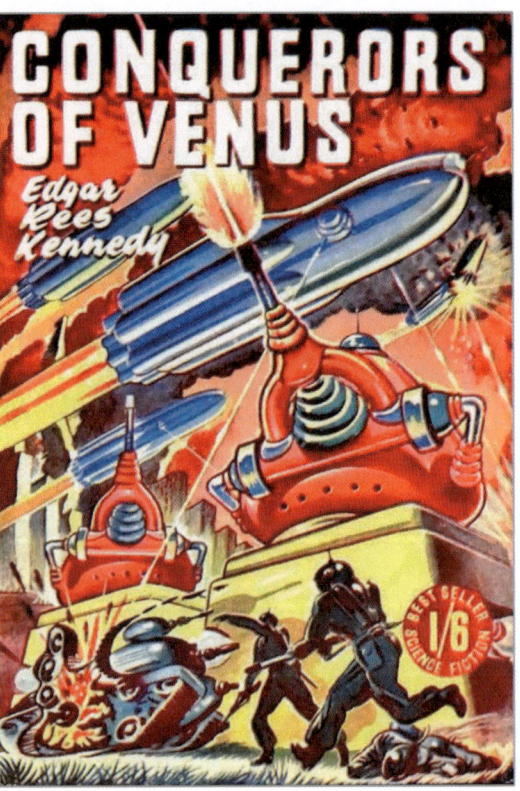

Turner's covers for *Pioneer, 1990* by Vargo Statten (Scion), *Magnetic Brain* by Volsted Gridban (Scion), *Sinister Forces* by Alvin Westwood (Brown Watson) and *Conquerors of Venus* by Edgar Rees Kennedy (Edwin Self), all published in the first half of 1953.

4: ODD STRIPS AND TIT-BITS

By mid-1953, Ron had become Britain's most popular SF cover illustrator, and his work was in constant demand. But, as a newly-freelance artist, there were other avenues he wished to explore. Initially, he had taken comic strips not too seriously, despite the relative success of his early ventures, but in light of the near-collapse of Scion the previous year, he now felt the need to establish himself fully in that medium, in case the cover work should ever cease. There was also another impetus. Running parallel to him over the last few years had been an artist he greatly admired: Frank Hampson, creator of Dan Dare for the *Eagle* comic.

Ron had been aware of Hampson's work from the very first issue of *Eagle* in 1950. Intrigued by the arrival in Romford of a Humber Hawk car bearing on its roof a large papier-mâché golden eagle – a publicity stunt devised by publishers Hulton Press to launch the comic – he had soon become an avid reader. Hampson's ideas of futuristic technology, his designs for spacecraft and machines, and his ability to tell a rattling good story involving believable characters, were qualities Ron couldn't help but find impressive. Hampson had shown the potential of a home-grown comic strip, and his continued and increasing success with Dan Dare was inspirational for Ron.

Ron had read and absorbed so much SF over the years that coming up with story ideas was not too much of a problem for him. His earlier contributions to an Odhams non-fiction book titled *Marvels of Modern Science* also helped, as he found that any obscure scientific or astronomical fact he'd come across could provide the germ of inspiration on which to base a tale. So, with plenty of creative ideas of his own that he wanted to realise, and with a large and eager market for this type of material, Ron was now keen, like Hampson before him, to produce strips of his own.

Ron's first freelance opportunity came after he provided a stunning line-and-wash endpaper, showing spacecraft and astronauts circling a space-station, for *Laurie's Space Annual* of 1953. So impressive did publishers T Werner Laurie find this piece that they also agreed to take from him an eight-page strip story for inclusion in the book. 'Death of a Planet!', despite its dramatic title, was a fairly uninspired tale of an alien invasion being defeated by, of all things, a group of interplanetary boy scouts! Ron's illustrations showed he was a little rusty after a two year hiatus from strips, his linework lacking any great detail. However, his creativity was as strong as ever, and the juvenile theme was saved by some dynamic compositions. But Ron needed more than occasional 'fillers' like this to get his comic-strip career in full swing; and luckily his agent, Hall, soon discovered that one of the paperback publishers, Comyns, was planning a new SF comic.

Encouraged by the recent appearance of a regular 24-page comic called *Spaceman*, published by Gould-Light and drawn and edited entirely by another ex-Odhams studio artist, Norman Light, Ron hoped that Comyns might be willing to devote issues of their new title exclusively to his work, and he enthusiastically set about creating his own space hero, Captain Sciento. Throwing all his creative energy into the project, he finally submitted a cover scene and two stories, 'The Solar Condenser' and 'The Missing Levitanium', as material sufficient to fill an initial 24-page issue. Comyns, however, obviously believed in the 'safety in numbers' principle of using several different artists. Although impressed by Ron's work, they accepted only 'The Solar Condenser' for the first issue of their *Star-Rocket* comic, alongside contributions from others such as Ron Embleton.

The influence of Alex Raymond's Flash Gordon was evident in the Sciento tales, though Ron's character was not a youthful figure with blond wavy hair but – as the name implied – a more mature scientist/adventurer type, his natty black beard and moustache owing more to Gordon's adversary Dr Zarkov than to Gordon himself. In 'The Solar Condenser', communication with Venus has been lost and the United Interplanetary Organisation sends Sciento to investigate. It transpires that Varon, self-styled leader of Venus, has stolen a solar

condenser – a giant flying lens – with which he plans to 'fry' the Earth, making it ripe for conquest. Sciento intervenes, and after several encounters, sends the giant lens crashing Venus-wards to crush the still-grounded invasion fleet.

This story was a vast improvement on 'Death of a Planet!', not only in artistic detail but also in storytelling techniques and in the amusingly transatlantic tone of the dialogue. At one point, Sciento tells his daughter Stella, 'If the UIO knew I'd brought you along as second pilot, I'd get sacked. But what can a man do with a brat like you!?' 'Nuts', is her curt response. A degree of pseudo-realism is also added to the proceedings, with the aliens speaking in their native tongue, so that when the evil Varon orders his guards, 'Giegen mikton salsar vorus sur … extor sen doros', Ron provides the translation, 'Take these two away and exterminate them!', for the benefit of readers yet to get to grips with Venusian! But it is the superb artwork that grabs the attention, Ron's enthusiasm spilling off the page with his futuristic designs for everything from spacesuits to spacecraft. All are convincingly rendered with a level of technical detail that most artists of the time would never have contemplated; but then, most were interested in nothing more than picking up the basic rate of pay on offer and then moving on, lacking any of Ron's dedication and ambition to create something special.

The latter part of 1953 saw Ron still continuing to pick up a steady stream of cover work for various publishers. This included further Milestone commissions for Ted Tubb's Charles Grey novels; and, as had happened previously with *Fugitive of Time*, circumstances conspired to ensure that two of these became rare instances where his compositions bore no relation to their respective stories. Ron was asked to submit preliminary sketches for the two books, *Space Hunger* and *Tormented City*. In approving them, however, Milestone's

Left: The title pages of 'Death of a Planet!' from *Laurie's Space Annual* (T Werner Laurie, 1953) and the first Captain Sciento story, 'The Solar Condenser', from the launch issue of *Star-Rocket* (Comyns, 1953).

   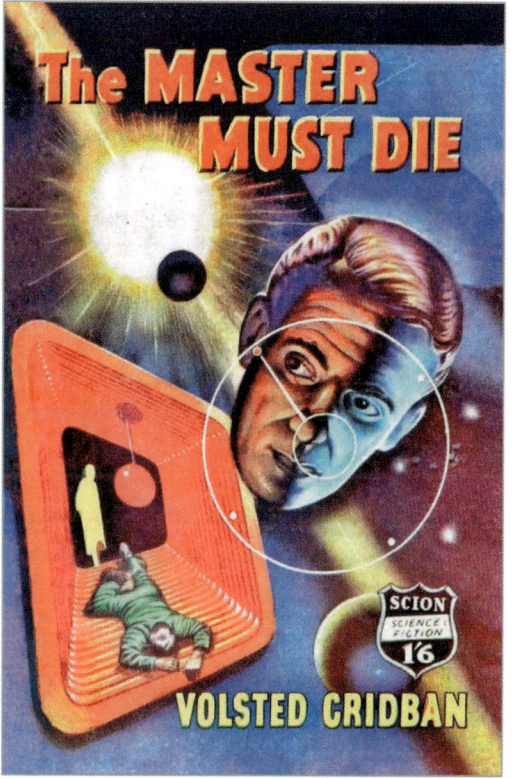

Turner's covers for *The Lie Destroyer* by Vargo Statten, *Man of Two Worlds* by Vargo Statten, *Exit Life* by Volsted Gridban and *The Master Must Die* by Volsted Gridban, all published by Scion in the second half of 1953.

The Unseen Assassin by Hank Janson (Top Fiction, 1953), combining a Reginald Heade female figure with a Ron Turner background.

art editor mistakenly assumed that the *Space Hunger* one was for *Tormented City* and *vice versa*, and marked them up as such. When the sketches were returned to Ron for him to complete the paintings, he simply lettered them as instructed: having been involved with other work in the interim, he was oblivious to the fact that the titles had been transposed!

Another commission Ron received in 1953, this time from Top Fiction Press, also presented his work in an unusual way. Top Fiction were the current publishers of Stephen Frances's hugely successful Hank Janson crime novels, boasting covers by classic 'good-girl' artist Reginald Heade, another of Greg Hall's clients. However, one particular Janson series entry, *The Unseen Assassin*, unusually had an SF theme, and Hall felt that on this occasion Ron would be a more suitable choice of artist. As the publisher wasn't prepared to lose Heade's trademark 'dame' – and doubtless neither was Heade – a compromise was reached, whereby Heade would provide the central figure of the girl, and the painting would then be passed on to Ron to supply a futuristic city background. This worked amazingly well, the skills of both artists combining to create a cover so expertly realised that few readers would ever have realised it was a collaboration.

In the meantime, Ron had secured a deal to provide SF covers for C Arthur Pearson, one of the more upmarket publishing companies of the period. Pearson's favourable rates of pay attracted some of the better SF writers of the day, and John Russell Fearn, during the brief period when he was in dispute with Scion, had approached their editor, Bob Brandon, offering to provide stories. Brandon had seized on this as an opportunity to launch a new SF range, *Tit-Bits* Science Fiction Library, hoping to emulate the success of Fearn's Vargo Statten and Volsted Gridban titles, with Ron again providing the covers. In the event, however, Fearn supplied Pearson with only two stories before being tempted back to Scion: *The Hell Fruit*, written under the pseudonym Lawrence F Rose and featuring the Martian detective Earmar Brown, intended to run as a

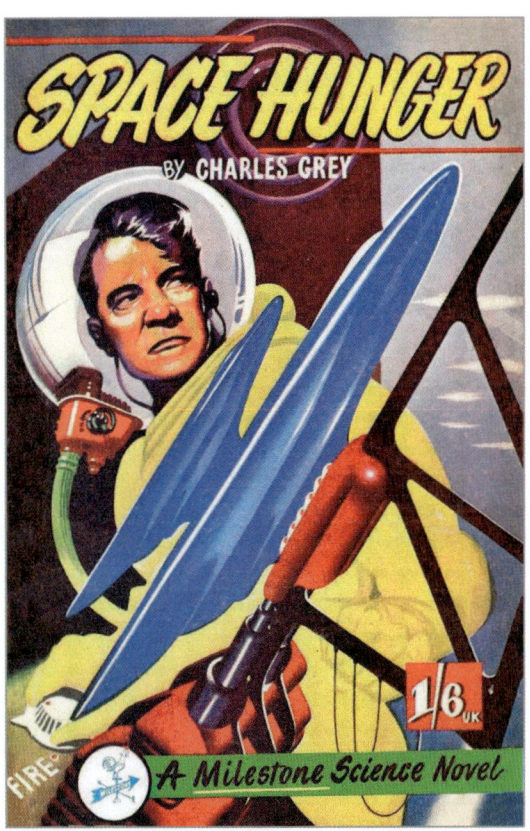

Right: Turner's inadvertently transposed covers for *Space Hunger* and *Tormented City*, written by E C Tubb as Charles Grey and published by Milestone in 1953.

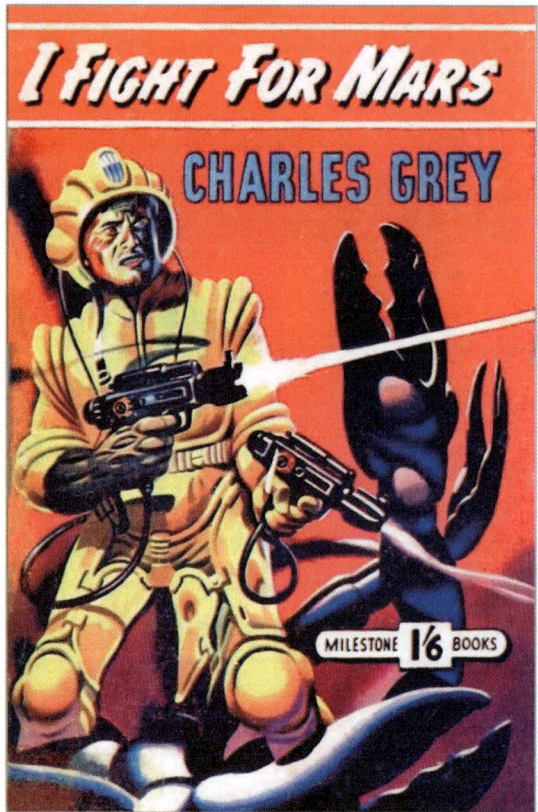

series character; and *Cosmic Exodus,* written under the pseudonym Conrad G Holt. The loss of Fearn was naturally a blow to Brandon, who had high hopes for his new venture. However, he decided to press ahead with the range, simply delaying its launch for several months until other writers, such as Ted Tubb, could be brought in to fill the gap.

Having lost Scion's best SF writer, Brandon had no intention of losing their best SF cover artist too, so Ron was kept on board, and the *Tit-Bits* Science Fiction Library range was finally launched in August 1953. *The Hell Fruit* was the first title, followed by *Cosmic Exodus* in September and two newly-commissioned titles, the pseudonymous *Doomed Nation of the Skies* by Steve Future and *The Star Seekers* by Francis G Rayer, in November and December respectively.

Ron, noting Brandon's admiration for his work and determined not to lose sight of his own goal, felt that now would be a good time to propose a sister range of monthly comic books, for which he would supply the contents. Ron's perception proved correct, as Brandon was immediately receptive to the idea. However, there was a drawback: these books would have to be in the same digest-type format already established for the novels, each running to 64 pages. This would be an enormous undertaking for Ron, as although the relatively small page size meant that he would need to draw only three or four frames per page, he would also be responsible for writing the stories, adding the lettering and providing the covers, all the while ensuring that he kept to a strict monthly deadline. Nevertheless, throwing caution to the wind, he eagerly accepted.

It was while he was working on the first issue of this new *Tit-Bits* Science Fiction Comics range for Pearson that Ron was approached by Comyns to do more strip work for them too. By this point, the second issue of their *Star-Rocket* comic had appeared, but lacking any contributions from Turner or Ron Embleton, and being filled instead by stories from unknowns who knew little about space science and even less about art, it looked pathetic by comparison with the first. Realising their mistake, Comyns decided that for the third issue they would take Ron's other Sciento submission, 'The Missing Levitanium', plus

Left: Two more 1953 paperback cover commissions: *Zhorani* by Karl Maras (Comyns) and *I Fight for Mars* by Charles Grey (Milestone).

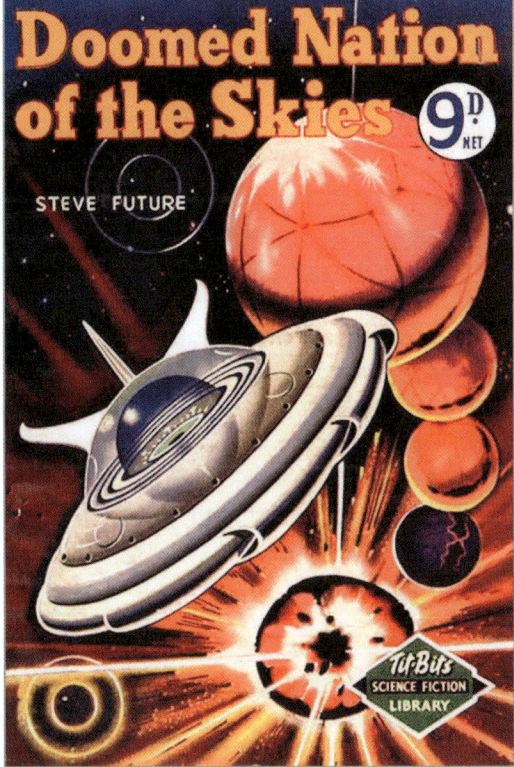

Turner's covers for the first four entries in the *Tit-Bits* Science Fiction Library: *The Hell Fruit* by Lawrence F Rose, *Cosmic Exodus* by Conrad G Holt, *Doomed Nation of the Skies* by Steve Future and *The Star Seekers* by Francis G Rayer (C Arthur Pearson, 1953).

a new 17-page story, 'Space Pirates', which Ron was also to feature on the cover. This issue would thus be made up entirely of Ron's work – the very thing he had wanted in the first place!

In order to cope with this latest addition to his workload, Ron realised that he would have to adopt a faster production method. For the *Tit-Bits* series, he had already decided to rely more on brushwork and less on pen than he had in the past. Now he hit upon the clever time-saving technique of producing shading by sweeping the hairs of a lightly-charged dry brush over the required areas of the page, avoiding the need for any conventional feathering effects. Also, whereas on the Sciento stories he had drawn six to eight frames per page, for 'Space Pirates' he switched to using the same three to four frames per page as for the *Tit-Bits* work. This probably wasn't what Comyns had expected, but a 17-page story had been their requirement, and that was exactly what Ron gave them.

Drawn using different artistic techniques and with different numbers of frames per page, 'The Missing Levitanium' and 'Space Pirates' made strange bedfellows, seeming at first glance to be the work of two different contributors; but ultimately their imagination and dynamics left no doubt as to the true identity of the artist.

The plot of 'The Missing Levitanium' revolves around cargoes of a Martian catalytic mineral, able to reduce the weight of steel to half that of aluminium, being stolen from Mars-to-Earth space-freighters. The gang responsible for the thefts then plan to blow up the mines on Mars with a rocket attack, so as to increase the value of their spoils. However, they reckon without Sciento and Stella, who rumble the plot and arrive in time to destroy the rockets' launch platforms. The story involves a certain amount of pseudoscience, but is remarkable for the fact that it shows Sciento's ship, *The Asteroid*, making a three-point landing, years ahead of the real-life Space Shuttle!

'The Space Pirates' is, however, the more impressive of the two stories. With its larger frames in the *Tit-Bits* format, it tells of a pair of space pilots, Trace Telemark and 'Smiler' Smolt, who enter their ship, *The Brigand*, into the Great Trans-Solar Space Race. *En route*, they come across a gang of space pirates plundering freighters. They are initially taken

Above: Turner's cover for the third issue of *Star-Rocket* (Comyns, 1953), promoting his 'Space Pirates' story inside. The artist probably drew this piece in black and white, leaving the publisher to add the colours.

prisoner, but manage to break free and seize control. They then capture the crooks, escape from their base before it's blown to bits and still manage to win the Space Race! The story rattles along at a cracking pace, with non-stop action that would not be out of place in a James Bond movie. As the two heroes close in on the pirate vessel in their unarmed racing ship, the spacesuited Trace steps outside carrying an oxygen cylinder. Still caught in *The Brigand*'s shallow gravity field, he hurls the cylinder into the pirate vessel's exhaust outlet, blasting it apart.

'Space Pirates' is a further step up from Ron's previous comic-strip tales, with more imaginative layouts, a stronger plot and better characterisation, demonstrating his growing confidence in storytelling. The story also shows his increasing emphasis on scientific and technical detail. In this adventure, he introduces us to the

Remote Controlled Air Vehicle, or RCAV – a rocket-propelled device designed to aid a disabled ship running low on oxygen by clamping itself to the hull and firing into it a tube through which air can be pumped. But in this tale, the gang use the device for their own evil ends, injecting a deadly gas to disable a freighter's crew and steal the cargo. It was stories such as this, based on or around known aspects of science and technology, that Ron now planned to develop for the *Tit-Bits* Science Fiction Comics series.

In the meantime, Bob Brandon had decided to extend Pearson's publishing output still further. The nature of printing made it more economical to keep the presses rolling, so another companion series, *Tit-Bits* Wild-West Comics, was added to the line. Ron's agent, Hall, never one to allow an opportunity to slip by, was more than willing to offer the services of other artists from his agency, and consequently Norman Light (of *Spaceman* fame) and George R Radcliffe, amongst others, became regular contributors to this new venture.

The Science Fiction Comics and Wild-West Comics series both saw their debut issues published on 6 October 1953; but it was the former that made the most impact and would continue to do so, for Ron's stories were instilled with a quality and flair that represented the best of '50s SF.

With the commitment of a regular series rather than the odd filler strip to produce, Ron realised he would have to steer away from clichéd 'invasion' and 'space pirate' plots if he was to keep his offerings fresh and exciting. Luckily, coming up with different themes and storylines posed little problem for him, as during his 'apprenticeship' on book covers he had absorbed a wealth of SF ideas from the stories he'd read, and these provided a good basis from which he could develop his own. Again, the scientific and technical elements, including such things as force-screens, hyper-space travel and atomic physics, were entirely Ron's own, and set his strip work apart from most other artists'.

Each issue of *Tit-Bits* Science Fiction Comics presented a lead story, after which that issue was titled, and one or two back-ups. In the first issue, *Planet-X1 – The New World*, the lead story tells of a planet, originally hidden behind Venus, that has now shifted into a new orbit and pushed our world further from the Sun, causing an ice-age to descend. Hostility builds up between Mars and Earth, as teams from each race to claim the new planet for themselves and test its suitability for migration. Eventually the Earth party, led by Clive Clinton and his co-pilot Spike Manley, discover that the planet is surrounded by a force-screen: an invisible barrier caused by 'inverted warping of the planet's gravity field, which is built up in direct ratio to the planet's mass'. They circumvent this, however, when Clive discovers that by 'switching the ship's power to hyper-drive and matching the frequency of the barrier' they are able to break through. Ron's pseudoscience, comparable to the sort of technobabble later heard in films and TV series such as *Star Trek*, was way ahead of its time as far as comic strips were concerned; but he delighted in giving his stories a degree of scientific verisimilitude, reflecting the enthusiasm he felt for his work at the time. He also included in the story

Below: the cover of the first *Tit-Bits* Science Fiction Comics issue, *Planet-X1 – The New World* (C Arthur Pearson, 1953).

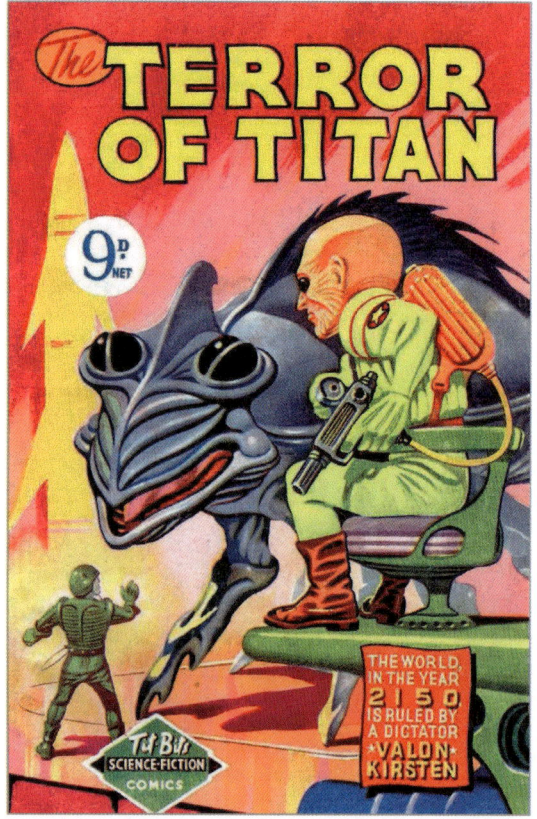

some suitably evil-looking Martians to complement the imaginatively-designed spacecraft taking part in the dogfights and other action sequences presented over its 31 pages. Comprising the other half of the issue, the back-up story, 'Giants of the Second World', leant more toward science fantasy, the titular characters being a group of subhuman barbarians who hold the secrets to a gravity-defying wonder metal located beneath the oceans of Venus.

The lead story of the second issue, *The Terror of Titan*, sees Ron's heroes battling fifty-foot Scorabs – scorpion/crab creatures with their nerve ganglia removed – as Martian dictator Valon Kirsten directs them by remote control to take over Saturn's moon Titan. This issue's back-up story, 'The Planetoid Peril', tells of a sudden increase in the prevalence of small asteroids, rendering space travel almost impossible, until the Space Lanes Clearance Company discovers that they are being controlled by ship-wreckers using a 'magnetic mass transference generator' to aim them at passing freighters.

In the lead story of the third issue, *Captain Diamond and the Space Pirates*, a comet is heading directly toward Earth, and a plutonium bomb intended to blast it off course is hijacked by a gang of crooks seeking a ransom. This tale introduces Ron's second recurring space hero creation, Captain 'Ace' Diamond, and his men from the Interplanetary Bureau of Investigation (an agency that would later reappear as the base of another space detective of a different writer's devising). In using another 'space pirates' plot, however, Ron had fallen back on a tried and tested formula; and, for the first time, the issue's back-up story was provided not by Ron but by a different artist, Norman Light. These were the first indications that Ron was now having trouble keeping up with the demands of the job.

The fourth issue, *The Scourge of the Carbon Belt*, confirmed those indications, as again Ron supplied only the lead story – another Ace Diamond adventure – leaving the remaining 32 pages to the talents of fellow Greg Hall-represented ex-Scion artist Jim Holdaway. Ron had started well on the series, but 64 pages per month was an output he just couldn't maintain: his

Left: Turner's covers for *The Terror of Titan* and *Captain Diamond and the Space Pirates*, the second and third issues of *Tit-Bits* Science Fiction Comics (C Arthur Pearson, 1953).

enthusiasm had exceeded his actual physical capability. However, with only the one story to concentrate on, Ron was this time able to devote all his attention to it, resulting in a great plot and some superb artwork – easily the most detailed of the whole series – including a tremendous cover (see page 59). The story involves a team of Earthmen discovering a rare fissionable mineral called Rivanium in the Martian Carbon Belt, only to be taken prisoner by the Terrons, a marauding band of savages riding incredible alien steeds. Ace and his crew then attempt to rescue the human team before the Martians can get to them first and discover the secret location of the sought-after mineral.

Ron gave this adventure plenty of dramatic action, both on Mars and in outer space, and incorporated some cleverly-designed hardware, including a mothership capable of releasing self-controlled surveillance 'pods'. He also reintroduced his innovative idea from the Sciento stories of giving the aliens their own lingo, with bracketed translations alongside – his logic being that unless the aliens could communicate telepathically, they were unlikely to be speaking perfect English! This 'pseudo-speech' added a certain charm and conviction to the story, and was quite cleverly constructed, not just a lot of nonsense words strung together. Ron took various foreign terms and phrases he had picked up during his war years and adapted them linguistically to correspond plausibly to the English 'translations'. Again he was ahead of his time in aiming for this degree of realism: some 35 years later, the TV series *Star Trek – The Next Generation* would have its Klingon characters similarly speaking in their own native tongue, with English translations given in subtitles.

In early 1954, while he was still working on the *Tit-Bits* series, Ron was invited to produce a cover for the George Newnes-published *Practical Mechanics* magazine. This monthly title had been around since the '30s, and although its main focus was the home workshop, it also carried the occasional speculative article, and the assignment here was to show a spaceship blasting off from the Moon. Despite the fact that he was already struggling to maintain the required level of output in his comic-strip work, this was an opportunity Ron

Above: Turner's cover for the March 1954 issue of George Newnes' *Practical Mechanics*.

couldn't pass up. Newnes was a highly-respected and well-established publisher paying top rates; and this piece, more than twice the size of his paperback covers, would be a lucrative commission that might also further his career.

Ron agreed to take on the task; but this meant that for the fifth *Tit-Bits* comics issue, *The Dome of Survival*, he had no choice but to relinquish the cover to George Radcliffe and one of the two back-up stories to Jim Holdaway. However, he was still able to complete two excellent strips of his own: the lead story and a second back-up one. In the lead story, an alien race on the point of extinction places its last members into a state of suspended animation, to wait millennia until life appears elsewhere in their system and revives them, whereupon they can claim their benefactor's planet for their own. In his back-up strip, 'The Inner World', Ron again chose to feature Ace Diamond. This time the Captain and his crew have been reduced in size so as to journey into the worlds within the atom in search of a missing scientist. They discover on the way that flying saucers are really visitors from the subatomic realm. Even though he was now taking on fewer pages each issue, Ron's stories were still light-years ahead of most of those supplied by his contemporaries.

For the sixth issue, *The Diemos Deadline*, George Radcliffe was called upon once more, this time to handle the now regular Ace Diamond adventure. Ron, however, reclaimed the cover duties and again provided both the title story and a second back-up: two completely original and innovative tales of quite cosmic proportions. In the lead story, a scientific taskforce execute a plan to terraform Mars by detonating its moon, Diemos, in a controlled atomic explosion from which the heat will release the atmosphere trapped beneath the Martian desert. Ron injects enough scientific detail into the story that when it's explained that Diemos has a core of uranium and an outer skin of beryllium, and that a chain reaction created in the uranium will produce a steady stream of heat to release oxygen on Mars, we actually believe it! Even though such a long-winded explanation isn't really needed, it's just another example of Ron's desire to add some scientific credibility to his stories.

Scientific concepts again form the basis of Ron's back-up story, 'The Ninth Moon', which introduces two new characters, Major Rex Raider and Captain Jon Karlson of the Interplanetary Patrol. The pair come up against alien planet-shifters intent on consigning Mercury, Venus and Earth to the Sun, so that the resulting explosion will provide the life-sustaining energy the aliens need to inhabit Jupiter's cold moon Callisto.

Producing these stories was obviously a labour of love for Ron, but although his mind was still teeming with ideas, it remained very demanding work, not only from the creative standpoint but also from the purely physical one of committing the ideas to board with brush and ink. Greg Hall continued to draft in support from his stable of other artists; but, with the exception of Norman Light, they weren't comfortable working in the SF genre, none of them possessing anything close to the flair that Ron had for it. Moreover, their involvement defeated Ron's original objective of producing his 'own' comic. But although the series hadn't turned out quite as he'd expected, he was still keen to persevere with it. Then, suddenly, it was cancelled!

The axe fell despite the fact that a cover and contents had already been prepared for a seventh issue, with Ron's work being supplemented by another Jim Holdaway back-up story. The series' demise probably came due to the poorer sales of the Wild-West Comics companion title, which had struggled to compete with the Amalgamated Press's far superior Cowboy Comics Library. The publishers doubtless considered it uneconomical to continue one series without the other, so both met their end.

Ron was devastated when he heard the news of the cancellation. He'd had high hopes for the comics series, and felt that his Ace Diamond character had the potential to become as familiar to readers as Dan Dare in the *Eagle* – not that he had any expectation of rivalling Frank Hampson's famous creation: in his eyes, Hampson was the

Turner's cover for *The Diemos Deadline* (C Arthur Pearson, 1954).

master. Simply to have continued producing a monthly quota of stories, even if they entertained only a few hundred readers, would have been enough to keep Ron happy. But it wasn't to be.

However, although Pearson never published the seventh issue, Ron's work on it wasn't entirely wasted. Some three years later, all of the *Tit-Bits* Science Fiction Comics tales bar the first were translated for the French SF periodical *Aventures de Demain!...*, and these included Ron's final story, 'The Diamonds of Death' – another Ace Diamond adventure – retitled 'Les Diamants de la Mort'. One of the problems with the *Tit-Bits* comics line, and possibly another factor in its downfall, had been its poor-quality printing, on coarse, pulpy paper. Luckily, *Aventures de Demain! ...* had much better reproduction, so Ron's ambitious efforts could at last be fully appreciated – at least by French readers!

Although the loss of the *Tit-Bits* comics came as a blow to Ron, it didn't dampen his enthusiasm; quite the opposite, in fact, for the whole exercise had shown him that he could successfully produce the type of work for which he had been aiming. The limiting factor was the time it took him to do so. With this in mind, he would now seek a less pressured outlet for his creative talents.

Meanwhile, Ron's decision to accept the initial offer of a *Practical Mechanics* cover paid off handsomely, as over the next few years Greg Hall was able to secure for him a steady stream of other work for that publication – not just further covers, but also internal illustrations. Not all of these involved astronomical subjects. The practical focus of the magazine meant that one month Ron might be depicting the London Planetarium or the first man-made satellite, while the next it might be fishing tackle or a tea-making machine! One of his most impressive internal illustrations was for the July 1960 issue, for a feature about the theoretical possibility of 'life spheres' replacing lifeboats. Taking into account the attributes that would be required of such vessels, Ron enthusiastically produced a superb cutaway design to incorporate them. In hindsight, this piece would have looked even more impressive if, rather than appearing in black-and-white inside the magazine, it had been in full colour on the cover – for which Ron was instead asked to produce a less-than-inspiring depiction of model aircraft!

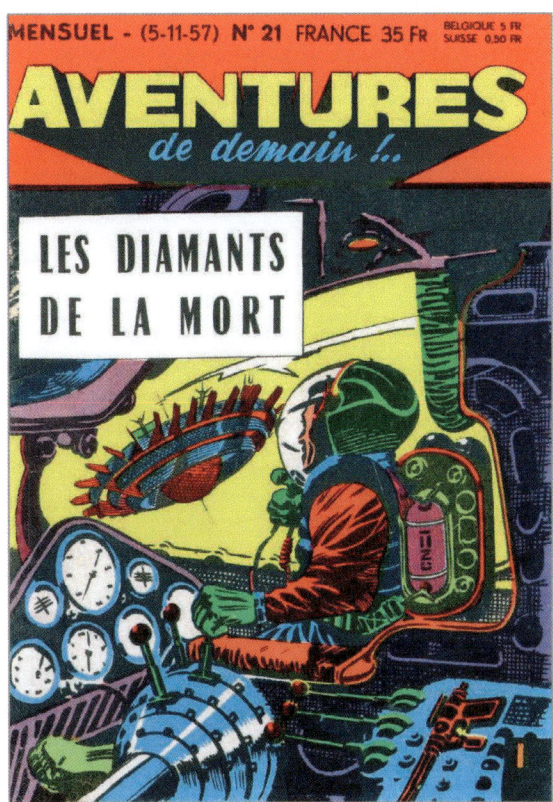

Above: Turner's story 'The Diamonds of Death' appears in a French translation in November 1957 in *Aventures de Demain!...*

Painting being his preferred medium, Ron always liked the cover commissions best. Although he approached each with equal professionalism, on those that involved scientific or technological possibilities he would allow his imagination to run wild, and then *Practical Mechanics* could at first glance almost be mistaken for an SF publication!

So inspired was Ron by the magazine's articles with a futuristic slant that he even submitted some of his own, along with suitable illustrations – although always using a pseudonym: for instance, a speculative piece he wrote about a future Thames Heliport appeared in the March 1962 issue under the byline 'L Turner'.

Ron was also from time to time called upon by Newnes to provide illustrations for the sister publications *Practical Householder* and *Practical Motorist*; assignments he again accepted as a challenge to his ingenuity. And, ultimately, it was all lucrative work that helped to keep his order book full.

THE FANTASTIC ART OF RON TURNER

Above: the impressive 'life spheres' design cutaway that Turner produced as an internal illustration for the July 1960 issue of *Practical Mechanics*. Below: his covers for the September 1954, April 1955 and September 1955 issues, demonstrating the wide range of subject matter he was required to tackle for this George Newnes-published periodical.

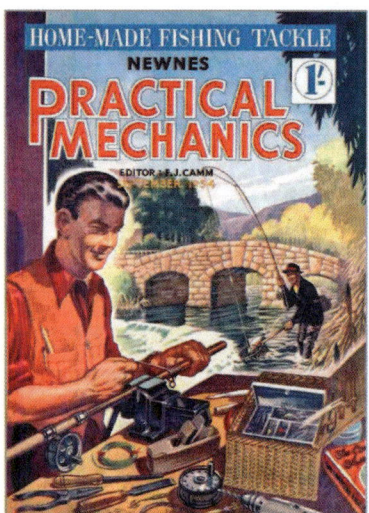
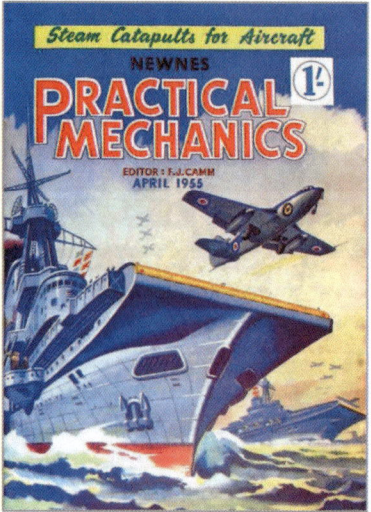
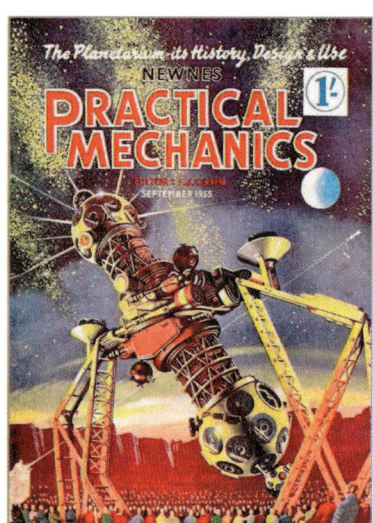

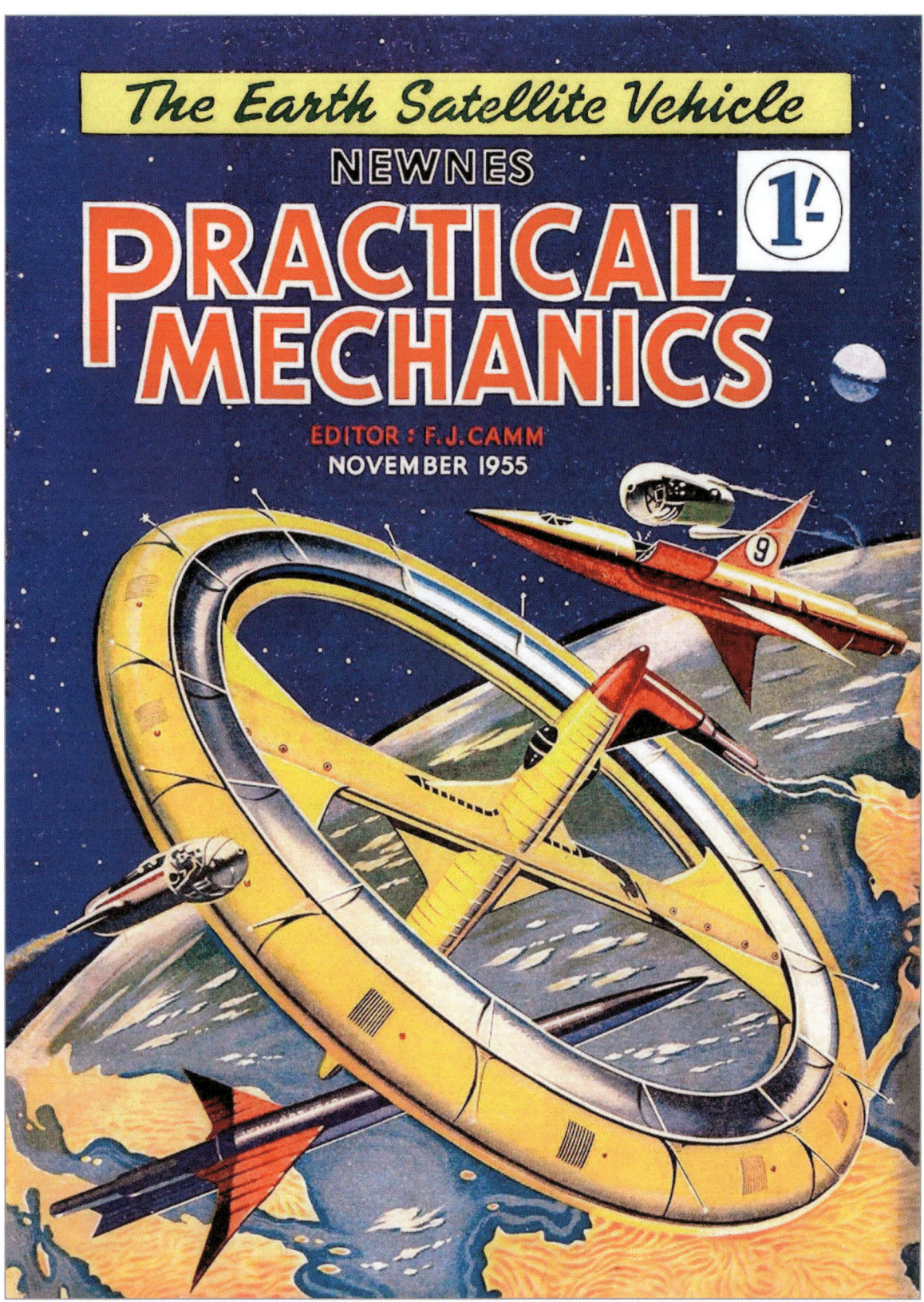

Turner's imaginative, science-fiction-style cover for the November 1955 issue of *Practical Mechanics*.

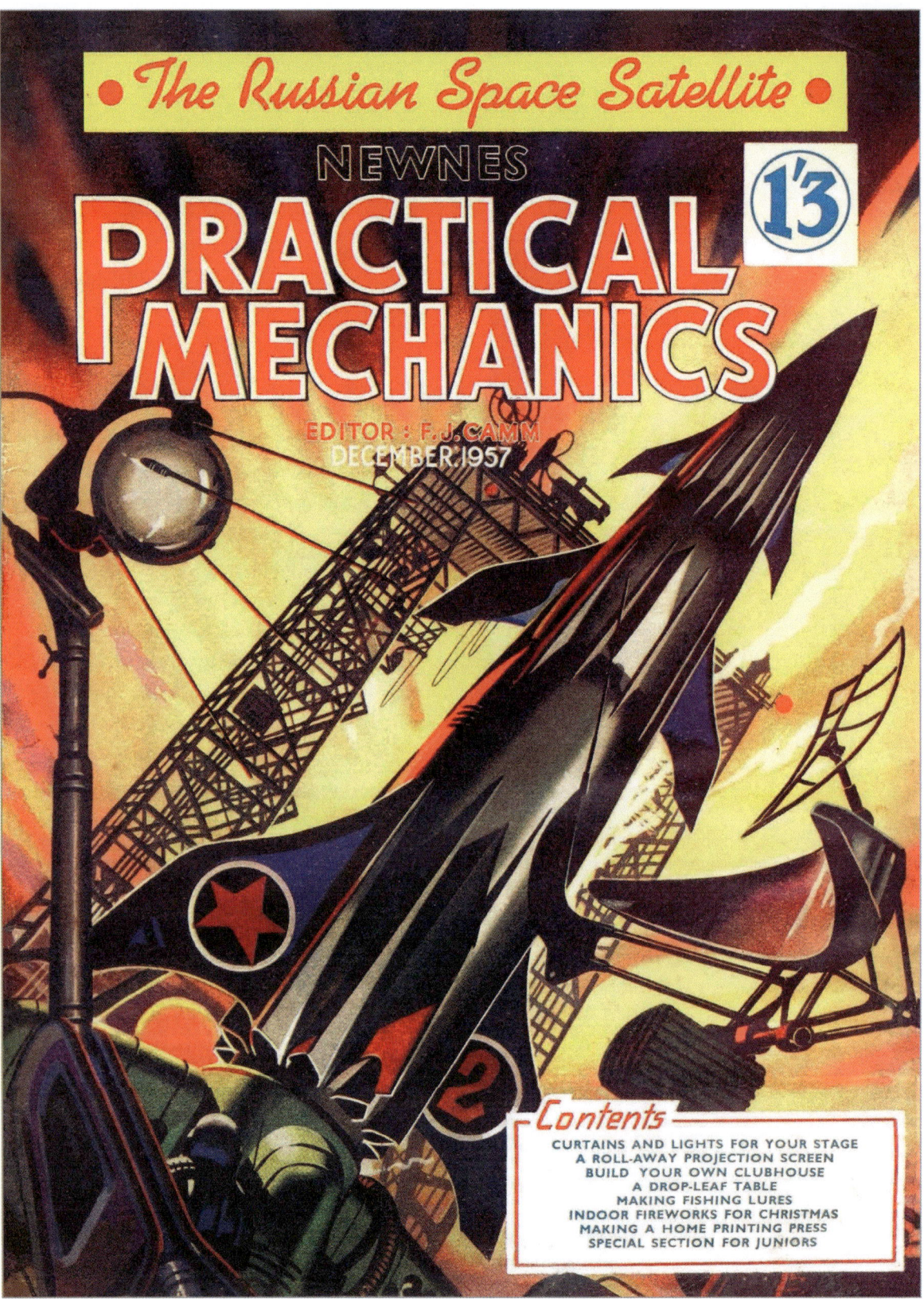

Turner's cover for the December 1957 issue of *Practical Mechanics*.

5: FURTHER 'ACE' ASSIGNMENTS

By early 1954, Ron's work had become so popular that he had started to receive fan mail from around the world, and he gratefully took the time to correspond with his ever-growing band of devotees. One letter in particular meant a great deal to him. It related to his recent cover for the Volsted Gridban novel *The Genial Dinosaur*, and it was from the book's author, John Russell Fearn, congratulating him on his perceptive interpretation of the story, involving a prehistoric beast on the loose in contemporary times. This reaffirmed the fact that it was not only Ron's skill and imagination that accounted for his success, but his determination to ensure that the cover was always a faithful reflection of the book's contents. That said, his cover for *The Extra Man*, written by Ted Tubb under his Charles Grey pseudonym and published by Milestone in February 1954, was another rare exception to the rule.

This was again entirely the fault of the publisher. Tubb had submitted a manuscript for *The Extra Man* and Ron had dutifully provided a cover for it. However, so happy were Milestone with what Tubb had written that they then decided to issue the book in hardback rather than paperback, and asked him to expand it to fill 160 pages rather than the usual 128. Tubb agreed, but first needed to complete another novel he was currently working on. When he delivered that other novel, rather than commission a separate cover for it, Milestone simply called it *The Extra Man* (later assigning Tubb's hardback a new title) and used Ron's existing piece, with no consideration for the fact that it now bore no relation to the contents; a thoughtless act that did Ron's work a considerable disservice and was completely out of his hands.

Below: *The Genial Dinosaur* by Volsted Gridban (Scion, 1954) and *The Extra Man* by Charles Grey (Milestone, 1954).

During 1954, Greg Hall continued to secure for Ron a succession of SF cover commissions, including a record number of six in May. But although financially the work was rewarding and more than enough to fill the gap left by the demise of the *Tit-Bits* comics, creatively Ron still had plenty of other ideas he wanted to explore. Toward the end of 1953, publishers Hulton had brought out a *Dan Dare* pop-up book, and so impressed was Ron by this that he was inspired to create a dummy for a similar book of his own. Titled *Into Space With Ace Brave!*, this featured a new space hero he had devised. The construction and presentation of the pop-ups initially proved quite challenging, but once he had worked out the details, Ron realised they wouldn't be too difficult to execute – simply time-consuming. All that was needed now was a publisher receptive to his idea; and, at his urging, Hall soon found one in children's book specialists Birn Brothers, whose output already included pop-ups.

With his dummy approved, Ron set to work on the artwork proper. This involved his new character, Ace Brave, Space-Master, 'speaking' to the reader, describing his duties and relating dramatic incidents from his career via four splendid pop-ups, separated by standard flat pages covering such topics as 'The Space Suit', 'The Weapons of Space' and otherworldly lifeforms. Born of Ron's scientific and technical knowledge, plus his great imagination, the illustrations were packed with amazing detail and looked totally convincing. One thing Ron had overlooked, however, was that the book would have no flyleaf, so although he had provided illustrations for the first and last pages, these would be stuck directly to the cover boards as endpapers and not be seen – except where, on some copies, the glue holding the endpapers did not extend right to the edges, allowing a small glimpse of the two further scenes – which, as far as could be judged, would have been every bit as exciting as the others.

Below: *Into Space With Ace Brave!* (Birn Bros, 1954).

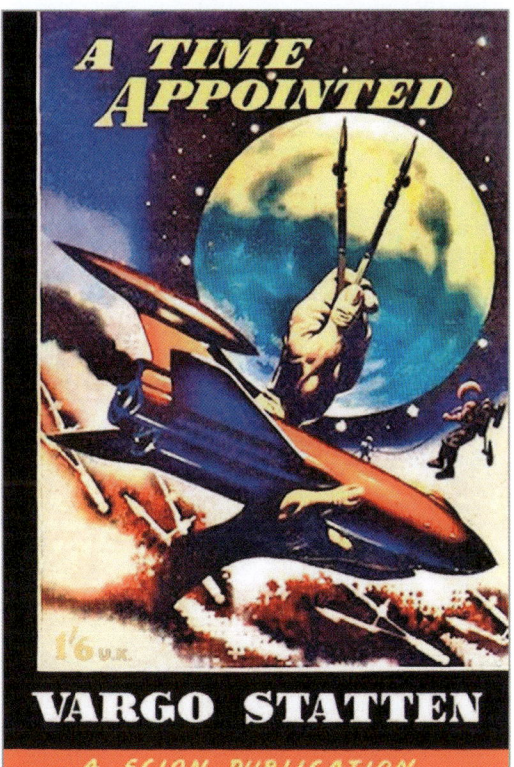
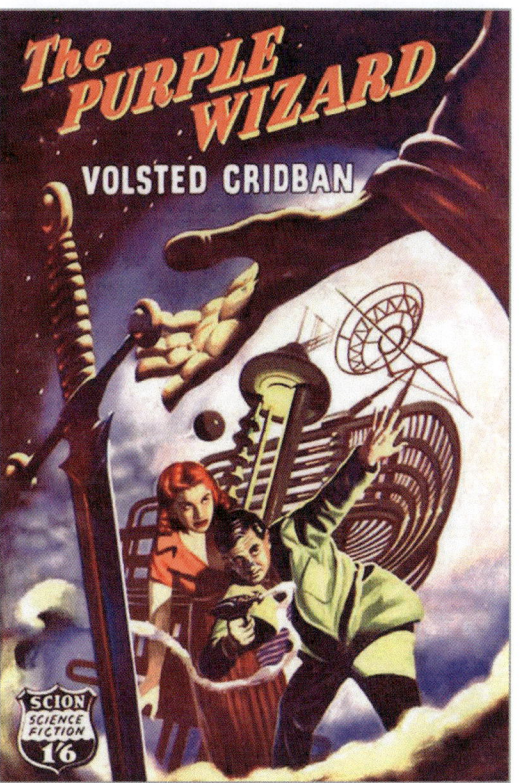

More cover commissions from Scion for the early months of 1954: *The Grand Illusion, Wealth of the Void* and *A Time Appointed* by Vargo Statten and *The Purple Wizard* by Volsted Gridban.

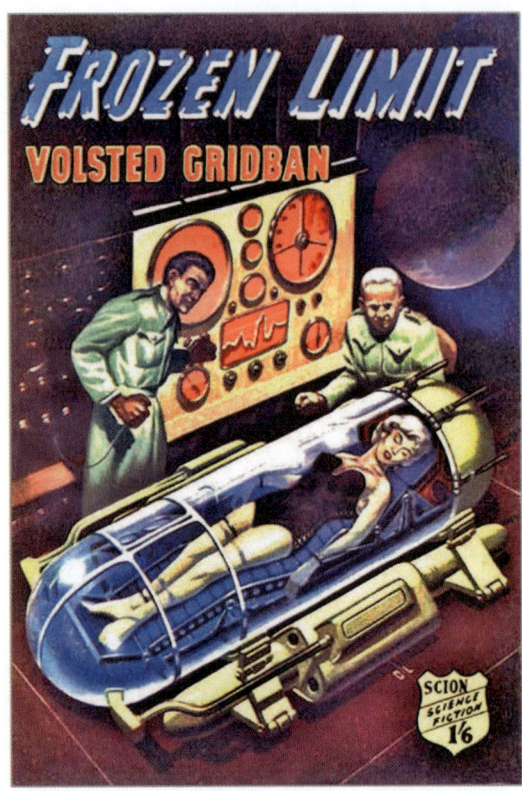

Four more 1954 cover commissions from Scion: *The Multi-Man* by Vargo Statten and *Frozen Limit, I Came – I Saw – I Wondered* and *The Lonely Astronomer* by Volsted Gridban.

FURTHER 'ACE' ASSIGNMENTS

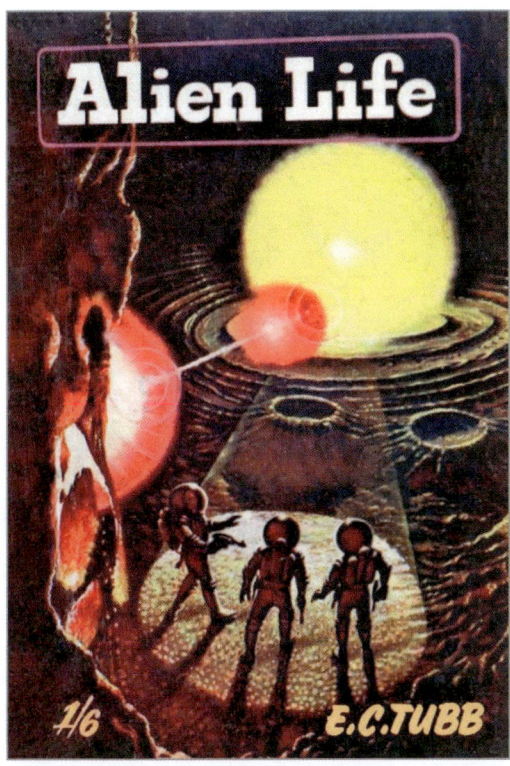
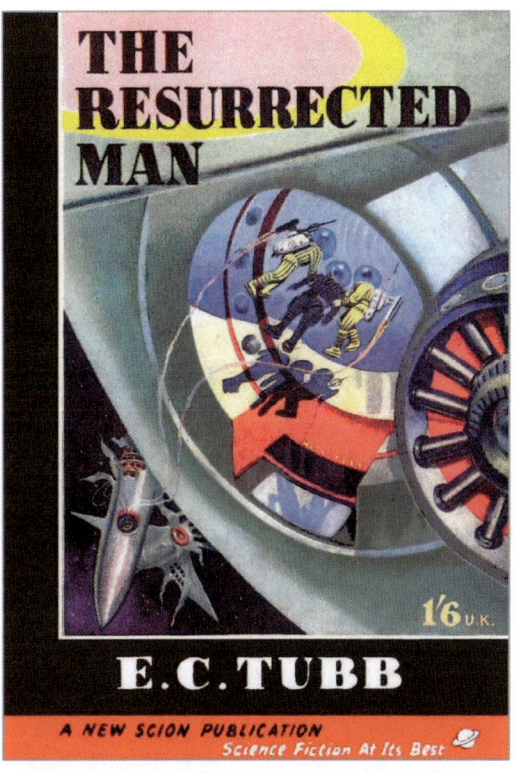

Another four Turner covers for novels published in 1954: *Alien Life* by E C Tubb (Paladin), *The Resurrected Man* by E C Tubb (Scion), *Voyage Into Space* by Erle Van Loden (Edwin Self) and *The Yellow Planet* by George Sheldon Browne (Edwin Self).

Turner's first published hardback dustjacket: *Project Jupiter* by Fredric Brown (Boardman, 1954).

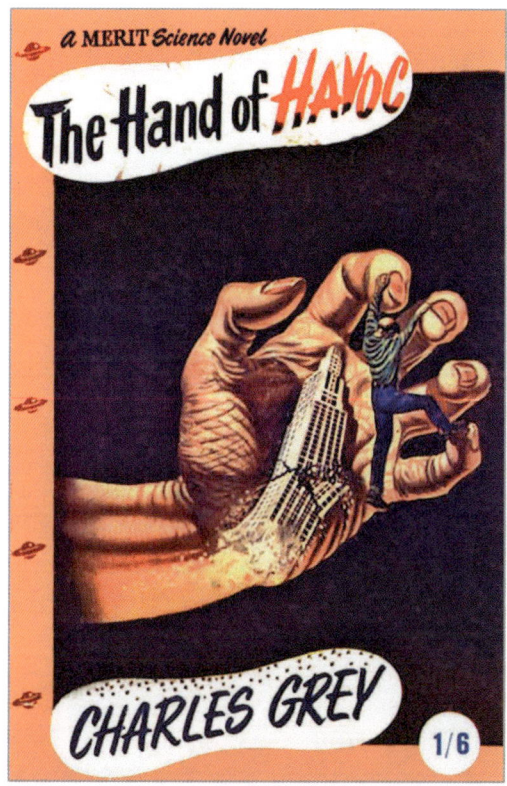
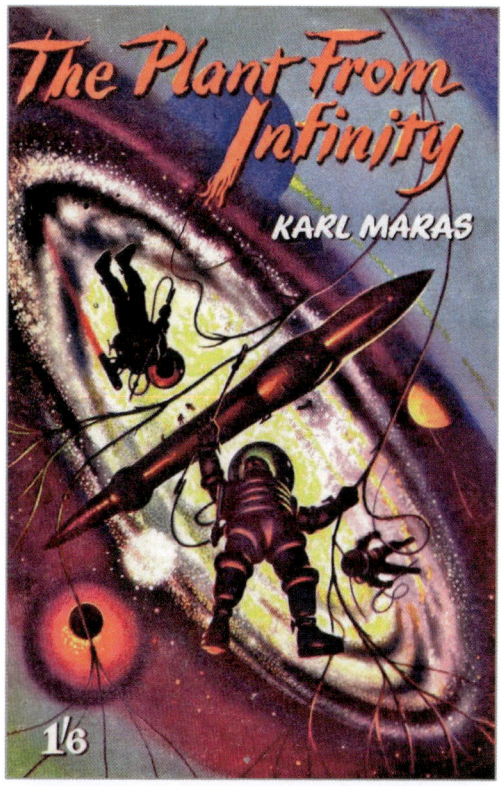

The Hand of Havoc by Charles Grey (Merit), *The Plant from Infinity* by Karl Maras (Paladin), *Enterprise 2115* by Charles Grey (Merit) and *1,000-Year Voyage* by Vargo Statten (Dragon): four more Turner cover commissions from 1954.

By 1954, Ron was living quite the high life, but although he had acquired his dream car, he was still working out of the bedroom of his family home in Romford, Essex, and lacked a proper studio. His status as an established and well-respected artist did not save him from having to contend with his mother's occasional objections to him leaving multicoloured paint stains on the bathroom washbasin! So, around May 1954, he moved into his own flat in Kensington. This was close to where Greg Hall was based, and not far from the premises of his main publisher, Scion, so the whole operation, from the commissioning of a cover to the collection of the finished artwork, could now run more smoothly. However, the move proved more time-consuming and disruptive than Ron had anticipated, and largely as a result of this, he was unable to complete one of the covers Scion had requested, for a novel called *Hell Planet* by Ted Tubb – who was now generally writing as E C Tubb rather than using a pseudonym. By the time this was realised, it was too late for Scion to commission anyone else, so instead they simply reused the cover that Ron had provided for another Ted Tubb book, *City of No Return*, published the previous month, with the new title placed over the top of the old one against a yellow background. This wasn't a happy situation; but it wasn't the last time a publisher would find that, due to some oversight, distraction or domestic problem on Ron's part, a piece of commissioned artwork would fail to appear.

Although C Arthur Pearson had cancelled the *Tit-Bits* Science Fiction Comics series, they continued to publish their *Tit-Bits* Science Fiction Library range of novels on a monthly basis, and Ron provided the covers for all twelve of those that appeared during 1954. He also received his first couple of hardback dustjacket commissions, and was asked to supply the covers for several issues of a new *Vargo Statten Science Fiction Magazine* launched by Scion at the start of the year. The SF paperback covers for Scion and other publishers also kept him busy; but he had the foresight to realise that these assignments would not continue indefinitely, and remained anxious to find a new regular outlet for his comic-strip work, which he felt would be more essential to his future.

Right: *City of No Return* and *Hell Planet* by E C Tubb, published by Scion in April and May 1954, with the same cover artwork.

FURTHER 'ACE' ASSIGNMENTS

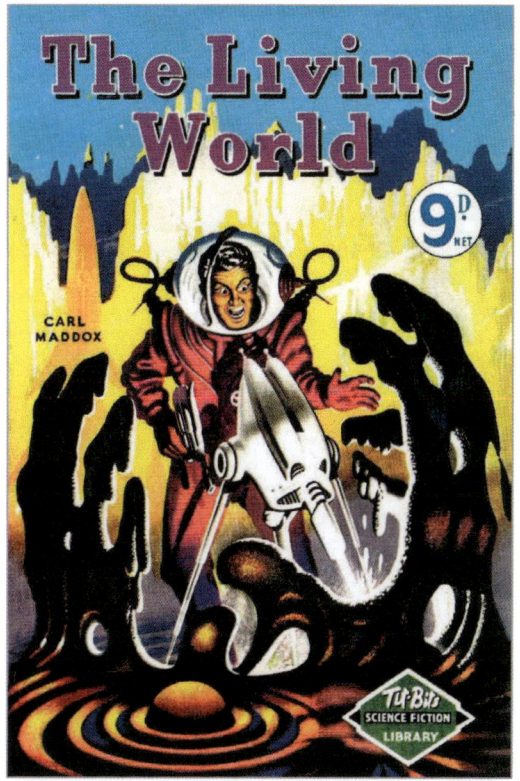
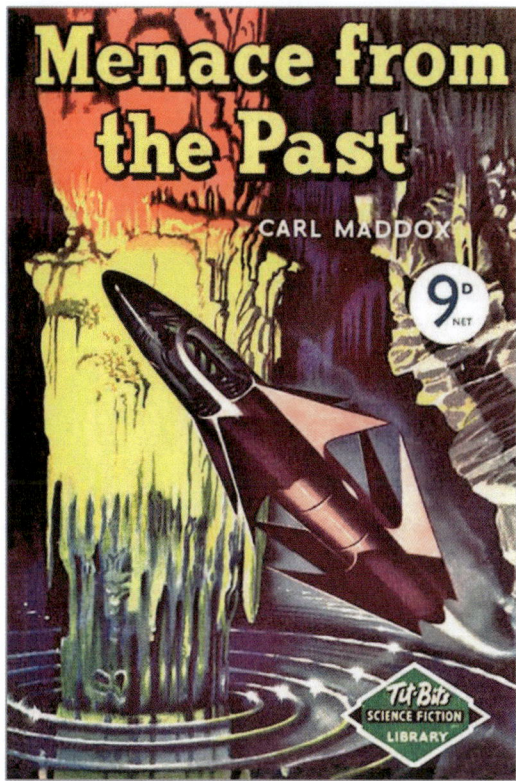
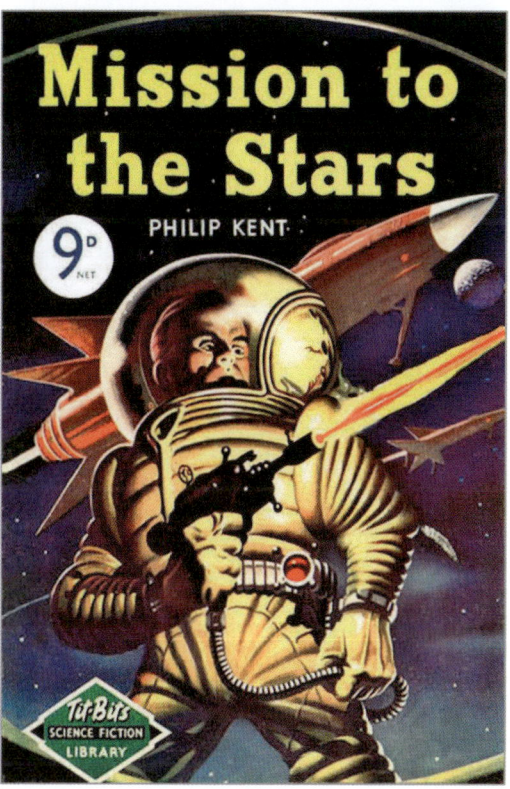

Turner's covers for the January to April 1954 entries in the *Tit-Bits* Science Fiction Library range: *Before the Beginning* by Marx Reisen, *The Living World* by Carl Maddox, *Menace from the Past* by Carl Maddox and *Mission to the Stars* by Philip Kent.

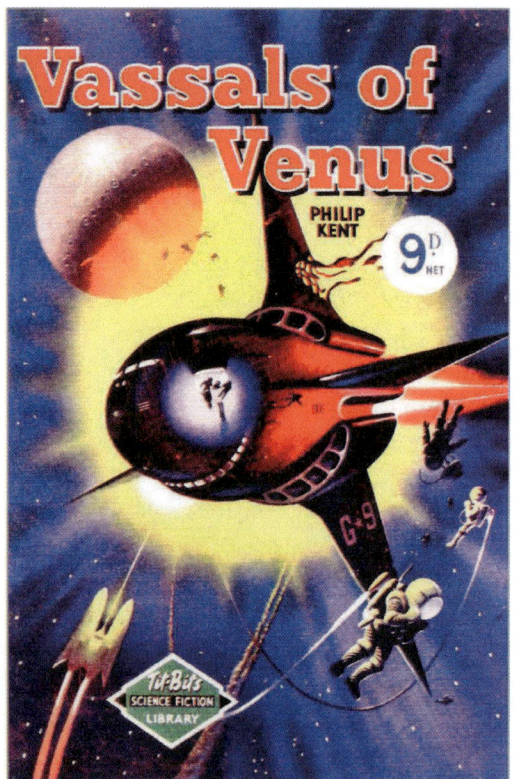
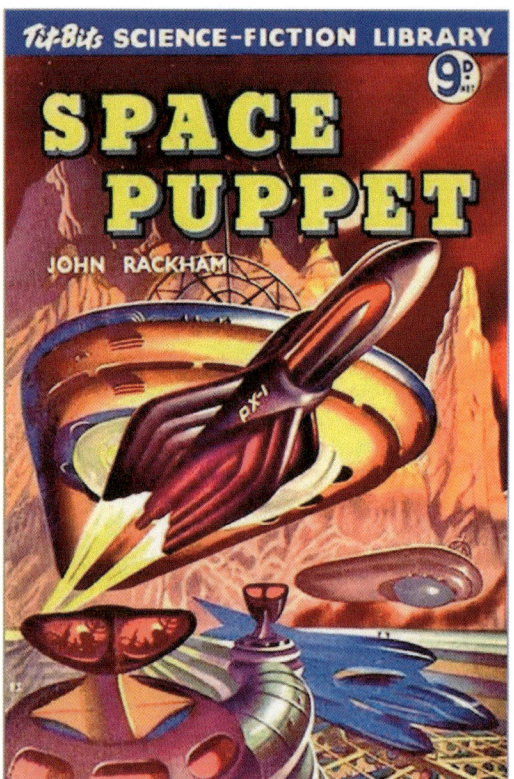
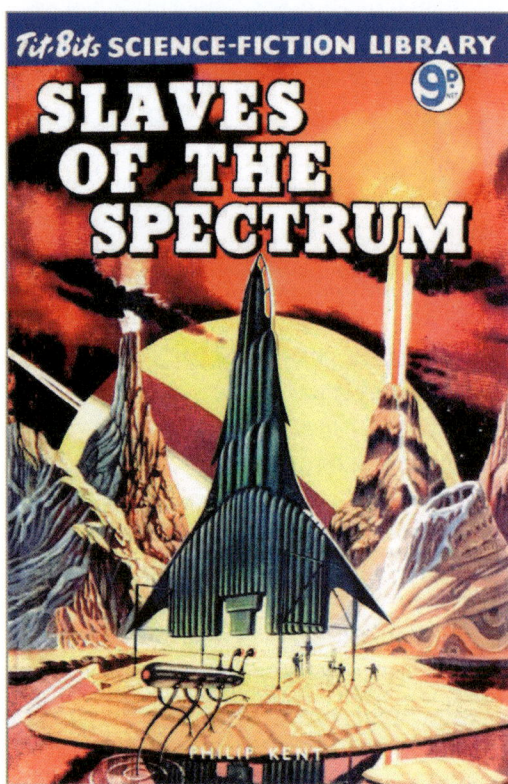
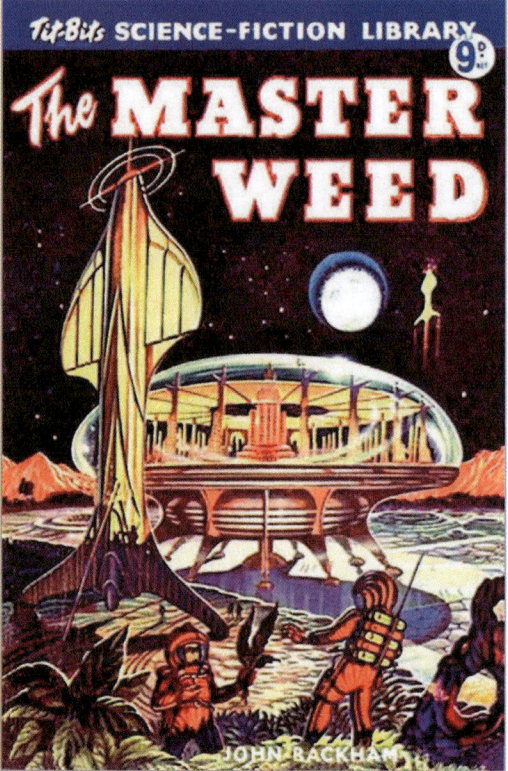

Turner's covers for the May to August 1954 entries in the *Tit-Bits* Science Fiction Library range: *Vassals of Venus* by Philip Kent, *Space Puppet* by John Rackham, *Slaves of the Spectrum* by Philip Kent and *The Master Weed* by John Rackham.

FURTHER 'ACE' ASSIGNMENTS

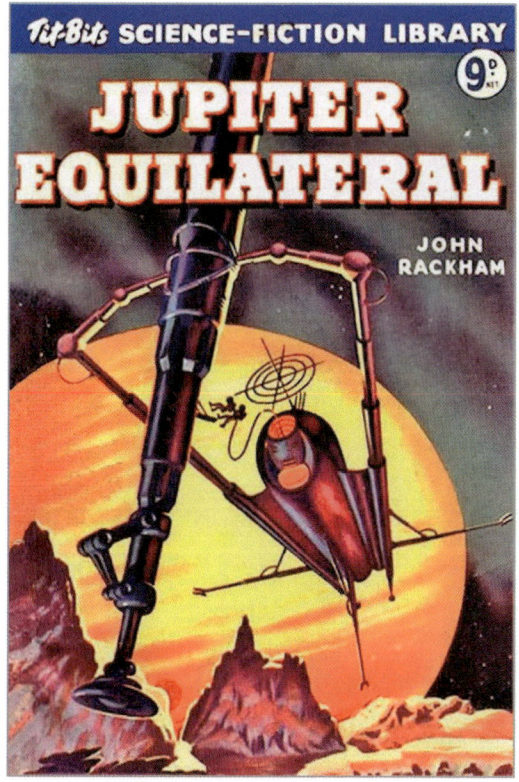
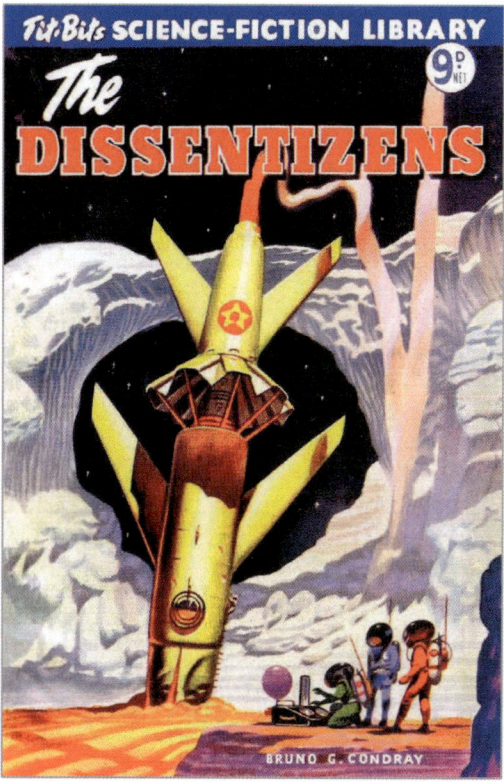

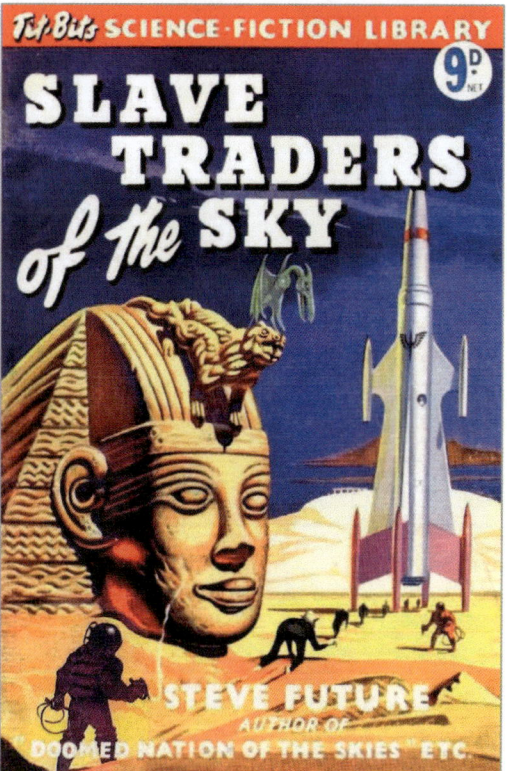

Turner's covers for the September to December 1954 entries in the *Tit-Bits* Science Fiction Library range: *Jupiter Equilateral* by John Rackham, *The Dissentizens* by Bruno G Condray, *Home is the Martian* by Philip Kent and *Slave Traders of the Sky* by Steve Future.

Turner's covers for Issues 1, 4 and 5 of Scion's *Vargo Statten Science Fiction Magazine*, aka *Vargo Statten British Science Fiction Magazine*, and Issue 2 of John Spencer's *Out of This World* magazine, all published in 1954.

FURTHER 'ACE' ASSIGNMENTS

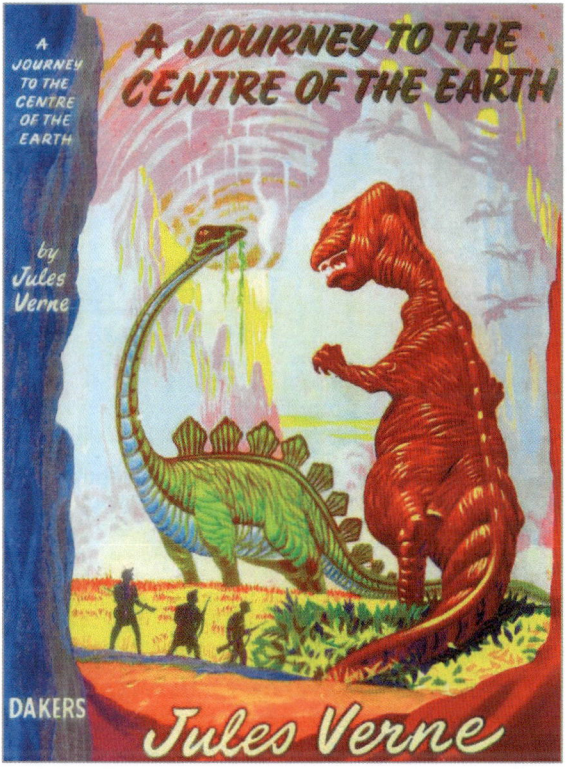

Ron didn't have long to wait for another regular comic-strip assignment to come his way; Greg Hall had been busy showing examples of his work to Fred Phillips, editor of *Lone Star Magazine*.

Based in Palmers Green, London, *Lone Star Magazine* had been launched in November 1952 by Die-Cast Machine Tools Ltd (DCMT) as a four-penny publication with Bob Mills as publisher. A second issue had appeared a few months later, then a third in May 1953, at which point it had become a regular six-penny monthly. Hopeful of securing strong sales, it was modelled very much on the most popular British comic of the day, the *Eagle*. Its artwork was variable in quality, despite boasting talented contributions from Ron Embleton and later Jim Holdaway, but it offered within its 24-page issues an entertaining variety of different ongoing strips, some in full colour, plus competitions and a club page. However, unlike the *Eagle*, which spawned tie-in merchandise simply as a byproduct of its success, *Lone Star Magazine*'s primary purpose from the outset was to promote sales of DCMT's range of toy firearms. To that end, the main strip was based upon 'real-life cowboy' Steve Larrabee, the Lone Star Rider – in reality Roy Green, an ex-army man turned actor. At the time, Green had become quite popular posing as the Larrabee character, with a roadshow, public park appearances, Radio Luxembourg broadcasts and TV spots. His adventures had even been recounted on the backs of cereal packets! He had therefore been seen by DCMT as the ideal person to help sell their toy guns and rifles. But, with SF being such a popular genre, and with the company also having ray-guns and other futuristic toys to promote, a space-themed strip was a must too, so editor Fred Phillips had come up with the character Space Ace.

Space Ace had actually debuted in a slightly different guise in the comic's launch issue, in the first instalment of a three-page serialised strip. There he was introduced as Ace Hart, Sheriff of Tarrant County, stratospheric pilot and amateur

Left: Turner's cover for *Peril from Space* by Karl Maras (Comyns) and dustjacket for a hardback edition of Jules Verne's *A Journey to the Centre of the Earth* (Dakers) – two more commissions from 1954.

scientist to boot. Having been knocked unconscious by a small radioactive meteorite, he then gains an unexplained immunity to its rays. A Professor McKay meanwhile discovers that the meteorite contains an element that could provide a new energy source to power space vessels. Having determined that it comes from the planet Zimbolus, he asks Ace to go in search of more, as commander of his new spaceship – unimaginatively designated the LS1 – with a crew consisting of chief pilot Bill Haines, physicist Dr Wang Fu, mining expert Silas Granger, engineer Monty Milne and – for comic relief – ship's mascot Marmaduke the Monkey (!). Ace functions here essentially as a space explorer, as he sets out to find supplies of the radioactive element. He encounters various perils along the way, before living up to his original sheriff status by apprehending criminals – the radioactive aspect of the plot being quietly forgotten about.

So far, so good. Then, however, editor Phillips became aware that a character called Ace Hart – Atom Man was already appearing in Manchester-based World Distributors' *Super Thriller Comic* title, and had been since 1948! Not wanting to risk any litigation, Phillips quickly had a rethink; and so, without any explanation or fanfare, from the third issue of *Lone Star Magazine* Ace Hart suddenly became Space Ace.

The strip was drawn initially by George Mottram, but then from the fourth issue by Terry Patrick, a childhood friend of Ron Embleton, with whom he had set up a studio in the early '50s, both being represented by Ron Turner's agent, Greg Hall. Embleton was the first of the pair to contribute to the magazine, taking on the *Steve Larrabee* strip in Issue 2, but Patrick soon followed, Phillips doubtless appreciating his style of illustration, which was cleaner, slicker and more suited to the subject matter than Mottram's overly cluttered presentation. Although initially the Zimbolus mission plotline was continued, the strip later presented other stories and featured some quite impressive artwork – although it is clear from some of the frames that Patrick resorted to a certain amount of cribbing from Ron's *Tit-Bits* work when original ideas weren't forthcoming.

Ron, having followed this strip from the outset, would have willingly taken over from Mottram himself, had Hall not put forward Patrick instead. But back in the spring of 1953 he had still been heavily occupied with more lucrative cover commissions for a multitude of paperback publishers, most notably Scion, and would have struggled to cope with the demands of a regular comic strip as well – as proved to be the case when he later took on the *Tit-Bits* comics series. By mid-1954, though, there were early signs that the cover work was starting to dry up, and the *Tit-Bits* comics had been cancelled. Consequently, when Hall delivered to Phillips the latest batch of Embleton's artwork, he took the opportunity to promote Ron as another potential contributor to the magazine. On seeing examples of the *Tit-Bits* layouts, Phillips immediately realised that here was an artist who could not only provide quality art and an entertaining story but, with his uniquely imaginative flair for SF, had the potential to help boost the magazine's sales and further promote the company's merchandise.

So it was that, with Terry Patrick finding work elsewhere, Ron took over *Space Ace* from Issue 17 of *Lone Star Magazine* in July 1954. With his arrival came a tremendous change to the strip, for although he was familiar with the established set-up, he decided to ditch it all. Out went Ace's strange backstory and weird assortment of crew members and in came wisecracking, moustachioed NCO Sergeant Bill Crag; a character whose name Ron had used previously in both the *Tit-Bits* stories and the *Ace Brave* pop-up book, and who provided a perfect counterpoint to the more serious and authoritative Ace – a nod, in fact, to the relationship between Dan Dare and Digby in Frank Hampson's work. Also at Ron's suggestion, the strip's page-count was increased from three to four per episode; this allowed him over the course of six monthly issues to tell, in serialised form, the same length and type of story he'd previously provided for the *Tit-Bits* comics.

Ron's first *Space Ace* story, 'The Island Universe', opens with an impressive frame showing the silhouettes of five strange spacecraft crossing the face of the Earth, as seen on a gigantic televiewer screen. The observer, rather than sitting in a chair, as might have been depicted by a less creative artist, is encapsulated in a large transparent control globe, elevated hydraulically in front of the screen. The imaginative design, detail

FURTHER 'ACE' ASSIGNMENTS

The spectacular title page of the first instalment of Turner's debut *Space Ace* story, 'The Island Universe', as published in Issue 17 of *Lone Star Magazine* (DCMT, 1954).

and composition of such a simple scene are still impressive today, and it's easy to appreciate the terrific impact the artwork must have made on young readers of the '50s. The plot of the story involves a race of aliens, the Metherons, using a sophisticated teleportation device to steal the Earth and move it millions of miles through space to their own universe, where they intend to turn it into a mini-sun, providing light, heat and power to support their dying home world. The tables are turned by Ace, however, and the aliens' world ends up on the receiving end of a planet-shattering warhead!

Ron really allowed his imagination to run riot on this story, devising the delightfully grotesque Metherons and including plenty of action, with rocket-propelled robots, futuristic cities and machines, fistfights, gunfights and dogfights in space. Other than some slight debts to Frank Hampson in the depiction of the spacesuits and of the alien leader, who appears in a floating sphere in the manner of Dan Dare's adversary the Mekon, the designs are all strikingly innovative. They also demonstrate just how much thought Ron put into his work. The Methrons' headgear, for instance, bears a stylised representation of a heron, and while this might seem to be simply an attractive emblem, it actually had some significance to the artist: as a student of wildlife, he knew that herons are shrewd, intelligent and determined creatures; qualities he felt would also typify the aliens. This rationale would of course have been completely overlooked by the casual reader – and certainly lost on a ten-year-old schoolboy! – but it was the type of detail Ron felt motivated to include, if only to satisfy his own sensibilities.

Also highly original are Ron's layouts for the story, which rather than following a uniform pattern are made up of frames in a variety of different shapes and sizes: long, narrow, circular, oval, triangular and borderless. The pace of the action benefits, too, from Ron having abandoned the alien lingo of his *Tit-Bits* comics tales in favour of telepathic communication. The very concept of teleporting a planet to another solar system and exploding it to provide energy seems quite original for the time; but, as was often the case, Ron might well have had the germ of the idea squirreled away in his mind from the various SF books he'd read or the technical volumes for which he'd provided illustrations when working at Odhams.

Ron's second *Space Ace* story, an untitled Titan-based tale, ran from January to April 1955, by which point his income had become almost entirely dependent on his comic-strip work. The start of the year had seen him provide the covers for three more of C Arthur Pearson's *Tit-Bits* Science Fiction Library titles, but that range had then been discontinued. The once-plentiful cover work for Scion had also come to an end with that company going out of business, leaving in its wake just a few further issues of the *British Science Fiction Magazine* – the Vargo Statten pseudonym now being used as an editor credit rather than in the title – the rights to which Scion had given to their printers, Dragon Press, in lieu of paying off a large financial debt. Sadly, the end of paper rationing had meant that Scion and their fellow indie publishers were unable to compete with the increased output of more well-established and respected imprints like Penguin and Pan, causing them to drop out of the market, so that by February 1955 these 'small fry' operations had virtually disappeared. The writing may have been on the wall for some time, but the loss of most of his former publishers still came as a shock to Ron, after five years spent happily creating a steady stream of paperback covers with little editorial interference. He was also concerned that the public appetite for the SF genre, in which he had made his reputation, might now be starting to wane. He did still manage to pick up the occasional cover commission elsewhere, including those further financially rewarding pieces for the handyman magazine *Practical Mechanics*, but he now saw his future lying very much in the comic-strip field.

Initially Ron decided to make the Titan-based story more of a gentle science fantasy than 'The Island Universe'. In contrast to the latter's intergalactic theme, it sees Ace and Bill being assigned to locate a survey party lost on Saturn's largest moon. The intrepid pair quickly discover that the missing party have been captured by the moon's natives, but then find themselves consigned to an arena to face a prehistoric throwback of a creature, the gargantuan Gark. However, having run for only four parts instead of the usual six as originally intended, the adventure suddenly segues into

FURTHER 'ACE' ASSIGNMENTS

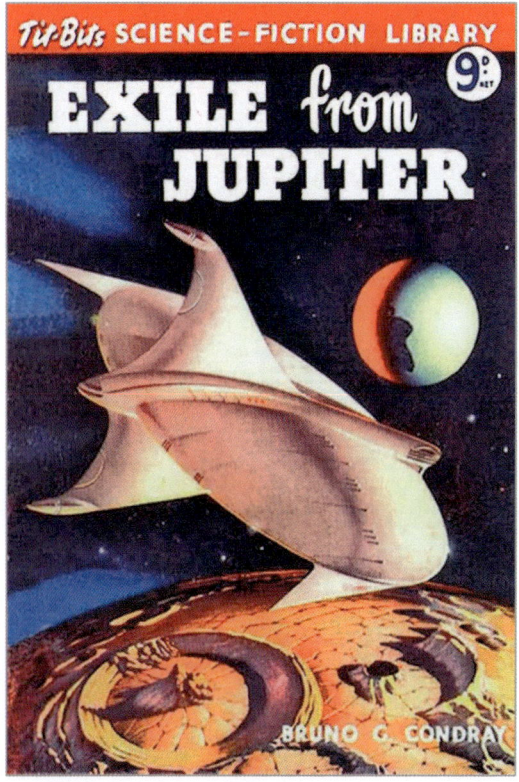
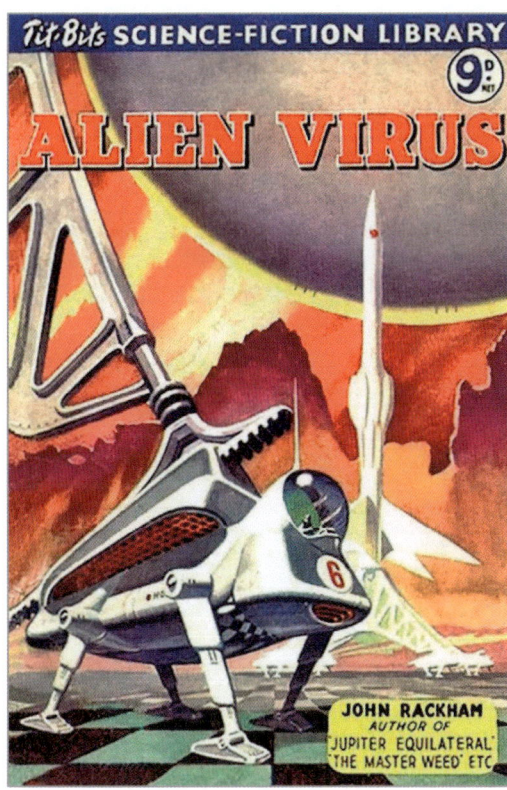

From early 1955, Turner's covers for Issue 6 of John Spencer's *Supernatural Stories* and the last three of Pearson's *Tit-Bits* Science Fiction Library range: *Exile from Jupiter* by Bruno G Condray, *Alien Virus* by John Rackham and *Dimension of Illion* by Irving Heine.

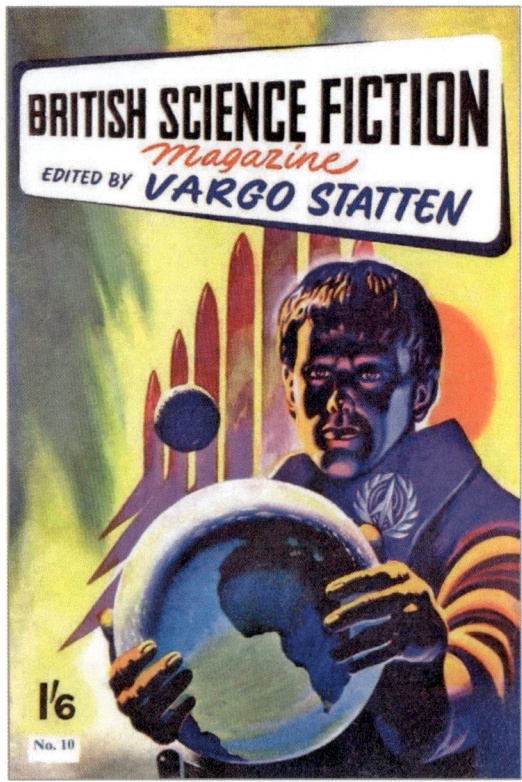

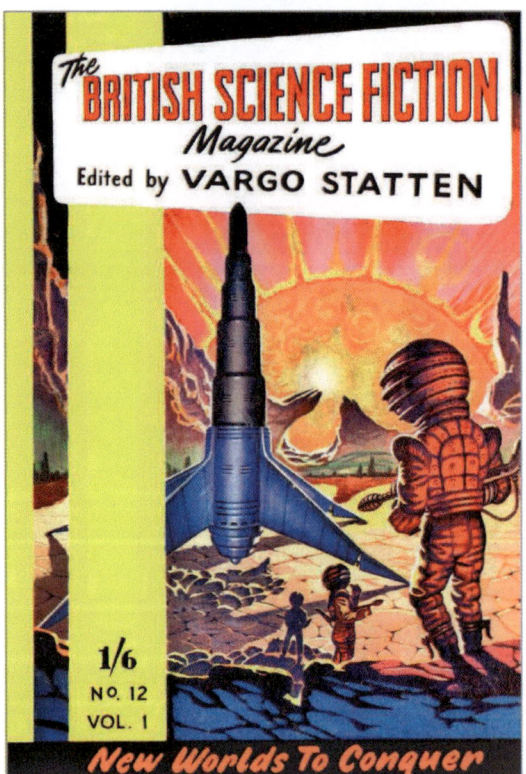
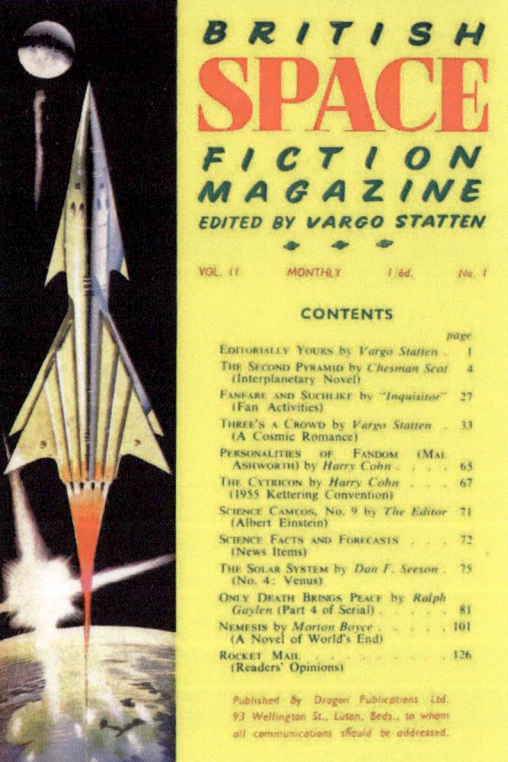

Turner's covers for Issues 10, 11 and 12 of the *British Science Fiction Magazine*, and Volume II Issue 1 of the retitled *British Space Fiction Magazine*, published by Dragon in 1955. All seven issues of Volume II used the same artwork, and the magazine was cancelled in 1956.

FURTHER 'ACE' ASSIGNMENTS

a different one entirely. Possibly concerned that his editor might be beginning to doubt the wisdom of continuing with *Space Ace*, Ron had decided to bring the Titan-based story to a premature end (leaving a few plot points unresolved in the process) and drop Ace and Bill into a tougher, more action-packed space adventure.

Filling the other two issues originally meant to wrap up the Titan tale, the next, again untitled, sees Ace's ship captured by a larger craft and taken to the Master, ruler of the outer galactic planet Zylon, whose fighting forces have been overcome and compelled to work as slave labour on a neighbouring world. The Master's ships are unable to break through the force-screens encircling their planet, but Ace's vessel, being of terrestrial origin and using different technology, is able to pass freely. Ace and Bill destroy the forcefield generator, allowing the Master's ships to break through and rescue the enslaved forces, bringing the story to a dramatic conclusion with a great space battle.

Ron had most certainly reaffirmed his SF credentials, and any fears he might have had about *Space Ace* being discontinued proved unfounded. Keen to maintain the momentum, he threw all his creative energy into the next untitled six-parter, which saw him back on top form with an adventure that had everything going for it. Within the first few pages, he had presented another dynamic space battle, quickly followed by a psychotic robot, a sea monster, a gigantic Wellsian walking machine and finally the return of his wonderfully bizarre aliens, the Metherons, whose plan this time is to destroy all nine planets of the solar system.

This was easily Ron's finest tale so far; and as with the previous ones, he had given its contents a great deal of thought. To take one example, he had decided to call the Metherons' chosen planet of operations Libra as, in astrological terms, Libra is represented by the

Left: Turner's last book cover commissions of 1955: *Deep Freeze* by Jonathan Burke (Panther) and the hardback *The Man With Absolute Motion* by Silas Water (Rich & Cowan).

scales of justice – and justice was what the aliens now sought, after Ace's destruction of their home world in 'The Island Universe'. Ron also included in one frame what almost amounted to a technical drawing, showing the various features of Ace's new multi-functional ship, capable of operating on land, sea and air as well as in space. This was something quite unusual to see in a comic strip; but, having designed the craft, Ron felt it more effective and satisfying to illustrate its features than simply to describe them. His storytelling and characterisation abilities had also much improved, as evidenced during the space battle when the Irish commander amusingly barks: 'Be the livin' blarney, if they so much as scratches the paint of me beautiful ship, it's their tail fins oi'll be tearin' out!'

Another superb six-month outing for Ace and Bill followed. In this adventure, once more untitled, the Earth is visited by a mysterious spherical craft crewed by a group of alien trophy-hunters intent on bagging items from across the cosmos to display in their space museum. The aliens have already collected some examples of Earth buildings, machines and animals, but their fortunes change when they also abduct Ace and Bill, along with their spaceship. Observing the two men, one of the aliens comments to his companion: 'Most odd. Rather like the ones we found on the jungle continent – only these haven't got tails, and they don't look so intelligent!' This remark, although on the face of it just a joke, is actually a veiled comment by Ron on man's supposed superiority to animals, a subject on which he had strong opinions. The point is further emphasised by the fact that the creatures seen in the aliens' collection are all terrestrial ones: rather than indulging in portraying a host of alien beasts, as one might have expected, Ron chose to use the story as a vehicle to express his distaste for wildlife being held in captivity.

Not only does this adventure have some amusing yet thoughtful dialogue, it is also has some inventive plotting. As the alien ship on which he and Bill are held captive passes close to Jupiter, Ace manages to explode an atomic mine, sending it careering off course to plunge into the oceans of the planet's second moon, Callisto. There, the pair realise that one of the aliens' collected trophies, a submarine, is not unlike a spaceship, in that it is a sealed chamber containing breathable air. Consequently they adapt it for space travel and manage to return to Earth. But, as if he felt the need to demonstrate the viability of this idea, Ron also supplied as a bonus a detailed cutaway illustration of the sub's conversion, with the explanation that instead of water being pumped through its propulsion jets, power from the motors could be discharged in order to achieve the same effect as a rocket! Again, as in his *Tit-Bits* stories, Ron was demonstrating his unique ability to relate, in comic-strip form, ideas that were highly imaginative yet still grounded in real science and technology; further evidence of the thought he put into them.

However, this alien trophy-hunters tale was to be the last of Ron's lengthy, serialised *Space Ace* stories. By June 1956, his professional commitments were being overshadowed by more domestic ones. In the process of house-buying, he missed the deadline for delivering the first instalment of his next planned story, involving a mission to the planet Marinios, and as a result, despite it being promoted on the cover, *Space Ace* was absent from *Lone Star Magazine*'s July 1956 issue. Ron did manage to complete and deliver the second instalment, but more domestic distractions then ensued, preventing him from continuing. The story had to be abandoned; and although Ron was ready to return to action a few weeks later, another artist had already been engaged to fill his slot until the end of the year.

When he resumed work on the *Space Ace* adventures from the first issue of *Lone Star Magazine*'s third volume, published in January 1957, Ron might perhaps have had ideas of reviving his abandoned Marinios story, but in the event that didn't happen. In its earlier years, the magazine had boasted quite an impressive roster of other artists, including Ron Embleton and Jim Holdaway, but since then they had all moved on to pastures new, leaving Ron's *Space Ace* as the only decently drawn strip in the whole publication. Perhaps not surprisingly, therefore, with his undeniably key

Opposite: example opening pages from instalments of Turner's four untitled *Space Ace* stories published in *Lone Star Magazine* across 1955 and the first six months of 1956.

contribution missing for the last six months of 1956, sales had begun to fall. Consequently DCMT, realising that the promotion they were gaining for their products was being obtained at too great a cost, had caved in and sold out to their former distributors, Atlas. Under its new owners, the publication, despite its title, became more of a comic than a magazine. Changes were made both to the size and to the content; and where *Space Ace* was concerned, a decision was taken to abandon serialised stories in favour of each issue presenting a self-contained adventure told over seven or eight pages. For Ron, this meant that he no longer had the pressure of maintaining continuity from one issue to the next; and, under his present circumstances, that was something he found more than agreeable. On the other hand, whereas his previous *Space Ace* serials had dealt with some quite complex and original ideas, these shorter stories afforded him less scope, obliging him to fall back on simpler subject matter, usually involving the standard comic-strip fare of psychotic aliens, marauding space crooks or tyrannical rulers.

The faster turnover of themes and ideas dictated by the monthly schedule again led Ron to draw inspiration from some of the novels he had previously read when producing covers for publishers such as Scion and Milestone, as well as others he had picked up purely for his own enjoyment, by authors such as Isaac Asimov and Arthur C Clarke. This meant that, while his storylines could occasionally become repetitive, he was at least able to inject some more imaginative elements into them. Thus, in the course of their exploits, Ace and Bill also encounter flame creatures and amphibious aliens; visit other planets through trans-dimensional portals; discover a hollow world powered by a central artificial sun; and even travel back in time. In one particular tale, they learn that the Egyptian pyramids were built by an alien race – an idea that Ron came up with a good ten years before author Erich Von Däniken would make a fortune out of his postulations on the subject!

For a one-off seven-page *Space Ace* story, Ron would typically draw 38 to 40 frames in total. Once he had decided on a storyline, he would write it up in just a brief script, more of a note to himself: 'A and B land on planet', 'A and B attack guards', etc. No definite dialogue would be written at this stage, though blank balloons and captions boxes would be drawn in as the artwork progressed, allowing plenty of room for whatever he eventually decided to put in them. In many cases it would turn out that the dialogue didn't completely fill the balloons; but he found this an efficient way to work, and preferable to discovering later on that the balloons were too small, landing him with the laborious task of having to stick larger ones over the top.

To complete each *Space Ace* story, Ron usually took a week off from any other assignments he had on at the time – unless he was up against a tight deadline, in which case the *Space Ace* work would have to be postponed, sometimes even causing it to miss its monthly slot in the magazine and leaving the publisher no choice but to reprint an older story or run a different strip entirely in that issue. Financially, this made little difference to Ron, as *Space Ace* was poorly paid, and he had to give priority to more lucrative work. He gladly stuck with *Space Ace*, however, as it was the only assignment over which he had total control, with little or no editorial oversight – as evidenced by the fact that even spelling mistakes and grammatical errors often slipped through uncorrected.

During the years when he was working on the monthly strip, Ron was also asked to supply *Space Ace* content for a succession of *Lone Star Annual* hardbacks published for the Christmas market. His contribution to the 1956 edition amounted to no more than a front endpaper illustration, but in other cases he produced complete strip stories. The first of these, for the 1955 edition, was especially noteworthy, in that it ran to thirteen pages, giving Ron an opportunity to devise a rather more involved one-off plot than usual. Titled 'The Pallasium Pirates', the story has three alien crooks attacking a mining operation on the planetoid Pallas, netting them a fortune in the valuable mineral Pallasium. Their ship is hit by a defence battery, however, and this causes a radiation leak that allows Ace to trail them to their hideout on Titan. There they are attacked by distinctly unfriendly natives sitting astride weird alien mounts, but Ace uses a Pax rocket to pacify the attackers and save the crooks, before they are hauled away to face justice. The Titan natives on their giant, dinosaur-like steeds – something of a Turner trope – are magnificently conceived, as is the idea of the Pax rocket that transmits waves of neutralising calm to stop the natives in their tracks. The inclusion of loads of action makes this one of the better annual stories that Ron would produce, and there is some lively dialogue, such as Bill exclaiming to Ace, as their ship is screaming through the narrow canyons of Titan, 'Suffering, sun-baked satellites! This is one way of rubbing the stardust off the hull!'

'The Pallasium Pirates' is notable for one other reason, too. Ron rarely featured women in his *Space Ace* stories, apart from as bystanders in crowd scenes, but in this case he made an exception, for it was while attending a local dance at around this time that he met his future wife, Ruby Baker; and, not wanting to let the experience go unrecorded, he decided to make it the basis of a subplot, ending the story with a most unlikely ballroom sequence! He even effectively namechecked Ruby by calling one of his characters (albeit male) 'Red Baker'.

Right and below: example pages from the *Lone Star Annual* 1955 story 'The Pallasium Pirates', showing the alien conspirators, the Titan natives on their steeds and the closing ballroom sequence.

The only other *Space Ace* tale of Ron's to include a prominent female protagonist would have been his abandoned Marinios serial, in which he had planned to feature the daughter of the planet's ruler. It would have been interesting to see how this developed, had it been completed; but doubtless Ron would have made the daughter a more modest character than the sensuous temptresses he drew in some of his later strip work – otherwise, on this occasion there would most certainly have been some judicious editorial intervention!

So enduringly popular did Ace's exploits prove to be that in 1960 Atlas launched a separate *Space Ace* comic, with Ron's monthly stories transferring from *Lone Star Magazine* to the new title to appear alongside content from other contributors. The comic's young readership were offered the chance to join the Space Ace Club and, for one shilling, enrol in the Space Ace Cadets, entitling them to receive membership cards, lapel badges and code books with which to decrypt secret messages, in the grand tradition of such clubs of the period. This was quite something for a strip that had begun as a back-up to a Western feature; and the fact that it had survived, flourished and now succeeded in its own right was due entirely to Ron's creative dedication.

Unlike on *Lone Star Magazine*, though, Ron now had the responsibility of providing the lead story each issue, and while on the one hand this was a well-earned reward for his loyalty, on the other hand it meant he was now under even greater pressure to deliver on time. Perhaps because of this, the quality of his *Space Ace* art did unfortunately become very variable toward the end of the comic's run, changing literally from month to month as competing commitments took their toll.

In all, Ron's *Space Ace* stories spanned some nine years, from his first contribution to the strip in 1954 to the character's final outing in 1963. But of course this was by no means the only work he took on during that period; and 1954 also saw him take the first steps toward becoming the regular illustrator of another SF hero who would reach a far wider audience and serve to establish him as firmly in the comic-strip world as the Vargo Statten covers had in the paperback market.

Left: the title pages of two of Turner's later *Space Ace* stories, 'Station X04' and 'Terror on Titan', published in 1959 in Atlas's *Lone Star Magazine* and *Lone Star Annual* respectively.

6: RANDOM ELEMENTS

Launched in February 1953, Super-Detective Library was the latest of the Amalgamated Press's ranges of 64-page picture-story digests, following on from Thriller Comics (later to be retitled Thriller Picture Library), presenting tales of historical derring-do, and Cowboy Comics (later to become Cowboy Picture Library), offering typical Western fare. The new range would showcase, in illustrative form, popular detective fiction of the time. It had fallen to group editor Edward 'Ted' Holmes to oversee the venture, and while it might have seemed fitting that a man of that surname should be associated with a detective title, as far as Holmes was concerned, crime fiction had had its day back in the '20s and '30s, and he felt that making it the subject of a new range was not good marketing. Holmes' RAF experiences during the Second World War, and the advancement of rocketry since then, had opened his mind to the possibilities of the future, and he had developed a keen interest in science fiction. The genre had been growing in public popularity, with films such as *Destination Moon* and *The Day the Earth Stood Still* attracting large audiences and *Eagle*'s *Dan Dare* and *Lion*'s *Captain Condor* finding receptive comic readerships, and he had tried without success to persuade his managing editor, Montague 'Monty' Haydon, that a 64-page SF range – similar to Ron's *Tit-Bits* Science Fiction Comics – would have more appeal than a crime fiction one and therefore be a good money-spinner. Haydon's belief, however, was that SF was too juvenile and would never attract the more mature readership that had brought success to the Amalgamated Press's other Picture Library titles.

But Holmes wasn't to be outdone. Apart from editing the Super-Detective Library range, he also contributed stories of his own, and he soon began to sneak in the occasional tale with an Earth-based SF premise, ensuring that a word such as 'mystery' or 'riddle' was included in the title in an attempt to justify their inclusion. As this met with no interference from Haydon, Holmes gradually started commissioning more otherworldly stories, until their settings and themes sometimes resembled those found in *Flash Gordon*. But this didn't last. Holmes' ruse was rumbled, his knuckles were rapped, and he was instructed to end these interplanetary escapades, as they had no place within detective fiction.

In the meantime, Ron had been reading these stories with keen interest, and with his *Tit-Bits* comics now cancelled, saw them as a possible new outlet for his work. The idea had other attractions too: unlike the small-time publishers he'd been associated with previously, the Amalgamated Press provided their artists with scripts, layouts and even drawing materials; and, most important of all, they paid better. It was with these considerations in mind that, in May 1954, Greg Hall approach Holmes with examples of Ron's *Tit-Bits* strips, confident of securing him a commission – until he learnt of the embargo on further SF stories. Once Holmes had seen Ron's work, however, and realised what he would be turning away, he became more determined than ever to find a way to continue to run SF material. The answer came to him when he read one of Ron's *Tit-Bits* stories, *Captain Diamond and the Space Pirates*, in which the hero belonged to the Interplanetary Bureau of Investigation, a *crime* unit. He realised that if he were to have stories set in the future, with guns changed to blasters, cars changed to spaceships, and the detective given space crimes to solve, Haydon could have no legitimate objection to the SF trappings. This proved to be the case and, with Haydon's consent, Holmes eagerly set about creating the character of a space detective. But having settled on the character, he now needed a name for him: something slick and alliterative like 'Dan Dare'.

One of Holmes' regular SF writers was Conrad Frost, who had supplied most of the stories in that genre to appear before Haydon's embargo. Frost also wrote daily and weekly newspaper strips, and had recently created a character called John Random for his ongoing *Ace O'Hara* SF strip in the *Daily Sketch*. Holmes liked the surname 'Random': it could imply the character being ready to take on any case, anytime, anywhere. 'Slick' then led him to think of 'Rick'. Holmes and Frost had an agreement, when it came to devising names, that if they hit upon one that still stuck in their minds the next day, then it would be in. 'Rick Random' stuck, and so the new space detective had his name.

But as impressed as he was with Ron's imaginative ideas and presentation, Holmes felt that his figure work and general line technique needed some improvement. So, having scripted the debut *Rick Random* adventure, *Crime Rides the Spaceways*, he assigned the task of illustrating it not to Ron but to one of the Amalgamated Press's best regular artists, Bill Lacey, who may have lacked Ron's unique flair for SF but could turn his hand to any subject. Holmes then sent Ron examples of Lacey's artwork to demonstrate the type of clean character and linework he was after, with instructions to produce for his approval the first four pages of a follow-up story.

Holmes wasn't to be disappointed. Although a past master of colour illustration, Ron had a natural inclination to want to learn and develop, and a determination to win the commission, so having the opportunity to study Lacey's techniques led to an overnight improvement in his own work. Holmes, delighted, had no hesitation in allowing him to complete the second *Rick Random* story, *Kidnappers from Space*. And although Ron hadn't drawn the first, he had still managed to contribute to it indirectly, as Holmes had decided to make his Interplanetary Bureau of Investigation (IBI) the base of operations for the new space detective, incorporating it into the series from the outset.

Ron's enthusiasm for *Rick Random* was obvious from the very start of *Kidnappers from Space*, published as Super-Detective Library Number 44 in December 1954, for it had a tremendous opening frame showing the space tide – a vast interstellar vortex – sweeping through the cosmos, drawing ships, spacemen and even planets to their doom. The story begins as a fairly basic kidnapping yarn, with a gang of space crooks abducting the young son of a millionaire industrialist, Jon Bryant. However, when the crooks' spacecraft gets caught in the space tide and crashes on a strange planet, with only the child surviving, it turns into a more surreal tale involving medieval-style kingdoms, winged horses and a legend concerning a child who will mysteriously arrive and later become the

Above: the opening page of the first Turner-illustrated *Rick Random* adventure, *Kidnappers from Space*, published as Number 44 in the Super-Detective Library range.

planet's ruler. It's possible that this latter part of the story was adapted from a previously-vetoed full-length SF/fantasy entry by Conrad Frost; the addition of a new beginning with a detective investigating a child abduction would have made it more acceptable to Monty Haydon. At any rate, the script was charged full of imaginative possibilities, from the technical to the fantastic, and gave Ron plenty of artistic challenges, which he was more than happy to accept.

For this story alone, with his creative juices running high, Ron came up with numerous different spacecraft designs, none of which he would ever use again. While many artists would doubtless have been quite content to recycle their ideas, Ron had a low boredom threshold and relished the opportunity to create any number of 'throwaways' – a feature of his art throughout his career. Not for him the clichéd 'cigar-tube with fins' type of spacecraft; his designs, whether flat, bulbous or globular, were always convincingly functional, with realistic control panels crammed with knobs, buttons, dials and switches – a style of presentation born of his experience producing technical drawings for Odhams, coupled with his creative take on the sophistication and complexity that, in the '50s, he imagined would be associated with space technology.

Had the artwork for *Kidnappers from Space* fallen short of the mark, Holmes would have brought Bill Lacey back to handle the next *Rick Random* entry, but in the event he was more than happy with what Ron delivered. So it was that, less than six months after starting work on *Space Ace* for *Lone Star Magazine*, Ron picked up another ongoing comic-strip commitment, and this a more prestigious one, as the regular artist on the Super-Detective Library's *Rick Random* adventures. These two tasks combined would require him to produce artwork at a much greater rate than he had even on the *Tit-Bits* comic books; but he still found time to take on a small additional project at the end of 1954: a one-off strip for *Blighty*, a men's pin-up and cartoon magazine of the period.

Blighty had started out as a free morale-booster distributed to the troops during the First World War, but had been revived in 1939 as a commercial proposition featuring, amongst other things, the cartoons of Arthur Ferrier, an artist who specialised in slightly risqué 'leggy lovelies' and who was also represented by Ron's agent, Greg Hall. Impressed by Ron's much improved figure work of women in the first *Rick Random* story, Hall immediately saw an opportunity for him too to produce a strip for *Blighty*. A meeting with the editor confirmed this possibility – provided that the story was centred on a pretty girl. What emerged was 'The Ghost of Limbo', a one-page, 14-frame SF strip with a twist in the tail, published in December 1954 in the magazine's Xmas Extra edition. Whether or not this was written by Ron, as well as illustrated by him, is unknown; but it may be significant that its opening frame, showing a vast whirlpool of space filled with derelict spaceships, almost mirrors that of the *Rick Random* adventure he had just completed.

Another one-off *Blighty* commission followed six months later, with Ron illustrating a story called 'The Venus Lady' for the magazine's 1955 Summer Special. Again, the identity of the story's writer is unconfirmed; but the opening scene, featuring a street brawl in a futuristic Western town, is not dissimilar to some of the frames Ron had been drawing for the current *Rick Random* story, *The Gold-Rush Planet*, so it is certainly possible that he was responsible, having managed to adapt his skills to this particular type of subject matter.

It was in the spring of 1955 that Ron started work in earnest on his new *Rick Random* assignment, juggling this with *Space Ace* and his handful of remaining cover commissions. Two or three Super-Detective Library titles appeared each month, so although *Rick Random* did not feature in all of them, Ron would still have several scripts to illustrate for publication over the remaining months of the year.

First up, appearing as Super-Detective Library Number 49, was *The Man Who Owned the Moon*, another superbly-crafted Conrad Frost story. The

Below: an example page of Turner's artwork for *The Man Who Owned the Moon*.

plot this time concerns an industrialist whose lease on part of the Moon enables him to set up a small colony there and develop it into a kingdom, establishing himself as Emperor of Luna – a position that ultimately gives him the power to threaten the Earth. Ron was presented here with the opportunity to draw some marvellous full-page scenes of the beautiful city of Lunaport, a regal setting with domes and minarets, and to depict characters in 12th Century-style court costumes. He delighted in creating the city's architecture, taking elements of art deco design and adorning the buildings with bas-relief interpretations of René Lalique-style figures. He also had structures supported by male and female statues; but rather than draw these as rigid columns in the manner of classical Greek caryatids, he took a more imaginative approach, showing Herculean men bearing the weight on their backs, and athletic women in graceful poses with their arms outstretched to serve as buttresses. As in the previous story, the placing of classical elements against a background of spacecraft and futuristic weaponry created a striking juxtaposition, inspired by Alex Raymond's similar treatment of *Flash Gordon*'s settings, and worked extremely well.

By the time he turned in his finished artwork for *The Man Who Owned the Moon*, Ron had really got to grips with the Rick Random character and was keenly anticipating tackling the next story – but things were not to proceed that smoothly. Back when he had first approached Ted Holmes about using Ron, Greg Hall had also persuaded him to take a chance on another of his clients, Jim Holdaway. Keen to run a series based on John Hunter's seafaring adventurer Captain Dack, Holmes had agreed that Holdaway could illustrate this. The first story, *Meet Captain Dack*, had been completed to his satisfaction and published as Super-Detective Library Number 43. However, when Holmes sent Hall the script for the second story, *The Mystery of Peril Island*, Hall returned it with an apology that Holdaway was no longer available, having taken up a too-lucrative-to-refuse offer of alternative work in the advertising field. Hall had no qualms about this – it was, after all, his business to ensure that he obtained the most profitable commissions for his clients – but Holmes was infuriated that he had been let down and would now have to find a replacement artist at short notice. Hall, fearing that Holmes' irritation might jeopardise any further work for Ron, immediately suggested that he be given the assignment instead. In the circumstances, Holmes had little choice but to accept. Not having seen any of Ron's non-SF work, he was doubtful of the results. But he needn't have worried. Although Ron was initially aggrieved at being moved off *Rick Random* to handle a less appealing subject – particularly at a time when he was already becoming concerned about a possible cooling of interest in SF – he took it as another challenge to his creativity. Channelling his efforts into the depiction of the characters, their postures and expressions, he gave certain frames an almost cinematic quality, with extreme high- or low-angle viewpoints and an effective use of perspective to vary and enliven the more static scenes. His imaginative use of presentational devices such as a snake coiling round to form a frame, or the blade of a native's hunting knife separating one frame from another, further demonstrated his determination to inject interest

Below: an example page of Turner's artwork for the *Captain Dack* story *Mystery of Peril Island*, showing his unusual perspectives and much improved figure work.

into the storytelling and create appealing artwork regardless of the genre. However, although Holmes could not deny that Ron had turned in a first-class job, there was still one aspect with which he was not entirely happy. In his opening frame, Ron had presented a typically spectacular scene of Dack's ship, with small figures on the deck, heading out across storm-tossed waters, past Peril Island, with lightning flashing in the distance. Holmes, though, favoured a more character-focused image, establishing Dack at the wheel of his ship. Consequently he had a less talented staff artist supply a replacement first page, Ron's being scrapped in the process, denying readers the opportunity to see what would undoubtedly have been a more exciting start to the story.

With Ron busy working on *The Mystery of Peril Island*, and Bill Lacey also now reassigned to another project, the task of illustrating the third *Rick Random* script, *The Case of the Space Bubble*, fell instead to Oliver Passingham. Passingham's previous Super-Detective Library work had been confined mainly to the exploits of the girl detective character Lesley Shane, although he had handled one other futuristic tale in *Revolt on Venus* – the very story that had provoked managing editor Monty Haydon to veto any further departures into pure SF territory, and had thus indirectly led to the creation of the space detective. Although his talents weren't a patch on Ron's, or on Lacey's for that matter, the fact that he was a fast worker and happened to be free at the time was enough to secure Passingham the current commission.

Holmes wanted to have Ron back working on *Rick Random* as soon as possible after the completion of *Mystery of Peril Island*, but there would be a short wait until the next script was ready, so to keep him occupied in the meantime he gave him two Super-Detective Library cover commissions. One was for the latest *Lesley Shane* series entry, *The Mystery of Table 13*, and the other, ironically, was for the Passingham-illustrated *The Case of the Space Bubble*. Sadly, Ron would never get to supply the cover artwork for any of his own *Rick Random* assignments, the publisher's standard practice dictating that this work would always go instead to specialists such as Amalgamated Press stalwart Arnold Beauvais and,

Above: Turner's covers for the *Lesley Shane* story *The Mystery of Table 13*, published in April 1955 as Super-Detective Library Number 51; and the *Rick Random* story *The Case of the Space Bubble*, published in May 1955 as Super-Detective Library Number 53.

later, renowned cover artist James E McConnell. *The Mystery of Table 13* and *The Case of the Space Bubble* were thus rare exceptions to the rule; but any unsuspecting fan who came across the latter and assumed that the contents would also be Ron's work would soon have realised their mistake, as the interior art, scripted with Ron's talents in mind, was extremely disappointing in Passingham's hands.

Ron did eventually receive the next *Rick Random* script, *Mr Five Face*, later to be retitled *The Five Lives of Mr Quex*, and quickly got down to work illustrating it. This was another tremendous story by Conrad Frost, focusing on Rick's investigation into a mysterious multimillionaire, Adam Quex, who appears to have been leading five different lives – Quex being an astute, if doubtless largely unappreciated, choice of name by Frost, as the word refers to a five-sided object, usually a coin. But as keen as Ted Holmes had been for Ron to resume his *Rick Random* duties, he was both disappointed and puzzled when he saw the finished artwork for the story. Whereas on *Kidnappers from Space* and *The Man Who Owned the Moon* Ron had followed Bill Lacey's lead in using an open linework style with little shading, this time he had taken the opposite approach of incorporating heavy shadow, fine line hatching and cross-hatching, and white hatching against a dark background – largely wasted effort, as when the art was reduced in size for printing, many of these effects would be lost and the fine linework would become just a black smudge. Although Ron was fully confident with colour illustration, he was never quite as sure of himself with black and white, and was always experimenting to find different ways of achieving certain tonal effects. In this case, it seems that, having seen Oliver Passingham's pages when producing the cover for *The Case of the Space Bubble*, he had been influenced to adopt some of that less skilful artist's techniques in his own work. What he had failed to take into account was that, although what he had produced was technically sound, this publisher's printers had less sophisticated presses than he had been accustomed to at Odhams, and they simply couldn't reproduce

Right: two examples of Turner's page art for the *Rick Random* story *The Five Lives of Mr Quex*, much of which was set on a huge space satellite transformed into an orbiting hotel.

the level of detail he had included.

Unfortunately, this wasn't the only problem that Holmes had with the artwork. One large frame showing a spaceship docking at Mr Quex's orbiting hotel satellite had been drawn by Ron in such a way that the ship's stabilising fins overlapped into the previous, much smaller frame. This went completely against the convention of the time that comic-strip panels should always be self-contained, certainly in a publication such as this, and just wasn't acceptable. Consequently Holmes had the smaller frame completely edited out and replaced with an explanatory caption, turning the larger frame into a full-page illustration. Although arguably the end result was none the worse for it, this was another clear indication that Ron's work was way ahead of its time.

Despite Greg Hall fearing that the extra aggravation this caused Holmes might put further *Rick Random* commissions in doubt, Ron was not about to be dropped from the series, for Holmes ultimately realised that the artwork's positive aspects still outweighed the negative ones. Futuristic story details such as an in-car fax machine that prints out a photo of Mr Quex for identification purposes, and a Knitmaster machine on which Rick's sister 'types' out a garment, were drawn more convincingly by Ron than any other artist, barring Hampson, could have achieved.

Ron's brilliance was clearly evident in his depiction of one other scene. The story's script made brief mention of Mr Quex having had his satellite's dome fitted with a five-centuries-old Michaelangelo ceiling painting obtained from a Venetian palace the multimillionaire had bought, and although it was not expected that this setting would be fully illustrated, Ron saw it as another challenge and decided to show it in a full-page frame. None of Holmes' other artists would have taken the time and trouble to produce such a beautifully detailed piece of work, and he knew it. The only downside was that on certain occasions Ron needed a little guidance on the more routine aspects of how to present his strip work, and

Left: further heavily-shaded pages from *The Five Lives of Mr Quex*, in which Turner depicts Rick Random using an in-car identification photo printer (top), and the Michaelangelo-painted ceiling adorning the dome of Mr Quex's satellite (bottom).

Holmes wished that he would listen more to what his editor told him. But Ron was quite dogmatic and had his own ideas about how things should be. This was an annoyance that Holmes was prepared to live with, and in fact he cut Ron considerable slack: whereas most other artists were required to submit pencils for approval before proceeding, Ron insisted on delivering his artwork fully completed; as far as he was concerned, if any adjustments needed to be made subsequently, then somebody else would have to make them. It shows just how much respect Holmes had for Ron's talents that he was willing to let him get away with this.

Ron's stubbornness meant that his artwork for the next *Rick Random* story, *The Gold-Rush Planet*, had the same shortcomings in Holmes' eyes as that for *The Five Lives of Mr Quex*, but again the editor was willing let this slide. *The Gold-Rush Planet* is effectively a cross-genre piece, as it places classic Western elements such as shootouts and a barroom brawl into an SF setting, with scenes such as pressure-suited outlaws being lassoed in space. Ron would generally rail against any detail in a script that he felt was at odds with the general tenor of the series – or indeed with the laws of astrophysics – but in this case, given the rather surreal premise, he just went along with the sheer fun of it. In plot terms, the adventure tells of two brothers, Ed and Cal Rankin, who lay claim to an asteroid called Arizon, then exploit the prospectors who rush there – in aero-cars rather than on horseback – to mine its gold. It's tempting to speculate that this may have been adapted from a script originally meant for the Cowboy Comics range, which Holmes was also editing concurrently, but given that *The Man Who Owned the Moon* had already taken a similar approach of placing anachronistic elements in an SF setting, it's likely that it was intended as a *Rick Random* entry from the start. At any rate, the juxtaposition of the Wild West with outer space made for an unusual presentation, and one that Ron again managed to carry off effectively.

In the next story, *The Moving Planet*, a rogue planet is on a collision course for Earth, and the one man who has the power to stop it is, unknown to the authorities, pursuing a sinister agenda of his

Below left: Rick rounds up the outlaws in *The Gold-Rush Planet*. Below right: the title page of *The Mystery of the Moving Planet*.

own. This enjoyable tale was a return to form for Ron, as his artwork featured less of the heavy shading and excessive detail that had caused problems and unnecessary work for Holmes on the last two stories. Instead, he had now started to experiment with the *chiaroscuro* technique of contrasting heavy blacks against stark whites to create an almost three-dimensional effect. This essentially mirrored the approach he had taken in his colour work – contrasting dark tones against lighter ones without hard separation lines – and lent itself easily to brushwork. It would become characteristic of his style.

In early 1956, when presented with the script for the next *Rick Random* story, *The Secret of the Ocean Planet*, Ron had to inform Holmes that he doubted he could meet the deadline for it. These books generally took him around a couple of months each to complete, alongside his *Space Ace* work and other commitments, and he now had a more pressing engagement lined up on the domestic front: in March, he and his girlfriend Ruby would be getting married. In light of this, Holmes offered him instead the chance to take on a fill-in assignment illustrating a Cowboy Comics strip. Unlike the Super-Detective Library books, which each contained just a single story within their 64 pages, the Cowboy Comics ones presented two or three different tales of varying lengths. Realising that one of these would be a less time-consuming proposition than a *Rick Random* story, and would also bring in much-needed extra income, Ron gratefully accepted the offer.

While Westerns were never a favourite subject of his, this would not be the first time that Ron had tackled a strip in that genre, even leaving aside the Western-themed *Rick Random* story he had recently completed. Back in 1954, not long after starting work on *Space Ace*, and shortly before taking on his first *Rick Random* assignment, he had been called upon by publishers DCMT to illustrate for Issue 19 of *Lone Star Magazine* the final instalment of a four-part *Steve Larrabee* serial called 'War Drums', its original artist, Ron Embleton, having jumped ship to concentrate on more lucrative work on Cowboy Comics. Although this additional task had landed unexpectedly in his lap, Ron cheerfully accepted the challenge of producing what would be not only his first Western strip, but also his first to use double-

Above: with a cover drawn by another artist, Issue 19 of *Lone Star Magazine*, published in September 1954, featured Turner's first Western strip, concluding the *Steve Larrabee* serial 'War Drums', alongside the third part of his debut *Space Ace* story, 'The Island Universe'. The Lone Star Cowboy's adventures were seen by publishers DCMT as the magazine's main *raison d'être*, and at this time *Space Ace* rarely rated a mention on the cover.

page spreads. He devoted a great deal of time and effort to the presentation, thoughtfully reflecting the rugged Western setting by giving some of the frames rough borders and the captions ragged edges, even flipping some of their corners over to create a more dramatic effect. Working long hours into the night, he eventually achieved results to his satisfaction.

The Cowboy Comics story that Ted Holmes offered Ron was a 40-page one called *The Apache Uprising*, the latest in the long-running *Buck Jones* series. Supplied with examples of some of the series' earlier entries, drawn by its regular Western artists, Ron eagerly set to work, ever willing to study different styles and techniques. As on his last non-SF strip, *The Mystery of Peril Island*, he focused on achieving a realistic depiction of the characters' postures and expressions and creating interest by presenting scenes from a variety of unusual angles, testing his inventiveness in this way in lieu of the type of imaginative content he would normally be called upon to provide in his SF work. He turned in a competent enough job. By sticking to a layout comprising mostly of two frames per page, rather than the three or four he usually drew on the *Rick Random* stories, he gave himself more scope for interpretation, and produced an open and well-balanced presentation – despite a problem capturing Buck Jones' likeness, which required a little in-house adjustment.

One unexpected bonus stemming from this cowboy strip was a cover commission shortly afterwards for a Western paperback, *Vengeance Trail*, written by Ted Tubb under the pseudonym James S Farrow and published by Badger Books. As Ron had feared, the public demand for SF stories was now waning, so small paperback publishers like Badger had switched to other genres. Consequently, in stark contrast to the situation a couple of years earlier, *Vengeance Trail* would be Ron's only paperback cover commission for 1956, and he was more than happy to take it on. As this novel was part of a series, the potential to supply further Western covers may have been there; but Ron already had more of his favoured SF comic-strip work than he could comfortably manage, so it remained a one-off.

The Secret of the Ocean Planet having been eventually farmed out to Bill Lacey, Ted Holmes was determined that Ron should illustrate the next *Rick Random* title, *The Planet of Lost Men*, concerning miners kidnapped from Earth and taken to a far-off planet to work as slaves, digging for a precious mineral. With plenty of action involving monsters and robots, this should have been an exciting adventure for Ron to draw, but in fact it must rate as the worst *Rick Random* strip he was ever involved with. It was always Holmes' intention that these books should be a good read as well as a visual treat, but on this occasion the huge amount of scripted text that Ron was asked to allow space for left little scope for decent illustration and proved incredibly frustrating for him as he tried to do his artistic best. It was as if the story was far too long to be condensed into a 64-page strip; but, given that like the previous ones it had been written by the

Above: *Vengeance Trail* by E C Tubb, writing as James S Farrow (Badger Books, 1956).

usually reliable Conrad Frost, the fault presumably lay instead with the script editor, who may well have rushed it through to Ron to ensure that, as Holmes' favoured *Rick Random* artist, he would not miss an issue this time.

It would not have been unusual for Ron to have made minor story adjustments of his own. He would often read through a script and look for opportunities to replace descriptive passages with more visual ideas, sometimes even combining two or three frames into one. In this instance, though, the amount of text provided was so excessive that this was scarcely possible, so he simply drew the frames as best he could and left it to the editor to worry about where the lettering should go, expecting that it would be pared down considerably in the process. In the event, though, the text was barely touched at all, resulting in great slabs of dialogue and narrative obscuring much of the artwork. In fact, the book was so wordy that it took three letterers to complete it, and it was published a month later than planned!

This was intensely aggravating for Ron. Fortunately, though, no such problems beset the next *Rick Random* story, *Invaders from the Ocean Planet*. As this was a sequel to the Bill Lacey-illustrated tale *The Secret of the Ocean Planet*, Holmes had to send Ron copies of Lacey's artwork for the purposes of continuity. In doing so, he took the opportunity to emphasise the importance of having good likenesses and sound technique, to ensure the same level of quality. Ron had been something of a loose cannon in recent times, with his desire to experiment. However, this current story having a much better, tighter script than *The Planet of Lost Men* encouraged him to get back on track, and he now settled down to producing a fairly reliable and consistent standard of work, which he would maintain for the rest of the series – apart from the occasional overindulgence.

A totally justified piece of indulgence graces the title page of *Invaders from the Ocean Planet*, and arguably stands as one the most impressive opening frames of the whole *Rick Random* series. The script called for the story to begin with a scene showing people on board a huge satellite in orbit around the Earth, gathered at large viewports to observe a fly-past of historic spacecraft. This was to be followed by a scene showing images of the fly-past being displayed on screens back on Earth. But Ron was never happy drawing people, always preferring to show settings or hardware if at all possible. He reasoned that, given that the event was being televised, the opening splash page would have more impact if it he set it in space and had the spacesuited cameramen actually *shown*, seated atop the satellite on a platform, with all the technical paraphernalia that would involve. The observers looking through the viewports would still be seen, but now at a much smaller scale and from *outside* the satellite.

Following his marriage back in March, by the summer of 1956 Ron was heavily involved in house-hunting, and this again made it difficult for him to focus on his professional obligations. Under pressure to continue illustrating *Rick Random* for the Amalgamated Press, he let his less-well-paid *Space Ace* work for *Lone Star Magazine* slip, and it

Top: an example page of the very text-heavy *Rick Random* story *The Planet of Lost Men*, published by the Amalgamated Press in June 1956 as Super-Detective Library Number 79. Bottom: the title page of the next story, *Invaders from the Ocean Planet*, published the following month as Number 83.

was at this point that his planned story set on the planet Marinios had to be abandoned, leaving the concluding instalment of the previous tale, involving alien trophy-hunters, as the last he would get to produce for a multi-part adventure in that series.

Having been temporarily dropped from *Space Ace*, Ron was faced with the prospect of having less work than usual in the closing months of 1956, and consequently less income. There were no more *Practical Mechanics* covers immediately in prospect for him, and although publishers Newnes would be able to put some small illustration jobs his way toward the end of the year on their *Practical Householder* and *Practical Motorist* titles, these would not be enough to compensate for the shortfall. Fortunately, Ron's agent Greg Hall was able to find him a few alternative outlets for his work.

Coming across a copy of Beaverbrook's *Express Weekly* comic, Hall saw that it was running a series of cutaways similar to those produced by L Ashwell Wood for the centre pages of its great rival the *Eagle*. Ron was already familiar with cutaways, having first produced them for science and technology textbooks when employed by Odhams; and whereas those earlier pieces had been mostly small black-and-white illustrations, *Express Weekly* were running half-pagers in full colour, his favourite working medium. On the strength of his earlier *Practical Mechanics* covers, Hall soon managed to secure him work on the series.

For the 25 August issue, Ron produced a piece titled 'Sentries of the Sea', about lightships and lighthouses, and for the 22 September issue, one titled 'Skimming the Waves', about the hydrofoil. More unusual was the one he supplied for the 17 November issue, under the title 'Here

Left: the closing page of Turner's last serialised *Space Ace* story, published in *Lone Star Magazine* Volume 2 Number 6; and the colour cover of that same issue. The cover's mention of *Space Ace* reflects the fact that, by 1956, the SF strip was growing in popularity.

Right: Turner's 'Sentries of the Sea' and 'Skimming the Waves' cutaways, produced for issues of Beaverbrook's *Express Weekly* comic.

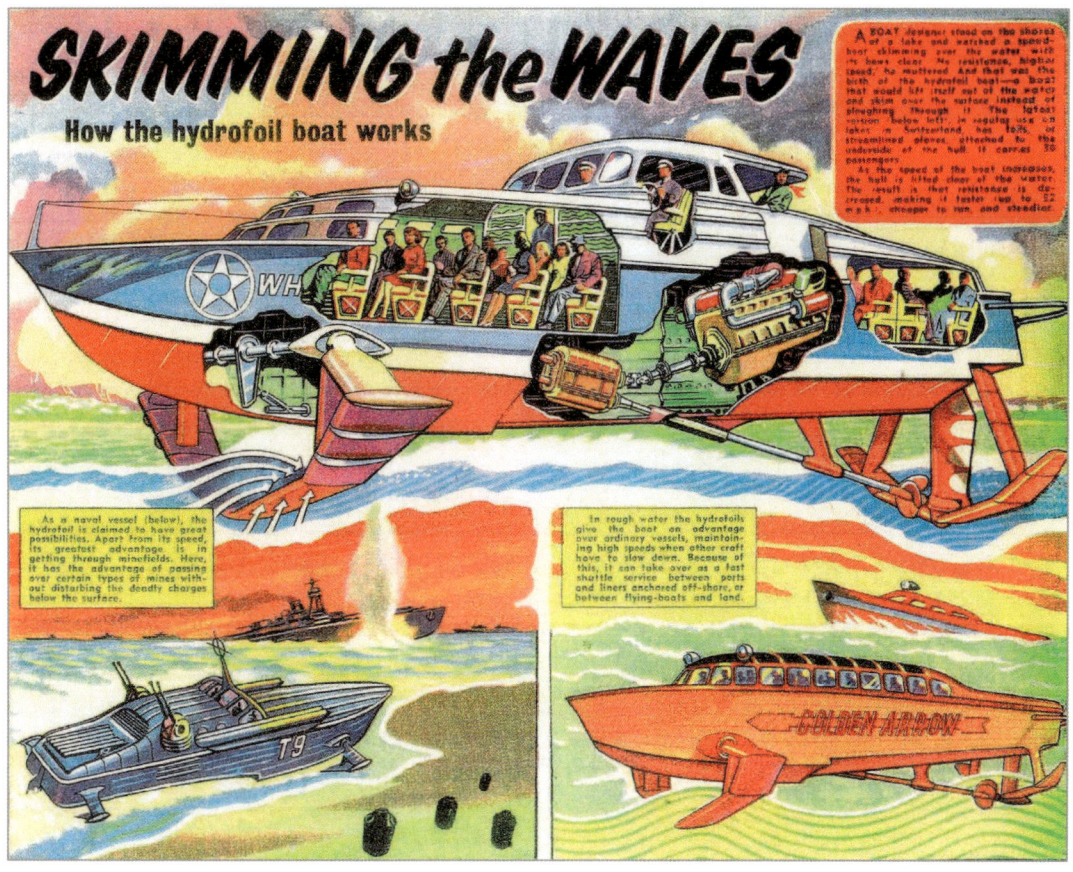

Come the Jet Cars'. Generally when tasked with producing a cutaway, an artist would be sent a photograph of the subject and details of its inner workings to use as reference. In this case, though, Ron illustrated a vehicle that hadn't even been developed in 1956. Given his passion for cars, and his interest in the future of transport in general, it would have been no surprise for him to have suggested this speculative piece. It gave him an excellent opportunity to present his own vision of what such a vehicle might look like and the features it might incorporate – including a TV screen instead of a mirror to transmit a rear-view image to the driver, something that existed only in his imagination at the time but can now be found in most modern cars. However, as enjoyable as Ron found this assignment, 'Here Come the Jet Cars' was to be his last contribution to the *Express Weekly* cutaway series. For now, he would remain largely reliant on his *Rick Random* strip work.

But just as change was taking place in Ron's private life, following his recent marriage, so change was also in the air at the Amalgamated Press. Conrad Frost having now accepted an offer to write both comic-strips and text stories for a new space-age weekly called *The Rocket*, he was succeeded as regular *Rick Random* scriptwriter by Bob Kesten, a big, bearded Canadian freelance journalist who had worked on newspapers back home in Toronto and often featured as an interviewer on CBC radio in the late '40s and early '50s. A strong, positive type, perhaps overbearing to a certain degree, Kesten was well-travelled, knowledgeable and enthusiastic, and had a great many interests, including SF. He had come to the UK initially to report back to Canadian TV viewers on the nation's recovery from the Second World War, but then decided to seek work in British broadcasting, approaching the BBC with various programme ideas. In 1956 he got the chance to present *Time to Spare*, a Home Service radio show concerning part-time occupations. However, he had a brash, showman-like style – one of his Canadian TV reports had opened with him telling of an unexploded wartime bomb found in London, only for the next shot to reveal him standing astride it! – and this did not go down well with his more staid BBC producers. Frequent arguments over the content and format of the programmes he worked on soon saw him left out in the cold.

Prompted by the popularity of the Light Programme's long-running *Journey Into Space*, Kesten had also sent the BBC an outline for a similar cliffhanger serial of his own. Although this was never commissioned, it alerted Kesten's British agency, Pearn, Pollinger and Higham, to his interest in science fiction. The agency's Gerald Pollinger was himself a big fan of the genre, always eager to promote it, so when he heard that Ted Holmes was searching for someone to succeed Conrad Frost on *Rick Random*, he put Kesten's name forward. Holmes offered Kesten the job; and, realising that he might have to fall back on his writing skills, if only for a short while, Kesten accepted.

Holmes supplied Kesten with examples of previous *Rick Random* stories as a guide. On reading these, Kesten was won over by the artwork, but found the plots dull. He felt that he could contribute something with a lot more pizzazz, including elements such as exotic aliens and high-concept machines that would really play to the artist's strengths. Via his agency, he sent Holmes two story outlines for approval. Both got the go-ahead, so he quickly proceeded to expand them into scripts, under the titles *Mystery in the Milky Way* and *Manhunt Through Space*.

Ron duly got to work illustrating the first of these. However, he was still in the throes of house-hunting – there was a baby on the way, and his one-bedroom flat was no place to start a family – and other domestic problems were also starting to weigh heavily on him at this time. Not only did he temporarily lose his *Space Ace* assignment, but in the end he also had to abandon work on *Mystery in the Milky Way* after completing only four pages. The story was then passed over to Terry Patrick, another of Greg Hall's artists, who had been responsible for the pre-Turner *Space Ace* strips.

Even after Ron had found a suitable house and the move had been completed, there was still a great deal of renovation and decoration to be done on the property, so a few weeks went by before he was ready to resume regular work. He then picked up the script for Kesten's second story, *Manhunt Through Space*, and was immediately impressed: the style of writing appealed to him far more than

Frost's and, determined to make up for lost time, he attacked the artwork with renewed vigour. *Rick Random* now being his sole focus of attention, he was able to put all his creative energies into the task, completing it ahead of Patrick delivering his pages for the previous story – which would consequently be published second. Whether Patrick had objected to Greg Hall dumping the assignment into his lap between other projects, or whether he simply couldn't compete with Ron, his work on *Mystery in the Milky Way* was distinctly inferior. He had given it a perfunctory treatment, lacking the quality even of his pre-Turner *Space Ace* serials. The stark contrast showed just how much effort Ron put into his realisation of the scripts, and the extent to which the success of *Rick Random* was reliant not only on his artistry but also on his storytelling abilities. Having previously written a great many strips himself, he could quite easily take the essence of a script and, by enhancing the visuals with a fantastical setting or a futuristic technological device, pave the way for more effective dialogue and narrative to be added at the lettering stage. In Ron's hands, *Mystery in the Milky Way* would doubtless have been a tremendous story, far superior to the version eventually published, and one can only imagine how displeased new writer Bob Kesten must have been with the results.

But in Kesten's hands, *Rick Random* would be truly transformed. Well-versed not only in classic SF literature but also in contemporary works by the likes of Asimov and Heinlein, the Canadian would incorporate some of their scientific and technical ideas into his stories, along with accurate astronomical facts for authenticity; and under his stewardship the adventures would no longer be confined to Earth's solar system – Rick would become an *interstellar* detective, visiting star systems that actually existed.

Ron was delighted with Kesten's scripts, which were less wordy than Frost's and so gave his artwork more room to breathe, allowing him free reign to exercise his creativity and devise a succession of highly imaginative planetary settings, futuristic machines, and especially alien creatures – an opportunity previously denied him, as although Frost's stories had featured alien characters, these had always been humanoid villains, with no more

Above: Turner's title page for *Manhunt Through Space*, the first Bob Kesten-scripted *Rick Random* story for which he completed the artwork. It was published by the Amalgamated Press in September 1956 as Super-Detective Library Number 90.

than minimal distinguishing features such as pointed ears, and the storylines had been of the basic murder/kidnapping/missing persons variety found in conventional crime fiction, just transposed to other worlds of the solar system. In *Manhunt Through Space*, Rick travels half way across the galaxy via 'hyperspace' to find a murderer, encountering on the way a whole host of weird and wonderful creatures in their own alien environments and with their own peculiar technologies. This gave Ron the scope to come up with plenty of innovative ideas and produce some eye-dazzling artwork.

Kesten's tales then continued in this star-spanning vein, with new planetary locations each time – an added bonus for Ron, given his dislike of repetition, as it avoided any need for continuity of design and allowed him to be as diversely creative as he wished.

By 1957, still enthused by Kesten's scripts, Ron had made *Rick Random* very much his own,

Above: in these example pages from *Manhunt Through Space*, a cigarette-holding Rick Random visits a glamorous female prisoner in her cell, then has a visi-phone conversation with his boss; and later greets a gathering of weird and wonderful alien beings.

taking full advantage of the opportunity to contribute his ideas, not only in the presentation of technological wonders such as beautifully-designed spacecraft and impressively-detailed alien machines but also in the realisation of all aspects of architecture and costume design, his low boredom threshold ensuring that, unless the script called for it, he never used exactly the same idea twice. Not since Frank Hampson with his *Dan Dare* strips had an artist succeeded in such consistent and convincing world-building.

But one significant difference between *Rick Random* and *Dan Dare* – and indeed *Space Ace*, in which Ron had also indulged his passion for creating imaginative spacecraft, aliens and architecture – was that its title character was depicted in a more mature manner. Ron often showed Rick with a cigarette in his hand, like a detective in a film noir movie, and the curvy female friends and foes he gave him were another nod to the hardboiled crime genre. Ron reasoned that publications like *Rick Random* were aimed at a more adult readership than standard comics, and he liked to present the female form in all its glory. Occasionally, though, he became so immersed in his work that he went a little too far: some of his images of beautiful women in flimsy see-through dresses and micro-mini-skirts were considered over-revealing for the market, and a little in-house re-dressing was carried out to ensure the more intimate details never saw print.

Ron was on safer ground when it came to the futuristic hardware Kesten included in his scripts, which gave him a great opportunity to devise his own versions of SF tropes such as visi-phones. The idea of a phone-like device showing an image of the caller had been around in SF for some time, but Ron's interpretation was unique: instead of the caller's face being displayed on a flat screen, it appeared as a three-dimensional image in a globe above the device's mouthpiece.

Kesten's scripts positively bristled with space-age technological ideas, including the thought-probe, a machine to read and relay information from a suspect's mind; the dorma-dex, a device enabling Rick to sleep-learn the language and culture of an alien race in a matter of hours; the grav-chute, allowing for movement between different levels of a building without the need for an elevator; and the anti-grav pack, substituting for a parachute. All of these ideas inspired Ron at a time when his creative powers were at a peak, and he produced a seemingly endless stream of compelling designs that added greatly to the appeal of the *Rick Random* series.

As Kesten's stories progressed, they began to edge more toward pure science fiction, with the crime elements virtually disappearing. In *The Time Travellers*, published as Super-Detective Library Number 97 in February 1957, Rick is sent on a quest through time, first into the distant past and then into the far future, in an attempt to track down a lost scientist who has changed the present. Then, in T*he Riddle of the Vanishing People*, published as Number 101 in April 1957, his mission is to seek more missing scientists, both humanoid and extraterrestrial, in a plot involving a teleportation device. These were again incredibly imaginative stories that Ron was ideally suited to illustrate, and he relished the task, sometimes working long into the night and over weekends in order to do them justice.

The series was improving by leaps and bounds, both in its storylines and in Ron's superb interpretation of them, and the next two entries were truly exceptional. The first, *Sabotage from Space*, published as Number 111 in September, sees Rick investigating a wave of mysterious suicides, which he discovers are being engineered via mind control by teleporting non-humanoid aliens, invisible in our spectrum, who want to decimate Earth's population in preparation for a planned invasion. The second story, *SOS from Space*, published as Number 115 in November, has Rick travelling to the distant planet of Gyzma after a strange cylinder – a hi-tech 'message in a bottle' – is found floating in space. Once there he runs into an alien apartheid system instituted by the evil, twin-faced Ebloni and solves a 10,000-year-old mystery concerning the disappearance of the planet's original race, supposedly extinct due to genocide.

SOS from Space was easily Kesten's best story so far, and had everything going for it: space battles, bizarre aliens, weird creatures, beautiful women and an intriguing mystery to solve. One can only imagine how good his next script would have

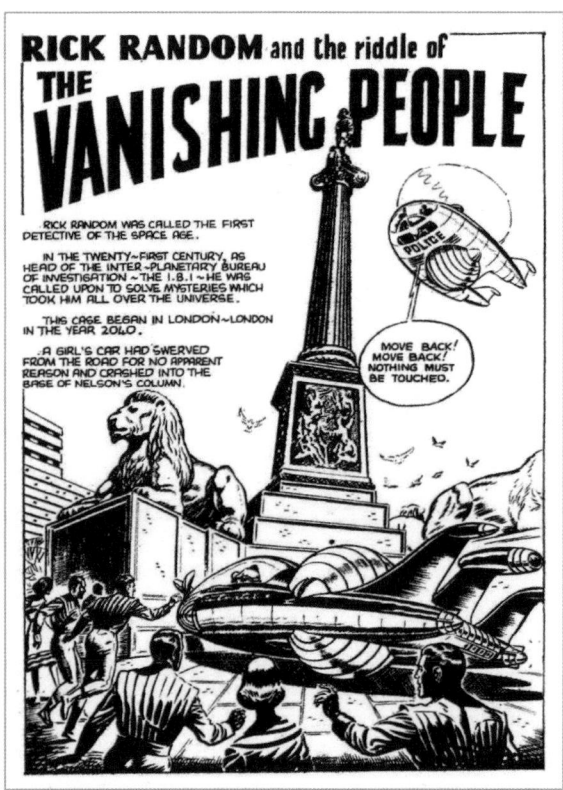

Above: Turner's title pages for the *Rick Random* stories *The Riddle of the Vanishing People* and *Sabotage from Space*.

been, had he been allowed to continue in the same vein; but this was not to be, as more changes were in the offing at the Amalgamated Press.

At the start of 1957, Ron had gratefully resumed work on the *Space Ace* stories for *Lone Star Magazine*, so he was now back to having two ongoing comic-strip assignments to alternate between; and there was also the usual requirement to provide further *Space Ace* material for that year's *Lone Star Annual*. Still, though, he found time to complete over the course of the year four more full-colour *Practical Mechanics* covers, and even somehow managed to squeeze in the artwork for a non-series Super-Detective Library entry, *The Oasis of Mystery*, based on a story by crime author Victor Canning. All of his strips he graced with his usual enthusiastic presentation and dynamic visuals – but now also with an economy of linework. The fine hatching and cross-hatching techniques he had sometimes used in his earlier, more self-indulgent phase were long gone, and his *chiaroscuro* method of contrasting bold strokes of deep shadow against stark areas of white, in an almost film noir style, was very much to the fore. In some cases, his images had no constraining lines at all. This was particularly so in his figure work, where creases and folds in clothing helped to establish form and movement; a clever visual effect, fooling the reader's brain into supplying the detail. This technique, which could be accomplished with easy brushstrokes, proved an extremely fast and efficient way of working, thus allowing Ron to increase his output considerably. At the time, this was a particularly important consideration, as early in the year his second child had been born, and with another mouth to feed, he needed to be as prolific as possible.

Aside from science fiction, Ted Holmes also had a passion for photography, so when an opportunity arose for him to edit the Amalgamated Press's great photo-news weekly *Everybody's*, he jumped at it. This resulted in the company's new managing editor Leonard Matthews, who was already overseeing the Thriller Picture Library, taking full charge of the Super-Detective Library as well. Unlike Holmes, Matthews had no interest whatsoever in SF, and when he reviewed the recent *Rick Random* stories, he disapproved of Kesten's approach to the scripting. He did, though, appreciate Ron's talents, and felt that the series should continue, but with the more fantastical elements reined in. He insisted that the stories should be of detection with SF overtones, rather than the other way round: in essence, the same policy as had originally applied under his predecessor Monty Haydon. This would have a dramatic effect on the course of the series.

Previously during Kesten's time as scriptwriter, Ted Holmes had delegated day-to-day responsibility for the strip to an Amalgamated Press subeditor named Angus Allen. In the reshuffle, however, Allen's place was taken by Andy Vincent, who had been an assistant editor on the Super-Detective Library in its earliest days and was someone Matthews could rely upon to follow his mandate.

The new regime took over toward the end of 1957, and there was then a longer-than-usual wait before the next *Rick Random* story appeared, possibly due to Kesten having to adapt a previously-prepared script to comply with the new directive. When it eventually saw print in April 1958, this tale of Rick's search for a missing Governor on *The Planet of Terror* failed to match the standard of its recent predecessors. Ron had attempted to enliven proceedings by including in his artwork some delightful alien characters, but prior to publication these had been 'humanised' with in-house paste-overs. Kesten had nevertheless managed to sneak in sequences involving an encounter with a giant, prehistoric-type creature and a battle with a sea-monster, so Ron wasn't entirely cheated of the more imaginative aspects; but perhaps because of this, Andy Vincent felt that the story still wasn't fully in line with the new policy, and began casting around for other writers who could provide the type of material he felt was needed.

Conrad Frost, who had supplied most of the early *Rick Random* scripts, was now free again, his work on the SF weekly *The Rocket* having ended with that publication's cancellation, and he was invited to come back on board. Agreeing, he produced and was paid for a script with the working title *Murder at the Space Hotel*. As events transpired, however, this would never be used, as another writer had appeared on the scene whom Vincent realised could provide just the type of story that Matthews was

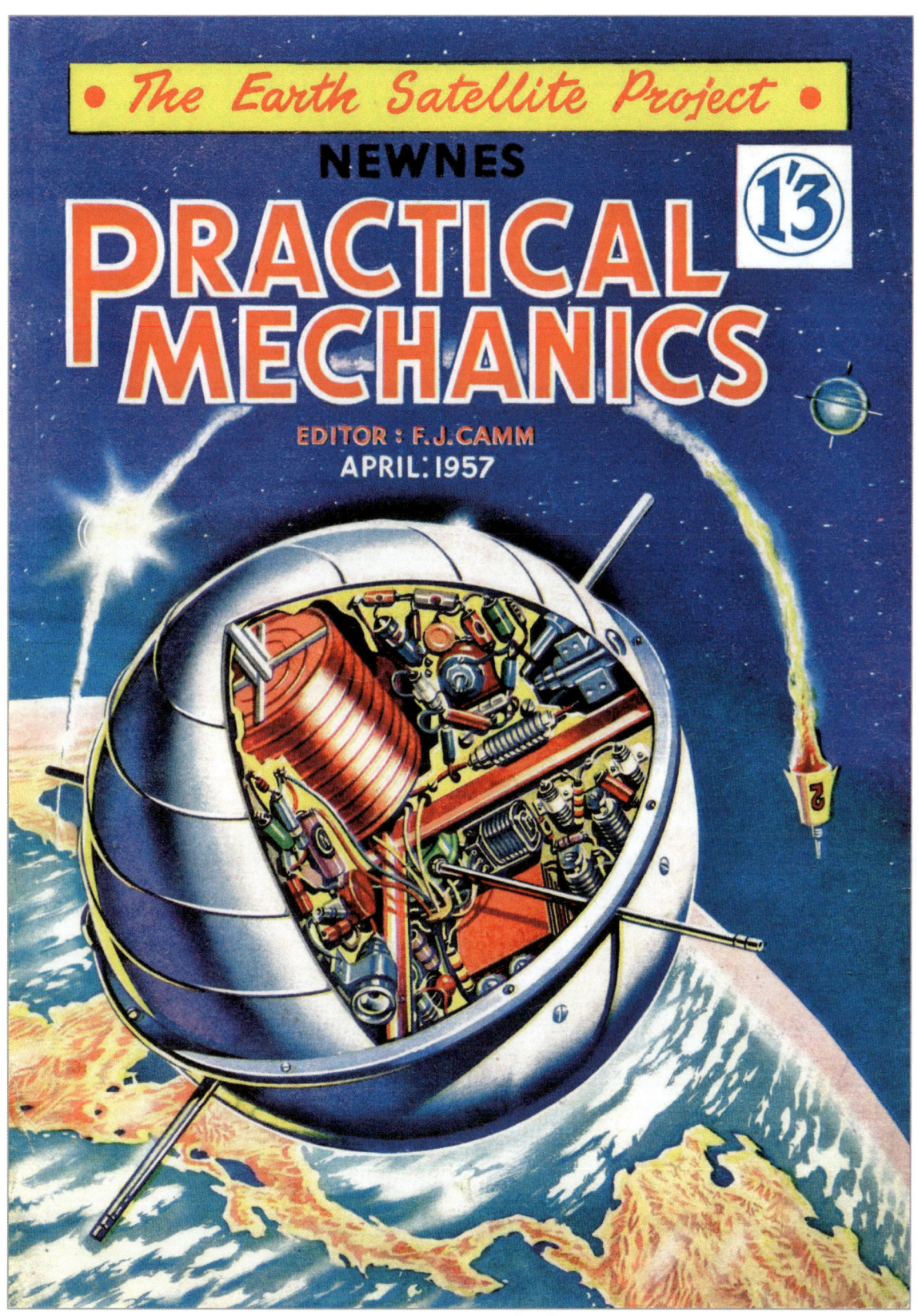

Turner's cover for the April 1957 edition of Newnes' *Practical Mechanics*.

seeking. That writer was Harry Harrison.

Harrison had both written and drawn SF strips in his native America and knew the medium inside out; but now, disliking the restrictions imposed on the industry by the recently-formed Comics Code Authority, he had decided to move to the UK. Arriving in the autumn of 1957 to attend the London WorldCon, the first SF convention to be held outside of America, he met Sydney Jordan, creator of the *Daily Express*'s long-running *Jeff Hawke* strip, and agreed to provide a story for him. But Harrison was also introduced to Andy Vincent, who was impressed by his credentials and felt sure that he could supply the 'harder' type of SF that Matthews favoured. Consequently Frost's script was passed over and Harrison was engaged to continue the *Rick Random* series.

Harrison's first story, *The Space Pirates*, published in May 1958 as Super-Detective Library Number 127, was a 'whodunnit' involving disappearing spaceships, and while it lacked the flair and visual potential of Kesten at his best, it was nevertheless an intriguing and well-crafted tale. At one point, the script described a spaceship passenger as 'Jal – a man from another planet', and Vincent having omitted to specify in editing that this was to be a humanoid alien, Ron naturally drew him as a typically weird-looking extraterrestrial. Under Holmes' editorship, he had been given almost carte blanche with his interpretation of the scripts – but not so now. Matthews' new ruling ensured that, in another case of in-house editing, Jal was given a terrestrial makeover prior to publication, and Ron's exotic alien would never see print.

Harrison's second script, *Rick Random's Perilous Mission*, involved a murder investigation at a whale farm in the mid-Pacific, a setting not dissimilar to that of Arthur C Clarke's 1957 novel *The Deep Range* – an idea possibly suggested by Vincent to ensure there was not the slightest opportunity to include aliens or even spacecraft in the artwork. The story did however feature a number of futuristic machines for Ron to interpret in his own inimitable style, and the opening frame he produced was easily one of the most dramatic and effective of the whole series, showing an underwater scout craft discovering the body of a farm operative floating in the shadow of two huge

Above: Turner's highly impressive opening frame for *Rick Random's Perilous Mission*, published in June 1958 as Super-Detective Library Number 129.

blue whales.

Although Harrison's scripts were now meeting Leonard Matthews' requirements, his contributions to the series were temporarily interrupted as, feeling stifled by the smog-bound atmosphere of North London, he decided to move to the sunnier climes of Italy. Suddenly Bob Kesten was back in favour and approached to provide a fill-in script – albeit with the stipulation that this should be in line with Harrison's style. The result was *The Mystery of the Frozen World*, a story that certainly conformed to Matthews' dictates, as again there was not an alien or a monster in sight. Somewhat disheartened by the vetoing of his usual galaxy-hopping contributions, Keston had fallen back on the familiar theme of teleportation, supplying a rather mundane bank-robbery plotline inspired in part by elements of two Earthbound SF novels: *The World Wreckers* by Sydney J Bounds and *Robbery Without Violence* by one-time Vargo Statten novelist John Russell Fearn. The resulting tale was rather dull by

Kesten's standards and lacked the visual possibilities of his earlier work, but was nevertheless enlivened by Ron with more than his usual quota of stunning full-page scenes. The use of these would usually be indicated in the script, with layouts provided, but Ron would often choose to go his own way, working out which scenes would have the most impact at full-page size and rearranging the other frames to suit. Whereas a less ambitious artist might have been quite content simply to draw close-ups of individuals where specified, Ron preferred to pour his creativity into the settings rather than the characters. Thus, in his hands, a scripted three-panel sequence of 'talking heads' in a spaceport might be transformed into a stunning single-frame depiction of the location in all its Turneresque glory. Space-freighters, trucks, loading equipment and architecture would be the focus, with the characters reduced to mere brushstrokes in long-shot. Not only would this approach give the scene a greater sense of perspective, it would also lessen the need for detailed figure-work – the least appealing aspect of strip illustration as far as Ron was concerned.

His move to Italy now completed, Harry Harrison resumed his *Rick Random* duties in time to provide the next script, *The Mystery of the Robot World*. The story's classical themes and Italianate settings, no doubt inspired by the writer's new location, gave Ron some excellent material to work with. The plot this time involves Rick being called in to investigate the murder of the Prime Minister of Arcadia, a Utopian world where the population's every need and desire are by met robots; a scenario affording Ron the opportunity to present some impressive mechanical monsters – five types in all!

Ron considered Harrison's scripts inspiring, and the admiration was mutual: Harrison later stated that Ron's art 'filled him with fire'. As an artist himself, Harrison wrote from an artist's perspective, putting in material that naturally leant itself to Ron's visual style. A good example of this in *The Mystery of the Robot World* is a scene where Rick and his companion are fleeing from the Arcadian police through a modern art gallery. Although insignificant to the plot, this presented Ron with a great opportunity to include some futuristic statuary – something Harrison had noted he delighted in doing in his previous stories.

Above: two of Turner's impactful full-page scenes from the *Rick Random* story *The Mystery of the Frozen World*, published as Super-Detective Library Number 133 in August 1958.

However, when at the end of 1958 Harrison turned in his fourth *Rick Random* script, *The Terror from Space*, it was less impressive. The only mystery it posed was why Rick's boss was apparently out to kill him – this being explained as the work of shapeshifting humanoid aliens replicating and replacing world leaders to pave the way for an invasion. Otherwise, it was essentially a rehashed Second World War story, featuring French resistance workers, commando-style fighting on Gibraltar and a torpedo-boat escape. If it seemed that Harrison wasn't trying too hard with this tale, it might well have been because he had by now had a better offer from *Flash Gordon* illustrator Dan Barry to return to the States and write scripts for him instead. The Amalgamated Press tried to dissuade him from leaving, offering to increase his fee from £35 to £50 per story, but it was too little, too late.

With Harrison's departure, Kesten was once more back in favour and asked to provide another story. However, irritated at having been sidelined, and having now found more lucrative work writing material for a fellow Canadian, the comedian and actor Bernard Braden, he was less than enthused, and delivered a script so lacking in inventive material that even Ron's talents failed to enliven it. *The Threat from Space* tells of a comedian, Ally Akbar, being kidnapped by aliens and hypnotised to pass coded invasion details to 'fifth columnists' via his act – another plot that could have worked just as well in a Second World War setting! The fact that Kesten had recently scripted a piece called *My Friend Ally* for Braden's one-man BBC series *Personal Playhouse* might lead one to suspect that he had simply given this a hurried makeover to fulfil the irksome *Rick Random* commission. At any rate, the story's uninspiring subject matter, added to the fact that it consisted almost entirely of 'talking heads', resulted in a very substandard offering. The only scope Ron might have had to improve matters – by depicting the aliens in a highly imaginative way – had been denied him by the stricture to keep to humanoid extraterrestrials. As it was, the only way he could show their otherworldly origin was to give them a gigantic stature. Sadly, this disappointing story effectively signalled the beginning of the end for *Rick Random*.

Over the past year, Ron had picked up only a couple more book cover commissions – one for a paperback, *A Mirror of Witchcraft* by Christina Hole, published by Pedigree, the other for a hardback, *Ace Carew* by Edward R Home-Gall, published by Dakers –

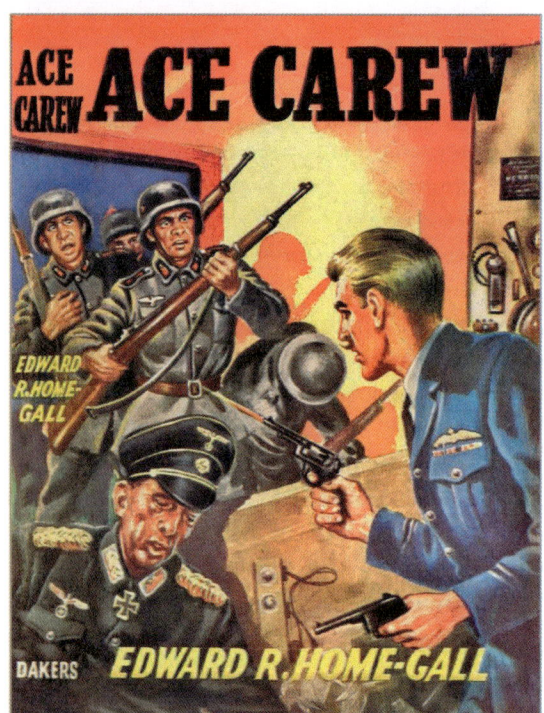

Above: Turner's covers for *A Mirror of Witchcraft* by Christina Hole (Pedigree, 1958) and *Ace Carew* by Edward Home-Gall (Dakers, 1959).

but his regular *Space Ace* strip work for *Lone Star Magazine* had continued unabated. At the very end of 1958 he even made two further contributions to the magazine's flagship *Steve Larrabee* cowboy series. The first of these appeared in that year's *Lone Star Annual*, for which he contributed not only the front endpaper illustration and two eight-page *Space Ace* stories but also a sixteen-page adventure for the Lone Star Rider. The second came in the December issue of *Lone Star Magazine* itself when, having been asked to fill in for the regular artist, he devised a story called 'The Apache Pass Aqueduct'; and even here he gave himself some unusual technology to illustrate as, eschewing clichéd Western subject matter such as cattle-rustling, shootouts and bank raids, he settled on a plot involving the building of an aqueduct to channel water into a valley where gold prospecting is under way, thus preventing a crooked land-owner from taking advantage of a spring on his property.

Upmarket publishers George Newnes also continued to put a steady stream of work in Ron's direction during 1958 and 1959. In a few cases this involved providing illustrations for their *Practical Motorist* and *Practical Householder* titles, including the covers for two supplements that came with issues of the latter, but for the most part it consisted of further cover commissions for *Practical Mechanics*. The three covers that Ron supplied in 1958 were, as usual, full-colour paintings. The six in 1959, on the other hand, were just two-colour pieces, the magazine having switched to that more basic style of presentation at the start of the year.

This may well have been an enforced change, as there was at that time an industrial dispute in progress in the British printing industry over union demands for a maximum forty-hour working week for their members. In May, this dispute escalated into a full-scale print-workers' strike, which lasted

Top left: Turner manages to inject a little visual excitement into this example page from the under-par Bob Kesten-written *Rick Random* story *The Threat from Space*, published as Super-Detective Library Number 153 in June 1959.

Bottom left: the title page of 'The Exiles', the *Space Ace* story written and illustrated by Turner for the July 1958 issue of Atlas's *Lone Star Magazine*.

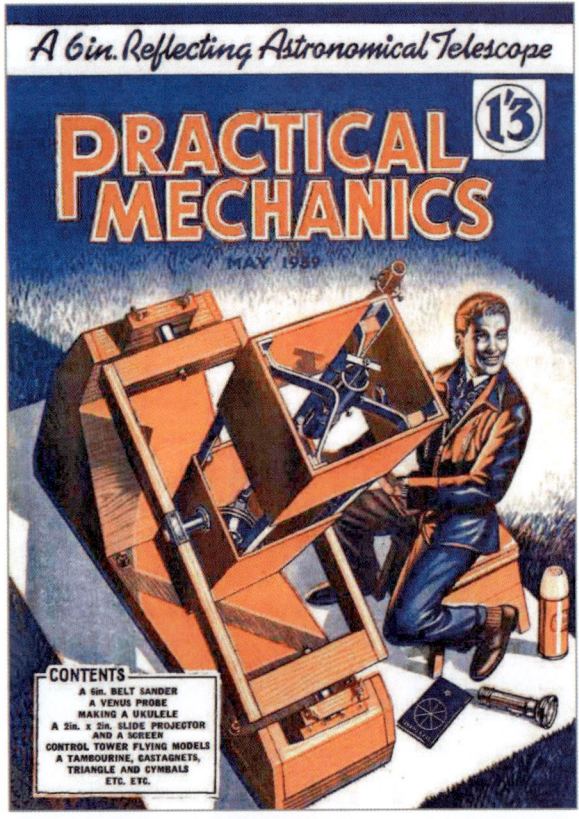

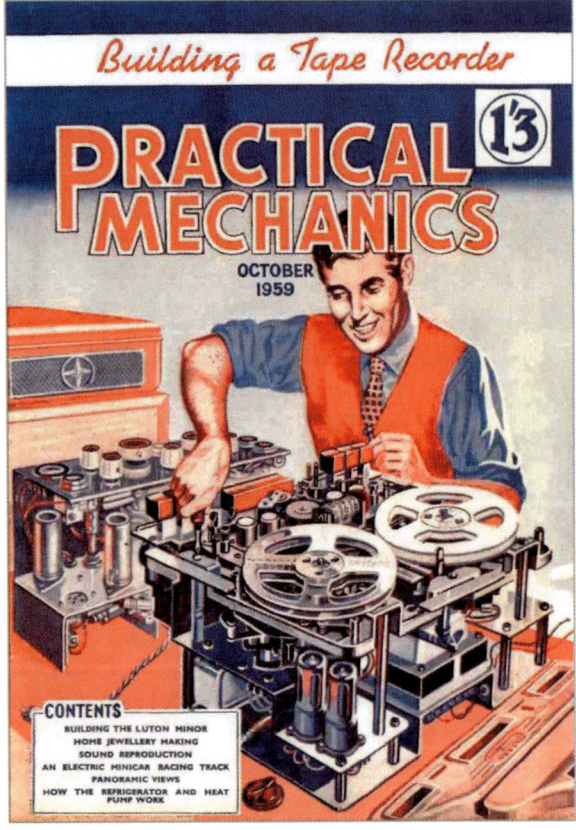

some weeks and caused significant disruption for publishers. One consequence of this for the Amalgamated Press was that, although they were still able to maintain a monthly schedule with their titles, the summer of 1959 saw them taken over by the Mirror Group and renamed Fleetway Publications, after their Fleetway House premises.

It was under the new owners that the next and final *Rick Random* series entry appeared. Published in December 1959 as Number 163 in the now rebranded Super-Detective Picture Library, *The Kidnapped Planet* was again more of a futuristic war story than a detective one, involving Rick attempting to rescue an old friend on the planet Antares from the clutches of the invading Bakusti – more gigantic humanoid aliens! Thankfully, this swansong adventure was at least something of a return to form for scriptwriter Bob Kesten, featuring plenty of action in space and futuristic hardware for Ron to design.

The series might have continued to improve from this point, had it lasted longer; but this was not to be. With the public appetite for science fiction still waning, the new regime felt that Rick's adventures had now run their course. Moreover, although the Super-Detective Picture Library would continue to be published until the start of 1961, and this was not quite the end of Ron's association with it, from this point on it would rely more on reprints than on original material.

The demise of *Rick Random* at the end of 1959 happened to coincide with the end of Frank Hampson's involvement with the *Eagle*'s *Dan Dare*. It came as a blow to Ron to learn that Hampson was no longer responsible for his own creation. Hampson had been a hero to him – a pioneer of the British SF comic strip – and with 'the skipper' now gone, he felt somewhat cast adrift. Not only was this the end of a decade, it was also the end of an era. The last three *Rick Random* stories having all had Second World War overtones, they indirectly presaged a big change that was on the way for boys' comics, and one that would ultimately change Ron's own attitude to strip work.

Left: Turner's covers for the May 1959 and October 1959 issues of *Practical Mechanics*, in the new two-colour style adopted that year by publishers George Newnes.

7: WAR IS HELL!

In the years immediately after the Second World War, there was a strong desire amongst the general British public to put the conflict out of their minds, and this was one of the things that led readers to turn to the escapism of science fiction. By the mid-1950s, however, science fiction was losing its appeal, due in part to it being overtaken by real-world space-race developments, and there was a growing interest in revisiting those dark wartime days. So it was that, little more than a decade after the war ended, it began all over again, in the realm of popular fiction.

With Second World War films such as *The Cruel Sea*, *The Dam Busters* and *Reach for the Sky* breaking British box-office records, it was not long before the Amalgamated Press picked up on the new trend. In September 1958, they expanded their output of 64-page picture-story titles with the launch of the War Picture Library; and, reviewing the situation after their takeover of the company in the summer of 1959, the new Mirror Group owners quickly realised that this was outselling the Thriller Picture Library and Super-Detective Picture Library ranges, which now seemed rather dated. As the Thriller Picture Library already dealt in stories set in the past, the situation there could be remedied simply by shifting its focus to the modern history of the war years, in new series such as *Battler Britton* and *Dogfight Dixon*. Where the Super-Detective Picture Library was concerned, though, a more significant overhaul was needed to justify its continued existence. Thus the decision was taken to drop the futuristic adventures of *Rick Random* and introduce the retrospective ones of *John Steel – Secret Agent WWII*.

The first *John Steel* story was published in September 1959, and when the final *Rick Random* one saw print three months later, Ron was offered the chance to transfer to the new series. Initially, after years of working on his preferred science fiction strips, with just the occasional brief foray into the Western genre, he wasn't too keen to illustrate war stories, for although he could take inspiration from his own wartime experiences when it came to hardware and locations, he would still need to do some research. However, the *John Steel* tales were well scripted by Bob Kesten and others and so, armed with volumes of the Odhams-published *The Second World War In Pictures* to use as reference, Ron set to work with a certain amount of determination, his professionalism ensuring that the quality of the art was just as high as on his *Rick Random* strips, with a great deal of thought and effort being put into some exciting action sequences.

But Ron still wasn't entirely dedicated to this new series. Moreover, in March 1960, he became a father for the third time, and now with a daughter as well as two sons to support, he needed the quickest and most lucrative work around. Consequently he prevailed upon his agent Greg Hall to gain him more Newnes commissions, and this resulted in him producing, over the course of the year, a further nine two-colour covers for their *Practical Mechanics* monthly. The *John Steel* work had to take a back seat, and in the end Ron illustrated only three entries in that series. Even his *Space Ace* work had to be dropped for a few months – until Ace was made the title character of his own comic in August 1960.

Despite the revamp, sales of the Super-Detective Picture Library continued to fall, and in January 1961, coinciding with the debut of another war-focused range, the Battle Picture Library, it was finally axed. Ready by this point to start taking on more Fleetway work again, Ron accepted the assignment to illustrate its very last entry, which curiously introduced a character not dissimilar to John Steel in a story called *School for Spies* under the new heading *The Shadow – Mystery Man of WWII*.

Following the demise of the Super-Detective Picture Library, the *John Steel* stories themselves were absorbed into the Thriller Picture Library. It was understood that Ron would continue to be offered work on them; but as the next script was not yet ready, he was first asked instead to tackle a *Dogfight Dixon* tale. This series having as its theme

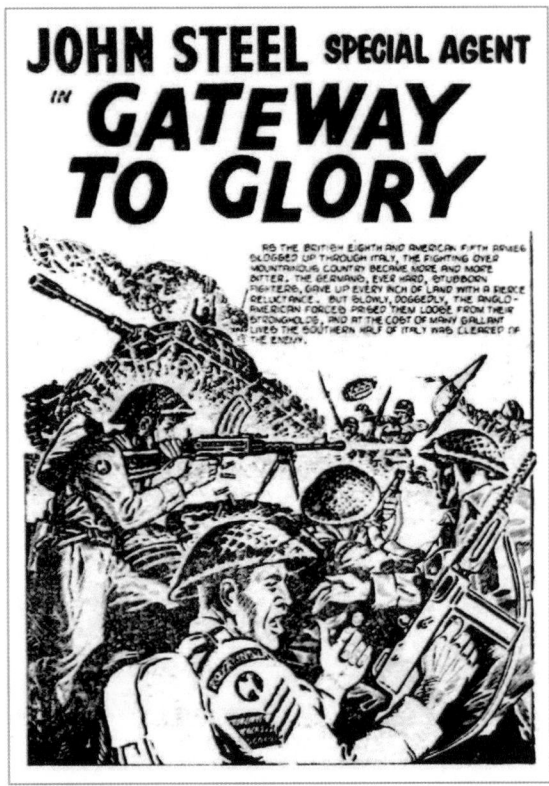

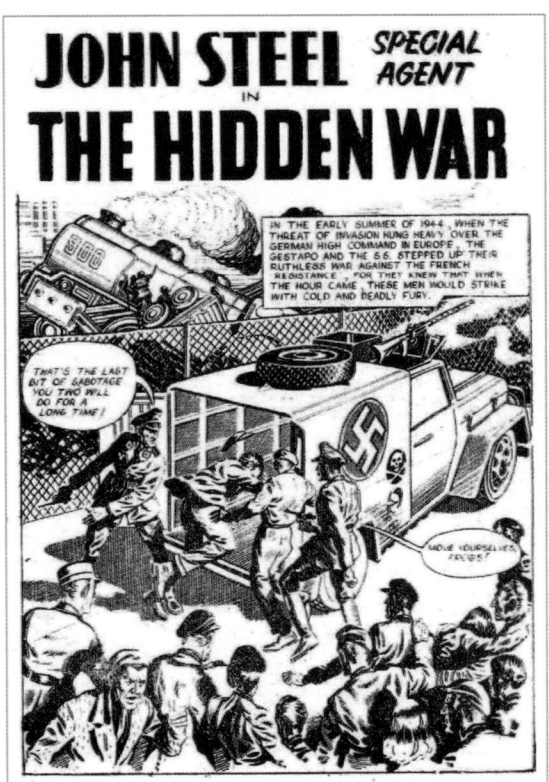

The title pages of the four war stories that Turner illustrated in the final months of Fleetway's Super-Detective Picture Library: *Gateway to Glory*, *Operation 'Tina'* and *The Hidden War* in the *John Steel* series, and *School for Spies* in the one-off *The Shadow* swansong.

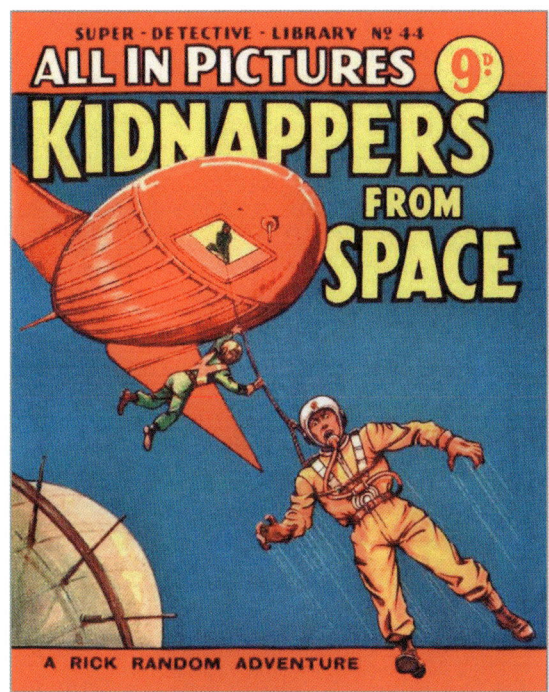

Above: a six-year evolution in content and design. With covers painted by other artists, Super-Detective Library Number 44, published in December 1954, presenting Turner's very first contribution to the range, the *Rick Random* story *Kidnappers from Space*; and Super-Detective Picture Library Number 188, published in January 1961, presenting his very last, the one-off *The Shadow* story *School for Spies*, set in the Second World War.

the flying aces of the First World War, it would mean more dreaded research, but Ron was now coming to terms with the fact that the SF strips were over and done with as far as Fleetway were concerned, leaving the war stories as his only option; and provided they were well-written – which they generally were, some of them ironically by future SF luminary Michael Moorcock – then he was prepared to give them his best shot. However, he had completed only around twenty pages of the *Dogfight Dixon* strip when suddenly Greg Hall called him and instructed him to stop work on it. The commission had been accepted on the understanding that Ron would receive the same page rate as he had on the Super-Detective Picture Library books, but as part of their ongoing economy drive the Mirror Group had recently engaged several new European artists who were willing to accept much lower fees, and Hall had just learned that the established British artists were now expected to follow suit. Not at all happy with the situation, the agent protested that Ron's far superior standard of work justified a higher rate; but this argument cut no ice with the editor, who responded that he simply wanted passable art that told the story. Consequently Hall took Ron off the book, and the pages he had already completed would never see print.

Ron was intensely disappointed to have lost this challenging but enjoyable project. He'd approached the strip in good spirits, carried out his research and produced some extremely detailed work with which he was well satisfied, considering it some of the best he'd ever done for a non-SF subject. But now, the three weeks' effort he'd put into it would be wasted – added to which, he wouldn't receive a penny for it. Had he been consulted, he would probably have been prepared to accept the lower rate on offer. For Hall, though, this was a matter of professional ethics, and he would now seek a replacement commission at a rate he considered acceptable. He soon found it; but Ron was less than pleased with what it entailed.

It was back to the Second World War again for this new assignment, on a series called *Scoop Donovan – War Cameraman* for the *Film Fun* comic, also published by Fleetway. However, it was not the subject matter that troubled Ron, it was the fact that this was his first strip for a weekly publication, necessitating a drastic change of working practice for him. Quite apart from the obvious challenges the faster turnaround presented, the different format of the strip meant that he was now faced with the unenviable task of having to cram twenty or so small frames into two-and-a-half standard pages, depriving him of the scope and freedom of expression he'd enjoyed on the Picture Library books. He was not impressed with the scripts, either; they paled by comparison with the ones he'd been used to working on, and often contained excessive captions and dialogue, restricting him from presenting the stories in the way he would have liked. Consequently the weekly work became something of an ordeal.

Nevertheless, Ron brought his usual ingenuity to bear and was occasionally able to lessen the problems by merging two scenes into one, so that certain sections of narrative could be cut. Donovan's missions involved him capturing action footage from battlegrounds all around the world – naturally getting into various scrapes along the way – and Ron needed as much space as he could create to illustrate these scenes in a way that did them justice. But it was really only on the rare occasions when the strip was allowed to run to three pages rather than the usual two-and-a-half that he had the leeway to produce work that satisfied him.

Ron's first *Scoop Donovan* strip appeared in the 7 January 1961 issue of *Film Fun*, and by the middle of the year, having skipped only one week in the interim, he had already grown tired of illustrating these tedious wartime yarns, with their strict weekly deadlines. Anxious to be able to move on from this frustrating assignment, he had asked Greg Hall to find him less taxing but more inspiring alternative work. Hall had agreed to try, but old-style comics like *Film Fun* and *Knockout* had nothing else available in Ron's line, and in any case were beginning to rely more and more on reprints of US material in preference to original content. Newer titles like Fleetway's *Lion* and *Tiger* did run SF strips, such as the former's *Captain Condor* and the latter's *Jet-Ace Logan*, but these and any other weekly series that might have been suitable for Ron were already taken by other artists. There was, though, one new weekly on which it seemed he might stand a chance of gaining a commission. This was *Buster*, launched by Fleetway in 1960.

Modelled on the large-format D C Thomson comic *Topper*, *Buster* led off with a front-page strip featuring the title character, supposedly the son of the *Daily Mirror*'s famous cartoon layabout Andy Capp. Inside, it offered a mix of adventure strips for older children and funnies for the younger ones. But one thing it didn't have was any SF. Hopeful of persuading editor Jack Le Grand to introduce such a strip, Ron set about devising a sample page, reasoning that if he had to work on a weekly series, then it might as well be in a genre he enjoyed, with narrative and dialogue over which he might have some influence, as on *Rick Random*.

Ron still hadn't quite got over the shock of Frank Hampson leaving *Dan Dare*, so it is perhaps unsurprising that his sample page featured a main character with a striking resemblance to Hampson's 'Pilot of the Future', even down to the same jagged eyebrows. The basic premise was that this new, if familiar-looking, hero would embark on a series of escapades in space and on other planets, accompanied by a young sidekick – a lad with whom the comic's more juvenile readers might identify. Ron put a lot of effort into illustrating this page, and the end result was outstanding, with a dramatic opening frame of the two adventurers heading out toward the reader aboard their amazing spaceship. But Le Grand wasn't impressed. He disapproved of the homage to *Dan Dare* – effectively a nod to a rival comic – and disliked the design of the spaceship, which looked something like a flying Cadillac, all steel and gleaming chrome. While this might have been fine five years earlier for *Rick Random*, it now appeared somewhat dated – not at all what a recently-launched comic needed. Ron had previously been spoilt by publishers such as Atlas, who had been prepared to accept whatever he dreamt up, with little or no editorial intervention. Fleetway, by contrast, liked to keep a tight rein on their artists, and to engage those they could rely upon to stick to their house style. Consequently Ron's proposal was rejected.

Disappointed, Ron realised that, at least for the time being, he would just have to knuckle down and continue working on *Scoop Donovan*. He could not have known that a chance encounter by his agent would soon lead to a more enjoyable commission, and one quite unlike any he had ever had before.

The *Dan Dare*-like sample page that Turner produced in 1961 for consideration by the new Fleetway comic *Buster*.

A page of Turner's artwork for the *Scoop Donovan – War Cameraman* series that ran in Fleetway's weekly *Film Fun* comic.

WAR IS HELL!

Another of Turner's title pages for *Film Fun*'s *Scoop Donovan – War Cameraman* series.

Featuring Ron Turner paintings, the covers of the January, March, April and May 1961 issues of George Newnes' *Practical Mechanics*.

8: THE NUMBERS GAME

It was while out walking one morning in the summer of 1961 that Ron's agent Greg Hall met William Lee, a former publishing acquaintance who was now a commissioning editor at Craft Master, a company that specialised in marketing painting-by-numbers kits. On learning that Lee was looking for artists, Hall quickly informed him that Ron was available. Familiar with Ron's work, Lee was only too pleased to take him on. Thus a deal was struck for Ron to provide the original masters from which new additions to the company's painting-by-numbers range would be produced. Ron was delighted. Essentially a painter, he was keen to get back to doing more colour work, after all the black-and-white illustration he had been occupied with of late. The subject matter would be very varied: animals, ships, cars, portraits, landscapes, even a few nudes. The only downside was that it would not extend to spacecraft, aliens or any type of action scene. However, Ron was not concerned about that. He was only too pleased to have been presented with this unexpected new outlet for his talents.

Even so, Ron did not yet feel comfortable enough to give up his well-paid *Scoop Donovan* assignment. He remained open, too, to accepting further, even better-paid *Practical Mechanics* commissions, and was pleased to be asked to provide the covers for ten of 1961's twelve issues – particularly as publishers Newnes had now reverted to having these printed in full colour. There was, though, a limit to how much work he could realistically cope with. Something had to give, and that turned out to be his long-running SF strip *Space Ace*. This poorly-paid job had always been more of a labour of love than something he did for financial gain, and having to write, illustrate and letter a new story each and every month had now become too much. Consequently, Issue 13 of the *Space Ace* comic, published in August 1961, proved to be the last – although its title character would continue to appear for a couple more years yet in stories that Ron found time to contribute to publisher Atlas's annual-type books aimed at the Christmas market.

Ron found the production of the Craft Master painting-by-numbers masters quite an intense process. First, working mainly from photographic references, he would draw the subject onto card. Then he would add an outline around each of the areas that he wanted to be a different colour. Next he would place a sheet of clear acetate over the drawing and fill in the outlined areas using the appropriate colour paints, limiting himself to those that would be supplied with the kit. Finally, he would remove the painted acetate and note each of the outlined areas on the card with a number corresponding to the colour he had used for it. The painted acetate would then be reproduced as the box-lid artwork, while the card with the numbered areas would serve as the guide for the user to follow. This was intricate and time-consuming work, but it paid very well and, best of all, there was never any great pressure on Ron to meet a firm deadline. The only problem he ever had was with two still-life subjects: as an action artist, he had painted scenes of flowers with leaves and blooms twisting, turning and wrapping around each other, and these were rejected as being just 'too lively'!

As Ron's familiarity with this new type of work grew, so did the commissions, both in quantity and in physical size, and finally he did feel able to say goodbye to *Scoop Donovan*. His regular stint on the strip ended in December 1961, and he made just three more contributions to it in the early months of 1962. He continued to take on *Practical Mechanics* work, however, and on occasion was even moved to send in a reader's letter or submit a pseudonymous article of his own; it was at this time that his piece on a prospective Thames Heliport saw print. His paintings graced the covers of all of the first eight monthly issues of 1962. But times were changing, and these would be the last of his many cover pieces for the magazine, Newnes having now decided to switch to using photographs rather than artwork. Aside from a handful of small internal spot-illustration jobs for issues up to March 1963, this marked the end of Ron's association with *Practical Mechanics*, leaving his Craft Master work as, for the time being, virtually his sole source of income.

Turner's cover for the March 1962 issue of *Practical Mechanics*, containing his speculative article about a Thames Heliport.

The September 1961, December 1961, January 1962 and February 1962 issues of George Newnes' *Practical Mechanics*.

A selection of the master paintings that Turner produced for Craft Master painting-by-numbers kits between 1961 and 1965.

THE NUMBERS GAME

Further examples of Turner's master paintings for the Craft Master painting-by-numbers kits.

Another selection of the master paintings that Turner produced for Craft Master painting-by-numbers kits between 1961 and 1965.

From late 1961 to late 1965, Ron's working time was largely spent on his Craft Master paintings. However, he did still take on a few comic-strip assignments, reminding editors that he was still around. These included his very last *Space Ace* stories, which saw print in two annual publications from Atlas: the seventh *Lone Star Annual* in 1961; and *Book of Space Adventures* (titled as such on the cover but as *Boys' Book of Space* inside) in 1962. A further three *Book of Space Adventures* volumes followed in 1963, 1964 and 1965, including stories under the character's original name Ace Hart, but Ron was not involved with these.

Back in mid-1961, around the same time as he had made his rejected pitch for an SF strip in *Buster*, Ron had also submitted to the editor of *Tiger* a sample page for a proposed *Jet-Ace Logan* strip. That approach had been equally unsuccessful; but in 1962 he got the chance to illustrate, as a fill-in for another artist, a one-off 64-page *Jet-Ace Logan*

Below: Turner's original sample page for a possible *Jet-Ace Logan* strip for Fleetway's *Tiger* comic. In what appears to have been a private joke, he gave this the same title, 'Revolt on Venus', as the Oliver Passingham-illustrated Super-Detective Library entry that had led to a veto on straight SF in that range (see page 113).

Above: the title page of 'The Rain of Death', one of Turner's last two *Space Ace* stories, both of which appeared in Atlas's *Book of Space Adventures* in 1962.

story, the David Motton-scripted *Times 5*, for the Thriller Picture Library. The fee on offer for this was no greater than that for his scrapped *Dogfight Dixon* assignment, but as he was already by this point receiving an excellent income from his Craft Master work, that was perhaps of less significance now.

Concerning the alien Quintapeds and a duplicating device they use to clone a whole army, *Times 5* saw Ron on top form, and proved that the lack of any SF subjects in his regular Craft Master work had in no way dulled his imagination. On the contrary, it had left him eager to pursue such opportunities, when they arose; and not long afterwards, he accepted an offer to illustrate another *Jet-Ace Logan* story for the Thriller Picture Library. *Power from Beyond* was even better than *Times 5*; and its mention of a 'journey to the edge of creation' obviously struck a chord with Ron as, purely for his own amusement, he used his own

Above: the title pages of the Turner-illustrated *Jet-Ace Logan* stories *Times 5* and *Power from Beyond*, published as Thriller Picture Library Numbers 418 and 442 respectively.

likeness for a Professor character.

A further Fleetway commission followed just a few weeks later, this time to illustrate a story called *Claws of the Cat* for the Air Ace Picture Library – yet another war-focused range, launched at the start of 1960. Any additional Picture Library contributions were effectively ruled out, however, by Ron's obligations to Craft Master; and the lack of any other comic-strip work in 1963 and 1964 led Greg Hall to secure for him a few side projects with other companies producing art sets similar to painting-by-numbers, such as touch-tapestry and plush-craft – which involved creating a picture by hooking pre-cut, colour-coded pieces of wool into slots using a special tool. But if this period was a bit of a comic-strip nadir for Ron, things were about to change significantly.

By 1965, Gerry Anderson's SF-themed TV puppet shows such as *Supercar* and *Fireball XL5* were becoming increasingly popular and generating a slew of tie-in merchandise, including a weekly comic, *TV Century 21*, produced by Century 21 Publications and printed and distributed by City Magazines. Keen to get in on the act, Craft Master gained a licence to produce a *Stingray* painting-by-numbers kit. Unfortunately, Ron was overlooked to provide the art for this, despite his SF credentials, but it whetted his appetite for any Anderson-related comic-strip work that might be in the offing: he was a great fan of the Anderson shows, not so much for their stories or their characters as for the design and presentation of the incredibly effective action sequences that dominated each episode.

Hall approached *TV Century 21*'s editor-in-chief Alan Fennell with examples of Ron's previous SF work, and Fennell agreed to give him a try-out on a seven-page black-and-white *Stingray* strip for a *TV Century 21 International Extra*, to be published in October 1965. Impressed with the outcome, Fennell then offered Ron another fill-in strip for a *Stingray Special*, to be published a little earlier, in May, this time requiring two pages in black-and-white and two in colour. Ron was particularly delighted by the latter aspect, as it gave him the chance to create his first ever fully-painted strip. The results were superb, and Ron hoped to be asked to supply more of the same. However, his days as a fill-in artist were coming to an end, for his abilities had not gone unnoticed by *TV Century 21* art editor Dennis Hooper, who would soon be making him an offer he couldn't refuse.

Above: two of Turner's seven black-and-white pages for the *Stingray* strip he was asked to illustrate for the *TV Century 21 International Extra*, published in October 1965. Below: both of Turner's fully-painted colour pages for the *Stingray* strip he was commissioned to supply for the *Stingray Special* issued in May 1965.

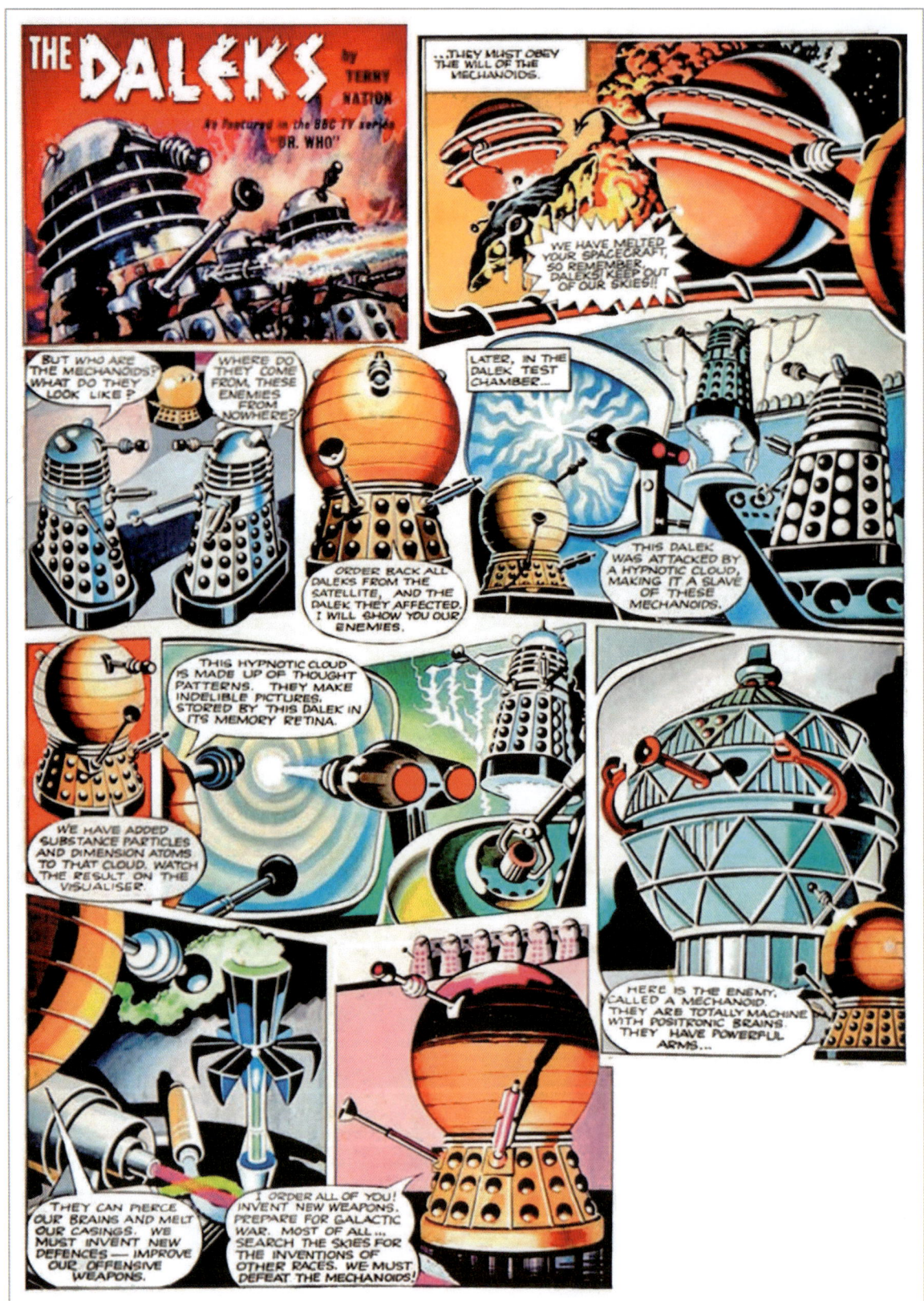

Turner's original art board for his second instalment of *The Daleks*, published in *TV Century 21* Issue 51.

9: A YEAR ON SKARO

From its inception, *TV Century 21* was intended first and foremost as a tie-in to Gerry Anderson's 'Supermarionation' TV shows. However, editor Alan Fennell, appreciating the huge popularity of the BBC's *Doctor Who*, now entering its second year on air, came up with the unusual idea of including, as an added attraction in the large-format comic, an ongoing strip built entirely around the good Doctor's arch-enemies, the Daleks.

Ex-*Eagle* artist Richard Jennings was engaged to provide the fully-painted colour artwork, and *The Daleks* ran on the comic's back page from the very first issue, published in January 1965. After almost a year, however, Jennings' contract ended, and he decided to move on. This left the current storyline with two instalments still to run, and art editor Dennis Hooper, impressed with Ron's colour work on the *Stingray Special* strip earlier in the year, had no hesitation in offering him the task of completing the job until a permanent replacement for Jennings could be found. As far as Ron was concerned, *The Daleks* was an even better proposition than *Stingray*, because it was pure SF, and he happily accepted and completed the work.

Ron then returned to his Craft Master assignments, little realising that those two initial pages for *The Daleks* would be pivotal to another change in his career. For, when Hooper saw the first page – concluding with an impressive interpretation of the Daleks' saucer being destroyed by their robotic adversaries the Mechanoids, its twisted shell dripping molten metal into space – he came to realise Ron's true potential and knew that, in him, he had found the ideal artist for the series.

Ron was consequently invited to succeed Jennings on an ongoing basis. However, this gave him a dilemma. Craft Master were already keeping him very busy, and he couldn't possibly work for both companies full time. But how could he refuse such an offer? Here was an SF strip, in full colour, based on a TV show he thoroughly enjoyed, and with rates comparable to those he was already receiving for his painting-by-numbers pieces. He needed time to consider. In any event, he wouldn't

Above: Turner's first page for *The Daleks*, published in Issue 50 of *TV Century 21*, dated 1 January 1966.

be able to take over immediately, due to his Craft Master obligations. While he deliberated, another ex-*Eagle* artist, Eric Eden, was engaged to illustrate the next seven-part storyline. Long before that seven weeks was up, however, Ron, had made his decision. His reservations about returning to the comic-publishing world, with its relentless deadlines, were outweighed by the excitement he felt at the prospect of taking on a major SF series, tailor-made for his creativity, after several years in the wilderness. So, he chose to accept Hooper's offer and wind up his regular Craft Master work.

With Eden still finishing off his stint on *The Daleks*, Hooper kept Ron busy by giving him a six-page black-and-white strip to illustrate for a *Thunderbirds Extra* special, to be published in March 1966. Then, early that year, seven weeks

Above: the openinig page of the untitled Turner-illustrated *Thunderbirds* story included in *TV Century 21*'s *Thunderbirds Extra* special, published at the end of March 1966.

be interpreted by Ron in his own distinctive style. The result was a tour de force of his fertile imagination. With dramatic layouts and a clever use of colour, his ingeniously-designed machines, spacecraft and monsters were set against fantastic backdrops to totally stunning effect.

Some of Ron's most spectacular pages for the series saw him establishing some large and imposing element, such as a buildiing, a machine or a spacecraft, in the centre of the page, then placing other, less dramatic frames around it. An excellent example of this can be found in Ron's very first page as the strip's regular artist. For this he was required to illustrate a Dalek observatory, and rather than show two scenes – the first exterior and the second interior – he combined them into one by making the domed wall of the base transparent, an effect that was not only striking but also added an almost surreal twist to the presentation.

Ron's influences were clearly apparent in his design of the Mechanoids' robot spy, 2K, which he

Below: from *TV Century 21* Issue 59, Turner's first page as regular artist on *The Daleks*.

after he had produced those first two pages, Ron began his regular assignment on *The Daleks*.

With Ron now responsible for the artwork, the series soon became imbued with a new vitality. The rigid grid layouts that had previously confined it gave way to a more open style. Panels merged and borders were eliminated, the subjects forming their own frames or sometimes breaking out of them altogether, as spacecraft fairly blasted off the page toward the reader! But although Ron was no novice in the colour department, he soon found that producing work of this nature was far more demanding than painting a single scene for a book cover; now, to be aesthetically pleasing to the reader, the colours and tones had to balance not only within a given frame, but across the page as a whole. However, the challenges of the work were compensated for by the subject matter, for as the stories were centred on the alien planet Skaro, then apart from the Daleks themselves, everything could made a deliberate homage to the robot Maria from the classic film *Metropolis* – a firm favourite of his from the days of his youth.

As demanding as his work on *The Daleks* was, Ron also found time to take on some additional *TV Century 21* commissions. The comic was presented as if it were a future newspaper – it was dated 2066 instead of 1966, with the strips serving as its news reports – so amongst its other features was a 'news in brief' section. This required accompanying 'photographs' of futuristic machines and installations, such as a spaceport or a lunar base, and Ron provided several of these in the form of heavily-toned black-and-white illustrations. He even agreed to take on additional comic-strip stories for *Thunderbirds*, *Stingray* and *Fireball XL5* annuals and specials that appeared during the course of 1966. The majority of these were black-and-white commissions, to which an in-house artist was then given the task of adding colour – but unfortunately said artist approached the work with all the subtlety, care and attention of a six-year old with a spray gun, completely ruining Ron's meticulous layouts. Ron was dismayed at the results, but had no say in the matter; he had been commissioned, had produced the work as required, and had been paid accordingly.

A far more rewarding commission came from J Rosenthal Ltd, one of the toy companies licensed to manufacture products based on the Anderson series. This was for a set of four *Thunderbirds* '3D' painting-by-numbers kits – a type of work with which Ron was of course very familiar. Around the same time, Craft Master made further use of their own Anderson licence to produce a rival set of six *Thunderbirds* painting-by-numbers kits, each containing two pictures; and Greg Hall made sure that, unlike on the previous year's *Stingray* kit, Ron was asked to provide the artwork for these too.

Although Ron's enthusiasm was running at a

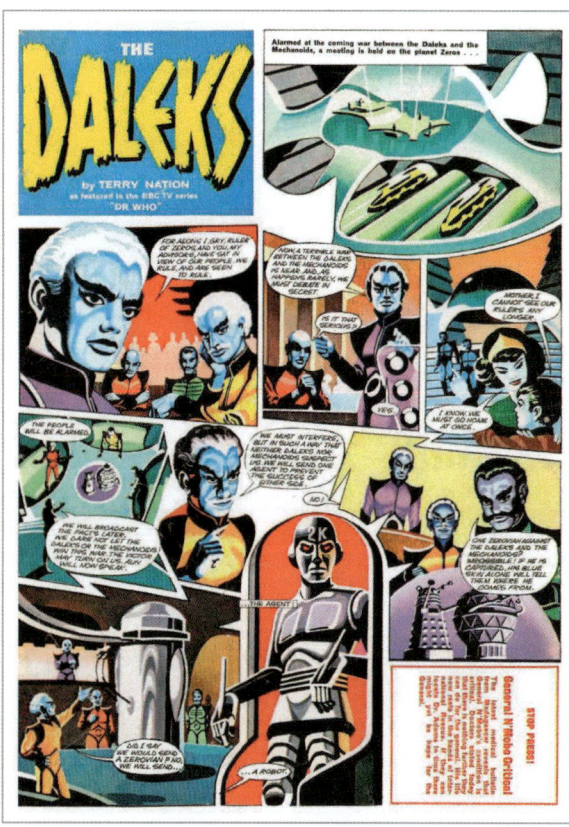

Top right: robot 2K debuts in *TV Century 21* Issue 63.

Bottom right: the title page of 'The Collector', a strip Turner illustrated in black-and-white for the 1966-published *Stingray Annual*, with colours added – poorly – by another artist.

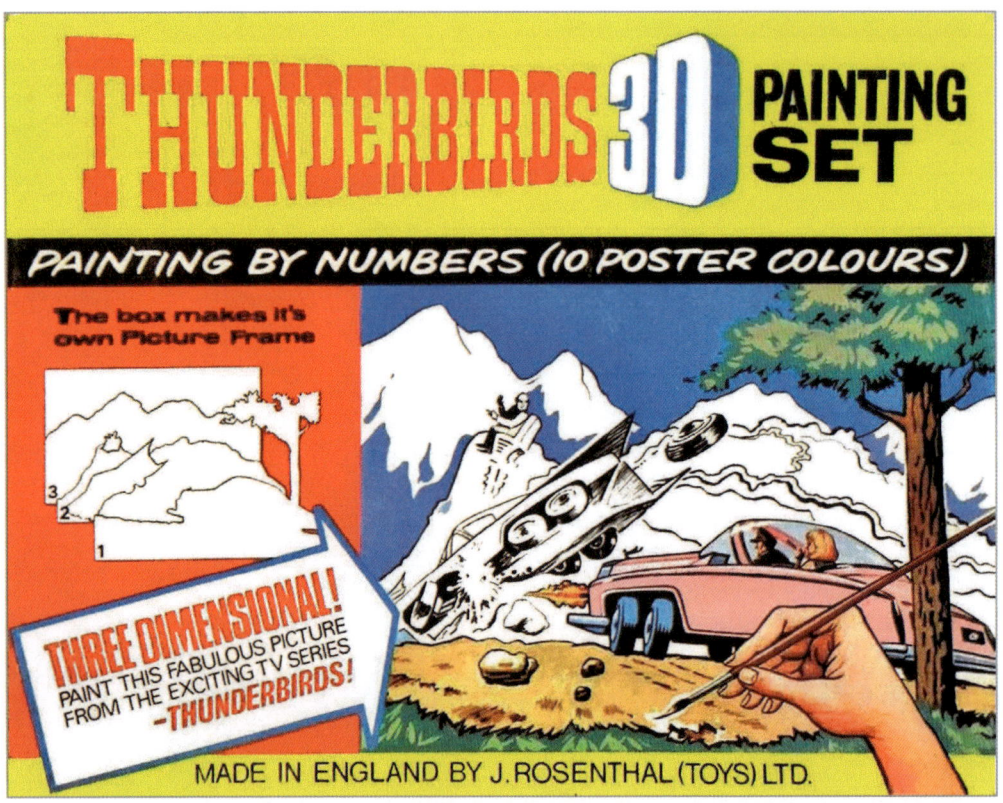

The box-front and back of a J Rosenthal Ltd *Thunderbirds* painting-by-numbers kit, showing Turner's four designs for the set.

high at this point, all of this extra work meant that he had to burn the midnight oil, and there were times when he would only just meet the deadline for completing the latest instalment of The Daleks. On one occasion, his efforts almost went to waste. Having gone out to his car to deliver the artwork to the publishers, he realised he had left his keys behind. Placing the artwork on top of the car, he dashed indoors to get them, then hurried back out again and drove off. He hadn't gone very far before he was pulled over by a police car. The recipient of several speeding tickets in the past, he thought this was another complication he didn't need, but in fact he did: a police sergeant had seen the artwork fly off the roof of his car as he had set off, and had caught up with him to return it! Fortunately, it showed no sign of any tyre-tracks, which would not have endeared him to his editors.

His work on The Daleks so delighted Ron that he looked upon each week's script as a challenge, always seeking new and inventive ways to present elements to their best advantage, so that even a potentially dull episode would pack a great visual punch. He even gave the Daleks themselves a makeover, so that some of them now had a more practical claw arm in place of the usual 'sink plunger' appendage and a more stylised variation on the 'egg whisk' armament. The Daleks' hoverbouts – the airborne disks on which they travelled in the strip – underwent an even greater revamp. As previously depicted, the platform stood nearly two feet from the ground, and Ron rationalised there was no way a Dalek should be able to board it. Again, therefore, he conceived a more practical version that allowed access from ground level, incorporating elements of the Dalek's own design so as to produce a customised carrier. There was still no indication of any propulsion system, but by showing the motive force blasting from beneath, Ron emphasised the Daleks' power, both figuratively and literally, in a more direct and dynamic fashion than before. If Ron hoped this design would be adopted by later artists, or even by TV producers, he would be disappointed; but he was pleased as far as his own work was concerned.

Ron felt this kind of indulgence was justified, as there was so much he wanted to do with the strip and, being averse to repetition, he found it very difficult to resist his creative urges if he could see a better way of presenting something – particularly if it was to greater dramatic effect. Devoting all this extra thought and creative energy to his work came at a price – it was very time-consuming, a factor his editors might not have appreciated – but such was his dedication to the strip that he wasn't prepared to let a page go until he was entirely satisfied with it. The only drawback was that, in his eagerness to present the action in new and exciting ways, Ron sometimes overlooked minor points of continuity. The number of hemispheres on a Dalek's skirt section would change from week to week, for instance, and the Dalek Emperor's appearance also evolved as time went by, the bands across its huge dome section varying in number from three to four and finally disappearing altogether to be replaced by a blank screen-like feature as Ron, either consciously or unconsciously, remodelled the design. To the casual reader, though, these lapses would probably have gone unnoticed; and if Ron's editors spotted them, they were doubtless willing to let them go, given the overall standard of his work.

But then, around a month before Christmas 1966, there came a bombshell: the strip was to end in Issue 104, after a two-year-long run. The publishers had to pay the Daleks' creator, writer Terry Nation, a hefty fee for the rights to use them, and had decided this was an expense they could do without – particularly as they had a growing number of Anderson properties to promote and wanted to introduce a new strip, Zero X, based on a character from the about-to-be-released Thunderbirds Are Go! movie. The news of The Daleks' cancellation came as a great shock to Ron, who felt that there was still plenty of mileage left in it. However, the storyline was at least brought to a logical conclusion, with the Dalek Emperor threatening to conquer Earth, serving as a lead-in to the events of the 1964/65 TV story 'The Dalek Invasion of Earth'.

Ron's disappointment at the loss of The Daleks was tempered by the intriguing thought that he might be given another regular TV Century 21 assignment, even if he doubted it would be one of equal appeal. However, this wasn't to be. As superb as his artwork was, Hooper couldn't afford to offer

Above: Turner's original art board for the final instalment of *The Daleks*, for Issue 104 of *TV Century 21*. Added prior to publication were a standard title logo strip at the top, and in the bottom right-hand corner one of the comic's usual 'Stop Press' panels – this time announcing that there would be a free gift accompanying the next week's issue.

him another regular strip, given his continuous improvisations, which always carried the risk of creating an unnecessary problem or causing a delay. Inwardly, Ron was pleased to be free of the weekly deadlines, but in practical terms he still needed to find alternative work. Fortunately, Hooper was at least able to offer him a one-off commission: to illustrate, for a forthcoming *TV Century 21 Spring Extra* devoted to *Thunderbirds*, a strip comprising four black-and-white pages and a full-colour centrespread. This centrespread would be the largest full-colour strip page Ron had ever produced, and he approached it in the same way as he had his most impressive instalments of *The Daleks*, choosing to highlight key elements and build the less dramatic frames around them. Consequently, young *Thunderbirds* fans, having turned the page from a relatively dull monotone layout, were suddenly greeted by some spectacular images of Thunderbird 1 streaking into the sky and the Mole burrowing out toward them, all in full colour! Ron certainly knew how to present a stunning piece artwork. Sadly, however, his indulgence had the perhaps inevitable downside of causing him to miss the deadline for the piece.

This was not an issue that Hooper could raise with Ron in person; in fact, he had never even met him, as Greg Hall insisted that all publisher-to-artist communication be channelled via his agency. Quite apart from considerations of professional propriety, Hall realised that if Hooper were to put any editorial criticisms direct to Ron, when Ron was giving his all to produce the best work he could, this would more than likely result in an argument and the loss of any further commissions. In the end, Ron was granted an extension to complete the *Thunderbirds* strip. However, as time went by and the artwork still failed to appear, Hooper became increasingly concerned. Unaware of Ron's history of falling out with editors, leaving Hall to play piggy-in-the-middle in an attempt to keep both sides happy, he was puzzled by the agent's refusal to allow any direct contact with the artist, and even began to wonder if Ron actually existed, or was just a cover

Below: Ron Turner's superb full-colour centrespread for the *TV Century 21 Spring Extra* devoted to *Thunderbirds*, published in March 1967.

for Hall to produce the work himself!

Fortunately, the strip was finally delivered to Ron's satisfaction and his editor's relief. However, the relationship had been soured, and although a steady stream of further commissions would follow over the next three years, these would almost all be for stories in Century 21 annuals rather than in *TV Century 21* itself, and almost all in black-and-white – with colour overlays sometimes added in-house – rather than in full colour.

There was to be no return to regular Craft Master work either – although, as Ron had by this point established himself as their go-to artist for Anderson-related subjects, they did invite him to supply six pieces for another set of licensed painting-by-numbers kits, this time based on *Captain Scarlet*. As welcome as this was, Ron still needed another regular comic-strip assignment if he was to maintain a good, steady income; so Greg Hall, realising that his old client Fleetway might now offer his only hope of securing such work, began checking out the company's current output, hoping to find a suitable vehicle for the artist's talents.

It had been over five years since Hall had last dealt with Fleetway on a regular basis, and Ron's decision to abandon *Scoop Donovan* hadn't exactly endeared him to them. However, the agent finally found what he was looking for in a strip called *The Robot Builders*, which had been running for the past year in *Tiger and Hurricane* (the two previously separate comics having been merged in 1965). He approached editor Dave Gregory with examples of Ron's pages for *The Daleks*, arguing that his recruitment to *The Robot Builders* could improve it considerably. Gregory, who also knew of Ron's work from his time on the Picture Library ranges, agreed, and decided to take him on from the start of a new story in early 1967.

The strip usually comprised two black-and-white pages each week, but was occasionally extended to three if it was to be featured on the comic's cover, with colour added in an overlay rather than painted. Initially Ron was apprehensive about this new work, recalling how *Scoop Donovan*, his last regular black-and-white strip, had been so text-heavy it had left him little room for decent artistic interpretation. However, he needn't have worried, for *The Robot Builders* was a complete contrast: it had very little wordage, with some frames requiring no lettering at all.

The stories, involving Dave and Damon Arrow and their android pals Steve and Eggy fighting criminal masterminds with the aid of giant purpose-built robots, were wild and unscientific, even surreal at times, but their highly inventive and fast-paced action sequences featured an incredible array of futuristic machines and mechanical creatures. They could have been written with Ron in mind, and he was suitably inspired. Without the time-consuming element of colour to worry about, he soon began to explore the other illustrative possibilities the strip offered him; and his presentation was apparently influenced to a certain degree by the work of a renowned American artist.

The previous year, 1966, had seen a great *Batman* revival, led by the Adam West-starring US TV show of that title. This had prompted publishers DC to reprint many of the Caped Crusader's classic comic-book stories, some of them illustrated by their leading and most respected artist, Dick Sprang. Sprang had a very dynamic style, his trademark

Below: Turner's new regular comic-strip assignment for 1967: *The Robot Builders* in Fleetway's *Tiger and Hurricane* comic.

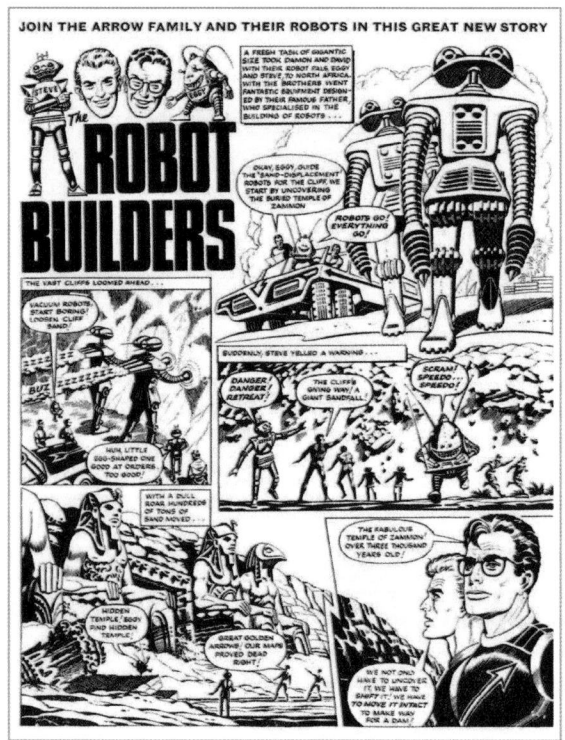

Above: the Turner-illustrated *The Robot Builders* strip is promoted to the front cover of the 25 March 1967 issue of Fleetway's *Tiger and Hurricane*.

effects including speeding cars trailing dust-clouds in their wake, small figures dwarfed by mighty structures, and scenes shown from unusual angles; and while Ron would never openly admit to having taken any cues from an American artist of the superhero genre, which he detested, elements of that style do seem to have crept into his own work at this time – even down to speeding cars trailing dust-clouds. Could he have been unconsciously influenced by *Batman* comics brought home by his sons? Whatever the case, while the influence may have been Sprang's, the treatment was distinctively Ron's, and he made *The Robot Builders* very much his own, packing it with so many incredible ideas that no reader could have been left in any doubt that an exceptional new artist had taken over.

It wasn't just Ron's imaginative ideas that made this strip so impressive but also the amazing amount of detail he was able to give it. He had now developed a new shading technique to represent in black-and-white all the different colours he would have used had he still been working in that medium. This was again a very time-consuming process, and may well have led to more deadline problems; but he never wanted to submit an instalment until he was fully satisfied with it. The nature of the strip meant that story elements and settings were constantly changing, and Ron would consider each frame individually to decide on the most effective viewpoint from which to present the action, whether it be bird's eye, worm's eye or some other striking perspective. All were drawn with spot-on accuracy. The strip also gave Ron the chance to utilise his design skills to the full in realising all the various types of machines involved, often showing the robotic creations with small figures positioned beside them, emphasising their proportions.

The Robot Builders had been a great assignment for Ron, but Fleetway were always looking to keep their comics fresh, and in October 1967 they gave *Tiger and Hurricane* a full makeover. *The Robot Builders* had been a year old already when Ron had taken on the artwork duties, and sadly it was one of the strips now selected for cancellation. Ron's time on it had lasted only about six months, and it must today count as both his least known and his most underrated work; for while his instalments of *The Daleks* have been reprinted more than once over the years, his equally fine contributions to *The Robot Builders* have yet to be republished and are now largely forgotten.

The only SF strip that *Tiger and Hurricane* still ran after the revamp was *Jet-Ace Logan*, but that had been drawn for many years by the gifted John Gillat, and for editor Dave Gregory to have ousted him in favour of Ron would have been unthinkable. Thus it was that Ron found himself out in the cold once more, and feeling distinctly undervalued after all his efforts. On the other hand, he had by this point really had enough of the deadline treadmill. His four years of regular Craft Master work, on which he had enjoyed the relative luxury of plenty of time to complete each piece, had left him even less willing than before to tolerate the demands of weekly strips. This attitude, however, greatly limited his future work prospects, and Greg Hall now faced an uphill struggle in trying to find another outlet for the talents of his creative and conscientious, yet sometimes over-indulgent, artist.

THE FANTASTIC ART OF RON TURNER

Turner's *The Robot Builders* strips for the *Tiger and Hurricane* issues of 3 June 1967 (top) and 8 July 1967 (bottom).

10: HIGHS AND LOWS

By the summer of 1967, such was Ron's association with all things Anderson that it even earned him a special invitation to take a tour of the Century 21 Studios in Slough, where the feature film *Thunderbirds 6* was currently before the cameras. He had a keen interest in the nuts and bolts of the production and was fascinated to see how much time, energy and technical wizardry went into the shooting of a short sequence of Thunderbird 2 swooping down over an island. Although his visit had been planned to last only a few hours, he spent so long talking to the technicians involved that he ended up staying the whole day!

Sadly, this high point for Ron was quickly followed by the low one of Fleetway's cancellation of *The Robot Builders*, which left him for the first time in years without any regular work in hand. He had lost his spot as a *TV Century 21* artist back in the spring, and although the publishers were still appreciative of his abilities and willing to offer him other assignments – indeed, he had already completed a number of strips for that year's *Thunderbirds*, *Captain Scarlet* and *TV Century 21* annuals – it would not be until the early months of 1968 that they would be looking to commission material for their next batch of tie-in hardbacks. Consequently, the only jobs they had on offer for the time being were on junior activity books of the painting, puzzle and dot-to-dot variety, all planned for publication in the new year and featuring the title character of the forthcoming Anderson show *Joe 90*. Realising that he had no other option, Ron agreed to take these on; and, in his usual way, he looked upon the work as a challenge to his ingenuity.

For the *Joe 90 Puzzle Book*, Ron had to fill eighty pages with puzzles, and although he was supplied with a general idea for each of them, much of the presentation was left up to him. A more enjoyable project was the *Joe 90 Dot-to-Dot Book*, which involved illustrating a single eighty-page adventure – although Ron would have liked it even better had it been a standard annual story and not required him to put in all those dots! The work was tedious in that regard, and also unsatisfying, as it naturally resulted in fragmented pictures, far less impressive than he would normally have been able to achieve – although he did at least manage to include full illustrations of certain pieces of hardware, confining the dots to less inspiring aspects such as buildings and figures. Another drawback of the dot-to-dot format was that, contrary to expectations, each picture took him longer to complete than a comparable piece of standard black-and-white artwork. First he had to produce a simple pencil drawing of a suitable subject; then he had to consider which of the lines in that drawing were to be represented by dots; next he had to ink a dot and a number at either end of each of those lines; and finally he had to erase the lines to which he had added the dots and numbers and ink all the remaining ones in full. But Ron enjoyed challenging work; it kept him busy,

Below: the title page of the Turner-illustrated *Joe 90 Dot-to-Dot Book*, published in the spring of 1968.

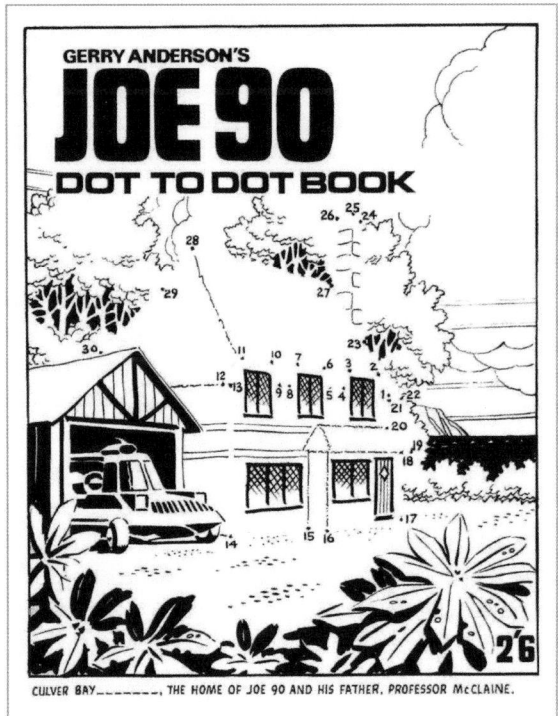

and he was thankful for the fact that the deadlines for these activity books were flexible.

One other title of the same type that Ron took on at the end of 1967 was the *Joe 90 Sticker Fun Book*. This contained an eight-page black-and-white strip story plus two sheets of full-colour gummed stickers. Each sticker showed a section of one of the pictures, so that it could be placed over that section and add colour to it. However, the stickers did not cover the whole scene, so the young reader was effectively encouraged to colour in the rest by hand.

These *Joe 90* commissions were soon followed by a similar assignment on an eighty-page dot-to-dot book based on the new ITV spy show *The Champions*, which although it had no Anderson connection was being lined up by the publishers to feature in an ongoing strip in a *Joe 90: Top Secret* comic planned for launch at the start of 1969. Again, the dot-to-dot format's inherent limitations marred an otherwise exciting piece of work, but it was at least another addition to Ron's order book, helping to bridge an awkward hiatus in his career.

All these activity book tasks took Ron in total about six months to complete, seeing him through to the spring of 1968. Then, true to their word, Century 21 Publications began commissioning him for contributions to their latest batch of annuals. Finally Ron was able to return to more substantial work, as he was once again called upon to illustrate selected strip stories for the latest *Thunderbirds*, *Captain Scarlet* and *TV21* volumes (the '*Century*' having now been dropped from the title of the latter), and this year also the entire strip content for the first *Joe 90* one. In all, this required him to produce more than fifty full-size strip pages.

The main craft and other machinery featured in these strips were generally of predetermined appearance, in that they had to match their on-screen counterparts, but for once Ron was quite happy about this, as he felt the majority were already extremely well-designed – and there was still some scope for him to exercise his creativity, as most of the scripts also introduced new items of hardware not seen in the TV shows, and on these he had free reign, provided he remained faithful to the overall Anderson style.

By now, Ron was fully immersed in that style and thoroughly enjoying his freedom from dreaded weekly deadlines. However, these annual projects would occupy him for only around four months, so he still needed other work if he was to maintain a decent income. If he had hoped that another Craft Master assignment might be in the offing in 1968, perhaps on a set of *Joe 90* painting-by-numbers kits, then he was to be disappointed, as the public demand for such kits had fallen and the company was now on the brink of liquidation. With no other offers in prospect, the outlook looked grim.

That an artist of his calibre should find himself in such dire straights made Ron question the continued viability of his career and wonder what the future held for him. One possibility he considered was to move away from book and magazine illustration altogether and try to gain a toehold in the highly lucrative field of advertising. To this end, Greg Hall approached several agencies with examples of his work. One of them, representing Cadbury's, seemed interested at first, but when Ron mocked up some specimens of how he might present the chocolatiers' classic 'glass and a half of milk in every bar' slogan, these failed to impress. His approach was just too 'lively' for the agency's liking, one particularly crass criticism being: 'Far too many bubbles in the milk'! Ron realised that the demands of this type of work were not quite what he had expected; and as Hall was also less at home dealing with the young whizzkids of the advertising world than he was with the old warhorses of the publishing business, the idea was soon abandoned.

Still no new commissions were forthcoming for Ron. In anticipation of further activity books being produced for publication in 1969, he began work on another series of *Joe 90* dot-to-dot illustrations; but these were brought to an abrupt halt when he learned that the publishers had cancelled the range, feeling that it had lost its appeal. The 31 pages of artwork he had already completed would eventually see print ten years later when, having been inherited by parent company IPC (International Printing Company), they were reworked as a *Whoopee! Annual* filler story under the title 'The Missile Menace'; but back in 1968, this just seemed to Ron like wasted effort.

In the end, it was not until the spring of 1969, when the next round of Century 21 annual

Above: the complete Turner-illustrated strip story 'Day Return from Death', as featured in the 1968-published *Thunderbirds Annual*.

commissions got under way, that Ron at last returned to gainful employment. This year he took on strips for the *TV21 Annual*, a joint *Captain Scarlet/Thunderbirds Annual* and not only a *Joe 90 Annual* but, tying in with the new comic, a *Joe 90: Top Secret Annual*, the latter of which also gave him the chance to tackle stories for *The Champions*, *Star Trek* and *Land of the Giants*, three other TV shows featured in the comic. Altogether this came to more than sixty pages of artwork, enough to keep him busy for a good five months, and his spirits were lifted. However, there was still no other work on the horizon, and he worried he would soon end up back in the same position he'd been in twelve months earlier.

Fortunately, Greg Hall did manage to find him a job illustrating another Air-Ace Picture Library story, *Fighter Ace*. The focus of this range inevitably meant that it involved an endless succession of aerial combat scenes, but while other artists might have fallen into repetition, Ron found the subject matter stimulating and came up with some varied and unusual angles from which to present the action, so that the artwork fully complemented the exciting and well-written script. Ron would have been quite content to continue working on these 64-page titles, with their more mature content and manageable deadlines, each keeping him busy for a couple of months, but they paid only a fraction of what he had once earned on weekly comics, so Hall was always on the lookout for other possibilities. In any event, the publisher's ever-increasing reliance on reprinted material meant that further Picture Library opportunities were likely to be scarce; and, indeed, another five years would pass before Ron would again contribute to any of these ranges.

It was while contemplating his future prospects that Ron turned to an option he had not pursued before: a newspaper strip. Four frames a day was a requirement he could quite comfortably handle, and newspapers paid far better even than weekly comics. Mindful of public interest in the recent Apollo 11 Moon landing, he decided to produce a sample SF strip based around an Interplanetary Rescue team. The stories would involve the team dealing with all manner of emergencies in outer space, using various types of futuristic equipment and machines that Ron could happily devise. The idea seemed promising, so Hall proceeded to hawk it around Fleet Street. However, the basic premise was obviously inspired by *Thunderbirds*' International Rescue set-up, and even though Ron had given it a fully outer-space setting, editors found the similarity too great. So, again, his efforts were to no avail.

But then, just when Ron felt that things could only get worse, there came light at the end of the tunnel. In the autumn of 1969, both Fleetway and Ron's old firm Odhams were fully absorbed into parent company IPC, resulting in sweeping changes across the board. Not only did some comics fold and others take their place, but managers and editors were also replaced; and Hall quickly realised this was a situation that could work in Ron's favour, giving him the chance for a fresh start.

Below: a sample produced by Turner for a prospective SF-themed daily newspaper strip.

11: KIDS' STUFF

One of the first comics to be launched under the new IPC banner was *Whizzer and Chips*. Edited by young newcomer Bob Paynter, it majored on 'funnies', but Greg Hall managed to snare for Ron the illustration duties on the one adventure strip it would contain: *The Space Accident*. Despite Ron's reluctance to return to regular weekly strip work, Hall knew that in the present circumstances it was an assignment he couldn't afford to refuse. This strip also had the advantage that the publishers would be giving Ron's black-and-white artwork a mono-colour overlay, so there would be no need for him to do any extensive shading himself – something that Hall felt would help him to keep to the weekly deadlines and thereby create a good impression with the editor.

In the event, the strip proved a great disappointment for Ron as, despite its promising title, *The Space Accident* had little SF content and was really nothing more than a childish fantasy. The plot involved two boys discovering a crashed spaceship and, after absorbing a strange substance from it, finding they have acquired the power to cause living creatures to grow to an enormous size. With a weekly diet of scripts involving giant cats, dogs, mice and spiders, Ron had little to inspire him, and he gave the material only the most basic treatment. Having to contend with nonsense such as this only served to heighten his disappointment at the rejection of his *Thunderbirds*-inspired Interplanetary Rescue newspaper proposal, and he began to wonder if this was something that might perhaps be adapted for *Whizzer and Chips* as a replacement for the tedious strip he was currently saddled with.

Hall duly put Ron's idea to Bob Paynter; but as the comic had a target readership of 8- to 12-year-olds and required its strips to feature juvenile leads, which would be implausible in the context of an outer-space rescue team, it was quickly ruled out. Nevertheless, perhaps realising that the artist's talents could be far better used than they had been so far, Paynter did offer him an alternative: a new strip with strong similarities to *Supercar*, coincidentally one of the Anderson series he had never drawn. The strip in question was *Wonder-Car*, involving a multifunctional vehicle that could travel on land, in the air and on or under the sea. Unlike Supercar, however, Wonder-Car could also walk on stilt-like legs and drill through solid rock! And amazingly, following the principle of having juvenile leads, but in this case seemingly turning a blind eye to plausibility issues, it was operated by three youngsters!

And so, as the 1960s gave way to the 1970s, Ron began work on *Wonder-Car*, taking the initial brief he was given for the titular vehicle and developing it with his usual ingenuity; reasoning, for instance, that it would look better and operate more effectively if it had three small drill heads instead of a single large one as originally indicated. All of his suggestions were accepted, resulting in a superb design.

Below: one of Turner's artwork pages for *Wonder-Car*.

To start with, Ron gave *Wonder-Car* the same basic treatment as he had *The Space Accident*. This was at the insistence of Hall, who was concerned that if he put too much effort into it he might struggle to meet the weekly deadlines. But, as time went by and the strip came to feature exciting action scenes involving pirate submarines, giant octopuses, dinosaurs, robots and – finally – even an adventure in outer space, Ron's enthusiasm for the subject matter inevitably led to him giving it more attention and an improved presentation. The youngsters' uncle being an inventor, the stories offered plenty of chances for Ron to design futuristic machines, and their various worldwide settings allowed for him to give them some diverse and exotic backdrops. So, although the scripts were by their nature very juvenile and never had the depth of the better ones he had worked on in the '50s and '60s, Ron was quite happy with this assignment; and the fact that, as on *The Space Accident*, the publishers generally gave his artwork a colour overlay meant that it wasn't as labour intensive as some of his previous strips, leaving him with the capacity to take on other projects – if any were forthcoming.

Ron might have expected that 1970 would bring the usual crop of Anderson annual commissions, but sadly these failed to materialise. The latest 'Supermarionation' show, *The Secret Service*, had met with little success, and all of the others were now off the air, so the market for tie-in merchandise had dwindled. Moreover, Century 21 Publications had been wound up in the summer of 1969, and although new *TV21* publishers Martspress would still issue an annual for 1971, the Anderson content was being dropped and Ron was not approached to contribute. This left Hall once again on the lookout for alternative possibilities, and he thought he had found one in the recently-launched *Scorcher*, IPC's first single-theme weekly comic – the theme in question being football. Unfortunately, Ron didn't share the passion that the comic's young editor David Hunt had for this subject – in fact, he disliked sport in general – so he was unwilling to take on a regular strip. Over the next three years, though, he would agree to illustrate for *Scorcher*'s holiday specials and annuals a few one-off stories in the comic's popular *Billy's Boots* series.

Right: the title pages of two of the one-off *Billy's Boots* strips that Turner illustrated for *Scorcher* holiday specials and annuals.

The premise here was that a pair of magic boots gave the 10-year-old title character the ability to play like a pro, so this was another juvenile fantasy rather than a straight football strip, and as such was at least a little more in tune with Ron's sensibilities.

Otherwise, Ron continued to busy himself with further *Wonder-Car* stories. *Whizzer and Chips* also spawned regular holiday specials and annuals, and Ron was asked to contribute to these too, sometimes on subjects other than *Wonder-Car*. Notably, for the *Whizzer and Chips Annual 1971*, published for Christmas 1970, he illustrated an eight-page non-series SF story called 'It Came on Firework Night', the first fully-painted colour strip he had been given since the end of his *TV Century 21* stint. This was the type of work he most enjoyed – and he was soon to get the chance for more of it, if only on a temporary basis.

The revamped *TV21* had for some time been running a weekly three-page *Star Trek* strip, illustrated in full colour by one of Ron's contemporaries on the original comic, Mike Noble. Now, though, Noble had decided to move on to work under his old *TV21* editor Alan Fennell on the about-to-be launched children's ITV comic *Look-In*, leaving the *Star Trek* strip without an artist. Consequently Ron was invited to fill in until a permanent successor could be found.

Having fallen out with the *TV21* editors four years previously, Ron was surprised to be asked back; but this may have been another case where he was helped by the change of personnel in the interim. His run on the *Star Trek* strip was to be for four issues published in October and November 1970, but he was keen for it to become a more permanent engagement. Back in the days when he had been illustrating *The Daleks*, he had had lots of other work on the go, whereas now he had only the weekly two-page black-and-white strip *Wonder-Car*, so he was confident that if he were to take on *Star Trek* on a regular basis he would not fall foul of the same deadline problems as before. Greg Hall, on the other hand, felt that the nature of *Star Trek* was such that Ron was bound to start obsessing over the detail of all the futuristic spaceship and hardware designs he would have to produce. Remembering the ructions suffered previously with the *TV21* editors, he was anxious to avoid any repeat. Moreover, the future of the revamped *TV21* was uncertain, and he was loath to risk Ron becoming so busy on *Star Trek* that he had to abandon his *Whizzer and Chips* work, thereby antagonising IPC just when good relations had been established. As far as he was concerned, if Ron was to take on any additional strip work, then it would have to be on an IPC title.

Consoling himself with the thought that he was now quite settled on the undemanding *Wonder-Car*, Ron reluctantly agreed that his *Star Trek* assignment would have to remain no more than a four-week fill-in. Consequently he produced in total only twelve pages of artwork for the strip; and although these were again fully-painted, by keeping the colours flat and basic and mostly avoiding the temptation to use the more delicate tones and airbrush effects he had employed on *The Daleks*, he managed to make the whole process a lot easier than it might have been, so that this time he was able to keep to *TV21*'s strict deadlines.

Below: Turner's fully-painted colour title page for the 'It Came on Firework Night' story in the *Whizzer and Chips Annual 1971*.

Turner's fully-painted title page for the cover-featured *Star Trek* strip in the 14 November 1970 issue of *TV21*.

The cover of the 21 November 1970 issue of *TV21*, the last to feature Turner's artwork for the *Star Trek* strip.

A piece of full-colour *Wonder-Car* artwork that Turner painted in 1971 for the *Whizzer and Chips Annual 1972*.

KIDS' STUFF

Although he had doubted that Ron could continue to fulfil his *Wonder-Car* commitments while also meeting a regular weekly demand for three pages of full-colour *Star Trek* artwork, Hall had no qualms about him taking on a certain amount of additional black-and-white strip work. Looking for something to fit the bill, he found it in *Robby Hood and His One Man Band*, a new strip for *Cor!!*, the second Bob Paynter-edited IPC title, launched in June 1970. To be presented with another juvenile fantasy, having only just given up on the enticing idea of continuing on *Star Trek*, was a big let-down for Ron. This Scott Goodall-scripted strip, in which young Robby teams up with the ghost of a medieval man who misunderstands the ways of modern life in true *Catweazle* fashion, was hardly appropriate material for someone of his abilities. Nevertheless, Ron agreed to take it on until something better came along. Unfortunately, for the time being, nothing did, and he had to resign himself to a long run of this and similar work.

In the end, Ron's stint on *Robby Hood and His One Man Band* spanned from November 1970 to April 1971. The next few months of 1971 were then taken up partly with his ongoing *Wonder-Car* work, but partly also with several new commissions he picked up for Christmas-market annuals. For the *Whizzer and Chips Annual 1972* he illustrated not only a seven-page *Wonder-Car* story but also three unrelated two-page strips; for the *Daily Mirror Book for Boys 1972* he produced a five-page colour strip called 'Calamity Rose'; and, in a brief return to Anderson-related work, he supplied two eight-page colour strips for the new *Thunderbirds Annual* published by Polystyle, who had now acquired the show's comic licence.

Once these jobs were out of the way, Ron took on another regular juvenile strip assignment, this time on the long-running comic *Tiger*, which had been launched by his old clients the Amalgamated Press back in 1954 but was now another IPC title.

Top right: the title page of a five-page colour *Tri-Man* strip, a rare series entry by Turner in the superhero genre he so disliked, published in autumn 1970 in the *Smash! Annual 1971*. *Smash!* was a former Odhams comic, acquired by IPC in 1969.

Bottom right: a page of Turner's artwork for the *Robby Hood and His One-Man Band* strip, from the 13 March 1971 issue of *Cor!!*.

The first page of 'Invisible Invader', one of two fully-painted strips Turner worked on for Polystyle's 1971-published *Thunderbirds Annual*.

The strip in question was *The Tigers*, about the scraps and scrapes of three kids from a boys' club, and Ron would illustrate this from October 1971 until its cancellation in October 1974. Meanwhile, after *Wonder-Car* was finally parked at the end of 1971, the following year saw his *Whizzer and Chips* association continue, first on the sequel strip *The Castaways*, which had the same group of youngsters left to fend for themselves after being shipwrecked on a desert island, and then on *Archie's Angels*, about a gang of junior pilots catching crooks, foiling bank-raids and so on, while flying miniature versions of First World War biplanes.

Archie's Angels continued into 1973, ending in June after an eleven-month run, although further stories illustrated by Ron would still appear in *Whizzer and Chips* annuals for a couple more years after that. Other work in 1973 included a five-page black-and-white puzzle strip called 'The Mystery of Grimm Grange' for an issue of the Williams Publishing comic *Quizzer*; and, more substantially, 'Malice in Wonderland', a ten-part strip story about a young boy whose secret agent father is being targeted by a strange mutant enemy called the Octopus, which featured from mid-October to mid-December in another Bob Paynter-edited IPC comic, *Shiver and Shake*.

In 1974, alongside his existing weekly engagement on *The Tigers*, Ron was invited to illustrate one-off strips for a plethora of IPC comic specials and annuals, including the *Whoopee! Summer Special*, the *Whoopee! Annual 1975*, the *Knockout Annual 1975* and the *Shiver and Shake Annual 1975*. Then, from June, he took on another weekly *Whizzer and Chips* series, *Danny Drew's Dialling Man*, concerning the exploits of a young lad with a giant robot that could be transformed into various different machines by turning a dial on its chest. This two-page strip would run until May 1976, and Ron would handle the artwork throughout.

Top left: the title page of 'Calamity Rose', the one-off colour strip story that Turner illustrated in 1971 for the *Daily Mirror Book for Boys 1972*.

Bottom left: one of Turner's artwork pages for *The Tigers*, this example taken from a story he illustrated for a *Tiger Annual*.

Example pages of Turner's IPC comic strip artwork for: 'Malice in Wonderland', a ten-part story that appeared in *Shiver and Shake* in 1973 (top left); an *Archie's Angels* story for the *Whizzer and Chips Annual 1974* (top right); a *Danny Drew's Dialling Man* story for the *Whizzer and Chips Holiday Special* from the summer of 1976 (bottom left); and 'March of the Mighty Ones', an eleven-week serial for *Monster Fun*, this particular page coming from the comic's 28 August 1976 edition (bottom right).

The next few years brought more of the same, as Ron continued to accept a steady stream of holiday special and annual assignments, alongside the occasional more interesting juvenile project. The latter included, in 1976, an eleven-week serial called 'March of the Mighty Ones' for another of the Bob Paynter-edited IPC 'funnies', *Monster Fun*. This story, about mechanical prehistoric creatures being brought to heel by a couple of kids, was more appealing to Ron than most, but it had all been done before – and better – back in 1967 when he had worked on *The Robot Builders*. Toward the end of 1976 he heard that he was to be offered a strip about an alien who crash-lands on Earth and then makes various attempts to return home; but any hopes he might have had of finally getting something more worthy of his talents were dashed when he discovered it was titled *Thingamajig* and was just another childish *Whizzer and Chips* entry. To add insult to injury, it turned out to be only three weeks' work while the regular artist was indisposed.

Affording little or no room for innovation, these 'by the numbers' strips were for the most part tedious, repetitive and a waste of Ron's talents, but by their nature were relatively easy to produce. At one point, Ron was handling three two-page strips per week, and with a family to support, he couldn't complain. Out of all these juvenile assignments, *The Tigers* was his favourite, for it was a *comic* strip in the truest sense of the word, with humorous situations requiring a lighter, less realistic tone and a more exaggerated representation of the human form. This gave Ron the opportunity for a little creative experimentation, and also led to him adopting a more 'cartoony' approach in some of his other assignments, including a few of his own devising such as 'William the Tele Fanatic' and 'Hugo Furst', two of the strips he supplied in 1971 for the *Whizzer and Chips Annual 1972*. Offered simply as filler material, these were rendered in a very loose and brief style, almost unrecognisable as Ron's; but as he sometimes felt aggrieved that his usual

Right: the title pages of Turner's 'cartoony' one-offs 'William the Tele Fanatic' and 'Hugo Furst' for the *Whizzer and Chips Annual 1972*.

highly detailed illustrations commanded only the same page rate as was paid to simple line cartoonists, this was one way in which he could redress the balance – and, in doing so, perhaps make a point! Afterwards, though, he happily returned to his normal way of working.

Mercifully, Ron did get some respite from the seemingly endless stream of 'kids' stuff' when, in 1974, after a five year break, he was asked to resume making regular contributions to the more mature Picture Library ranges, now published as IPC titles. This time, it was mainly the War Picture Library and the Battle Picture Library that would carry his work. These digest-sized books had recently returned to their original length of 64 pages after a period of being pruned back to 56, and initially Ron's task was simply to illustrate a succession of eight-page back-up strips to be run alongside reprints of earlier 56-page entries by other artists. As time went by, though, editor Ted Bensberg, recognising Ron's talents, began using him on a few full-length 64-page originals as well.

While this work often required little imaginative input, Ron was at least able to inject some realism into the stories, drawing on his own wartime experiences to give them authentic hardware and settings. And these Picture Library titles were certainly a welcome contrast to all the juvenile material he was having to handle at the same time. Their less restrictive deadlines meant that he was able to put a lot of thought into their presentation and make them much more detailed, producing a more satisfying end result. The downside was that this type of material allowed for nothing like the same degree of creativity as the SF strips he had worked on earlier in his career. As much as he missed those SF commissions, he had come to accept now that they were a thing of the past, and that he was unlikely ever to return to that genre. However, from his command module at *2000 AD*, the mighty Tharg was about to prove him wrong.

Right: Turner's title pages for the back-up strips 'A Debt Repaid' and 'No Hiding Place', published in War Picture Library Numbers 1018 and 1206 respectively.

Above: the title pages of the Turner-illustrated back-up stories 'Close-Up', 'The Fuehrer', 'Armed Raider' and 'Regan's Revenge', published in, respectively, Battle Picture Library Numbers 875, 893 and 896 in 1975 and War Picture Library Number 1291 in 1976.

Above: a sample strip page produced by Turner in 1977 as an ultimately unsuccessful pitch for the illustration duties on the *2000 AD* series *Harlem Heroes*.

12: BACK TO THE FUTURE

In the mid-1970s, writer Pat Mills brought a tough, gritty realism to two of IPC's leading boys' weeklies, the war-themed *Battle* and the controversial *Action*. The latter was an adventure comic, but completely different from any that had gone before. The product of a turbulent era of industrial strife, football hooliganism and social unrest, it presented a selection of violent and anti-authoritarian strips, triggering a public outcry that in October 1976 led to it being temporarily withdrawn at the height of its popularity. When it resurfaced two months later, it had lost its edge and become little different from any number of other boys' comics of the time, which may have lessened the heat but also resulted in falling sales. However, Mills knew that it had been the comic for a generation, and was keen to come up with another that would have the same uncompromising energy but packaged in a more publicly acceptable form. It was then that subeditor Kelvin Gosnell suggested publishing a science-fiction title. Films such as *Rollerball* and *Logan's Run* had recently created fresh public interest in SF, and the media world was buzzing with reports about the forthcoming big-budget *Star Wars*, so this was a commercially appealing idea. Moreover, Mills realised that, while the hard-hitting stories he wanted to present had been considered objectionable when set in contemporary times in *Action*, they would be less contentious if dressed in the fanciful trappings of SF, particularly if leavened with a degree of dark humour. Thus *2000 AD* was conceived.

Greg Hall, his ear ever to the ground, soon picked up on the rumblings about a new SF comic in preparation; and, as with *Whizzer and Chips*, he was determined to get in on the ground floor and establish Ron as a regular contributor. Ron having been lost in the relative obscurity of the juvenile market for some years, Mills and Gosnell were initially unaware of his aptitude for SF, but Hall soon enlightened them. Even so, many of *2000 AD*'s proposed strips, including a *Dan Dare* revival, had already been allocated to other artists. The only suitable candidate remaining was *Harlem Heroes*, an action-packed futuristic sports strip based around a game called aeroball – a mixture of American football, kickboxing and basketball, but with the players flying around using jet-packs. Also under consideration to illustrate this strip was a young Dave Gibbons, and both he and Ron were asked to submit a sample page based on the debut story's opening frame, showing the hero team's airliner touching down in front of a crowd of waving fans and rival supporters. Never keen on figure-work, Ron chose to depict the action from a high angle, emphasising the sleek lines of the futuristic airliner, with the crowd almost incidental to the scene. Gibbons, by contrast, chose a lower foreground vantage point favouring the enthusiastic fans, with the airliner less prominent in the background; and, as dramatic as Ron's composition was, it was this more character-driven, US-style of presentation that won the commission.

Unmoved by the editors' explanation that Gibbons' style would be more acceptable to the youth of the day, brought up on US Marvel comics, an infuriated Hall continued to advocate for Ron, insisting that he was the best SF artist in the country and that what he didn't know about the genre wasn't worth knowing. His persistence eventually paid off when work *was* found for Ron on a *Judge Dredd* series entry where, for once, the hardware was just as important as the people.

Written by John Wagner, 'Robots' appeared in *2000 AD*'s ninth issue – Prog 9, to use the comic's own terminology – published on 23 April 1977. Like all the previous *Judge Dredd* stories, it was originally intended as a one-off. Mills, however, could see a lot more potential in its central premise of robots rebelling against humans and suggested to Wagner – with whom he had created the Judge Dredd character – that it be expanded into the series' first multi-issue serial. Consequently 'Robots' became just a prelude to the eight-part 'The Robot Wars', which ran from Prog 10 to Prog 17 inclusive over the next two months.

Essentially a social satire on the class divide, in the manner of Kalel Čapek's seminal *Rossum's*

Universal Robots, 'The Robot Wars' concerns a carpenter droid, Call-Me-Kenneth, leading an uprising of all service robots against their human masters. When the killing starts, law-enforcer Judge Dredd is called in and has to tackle the Heavy Metal Kids – huge demolition robots with wrecking balls at the ends of their arms. Dredd is captured, but his only ally, the walking vending-machine droid Walter the Wobot (so named because he speaks with a lisp), rescues him from Call-Me-Kenneth's HQ. Flying up to a weather control satellite, Dredd then programs an electrical storm of several million megavolts to come crashing down, disrupting the robots' circuits and bringing the revolt to an end.

Wagner's scripts included some violent confrontations, but these were treated imaginatively and with a certain amount of black humour, making them less gratuitous than the kind that had made *Action* so controversial; and the story was all the more enjoyable for it. With the emphasis on machines, and plenty of explosive action, this was ideal subject matter for Ron, and he began happily illustrating the exploits of Mega-City One's motorcycling magistrate. However, as each *Judge Dredd* instalment ran to five pages, this was too much work for one artist to cope with on a weekly basis, so while Ron handled the 'Robots' prelude and the three parts of 'The Robot Wars' that appeared in Progs 11, 13 and 16, the other five parts of the main story were divided up between Mike McMahon, the regular *Judge Dredd* artist; Carlos Ezquerra, the original designer of Dredd and Mega-City One; and Ian Gibson, an IPC newcomer. These other three artists gave their contributions a consistent look. Loose and sketchy, it was a reaction against traditional comic-strip illustration and, as far as the editors were concerned, entirely suited to the subject matter. Ron, however, distained this approach, which to his eyes lacked quality. Keeping his head down, he persevered with his own sleek, clean, shiny interpretation, which although of a high standard, failed to achieve the raw, radical, punk-influenced effect the editors were after.

Inevitably this resulted in a lack of continuity, as Ron departed from the other artists' vision for the robot characters, developing his own sturdy, gleaming, highly stylised designs. Walter the Wobot, for instance, was supposed to be a little vending

Above: Turner's very first page of artwork for *2000 AD*: the title page of 'The Robots' from Prog 9, published on 23 April 1977.

machine on legs, but under Ron's hand became a six-foot-tall construction; which, although superbly realised, was totally out of keeping. Similarly, the Heavy Metal Kids, which McMahon had given a slightly comical look, were transformed by Ron into far more menacing creations.

The final two pages that Ron contributed to the story, showing lightning bolts crashing down around the deranged robots as they attack each other before their circuits burn out, were truly amazing pieces of work. However, had any of the other three artists been responsible, this scene of huge robots knocking each other's blocks off would doubtless have been treated with a certain amount of grim humour, rather than in the straight, dramatic way that Ron presented it.

These were important considerations that the editors were keen to get across to Ron before they gave him any further commissions. Consequently, once 'The Robot Wars' was concluded, they indicated to Greg Hall that they would like to speak to his client and explain just what it was they wanted. Hall, however, refused to allow any direct

Above: Turner's dramatic depiction of the demise of the Heavy Metal Kids, as presented over the last two pages of the penultimate instalment of 'The Robot Wars' in *2000 AD* Prog 16. The one-page colour overlay, a regular feature of the strip, was added by the publishers.

contact, insisting that as Ron's agent he should be the conduit for all communication. This response was not well received. The situation was in stark contrast to that with the younger artists, who were readily accessible and would often get in touch to discuss the scripts or suggest changes to improve the comic – which, after all, was still a fledgeling title trying to build a readership. Nevertheless, Hall was given the benefit of the doubt and Ron was accorded another *Judge Dredd* assignment, on the one-off story 'The Solar Sniper', this time with script margin notes emphasising exactly what was neeeded and encouraging him to phone if he had any doubts or problems.

No such calls were made, and when the finished pages came in, nothing had changed. The artwork was superb by any other standards, but too slick and smooth for *2000 AD*'s liking, and it seemed that Ron just didn't grasp the issue. Again the editors tried to impress on Hall that Ron needed to modify his approach to blend in with their other artists' style. Hall's blunt response was that the other artists *had* no style – just a lack of ability! Ron, he maintained, would never draw down to their level; he was a professional, and the best SF artist they had!

Hall did pass the editors' comments on to Ron, but the response was as expected. Ron wasn't willing to compromise; and why should he be, he added, when he was relishing his return to mature SF and producing his best work in years? No, the editors would get what he gave them! In fact, maybe the younger artists could take a few pointers from *him* – for he felt they had much to learn!

Ron was not wrong to suggest that his fellow artists lacked experience. Although they would all go on to have highly successful and accomplished careers, in 1977 McMahon had only just left art school and neither Ezquerra nor Gibson had taken on any previous SF work. From the editors' point of view, though, Ron's inflexibility was becoming a nuisance, and they let Hall know that they were inclined to drop him. Hall was incensed. He had made Ron aware of the requirements, but

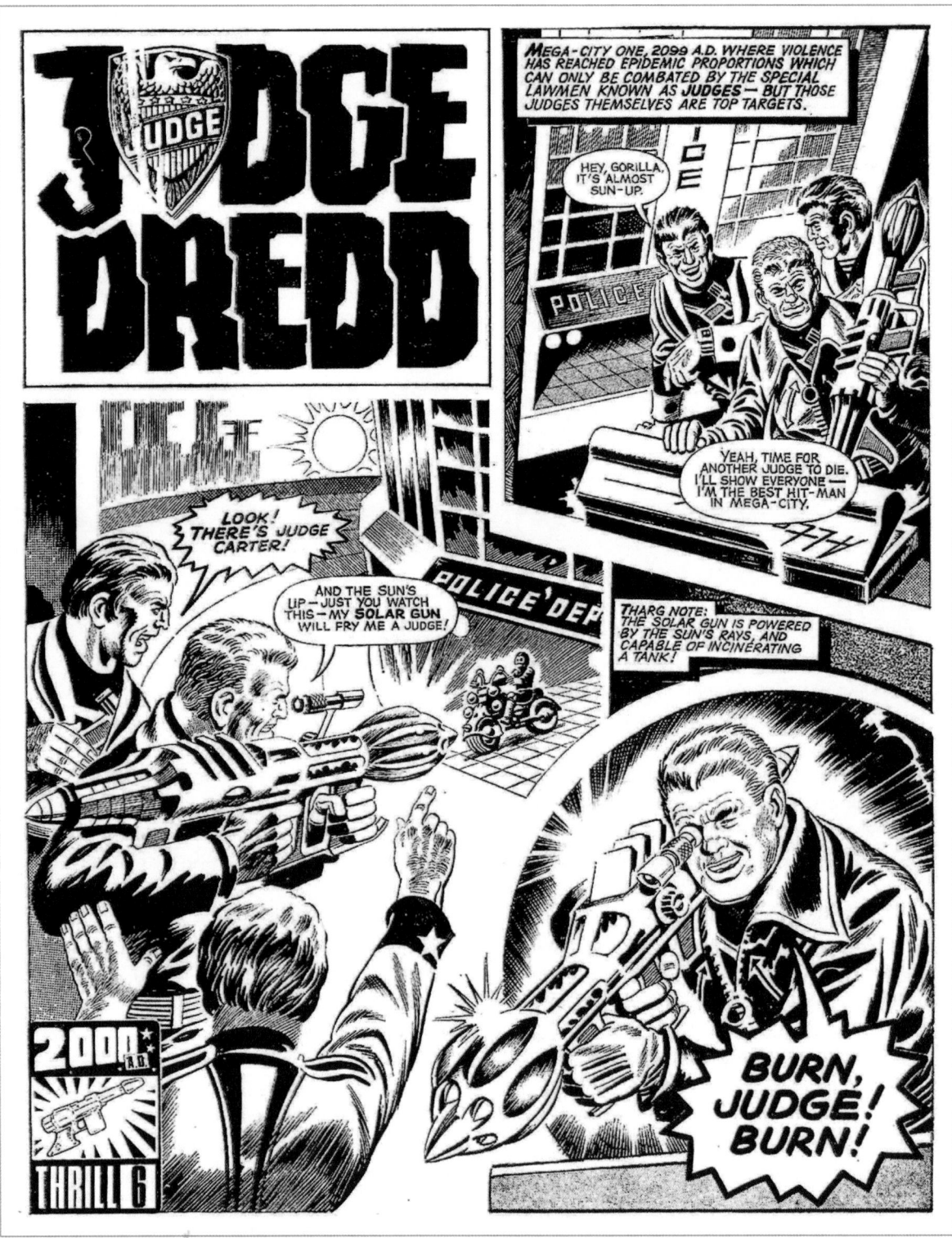

Above: Turner's title page for the *Judge Dredd* story 'The Solar Sniper', published in *2000 AD* Prog 21 on 16 July 1977. This story would prove to be the last he illustrated for the series.

considered them an insult to his abilities, and just couldn't understand the editors' concerns. After all, the work was SF, and Ron *did* SF, so what was the problem?

What both men had failed to appreciate was that *2000 AD* did not want its stories set in some gleaming, utopian future of the kind that Ron had once served up for a post-war readership craving escapism, but rather in a dark, grim dystopia that chimed with and railed against the depressing times through which the younger writers and artists – and their readers – were now living. Hall's criticism of the other artists' work, with remarks such as 'Ron was drawing SF strips before they were born,' cut no ice here. In fact, it served only to emphasise that, from the editors' perspective, Ron's style was 25 years out of date.

Fortunately, Ron did have other IPC work to fall back on. He was still picking up the occasional Picture Library commission and remained much in demand to illustrate strips for the yearly round of juvenile holiday specials and annuals. But to lose the more mature type of SF work that *2000 AD* represented, so soon after regaining it, would have been quite a blow to him. Feeling that there was now some kind of vendetta being waged against Ron by the clique of younger editors and writers, Hall threatened to take his protestations to group editor John Sanders, or even higher in the company if need be, until someone saw sense and agreed that his client's work could continue to feature in *2000 AD*. It seems unlikely that any such approach to Sanders would have been successful – he doubtless understood and supported what his editors were trying to achieve, and Hall's persistent demands on Ron's behalf were becoming tiresome – but luckily things did not quite come to that.

Around this time, it was decided that *2000 AD* should start to run some short, one-off, twist-in-the-tale stories under the series title *Tharg's Future Shocks*. As these could be set in some indeterminate future era, and thus did not necessarily have to conform to the overall tone of the comic, it was finally agreed that they might be suitable for Ron to work on. Hall accepted this compromise, and so, in September 1977, Ron happily illustrated two stories for the new series. However, the situation was still not ideal. *Tharg's Future Shocks* being essentially

Above: the title page of 'Super Spook', a black-and-white strip story that Turner illustrated for the *Cor!! Annual 1978*, one of the crop of juvenile assignments he continued to take on for IPC in 1977.

a fill-in item, the page-count was low and variable; the first of Ron's two contributions ran to three pages, the second to only two-and-a-half. Moreover, the series had been launched with the intention of giving up-and-coming young writers and artists a chance of getting into comic-strip work, so that their talents could be developed and ideally moulded to suit *2000 AD*'s requirements – none of which applied to Ron. In the end, it seemed that he and *2000 AD* were simply incompatible.

Hall was finally placated when a better fit for Ron's work was found on a regular series in the now 'defanged' *Action* comic. The series in question, running to four pages each week, was *The Spinball Slaves*, a futuristic sports strip with plenty of biker action similar to that featured in *Judge Dredd*. Although still disgruntled at having been dropped from *Judge Dredd* itself, Ron was pleased that his SF credentials were at last being acknowledged, and he settled down to work on his new assignment.

Originally titled *Death Race 1999* and then *Spinball*, *The Spinball Slaves* had started out as an extremely violent strip, and although it had been toned down considerably by the time Ron became involved, it still had its moments. Inspired by the film *Rollerball* and the classic arcade game pinball, the central story revolves around Joe Taggart and his motorcycle team – renamed from Kneagle's Eagles to the Black Gladiators at the start of Ron's tenure. Taggart has been wrongly convicted of the murder of the team's former manager, but in lieu of the death penalty, he and his teammates are now forced to play the hazardous game of spinball as free entertainment for the masses. With supercharged, spike-tyred bikes roaring around a giant pinball-table-like ice-rink in a *Judge Dredd*-style dystopian setting, the series offered plenty of action; but here there was no dark humour to leaven the violence.

The more brutal aspects of the scripts were not exactly to Ron's liking, but at least this time he was not having to share the artwork duties with anyone else, and so had complete control over the presentation. The downside was that he was now back on the treadmill of having to meet regular weekly deadlines. Anxious to avoid any return to the excessive working hours this had previously entailed, he decided he would have to modify his usual artwork technique. Out went the smooth lines of his *Judge Dredd* layouts, and in came a much looser style, using mechanical tone and airbrush effects to achieve the desired results far more quickly. Consequently, Ron's work on *The Spinball Slaves* was less clean and detailed than on earlier strips – and ironically closer to what *2000 AD*'s editors had been urging him to do on *Judge Dredd*! Although Ron himself was not entirely happy about having to take this approach, the 'dirtying up' of his style did much to help him achieve an effective depiction of the grim world the scripts envisaged, while making the work far less demanding for him.

As pleased as Ron was with the strip's high action content, repetitive scenes of the game being played out in a stadium packed with cheering crowds became increasingly tedious to illustrate as the weeks went by, and taxing too, as it was a constant challenge for him to try to come up with different ways of depicting very similar incidents. Although grateful for the work, he was beginning to wonder how long he could continue in this manner. Changes, however, were just around the corner.

Since its revamp at the end of 1976, *Action* had continued to lose readers – mainly to *2000 AD*, the comic it had effectively spawned – and sales had now fallen to the point where it was no longer commercially viable. But in the British comics industry, failing titles would rarely be cancelled outright: instead, for marketing purposes, they would be merged with others of a similar type. Thus it was decided that the David Hunt-edited *Battle* should become *Battle-Action* and pick up any of *Action*'s strips that it was felt could be successfully adapted into a war-themed format. At first, *The Spinball Slaves*, still essentially a sports strip despite its futuristic setting, was not one of those chosen to survive. This was not entirely unwelcome news to Ron, given his growing dissatisfaction with the formulaic nature of the work. Greg Hall, on the other hand, was furious to think that all the effort he had put in to gain his client a regular assignment would now be wasted.

Reconsidering, Ron reasoned that if an essential criterion for a strip to be included in *Battle-Action* was that it should be war-related, then surely *The Spinball Slaves* could be saved if only he could find some way to involve its characters in futuristic war scenarios. It was the old *Rick Random* situation all over again, where otherwise unwanted SF content could be made more palatable to an editor by placing it in a different genre context – in that case criminal detection, in this case wartime conflict. With this in mind, Ron set about devising a revised format in which Taggart and his team would become SAS-style troops working under cover of their spinball activities, with their motorbikes redesigned as fighting machines incorporating mini-rocket launchers, mortars, machine guns etc. Once satisfied, he had Hall submit his proposal to the powers-that-be at IPC; and, perhaps mindful of the fact that the irksome contention over his involvement with *2000 AD* had only recently been resolved, they readily agreed that the ideas had sufficient merit to justify the strip being given a new lease of life.

Above: from the 1 October 1977 edition of *Action*, the title page of the third instalment of 'The Black Gladiators', the first story that Turner illustrated for *The Spinball Slaves*.

Above: another impressive title page illustration produced by Turner for *The Spinball Slaves* story 'The Black Gladiators', this one from *Action*'s 15 October 1977 edition.

So it was that, from the first issue of the rebranded *Battle-Action* on 19 November 1977, *The Spinball Slaves* became *The Spinball Wars*, wherein Taggart and his team serve as conscripted members of the World Security Battalion, a secret organisation that wages war on threats to global peace, while continuing their spinball activities as the Black Gladiators. With the team embarking on games/missions worldwide, the series was now, frame after frame, page after page, action, action all the way. A certain amount of strong violence was still in evidence, with team members getting blown up, riddled with bullets or set on fire – all a long way from the gentle boisterousness of the boys' club bikers of *The Tigers* a few years previously – but with varied settings and plenty of thrilling incident, the stories now offered Ron many more creative possibilities than before.

Initially the plots were fairly formulaic, involving power-mad dictators or scientists holding the world to ransom with threats of nuclear attack or germ warfare, but soon scriptwriter Tom Tully freshened things up by introducing more fantastical elements such as killer robots, doomsday machines, rampaging monsters and alien invaders. By far the best story was 'The Megathon Menace', a nigh-on three-month-long potboiler concerning a seemingly unstoppable, indestructible juggernaut of incredible power, unleashed to start a Third World War! So, in the space of just a couple of years, a series that had begun as a sports strip had developed first into a war strip and now, exploiting its future setting to the full, an out-and-out SF strip!

Some readers were critical of the retooled series, feeling that such material had no place in a war-themed title and would be more suited to *2000 AD*, but most seemed to like it, and some even considered it the best thing in the whole comic. For Ron, the increased SF content meant that he was back in his element. Sadly, though, he was unable to enjoy this as much as he might have done, as the relentless pressure of producing four pages of artwork per week – a gruelling amount for any artist – led him to make further time-saving stylistic compromises, filling large areas of his layouts with heavy lines, deep shadows and dark silhouettes, so that he was never very pleased with them. This was a far cry from his days of working on *Rick Random*, when he had had the time to be truly creative and deliver work with which he was fully satisfied. But, as fate would have it, in a surprising development, *Rick Random* was just about to re-enter his life.

Around the beginning of 1978, *2000 AD* art director Kevin O'Neill was looking for fill-in strips to include in a *Sci-Fi Special* scheduled for publication that summer. To stay within budget, some of these would have to be reprint material, so the IPC vaults were being plundered. A fan of Ron's work, O'Neill came across the original art boards for two excellent 1957 stories starring his now legendary space hero Rick Random: *The Time Travellers* and *SOS from Space*. The latter he chose to appear in the *Sci-Fi Special*, while the former he decided to include in the *Dan Dare Annual 1979*, planned for publication in September. However, poring over all this old artwork prompted the intriguing idea that the *Rick Random* series might be successfully revived for a new generation of readers in the pages of *2000 AD* itself.

Below: *The Spinball Wars* debuts with the first instalment of a story called 'Tower of Doom' in the first issue of the rebranded IPC title *Battle-Action*, dated 19 November 1977.

With the arrival on the comic of new artists such as Brian Bolland, Gary Leach and Dave Gibbons, its original dark, gritty style had given way to a cleaner, sleeker look with which Ron's work was no longer so out of keeping, and his well-received treatment of *The Spinball Wars* meant that he was now back in favour. So, despite having fallen out with *2000 AD*'s editors two years previously, he was invited back into the fold to draw a new run of *Rick Random* adventures. The only problem was, he just wasn't interested!

Despite his obvious affinity with the subject matter, which would spare him the kind of interference he had faced on *Judge Dredd*, Ron didn't believe in the idea of resurrecting old characters. He had been aghast at the way his long-time idol Frank Hampson's most famous creation had been treated in its *2000 AD* revival, feeling that it was *Dan Dare* in name only, and had no wish to see his own character scripted in the same unsympathetic way. Like *Dan Dare*, *Rick Random* was a product of its time, he felt, and should be allowed to remain as a fond memory. As a science-fiction artist, he believed in looking to the future, not back to the past. Quite apart from these objections, there was also the practical consideration that to take on an additional commission requiring him to produce the envisaged six pages of artwork per week would be quite impossible, when at times he struggled to cope with the four he already had to supply for *The Spinball Wars*!

However, fixed on the notion of having Ron back working on the series with which he was so closely associated, the *2000 AD* team assured him that the scripts would be well written, in the style of the originals, and that he would be allowed plenty of time – months in fact – to produce the artwork. Ron was still unhappy at the idea of having to manage two strips at the same time, even though Hall reminded him that back in the '50s he'd done just that on *Rick Random* and *Space Ace*, but after much deliberation he finally relented. It was paying work, after all, and such was the insecurity of the publishing industry that new opportunities could quickly dry up, as both men knew only too well.

With Ron now on board, writer Steve Moore was tasked with scripting the first story of the revival. Having dutifully read through a stack of old *Rick Random* stories to get a flavour of them, he came up with the six-part 'The Riddle of the Astral Assassin', concerning the murder of alien delegates attending a top-level trade conference hosted, for security reasons, on a hollowed-out asteroid. This was essentially Agatha Christie's *Ten Little Indians* transferred to an outer-space setting, but Moore ensured there were plenty of large-scale dramatic scenes with futuristic elements that Ron could really go to town on, as he had on the original series.

Ron, though, approached the task with distinctly mixed feelings. While recognising that Moore had done a good job on the scripts, he still felt the pressure of having to produce two strips at once. He may well have worked this way in the '50s, but he'd been a lot younger and had much more energy back then. His initial reservations were quickly borne out as, even though he was allowed occasional weekly breaks from *The Spinball Wars*, he began to find the increased workload very draining. Things improved slightly at the start of 1979, when *The Spinball Wars* was cut from four pages to three each week, giving him more time to work on *Rick Random*. However, he still found it frustrating to have to chop and change between the two, disrupting his creative flow.

Ron's artwork for *The Spinball Wars* may have become, by necessity, loose and lacking in detail, but at least he had still found the time and enthusiasm to produce imaginative layouts and designs. Not so for the new *Rick Random*. His antipathy toward the task clearly showed in the fact that his depiction of the title character bore little resemblance to the original, but instead made him look more like the other series' Joe Taggart – complete with a spinball helmet as part of his fighting gear during the later action sequences! His designs for the strip's spacecraft, guns and other hardware were also uncharacteristically lacking in originality, showing that very little thought had gone into them. If it were not for the fact that some of Steve Moore's scene descriptions were based on Ron's own '50s concepts, the results might have been even worse.

This was all a reflection of Ron's dissatisfaction with the situation in which he found himself. His treatment of 'The Riddle of the Astral Assassin' was perfunctory – just enough to tell the story and no

Above: Turner's title page for the first instalment of *2000 AD*'s new *Rick Random* story 'The Riddle of the Astral Assassin'.

more – and, feeling unable to give the work the care and attention he normally would, he began to lose any interest he might have had in it. By the time he came to illustrate the fifth instalment, he had fallen badly behind schedule and found himself right up against the deadline, with his agent breathing down his neck for him to finish the pages so that he could rush them straight to the publisher!

It was in the wake of this that Ron began to wonder what on earth he was doing. Surely, he told himself, this was no way to earn a living? How could he possibly be creative and produce his best work under this kind of pressure? Suddenly he decided that he'd had enough. *Rick Random*, as far as he was concerned, was finished. Having just told *2000 AD*'s new editor Steve McManus that the pages for the story's final instalment would be with him shortly, Hall was furious. But Ron wouldn't be moved. Besides, he added, he'd recently had a problem with his car, and preferred to spend his time getting that fixed than hacking out artwork like one of the robots that *2000 AD* would have its readers believe worked on the comic!

In a vain attempt to salvage the situation, Hall continued to harass Ron for the artwork while simultaneously assuring McManus that it was almost ready. McManus was not a fan of Ron's work to start with – he had inherited *Rick Random* on taking over – so when the deadline came and went without anything being delivered, he angrily turned to a replacement artist. Carlos Ezquerra was not the most obvious choice for this type of subject matter, but he was quick and available and, adopting the pseudonym L J Silver, he managed to turn out the final instalment in time for publication.

This also proved to be, unsurprisingly, the final instalment of Ron's association with *2000 AD*, as Hall was informed in no uncertain terms that his client would never work on the comic again. Ron, for his part, realised that he shouldn't have agreed to take on the *Rick Random* strip in the first place. It was a classic case of bad timing. Had he been offered the assignment immediately after he was dropped from *Judge Dredd* and before he started work on *The Spinball Slaves*, he could have given it his full attention, and the outcome could have been superb. As it was, the new story paled in comparison with what had gone before, and the revival went no further, ensuring that *Rick Random* would remain forever rooted in the 1950s.

Fortunately, although he had been too busy to take on any of 1979's round of juvenile holiday special or annual strip work, Ron still had *The Spinball Wars* to turn to. Now that it had been cut to three pages per week, he was able to give it a lot more detail and produce some satisfying results. The SF themes had by this point been fully played out, but veteran scribe Tom Tully was renowned for being able to stretch an idea to incredible lengths, and he had the heroes become involved in ever more contrived situations, such as being kidnapped in an old Wild West town; encountering a dinosaur in the frozen wastes of Alaska; and being turned into zombies by an old African witch doctor. At the end of 1979, though, the series was finally brought to a close, with Taggart and his team suddenly receiving a free pardon. By now, Ron had really lost interest in this assignment too, so he breathed a sigh of relief to know that he was finally free of it. Next he wanted Hall to find him something far more interesting – something he could call *real* science fiction.

Above: the title page of the 5 April 1980 instalment of the Turner-illustrated *Journey to the Stars* strip in IPC's *Speed*.

13: A QUICK BURST OF *SPEED*

Seeking more suitable commissions for Ron, at the end of 1979 Greg Hall came across Marvel UK's *Doctor Who Weekly*, which would later be reformatted and become a long-running monthly but was then still in its infancy. Its lead comic strip was already being illustrated quite impressively by Dave Gibbons, but each issue also included a back-up strip recounting the evil deeds of one of the good Doctor's arch-enemies, and these were being handled by various different artists. Recalling the success of Ron's work on *The Daleks* strip in the '60s, Hall approached editor Dez Skinn, feeling that here was an ideal assignment for his client, featuring a mix of aliens, monsters and spacecraft. Skinn was familiar with Ron's *TV Century 21* work and, having previously been on staff at IPC, was also aware of his juvenile *Whizzer and Chips* and *Cor!!* strips. He agreed that Ron would be a good fit for the subject matter, and sent Hall the script for a four-page story involving the reptilian Ice Warriors. Ron was pleased to have this opportunity; for, after two years of pseudo-SF on the *Spinball* saga, this was more like the real thing.

But Ron had hardly begun work on the strip when, out of the blue, Hall received an offer for him to illustrate an ongoing series called *Journey to the Stars* for an in-preparation new IPC comic called *Speed*. Written by *Spinball* scripter Tom Tully, this was also SF, and each instalment would consist of two or, in weeks when it was cover-featured, three pages of full-colour artwork. The only problem was, the assignment was to begin almost immediately, and Hall knew that Ron would be unable to cope with it while still working on the *Doctor Who* strip. This presented him with a dilemma: which of the two should he turn down? His conscience told him that, as he already had a verbal agreement with Skinn, he should stick to that. However, his business sense told him the opposite. The black-and-white *Doctor Who* strip would pay less well than the full-colour *Speed* one, and was a one-off rather than a series, with no guarantee that it would lead to any further work. Moreover, Marvel UK being independent of its American parent company, it was a much smaller operation than the mighty IPC, and the future of its fledgeling title was inherently less secure. There were plenty of people at IPC with whom Hall had had problems, but at least he knew who they were and how to deal with them, whereas the Marvel UK set-up was completely unfamiliar to him. All things considered, he decided he had no choice but to accept the *Speed* offer and return the *Doctor Who* script to Skinn with an apology.

Skinn was infuriated. Too late now to engage another artist to illustrate the Ice Warriors strip in time for it to be published in its intended slot in *Doctor Who Weekly* Issue 13, he had no choice but to rush another story forward as a replacement; and, moreover, as the tagline 'The Ice Warriors Attack' had already been included on the issue's cover – which, being a glossy magazine-style one, was printed well in advance of the contents – he also had to give an apology for its non-appearance. In a repeat of what had happened on *2000 AD*, Skinn left Hall in no doubt that he would never employ Ron again.

Meanwhile, unaware of all these shenanigans and knowing only that the *Doctor Who* strip had been cancelled, Ron looked forward to starting work on *Speed*, the first issue of which was scheduled for publication toward the end of February 1980. Like its long-established IPC stablemate *Tiger*, it was to benefit from superior litho printing on good-quality paper, allowing for excellent reproduction of colour photos and fully-painted artwork. Unlike *Tiger*, however, its contents would not be confined to sports strips but would take in a variety of different genres, the only prerequisite being that each strip should feature fast-paced action reflecting the idea of 'speed', so as to justify – however tenuously – the comic's title. So, alongside football and motorcycling series there would be a Western, a war strip and an SF strip. With educational features and centrespreads planned to round out each issue, *Speed* was already being heralded as the new *Eagle*; in which case, *Journey to the Stars* would be its *Dan Dare* equivalent.

Above: the Turner-illustrated *Journey to the Stars* features for the first time on the front cover of IPC's *Speed* on 12 April 1980.

Above: another Turner illustration for *Journey to the Stars* graces the cover of the 10 May 1980 issue of *Speed*.

Ron may have been barred from the pages of *2000 AD*, but with *Battle-Action* editor David Hunt also in charge of the new title, he was always first choice to illustrate the SF strip. Hunt had no doubt that he was the right man for the job, and was happy to take him on. Sadly, as things turned out, while the war and sports strips would not have looked out of place in *Battle-Action* and *Tiger* respectively, *Journey to the Stars*, despite its promising title, was written as a childish adventure, more *Whizzer and Chips* than *2000 AD*. The first story involved the hero characters of an astronomer, his two kids and their dog being kidnapped by aliens resembling giant brains on legs, taken aboard their spacecraft and whisked off to a planet on the other side of the galaxy, where they escape and battle giant toad-men. Lacking any of the hard-hitting toughness of Tully's earlier *Spinball* scripts, this instead recalled the juvenile *Wonder-Car* series of the previous decade. The second story had more to offer visually, as the characters get caught up in dogfights in space, make landfall on a planet of robots and encounter a Dredd-like android law-keeper mounted on a hoverbike bristling with armaments, but it was still let down by juvenile dialogue and under-exploited situations. Somehow it seemed that Hunt had failed to learn the lessons of the success that *2000 AD* and *Battle* had enjoyed in running more mature strips, so that *Speed*'s contents spanned not only a range of genres but also a range of ages!

While this was not quite what Ron had hoped for, he was not too bothered: the work was still SF, in full colour and highly paid, and the scripts did at least have some imaginative content that he could get his teeth into. The weekly schedule was, as usual, a challenge: he sometimes found himself having to burn the midnight oil, and without the time to experiment with the kind of subtle airbrush effects he had used on the single-page instalments of *The Daleks*, he had to content himself with turning in flatter and more basic colour work than he would ideally have liked. However, he still found this medium easier than black and white illustration, where shading and tone could pose other problems; and when a printing dispute arose part-way through the run, taking the comic out of circulation for a time, this allowed him to get ahead

Above: Turner's *Journey to the Stars* artwork features on the cover of the 9 August 1980 issue of *Speed*.

with the work, relieving some of the pressure. He even had time to contribute *Spinball* and *Journey to the Stars* strips to some of that year's IPC annuals, and to illustrate another Battle Picture Library title.

Unfortunately, this happy situation didn't last. By the early 1980s, the average boy's pocket money was being spent more on video rentals and computer games than on comics, so this was a bad time for a new title to be launched. *Speed*'s sales soon fell to a level that made its initial high production values unsustainable, and in mid-August 1980 a switch was made to using the same cheaper paper and poorer-quality printing as *2000 AD* and *Battle-Action*, with most of the interior pages now appearing in black and white rather than colour. The revamp didn't end there, either: the contents were also refreshed, with several strips, including *Journey to the Stars*, being axed. A disappointed Ron failed to understand why the SF series could not simply continue in black and white. The official explanation he was given, that it was insufficiently

A QUICK BURST OF *SPEED*

Above: the title page of a *Spinball* strip that Turner Illustrated for IPC's *Action Annual 1981*, published in September 1980.

relevant to the *Speed* title, struck him as ludicrous: what could be speedier than a spaceship? The truth was that, despite Ron's excellent artwork, *Journey to the Stars* had been one of the comic's least popular strips, let down badly by its immature storylines. With better writing, it could indeed have been as much a highlight of *Speed* as *Dan Dare* had been of the *Eagle*, but sadly that was not to be. On the plus side, though, this did not mark the end of Ron's work on *Speed*, as editor David Hunt immediately offered him a new assignment, on a two-page motor-sport strip called *Winner!*.

Interested in grand prix racing and the drama of the track, Ron accepted this commission with enthusiasm. While he didn't relish the prospect of illustrating the crowd scenes he assumed it would entail, he looked forward to depicting some great action sequences like the huge car-crash that ended the first instalment. However, his expectations were confounded as, from that point on, the strip went off on a strange tangent. Suffering amnesia in the aftermath of the crash, the main driver character wanders away, and is then pursued by the authorities through one lame storyline after another, evading capture by taking to a variety of different vehicles such as a Mini, a go-kart and even a double-decker bus! Thus the strip became essentially just one long, drawn-out chase sequence.

Thankfully, Ron was also asked by Hunt to illustrate for the comic's back page a regular factual feature highlighting each week one of the pioneers of speed, such as inventor Frank Whittle, famed for his jet engine, and racing driver James Cobb, a one-time land-speed record-holder, and this was much more satisfying work. Sadly, though, the revamped *Speed* continued to lose readers, and in October 1980 it was absorbed into *Tiger*, which became *Tiger and Speed* for a brief time thereafter. Neither *Winner!* nor the factual pioneers of speed feature survived the merger.

Greg Hall approached *Tiger* editor Paul Gettens in the hope of Ron receiving another regular assignment, citing *Billy's Boots* as an example of his sports strip work, but Gettens knew that Ron had blotted his copybook on *2000 AD* and didn't want to use him. The same was true of new *Battle-Action* editor Terry Magee, who had just taken over from Hunt.

It seemed that, for the time being at least, if Hall wanted to find further work for Ron, he would have to look elsewhere.

Below: the Turner-illustrated *Winner!* was cover-featured twice by *Speed*, on the 8 September and 4 October 1980 editions.

14: A SPORTING CHANCE

Scottish comics publishers D C Thomson were usually a closed shop as far as contributors from south of the border were concerned, so their willingness to accept any work from Ron was doubtful, but with no other options readily available, Greg Hall tentatively sounded them out. Fortunately it was an opportune moment, as they were just then on the lookout for a temporary stand-in for one of the regular artists on their football-themed weekly *Scoop*. Quickly providing copies of Ron's *Billy's Boots* strips, Hall was able to persuade commissioning editor George Mooney that he was the man for the job. As a result, Ron was offered a three-month run on the comic, to work mainly on a long-running strip called *Stark*. But despite Hall having assured Mooney that Ron could cope with this assignment, Ron himself was less certain. His *Billy's Boots* strips had all been one-offs for holiday specials and annuals, and as sports subjects of any kind left him cold, the prospect of a lengthy stint on a weekly football title filled him with dread. However, he was in no position to be choosy. It was paying work, and there was always the chance that it might lead on to better things. So, despite his reservations, he agreed to take it on.

Things began well, but *Billy's Boots* had been a whimsical series aimed at a juvenile readership, whereas *Stark* was a more mature one requiring all its scenarios to be depicted accurately. Being no fan of football, Ron was unfamiliar with details such as the fact that the goalposts in a five-a-side match are shorter than in a regular one, and consequently he sometimes made mistakes that had to be rectified in-house. His treatment of the players was also criticised: picking up on the toughness of the stories, he had made them all look like ex-wrestlers, which was hardly realistic!

Mooney quickly realised that Ron was not cut out for sports strip illustration as he had been led to believe. Nevertheless, appreciating his artistic abilities and the dynamism he had managed to inject into the work, he asked Hall what else his client could do. Although this enquiry seemed promising, Hall prevaricated. Aware that Ron's layouts had required some in-house adjustment, he was concerned that he might not now receive the full fee he had been promised for the work. Mooney assured him this was not the case; but, unfamiliar with the way D C Thomson operated, and probably influenced also by the stereotype of Scotsmen being careful with their money, Hall preferred to wait until the fee had actually been received before signing Ron up to anything else. Mistaking caution for distrust, Mooney then decided that he could do without having to deal with awkward Southerners, and that Ron would, after all, be offered no more work for the company.

While relieved to have finished the *Scoop* assignment, which he counted as probably the most tedious and uninspiring of his whole career, Ron couldn't help but think that Hall's alienation of D C Thomson had been incredibly inept; a longer relationship with the publisher could have proved highly beneficial, as with others in the past. But the die had been cast.

Luckily, during the three months Ron had been busy with D C Thomson at the start of 1981, Hall had managed to secure another regular assignment for him. The previous year, alongside his work on *Speed*, Ron had illustrated a handful of the one-off war stories that *Battle-Action* now featured amongst its contents, and it had struck Hall that new editor Terry Magee, although unwilling to use him on any of the comic's ongoing series, might be prepared to give him further work on these self-contained tales. This proved to be the case, and Ron was allocated a fair share of the 1981 run of stories, the ambit of which extended beyond the First and Second World Wars to encompass other historical conflicts such as the Boer War, the Crimean War and the English and American Civil Wars – a variety of subject matter that Ron welcomed, despite finding it challenging in terms of the research needed to ensure accuracy in the depiction of the period costumes and settings.

Clearly Ron had not burnt his bridges with IPC altogether, and while he was working on these *Battle-Action* stories, he also picked up a couple of other strip assignments on that year's crop of tie-in

Above: the title page of a *Charley's War* series strip that Turner illustrated for the 1981-published *Battle-Action Holiday Special*.

holiday specials and annuals, and a commission for yet another 64-page Battle Picture Library entry, *Yellow Peril*, published in October.

Meanwhile, still seeking further commissions for his client, Hall had discovered that Marvel UK, pleased with the sales of their *Doctor Who* title since its revamp as a monthly in September 1980, were now planning to launch a similar magazine devoted to another hit BBC sci-fi show, *Blake's 7*. As Dez Skinn appeared not to be involved this time, Hall hoped that Ron might be considered for the lead strip; so, having got him to produce a sample page depicting the show's spaceship and crew, he submitted this to the editor, Stuart Wales. After some deliberation, Wales declined, saying that he preferred the work of another artist, Ian Kennedy, although he did promise to bear Ron in mind for any future opportunities that might arise. Whether or not that promise was sincere is debatable, as when Kennedy suffered a serious car accident a few weeks into illustrating the strip, putting him out of action for several months, Ron received no invitation to stand in for him. On querying this, Hall was given various excuses – the sample artwork had been lost, his contact details had been mislaid etc – but in truth it seemed more likely that his earlier falling out with Skinn had come back to haunt him, and that Wales had been warned by others within Marvel UK not to touch Ron's work with the proverbial bargepole!

Hall next looked at some other publications he had not approached before, but the only one that seemed to hold any real promise was the junior *TV Times* comic *Look-In*, which paid exceptionally good rates. Its strips were focused on current TV shows, meaning that an essential prerequisite for its artists was the ability to draw faithful likenesses, something that Ron would have been the first to admit was not his forte. However, he had made a good job of illustrating *Star Trek* for *TV21* in the '70s, and felt that he could do equally well if given a chance to take on *Look-In*'s current *Buck Rogers* strip. Unfortunately, when Hall approached the publishers, it turned out that they were quite happy with the artists they already had handling that strip. Instead, they suggested that Ron might perhaps be considered for a strip based on the fictional adventures of the pop group Bucks Fizz!

Disillusioned, but nevertheless needing the extra work, Ron produced a sample sheet depicting the group's four members in a variety of different aspects. However, his heart just wasn't in it, and although his close-up portraits of the four were spot-on, his attempts at capturing their features at a distance and from other angles were less successful and ultimately failed to meet with editorial approval. So, again, this initially promising prospect came to nothing.

Toward the end of 1981, Greg Hall got wind that a new IPC comic was in the works, with David Hunt lined up to edit it. Hunt had always put work Ron's way whenever he could on *Battle-Action* and *Speed*, so Hall was hopeful that he would do so again now – whatever objections others at IPC might raise. His confidence grew still further when, as the weeks went by, it became apparent that the new comic was to be a revival of that old classic the *Eagle*, with its flagship character, Dan Dare, set to cruise the spaceways once again.

When Hall contacted Hunt, however, he was dismayed to discover that not only were several other artists already under active consideration to illustrate the *Dan Dare* strip, but Ron wasn't even in the frame! The stumbling block was that, for once, the selection of artists rested not with Hunt but with his boss, group editor Barrie Tomlinson. For this wasn't to be just another comic: it was to be a prestige title, launched at a top London hotel and given an initial 350,000-copy print-run, with the publicity-generating *Dan Dare* being banked on to attract a huge and continuing readership. Tomlinson wanted to be sure that whichever artist was chosen to handle its headline SF strip could be relied upon to deliver three pages of quality colour artwork week in and week out, without any problems.

Furious that Ron wasn't even in the running, Hall pointed out that he had often produced three pages of artwork per week without any issues, and that having been inspired and influenced by *Dan Dare* creator Frank Hampson, he knew the strip like the back of his hand. Ron, he insisted, was unquestionably the man for the job! Tomlinson, to his credit, was not unsympathetic to these arguments. However, the intention was that the strip should remain faithful to the elements originally established by Hampson, and he was concerned that as time went by Ron might allow his enthusiasm to get the better of him and start to introduce his own stylistic flourishes and modifications, causing character and hardware continuity problems as he had on *Judge Dredd*. In short, Tomlinson felt that Ron was just too imaginative for his own good. What he wanted was a competent and dependable artist who would do exactly what was asked of him, without adding a lot of personal embellishments.

The argument continued, until finally Tomlinson did agree to consider Ron – provided he could meet with him and explain in person just how important it was that the strip remained true to Hampson's original likenesses and designs. Whether Tomlinson made this stipulation because he realised it would be unacceptable to Hall, and so end the matter, or whether he genuinely wanted to talk to Ron and have a chance to explain why IPC had sometimes had issues with his work before, is uncertain. Either way, predictably, Hall refused. His reasons were twofold: first, he doubted Ron would want to meet Tomlinson, having been stung by past editorial criticisms of his work; secondly, he was concerned that, in the unlikely event the meeting did take place, it would compromise his position as Ron's agent, and could even lead to the two men agreeing terms privately, cutting him out of the deal and depriving him of any income from it. Although Tomlinson dismissed this possibility, problems Hall had experienced with other clients over the years had left him wary, and he was immovable. Thus any possibility of Ron getting the *Dan Dare* strip was ended, and it went instead to Gerry Embleton.

Angry and humiliated that he'd lost the one commission he felt should have been Ron's without question, Hall resigned himself to accepting whatever other work the new comic might have to offer. To his dismay, however, he learned that it would include only one other illustrated strip, which had already been assigned to a Spanish artist, relying on photo-stories to make up the balance. To Hall's mind, this was a cheap cop-out, robbing artists of work and allowing IPC to profit off the back of the one illustrated strip that could be guaranteed to pull in readers. The rest of the comic might just as well be filled with blank pages! He urged Tomlinson to think again, insisting that an additional strip, handled by Ron, would enhance the contents and act as another selling point; but this cut no ice with the editor. Hall's only consolation was his conviction that the comic would eventually have to revert to using illustrated strips if it was to succeed, and that Ron would then be given work on it. He would ultimately be proved correct on both counts, although it would be many months before the second would be borne out.

With no regular weekly work in prospect, the early part of 1982 saw Hall resort to picking up whatever one-off assignments he could find for Ron back on IPC's roster of juvenile holiday specials and annuals – including, ironically, a five-page strip for the *Eagle Annual 1983*. Then, toward the end of the year, editor Ted Bensberg came to the rescue with some further commissions for the War Picture Library range, always happy to use Ron because his wartime service meant that he was one of the few artists who could be relied upon for accuracy in the depiction of local colour and technical detail. Ron, for his part, enjoyed working on these more substantial 64-page digests, with their mature storylines, realistic characters and natural dialogue, not to mention their relaxed deadlines now that most of the range was made up of reprint material.

However, returning to fine-line black-and-white work in a smaller format than usual, Ron found that his hand was not as steady with a brush as it had once been, and initially he was dissatisfied with the results. Fortunately, around this time, felt-tip pens had begun to swamp the art market. Realising that these could be the answer to his problem, Ron experimented with them until he came up with the right balance between pen and brush. The former couldn't deliver the same fluidity as the latter, but at least the flow was consistent, allowing him to concentrate on the drawing rather than on when the ink would run out. This enabled him to give his work far more detail and polish than would otherwise have been the case, and consequently the run of War Picture Library titles he illustrated over the next couple of years would feature some of his most accomplished black-and-white war art since his *John Steel* series for the Super-Detective Library back in the '50s.

Ron seemed quite content to continue with this stress-free type of work, it being quite conducive to his current lifestyle; but, sadly, much to his displeasure, it wasn't to last.

Above: the title pages of four stories that Turner illustrated for IPC publications in 1982: the football-themed 'Lee's Amazing Secret' from the *Cheeky Annual 1983*; a *The Leopard from Lime Street* series story from the *Buster Book 1983*; 'The Cosmic Key!', a part-dot-to-dot adventure from the *Whoopee! Annual 1983*; and a *Young Macdonald & His Farm* series story from the *Cor!! Holiday Special*.

Above: the title page of a story in kung-fu series *The Fists of Jimmy Chang*, illustrated by Turner for the 1982-published *Battle Holiday Special*.

Above: 'If You Go Down to the Woods Today …', Turner's dot-to-dot centrespread for the 1982-published *Cor!! Holiday Special*.
Below: the opening title spread of 'Tall Story', a *The Collector* strip that Turner illustrated in 1982 for the *Eagle Annual 1983*.

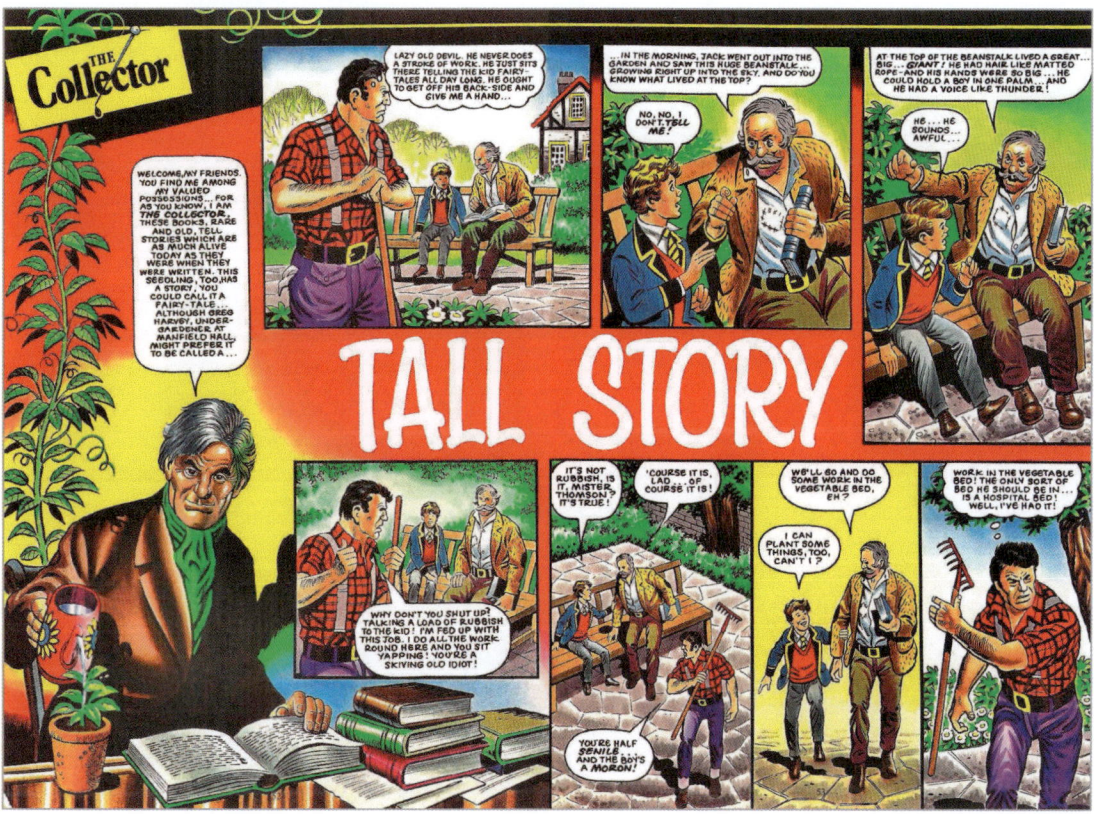

Above: a page from the War Picture Library title *Fire Trap*, published as Number 1962 in November 1982, with Turner's signature on one of the frames.

15: NO FORCED ACTION!

Battle-Action's strand of one-off war stories having now ended, and the next round of holiday special and annual commissions not yet begun, the latter months of 1982 saw Ron's output confined to his new run of War Picture Library assignments. However, these were poorly paid by comparison with weekly comic-strip work, of which no more was on the horizon, and his income suffered as a result. His conviction that a career as a commercial artist had so many pitfalls that it was unconducive to a happy married life was sadly proved correct when, the present situation having brought things to a head, he and his wife Ruby divorced.

Now with more pressing matters to attend to, such as selling the family home and finding somewhere else to live, Ron had no choice but to put what little work he had on hold for a while. Fortunately, the ever-resourceful Greg Hall was able to find him a less demanding alternative that would bring in some much-needed extra money while also providing him with temporary accommodation: house-sitting for a business associate while he was away working for a year in America. The house in question was a small one on Ash Island in the Thames, a real loner's retreat, which suited Ron admirably. He needed time to think and recharge his batteries after the recent turmoil in his private life, and this was the ideal place in which to do it.

Once settled, Ron persevered with his War Picture Library illustrations. Now relieved of most of his domestic commitments, and without any tight deadlines to work to, he was able to take his time over these, and it showed in the quality of the end product. Thoughtfully-composed frames and detailed character studies, achieved with his new technique involving the use of felt-tip pens, helped to make these some of his best ever contributions to the range. The first two titles, *Cold Courage* and *Fire Trap*, had a special significance for him, as both concerned the Second World War's Battle of Monte Cassino, in which he himself had seen action. He did his best to ensure that the artwork reflected his own personal experiences of the conflict; and there was one particular sequence in *Fire Trap* that really struck a chord with him, as it involved a group of soldiers coming under heavy German mortar fire and seeing their captain get killed – just like the traumatic incident when he had witnessed his own commanding officer get blown up by an exploding mortar. Such was the resonance this had with Ron that he was moved to do something he had done only a couple of times before, at the very start of his career, and certainly never before on a comic-strip illustration: he added his signature to one frame of the sequence. Whereas on those earlier occasions his motivation had been satisfaction with his work – on a couple of the early '50s Vargo Statten paperback covers – this time it was simply that the story had brought back such poignant memories for him that he felt he had to acknowledge the fact in some way – even if only to himself, and at the risk of it seeming like a mark of vanity to readers unaware of the circumstances.

The early months of 1983 saw Ron's situation improve with the arrival of the now-expected quota of commissions for IPC holiday specials and annuals, this year including strip illustrations for the *Buster Holiday Special*, the *Battle Annual 1984*, the *Eagle Annual 1984* and the *Shiver and Shake Annual 1984*. He was finding his current lifestyle idyllic, so when his house-sitting job came to an end and he had to give up his Robinson Crusoe act on the island, he decided that rather than seek a property on dry land he would explore the possibility of obtaining a riverside home. So it was that he came to take up residence on a rather dilapidated houseboat that he felt had potential, resolving to spend time and money renovating it to his own liking in between his professional commitments.

Around the middle of the year, Ron received a new commission to illustrate two out of a series of five eight-page mini-comics called *Action Force*, to be given away free with issues of *Tiger*, *Eagle* and *Battle* (the *Action* having now been dropped from the latter's title) to promote a new range of toy manufacturer Palitoy's Action Man figures. These figures looked like they could have come straight

All from 1983, the title pages for a *The Hunters* story in the *Battle Holiday Special*; a *Toby's Timepiece* story in the *Shiver and Shake Annual 1984*; and *The Collector* stories 'The Eyes of Harry Eden' in the *Eagle Holiday Special* and 'Yellow Fever' in the *Eagle Annual 1984*.

out of a blockbuster action movie, the concept being that they were an elite group of SAS-style agents operating on land, sea and air, and even in outer space, to oppose the arch-villain Baron Ironblood and his fanatical Red Shadows minions in their attempt at global conquest. In order to promote the range effectively, it was essential that every detail of the characters and their associated transport be illustrated accurately, so Ron received boxes of the toys to use as reference. Having completed the two stories he had been assigned, he then returned to his regular work, not expecting anything further to come of Action Force. However, comics in general had been experiencing a severe decline in sales over the past year, as other youthful interests such as computer games continued to hold sway, and *Battle* looked likely to be the next casualty of the dwindling market unless something drastic could be done to save it. Prior to the promotional giveaway, it had run a four-week *Action Force* series, and this experiment having been deemed a success, IPC now reached a deal with Palitoy whereby the toy company would absorb a large percentage of the production costs in return for the series becoming an ongoing one and the comic being retitled *Battle Action Force*.

Ron's work on the mini-comic stories having impressed, he was now invited to become the regular *Action Force* illustrator, with a requirement to produce four pages per week. Given that IPC were previously unwilling to have him back on a weekly strip, it is likely he owed this offer to Palitoy's influence. However, after three years of enjoying a relatively relaxed schedule, he himself was now reluctant to return to the treadmill of relentless weekly deadlines. Living on his own on the river, he had fewer financial responsibilities than before, and could manage well enough on the income he was already receiving from his occasional War Picture Library assignments and the seasonal batch of one-off juvenile strips.

But if Ron was content with this situation, his agent was not. Having struggled for some years to find him a new weekly strip assignment, Hall just couldn't understand why he would want to pass up the one that had now fallen virtually in his lap. Once again, this led to a falling-out between the two men. Hall accused Ron of being lazy, while Ron complained that four pages of artwork per week was a greater commitment than he had ever taken on before. When Hall reminded him that the *Spinball* saga had entailed a similar output, Ron countered that it had been for a short period only, and at a time when he had felt better able to cope with working at such a pace. Hall then pointed out that the *Action Force* commission might also last for a short period only, and urged him to take it while he could, if only to get back fully into IPC's good books; then they could see where it might lead.

Hall's repeated protestation that the rate of pay on offer was one that many artists would give their eye teeth for, coupled with his insistence that he himself needed to make a living, finally persuaded Ron to acquiesce. But although he had been browbeaten into accepting the commission, he had no enthusiasm for it. Even the initial story's outer-space setting failed to inspire him, and his resentment showed in some of the worst artwork he had ever produced. Instead of giving it his usual attention to detail, using a pair of compasses, French curves and a ruler to achieve smoothly-drawn, clean-lined panels, he dashed it off freehand, as quickly as possible; and in many ways it resembled his early work on the *Tit-Bits* comics, before Fleetway had lent him a guiding hand and helped him hone his skills on *Rick Random*.

Hall accused Ron of sloppiness, but Ron retorted that he was still producing better results than most of the other so-called artists the comic employed, so why should he bother to expend more effort? IPC would get what he gave them, and they could take it or leave it – preferably the latter!

By the time the third week's script arrived, Ron had calmed down somewhat and was being a little more conscientious with the work, but inwardly he was still fuming over the way he'd been cajoled into taking it on, and he told Hall that he would stick with it only if he could be relieved of some of the deadline pressure. Consequently other artists were brought in to give him breaks between stories.

It was not simply the heavy workload that made this assignment a challenging one for Ron, but the extra time he had to put in to ensure that the characters and hardware – such as spacecraft, assault vehicles, boats and other modes of transport – matched in exact detail the equivalent Action Man

Turner's title page for 'Ironblood's Revenge!', the first of the *Action Force* mini-comics, published on 16 July 1983.

toys. The need to incorporate established elements had also been an issue when he had worked on the Anderson strips, but whereas in that case he had wholeheartedly approved of the pre-existing designs, here he found them relatively poor – a prime example being the fact that the villain of the piece, Baron Ironblood, wore what appeared to be an upturned metal bucket on his head! On any other strip, Ron would have been able to rectify flaws such as this; but here the need to promote the toy range meant that his hands were tied, and he was powerless to make changes. His general dissatisfaction with the assignment wasn't helped, either, by the strip's hackneyed storylines, in which Ironblood served as a rehashed Hitler figure. Nevertheless, on some of the later stories he did return to his professional best and produce some impressive layouts.

The early months of 1984 saw Ron not only up against the clock with his weekly *Action Force* deadlines but also needing to finish off two more 64-page Picture Library assignments, and his fears about becoming overburdened with work were soon borne out as his health started to suffer. The situation wasn't improved by his circumstances, albeit self-imposed, of living on a houseboat, which meant he was regularly rocked about by passing river traffic! The constant stress of working in these conditions eventually affected him to such an extent that he suffered an angina attack. Under doctor's orders, he had to rest. And when he did return to work, it was with the strong advice not to take on any further commissions of a demanding nature – which meant no more *Action Force*, or any other regular weekly strips.

Although less than happy at this turn of events, Greg Hall now had no choice but to accept the situation. Consequently, Ron's *Action Force* run came to an end with the closing instalment of a story called 'Castle Death', published in the *Battle Action Force* issue dated 4 August 1984 – coincidentally, the day after his sixty-second birthday.

But although he would accept no more weekly strip work, or any further regular Picture Library assignments, Ron still had his less pressured holiday special and annual commissions to keep him gainfully employed. This year's bumper crop included strips for the *Action Man Annual 1985*, the *Buster Book 1985* and the *Eagle Annual 1985*, and a dot-to-dot story for the *Whoopee! Annual 1985*.

Below: Turner's covers for the 24 March and 4 August 1984 issues of *Battle Action Force*, the latter being the last to which he contributed.

There were also two contributions to the latest *Eagle Holiday Special*, one of which was an unusual departure for Ron, as not only did it take him into unaccustomed school strip territory, being an entry in the *Crowe Street Comp* series, but it also saw him make a special effort to capture the style of that series' original artist, Rex Archer. While a guest illustrator on a series would generally be expected not to stray too far from its established look, Ron's usual inclination was to put his own slant on the material, so that it was still recognisably his work. In this instance, though, liking the fact that Archer had taken a less 'cartoony' approach than most other artists who worked on humorous subject matter, he tried to emulate him more closely. Consequently, aside from a few trademark touches such as the style of lettering on the side a van and the type of speed lines used, there was little to identify him as the artist responsible. An enjoyable challenge for Ron, this produced an excellent, if atypical, result.

Once all these juvenile strip assignments were out of the way, though, there were no more in prospect until the following year; and if the previous excess of work had been stressful for Ron, then the current lack of it, coupled with all the spats they had been having of late, proved equally so for his agent. Sadly, it was now Hall who fell ill, suffering a stroke that left him incapacitated.

With his order book empty and his agent now out of action, Ron began to reflect on his situation. He was 62. If he could find another job – even something entirely different, and not too taxing, like school caretaking – it might be enough to keep his head above water until he reached the state pension age of 65. Then, with his love of life on the river, he could perhaps follow his dream and roam the waterways, stopping wherever and whenever he liked. However, if Ron thought his career as an artist was over, he was much mistaken. For, from a most unexpected quarter, a new opportunity was soon to come his way, and a new phase of his life would then begin.

Top left: the title page of 'Pirate Guns', published as War Picture Library Number 2056 in March 1984. This would be the last of Turner's many contributions to the Picture Library ranges.

Bottom left: one of Turner's pages for the *Crowe Street Comp* strip in the 1984-published *Eagle Holiday Special*.

PART 2:
1984-1998

Ron Turner at work in 1984 on a 'heroes' tableau' piece drawn as a private commission for author John Lawrence.

16: A QUEST BEGINS

In 1978, I attended the great Denis Gifford-organised Comics 103 convention in London and managed to acquire a good deal of published Ron Turner material of which I'd previously been unaware, including some of the classic *Rick Random* issues I'd missed out on first time around. This spurred me on to contact *2000 AD* and suggest that they revive *Rick Random*, with Ron as illustrator. The forces of fate are indeed strange, for not only had they already considered this idea, but a script had been written and was ready and waiting for Ron to work on, whenever he could fit it in between instalments of *The Spinball Wars*, which he was currently drawing for *Battle-Action*! This was like a dream come true for me – despite the fact that, when it eventually appeared in the spring of 1979, the new *Rick Random* story was not in the same league as the originals, and Ron, disillusioned with the scripts, had left another artist to complete it.

Encouraged by these events, I decided to write an appreciation of Ron's work, feeling it was high time he received some public recognition for the tremendous contribution he'd made to the SF genre on strips such as *Rick Random*, *Space Ace* and *The Daleks*. But although familiar with his work, I knew nothing of the man himself; and when I enquired of *2000 AD*, I was surprised to learn that they were equally in the dark – for, as art editor Kevin O'Neill informed me, Ron Turner was a very reclusive character whom no editor had ever met or spoken to. All dealings were conducted through his agent, a Mr Hall, who was reluctant to discuss his client and would allow no direct contact. This had prompted many questions over the years. Why didn't Turner show himself? Was he hideously deformed? Did he even exist as such, or was he actually Hall himself, working under a pseudonym? Hall was the only one who could provide the answers, and he wasn't giving anything away.

All this mystery served only to intrigue me further, and I determined to speak to Hall myself. Having obtained his phone number from O'Neill – who warned me that he could be a difficult man to deal with and that I should on no account reveal who had given me his details – I went ahead and contacted him. As predicted, Hall refused to let me speak to Ron. However, I soon discovered that this was just, as he saw it, a matter of professional propriety. When I expressed my disappointment that Ron was no longer working on *2000 AD* and explained my plan to write an article about him, this struck a sympathetic chord, and he was only too pleased to talk. Ron, he explained, was simply an intensely private person who preferred to go about his business in quiet anonymity and let his work speak for itself. He was also an artist of the old school, who had always worked through an agent and preferred to keep it that way. However, the business had now changed, and as the 'new wave' of editors at *2000 AD* liked to be able to discuss things direct with their artists, something Ron was unwilling to countenance, it was unlikely he would be supplying any further work for that comic.

Disappointed, but happy I had at least managed to obtain some information from Hall, I wrote my article, which duly appeared in the Spring 1980 edition of *Golden Fun* magazine. Subsequently I received some encouraging feedback from readers as far afield as Australia and New Zealand, but by far the most significant response came from much closer to home. Having happened upon my article quite by chance, Philip Harbottle, writer, collector and ex-editor of the '60s SF magazine *Vision of Tomorrow*, immediately contacted me, explaining that he was also a great fan of Ron's work, but that his interest stemmed from a different source: the marvellous covers that Ron had produced in the 1950s for Scion's Vargo Statten SF paperbacks, written by John Russell Fearn – something I'd not mentioned in my appreciation, for the simple reason I was unaware that Ron had worked on them. Phil soon enlightened me. The facts and figures he sent me about Ron's paperback cover work were indeed impressive, and they opened up for me a whole new field of collecting. Phil, for his part, had been similarly unaware of Ron's foray into the world of comics, assuming he had retired from the business when his book cover commissions had dried up, so discovering that this was not the case was great news for him – and learning that Ron was still around and still working was even better.

By now, in 1980, Ron was illustrating *Speed*'s *Journey to the Stars*, his first true SF strip in years, but Phil readily agreed with me that his talents were being squandered on such juvenile fare. Through dealing with John Russell Fearn's widow, Carrie, Phil had recently become literary executor of Fearn's estate, holding copyright in all his work, and he suggested this might yield suitable scripts on which Ron could reestablish his reputation with more mature SF work. Having put together some ideas that seemed to hold promise, he sent these to Hall, to be passed on to Ron. To his disappointment, Hall didn't even reply.

Feeling he had been wasting his time, Phil was ready to give up. I wasn't, though, so I contacted Hall myself, and urged him to give serious consideration to Phil's proposal. Hall was very wary, seemingly convinced that Phil was simply after financial gain for himself. I assured him this wasn't the case, and that there was a genuine desire to see Ron back working on strips that really played to his strengths. *Journey to the Stars* having now ended, Ron's current output consisted solely of one-off war strips and fill-ins for holiday specials and annuals, and when I complained that his true abilities were being overlooked by the current contingent of editors, this resonated strongly with Hall's own feelings, and we finally reached common ground.

To show my sincerity, I agreed to act on Hall's behalf in pitching the Fearn ideas not only to IPC but also to D C Thomson, Marvel and Polystyle. Sadly, nothing came of these approaches, but they did at least serve to demonstrate to Hall that Phil and I had honourable motives, and having finally accepted this, he confirmed that Ron was interested. With this added incentive, over the next few months we again bombarded IPC and D C Thomson with various story outlines. I then tried Fleet Street, and in particular the *Mail on Sunday Magazine*, for which Phil had prepared a script outline for a serialised strip adapting a four-novel Fearn series, *Emperor of Atlantis*. Unfortunately, the economic situation at the time was such that publishers were relying more and more on cheap reprint material and advertiser-sponsored strips, so our efforts proved largely unrewarding.

One of the few editors sympathetic to our cause was the *Eagle*'s David Hunt, a great admirer of Ron's work, who agreed to consider commissioning something from us. We took a long time selecting the most appropriate Fearn stories and preparing them for submission, but were then informed that they would need to be rewritten with 8- to 12-year-olds in mind – turning them into just the kind of juvenile fare we wanted Ron to be able to escape from. So, in the end, this came to nothing.

By this point, around three years had passed since we first started making our pitches to editors. Hall and I had remained constantly in touch during that period, and he had kept me regularly informed of Ron's situation. So it was that, in 1984, I learned of the downturn in Ron's health, and of his doctor's warning that he should accept no more stressful commissions, leaving him with no choice but to give up the weekly *Action Force* strip. This changed things dramatically. The priority was no longer to find Ron better or more appropriate work: now it was to find him any work at all!

The only bright spot on the horizon was the possibility that Ron might be in with a chance of contributing to D C Thomson's 64-page war comic *Commando*, or better still its SF companion *Starblazer*. However, in order for him to be able to cope with this, the deadlines would have to be as undemanding as they had been on his recent IPC Picture Library assignments, so this was something about which D C Thomson would have to be sounded out. The problem was, Hall had fallen out with the company back in 1981. At my suggestion, he agreed that I should contact them instead, the thinking being that if I presented myself as Ron's new agent, while he remained in the background, this might achieve the desired results. But if anything were to come of this, it would not be for some time – and Ron needed work right now.

Over the years, I had harboured the notion of commissioning Ron myself, to produce SF illustrations of my own devising and for my own pleasure. One idea that particularly appealed to me was to have all the main comic-strip characters he had drawn over the course of his career presented together in one action-packed scene: a kind of 'heroes' tableau'. This would involve the Daleks landing at London spaceport and being repelled by Rick

Random, Space Ace, the Wonder-Car team and Joe Taggart's Spinball bikers, amongst others. The scene would be fairly large and detailed and should therefore, I figured, be enough to keep Ron occupied for some time, as a stop-gap until something better came along. I sent my specifications off to Hall, expecting a grateful response – but far from it! Ron, it seemed, wasn't keen on the idea of accepting private commissions: if he was going to continue as an artist, he wanted *professional* work, and was prepared to wait until he got it. Eventually, though, appreciating what I was trying to do, he came round to the idea and agreed to take on the task, accepting that, whether private or professional, it was still work. In the meantime, hoping to secure him a *Starblazer* commission, I set about contacting D C Thomson.

Despite all the effort I had put in over the past few years to try to find suitable work for Ron, I had still never met him in person, my repeated requests to do so having been denied by Hall. It seemed to me that, by this time, I had plenty of justifiable work-related reasons to be in direct contact; besides which, I felt I deserved a chance to meet the man whose work I had fervently admired for more than thirty years. However, apparently believing that this would undermine his position as Ron's agent, Hall maintained that all script ideas and discussions should be channelled via him: Ron had never met with his editors or writers in the past, and that was the way he intended to keep it. This I considered a ludicrous insistence; and whether it was coming from Hall or from Ron himself, I decided it was high time things changed.

During my conversations with Hall, I'd hung onto his every word, and occasionally he'd inadvertently let slip a few clues as to Ron's whereabouts. Now, I don't know what type of place I had expected Ron to be living in; a large property with a studio annexe, perhaps, or a comfortable detached house with a dedicated workroom. What I hadn't expect to discover, courtesy of Hall, was that he was actually residing on a houseboat! Hall revealed that, following his divorce in 1982, Ron had decided to follow his dream and live on the river. Exactly where his houseboat was moored was never mentioned, but as Ron always delivered his artwork to his agent by hand, it didn't take a genius to work out that it must be not too far from where

Above: the 'heroes' tableau' piece, as used on the cover of a 1999 fanzine featuring a John Lawrence tribute to Turner.

Hall himself lived in New Malden, Surrey. This therefore placed it somewhere on the Thames. Checking through the phone books for the area, I eventually discovered a 'Turner' connected with a houseboat named *Sagittarius*. I felt sure this must be the right one; and further enquires finally gave me an address in Windsor.

So that was it. Despite Ron's inclination to remain out of sight, it seemed I had at last tracked him down – and his address was no more than about an hour's drive away from mine. However, it was the beginning of August and I was just about to drive my family down to the south coast for our annual holiday, so I decided I would have to let the matter drift for a couple of weeks and review the situation on my return. But, excited at the prospect of finally meeting Ron, I realised before the holiday was out that to pass through Windsor on the way back wouldn't require much of a detour. So, it was settled – Windsor would be our last stop before we returned home.

Above: a 'Mining on Titan' scene and a 'Repairing a Space-Station' scene: two of a small number of black-and-white illustrations that Turner completed in 1984 as private commissions for author John Lawrence.

17: A DREAM IS REALISED

It was on the sweltering hot afternoon of Saturday 18 August 1984 that my family and I arrived in Windsor and found our way to Willows Riverside Park – the address I'd discovered, backing onto the local moorings where I believed Ron's houseboat to be located. Reaching the towpath, we began to follow it, taking in all the various craft moored along the riverside. One boat after another went by without significance – until suddenly we came across a squat brown vessel and there, on the side, I spotted the name I was looking for: *Sagittarius*. But surely this was too easy, I thought. Maybe I'd got it wrong. Maybe it was another Turner who lived here. I really couldn't believe that after all this time I'd actually found Ron Turner, the SF illustrator whose fantastic images had thrilled me so much during my boyhood. But as I approached the gangplank leading to the cabin door, there on the side of the boat was the name again, *Sagittarius*, this time rendered in Ron's unmistakable script, with a small image of the zodiacal archer accompanying it in his equally inimitable style. Yes, this was undoubtedly it. If he was home, then I was finally about to meet the man himself. But then, as I considered my achievement, excitement slowly turned to doubt. Greg Hall had continually emphasised that Ron was an intensely private individual. To descend on him unannounced might leave him upset or even angry at my intrusion and possibly ruin any future association – something I certainly didn't want. On the other hand, as my wife pointedly stated, my wanting to contact Ron was for all the right reasons, and to have come this far and not follow through with it would mean that all my efforts had been wasted. Encouraged, I left my family on the towpath, boarded the boat and tentatively rang the doorbell. Long seconds passed, then cautiously the door opened a little to reveal a small, wiry man with greying hair, wearing only a pair of shorts. I nervously enquired if he was Ron Turner, the artist. He confirmed that he was, and I began to introduce myself, wondering how I would be received, only for him to interrupt me in mid-flow to explain that his agent, Greg Hall, had already told him all about me and my attempts to put work his way. Then, expressing surprise that I'd obviously taken the trouble to 'carry out a little detective work' in order to find him, he welcomed me inside. Somewhat relieved at his kindly welcome, I followed Ron into his studio-cum-living quarters, a small but comfortable area with on one side a bed-settee, table and chair and on the other a drawing board under a large window looking out onto the river. A thermometer on the wall indicated that the temperature was over 90 degrees, but such was the thrill of the moment that I was completely oblivious to the heat as I began to relate my long-time admiration for Ron's work, mentioning all the high points of his career and the fanbase he still had, and finishing with my disappointment that he wasn't drawing the new *Dan Dare* for the *Eagle*. The conversation then suddenly turned to Frank Hampson, Ron making it clear that he would rather discuss Hampson's work than his own! Hampson had obviously been as much a hero to Ron as Ron had to me; as he saw it, he had simply followed in the master's wake.

We talked a lot about Hampson and about Ron's other influences, and I then asked about his current work situation. He admitted that, apart from the large scene he'd recently completed for me, he'd had none for weeks, adding that he didn't really expect any more. It was at this point he broke the news that Hall had suffered a stroke and would have to retire from the business – something of which I'd been completely unaware, having only just returned from holiday. Then he dropped the bombshell that, with no work and no agent, he was also inclined to call it a day and take a less demanding job, perhaps as a school caretaker! Shocked and dismayed at the prospect, I quickly explained that I'd already contacted D C Thomson with the intention of securing him work on *Starblazer*, and was currently awaiting their reply. I also assured him that I would approach IPC for any annual assignments available, and commission him myself for further private work, adding that there would doubtless be others, including Phil Harbottle,

Above: Ron Turner at the entrance to his houseboat, the *Sagittarius*, with its hand-painted sign.

who would be interested. Just then my family, having grown impatient waiting on the towpath, arrived on deck – much to Ron's bewilderment, until I explained who they were and why they were there. Considering that Ron had been living the life of a virtual recluse, to find a group of complete strangers overrunning his boat must have been disconcerting to say the least, but he seemed to take it in good spirits, no doubt buoyed by my talk of finding him work.

Just as I was about to leave, I noticed some artwork stacked in one corner. It was still at the pencil stage, which I thought odd, as Ron had indicated he had nothing currently in progress. When I asked about it, he explained that it was the first dozen or so pages of his very last War Picture Library commission, a story called *Whiplash*, which he had abandoned as IPC had cancelled the range prior to its publication. He could have submitted these pages and been paid for what he had already done, but had thought it hardly worthwhile. In fact, he said, he was about to throw the pages away. Up to now, Ron had still perhaps not fully appreciated just how much I valued his work – but then he saw the expression of abject horror on my face at the thought of these pages being lost! He wondered if I would like to have them. Would I! I was absolutely delighted, and Ron modestly declared that at least this had made my trip worthwhile. I began to discuss the work further, but Ron then reminded me that my family were still waiting – his tactful way of indicating that my time was up. So I rejoined my family and departed, promising to be in touch with more commissions to come.

Looking back, I would like to think that my arrival that day in August 1984 came as a breath of fresh air to Ron. Given his dire work situation, he must have been feeling pretty low and worried about his future. But then, out of the blue, I had turned up with the offer of new commissions; and although I couldn't pay him anything like the same rates as IPC, the subject matter would at least be in his preferred SF genre. So, monetary considerations aside, he was suddenly back in business and had a renewed sense of purpose – something for which he would be forever grateful, as he would later stress to me many times.

The following week I phoned Greg Hall's wife, Joan, to enquire after his health and explain about my meeting with Ron. Fortunately the stroke hadn't affected Hall's speech or cognitive abilities, but it had left him needing to use a wheelchair, making life difficult for both of them. Hall had already heard of my visit to Ron, and was at pains to warn me that I would be dealing with a very temperamental individual who had quite inflexible ideas about how work should be handled. He then proceeded to recount a litany of problems he'd had with Ron over the past few years, even seeming to blame him for the stroke. He claimed that since his divorce Ron had become very choosy about which assignments he would and wouldn't accept; if he didn't like a particular script, he would simply put it in a drawer and forget about it. When he did accept work, he would often deliver it late, even if Hall had given him an artificially early deadline to try to avoid this. There would be times when Ron would tackle a job only under protest, with Hall sitting by, waiting for it to be completed. And when it *was* completed, it would sometimes be sloppily executed. Ron's last War Picture Library story had indeed been abandoned, but not entirely due to the range's imminent cancellation as he had claimed. Apparently he had lost all enthusiasm for it on learning that the script had been written by a woman, furiously complaining that she couldn't possibly have any idea what life was like as an infantryman! Hall's reminder that principles don't pay bills had left him unmoved.

Hall was clearly also quite bitter about Ron having quit the *Action Force* strip, insisting that it could have given him at least two years' good work if only he had knuckled down and got on with it. Recalling that Ron had coped with producing four pages of artwork per week at other points in his career, he couldn't accept that this was so great a burden as to have made him ill.

It seemed Hall simply hadn't grasped that Ron was now much older and that his circumstances had changed. Living on his own on a houseboat, with no young children to support and no mortgage to pay,

he no longer needed such a high income and had no incentive to suffer such a punishing schedule. Hall himself, on the other hand, was still reliant on the hefty percentage he received from the commissions, and the thought that Ron had thrown away the opportunity of working on a long-running strip had incensed him to such a degree that, as he saw it, it had brought about his current condition.

I could see both points of view, and although it was unlikely Ron would ever be willing to take on another four-page weekly strip, or even a three-page one, I reminded Hall that comics such as *Tiger* and *Eagle* were still running some two-page strips, which might be a reasonable compromise. I offered to contact IPC's group editor Barrie Tomlinson on his behalf and try to pick up an assignment that Ron would be prepared to accept, and so please both camps. Hall agreed, but warned me that on no account should I give out Ron's address if asked for it . If Tomlinson were to contact Ron direct to criticise or complain about some issue with the artwork, Ron would only react badly and, in so doing, lose the commission. On occasions in the past, Hall added, editors had noted in their scripts that Ron should ring them if he needed clarification of certain scenes, but this had been nothing more than a ruse to try to establish direct contact with him. Hall would therefore vet all scripts in advance and take out any of these 'invitations' before Ron saw them, so maintaining a healthy distance between editors and artist. He had had to be the diplomat, and although this had meant taking a great deal of flak from both sides, he had generally managed to keep things on an even keel and keep the commissions flowing in – until now.

Two days later, I attended a meeting I'd arranged with Barrie Tomlinson at IPC. Also present was Ian Vosper, editor of the sports comic *Tiger*. I had taken along some examples of the football strips Ron had produced for *Scoop* several years earlier, reasoning that although he wasn't keen on the subject matter, a sports series might fill a gap while I was still awaiting a response from D C Thomson about *Starblazer*. However, neither man was very impressed with Ron's work. They liked the layouts and the action scenes but clearly realised that Ron had no enthusiasm for football. The players all looked too clean – none had their hair unruly, socks down or shirt hanging out. In short, the treatment lacked realism. My argument that if such details were to be specified in the scripts, Ron would surely draw them, cut no ice with Vosper, who pointed out that if an artist had an affinity for the subject matter, he would put in all the necessary details, and more, without having to be told to do so. The two men felt that even if Ron were to be given precise instructions, after a few weeks he would probably fall back on his usual style of presentation; so, all in all, they were unable to use him on *Tiger*.

Tomlinson added that he had considered commissioning Ron for the *Eagle*'s new *Dan Dare* strip, but had been concerned that after only a short time his depiction of Dare's features would revert to his usual 'stock hero' type, and they would then have trouble getting him to change it, or else would have to ask another artist to make adjustments. Moreover, he felt that Ron's SF work was now a little dated. What they wanted for the *Dan Dare* strip was something more in the *Star Wars* line, insofar as spacecraft and hardware were concerned. This last assertion left me baffled, as my understanding was that a conscious effort was being made to use designs reflecting the style of Hampson's 1950s originals. However, it seemed that Tomlinson's real concern was the old sticking point that he wanted direct communication with the artist, to ensure that all editorial requirements were fully understood and that any issues that arose could be easily remedied.

Tomlinson then noted that – as Hall had told me – IPC had sometimes in the past included a phone number in their scripts and suggested that Ron get in touch with them if he wanted to discuss any points of uncertainty; but, for whatever reason, these invitations had never been taken up. They had even tried to arrange mutually convenient meetings, but again nothing had come of this. Tomlinson accepted that Ron had a great talent, but nevertheless felt that there were aspects of his work that needed attention, and until these could be talked through and addressed, it was difficult for IPC to consider taking him back on a regular series.

Hall having left me in no doubt that Ron would never be amenabe to such direct contact, I realised I was getting nowhere with this line of discussion, so I decided to try another tack. *Tiger* was at that time running a two-page SF strip called *Sintek*, which was so appallingly drawn that I felt sure Ron would be considered a preferable option, even if he didn't follow the scripts to the letter. But apparently not. Vosper insisted that the current artist, although a newcomer, was flexible, willing to learn, very approachable, and timely in delivering his work. Consequently, he would rather stick with him than have to deal with an artist who, although top-rate, could be problematical. This was a big disappointment to me, as the strip would have been ideal for Ron. However, Vosper's attitude made it quite apparent I would get no joy there.

As a last try, not wanting to go away empty-handed, I asked if there was any one-off strip work that Ron might be given. All of that year's holiday special and annual assignments having already been completed, the only hope Tomlinson could offer me was that *Battle Action Force* editor Terry Magee might have one or two self-contained stories needing an illustrator. While I was sceptical of the wisdom of approaching the very man Ron had recently let down when he backed out of the *Action Force* series, Tomlinson seemed keen to take me along to meet Magee, so although this was probably just a sop for having failed to give me anything himself, I figured nothing ventured, nothing gained.

However, my fears were soon borne out. When I explained who I was and what I was after, the stoutly-built Magee drew himself out of his chair, leaned over his desk and, towering over me, declared that there was no work he could give me. He ran a war comic, he thundered, and Ron's style was 'wholly inappropriate' to the subject matter! Taken aback, I countered that Ron was surely one of IPC's best war artists and, having actually served in the Second World War, must be better suited to this type of work than any young newcomer. Magee then came out with something that left me even more astonished: he said he would put any of his other artists up against Ron, for in his considered opinion, 'Turner is more suited to drawing elves and dragons!' To this day, I find that statement totally perplexing. Did he perhaps mean 'aliens and monsters' rather than 'elves and dragons'? Whatever the case, It was obvious Magee held very bitter feelings toward Ron, and quite clearly I was wasting my time.

I left, realising that my only chance now lay with D C Thomson and *Starblazer*.

A DREAM IS REALISED

A 'Futuristic City' scene: another of the private commissions that Turner took on in 1984.

A second 'Futuristic City' private commission scene illustrated by Turner in 1984.

18: A RETURN TO SF

Over the next few days, I contacted several friends who were fans of Ron's work, telling them of my meeting with him and of his current predicament. One who responded immediately was Phil Harbottle. Phil had for a number of years been privately publishing reprints of some of John Russell Fearn's short stories in digest-size booklet form, using for the covers either astronomical photos, spot illustrations recycled from the original publications or artwork of his own. The chance to get Ron back working on a Fearn subject after a gap of more than 30 years was one he couldn't pass up, so he commissioned him to provide black-and-white front and back covers for his next release, *The Slitherers*. This was just the first of many jobs Phil would put Ron's way, and was quickly followed by a request for him to produce a full colour recreation of his original 1954 cover for the novel *Hand of Havoc*, to be presented to the author E C Tubb as a surprise gift on his sixty-fifth birthday. Other comic and SF fans such as actor David Ashford and book dealer Norman Wright also rallied round, suggesting futuristic scenes they would like Ron to produce for them; and I had a few more commissions of my own to give him too. So, all in all, Ron was kept quite busy over the following weeks.

All this sudden interest seemed to have a revitalising effect on Ron, for he began to turn out some of his best work in ages. A 'Starship at the Edge of the Universe' scene drawn at my request was reminiscent of his finest *Rick Random* output; a sure sign that he was enjoying his return to the SF genre, and gratified to know that there was still an appreciative audience for his favoured type of work. My concern, however, was that this happy situation would be short-lived, for I still needed to find him a regular professional commission. Having still had no word from D C Thomson, I wrote again to editor Bill McLoughlin. This time I did receive a reply, though not exactly the one I was hoping for.

I had supplied samples of Ron's *Journey to the Stars* strip from *Speed*, this being his most recent SF work, but McLoughlin had picked up on its juvenile tone and told me he considered the style too 'comicy' for *Starblazer*'s readership, adding as a footnote that at present he was really looking for new writers rather than new artists. Having read some of *Starblazer*'s stories, I certainly agreed that he needed new writers: writers who could actually compose a proper sentence, never mind provide decent dialogue, story ideas and plot. But, aside from contributions from a couple of reasonable ex-IPC regulars, I found the title's artwork equally poor, so I could see no reason why Ron shouldn't be welcomed if I demonstrated that he was capable of handling more mature material. Feeling that something in the *Rick Random* line might impress McLoughlin, I sent him examples of that series, expecting a more positive response this time. Again, though, I was rebuffed. Obviously aware that the *Rick Random* layouts were over 25 years old, McLoughlin wanted to see something more up-to-date. The difficulty was, Ron hadn't worked on any mature SF strips in recent years. He could, of course, produce some new samples specifically for McLoughlin to consider, but what to base them on?

Phil and I put our heads together and initially thought about scripting some Fearn story extracts for Ron to draw. But then, picking up on McLoughlin's comment that he was seeking new writers, we realised we could take this one step further by reverting to the approach we'd first tried a few years earlier, proposing a full, serialised Fearn adaptation, scripted by us and illustrated by Ron. That way, we might be able to sell *Starblazer* a complete package.

Phil immediately set about choosing a suitable Fearn story, quickly focusing in on two novelettes originally published in American SF magazines. The first, *The Micro Invasion*, was based on a 1937 *Thrilling Wonder Stories* entry. However, although this was a great read, it contained several horrific elements such as bodies being ripped apart and men and women being vivisected on operating tables, which seemed to make it unsuitable both for D C Thomson and for Ron himself. The second candidate was *Special Agent to Venus*, which originally appeared in the October 1940 issue of

Above: the front and back cover pieces that Philip Harbottle commissioned from Turner in 1984 for his private first edition publication of John Russell Fearn's *The Slitherers*.

Fantastic Adventures. This was more in the line of a *Dan Dare/Rick Random* adventure, and seemed the better option, so I asked Ron to produce a few sample illustrations of key scenes, including a dogfight in space; an attack by weird, pterodactyl-like creatures; spacecraft approaching the ringed defence system of a planet; and the emergence of the planet's giant alien inhabitants – all elements that would show his work to its best advantage. However, when I sent these on to McLoughlin, his response was once more negative. Although he liked Ron's clean line-work, he disapproved of the *Dan Dare*-type storyline, which he felt again made the style too 'comicy' and not 'straight' enough for his needs.

More promising were McLoughlin's closing words, indicating that he might be interested in seeing any storylines I could supply in a tougher, edgier, more *2000 AD* vein. This encouraged me to think that *The Micro Invasion* might, after all, be suitable, bearing in mind that the gorier elements could be watered down or cut if necessary. But when I proposed this to McLoughlin, unfortunately my original assumption proved correct. He told me that D C Thomson would not approve this type of story, even with severe editing; and, to clarify matters, he enclosed a writers' guide setting out all the dos and don'ts of scripting for *Starblazer* – a guide that, when I read it, appeared to me not only restrictive but also hypocritical, as the comic actually included in its stories some of the very elements McLoughlin claimed to find objectionable. Despite having raised my hopes in his previous letter, McLoughlin ended by declaring that he deemed Ron's artwork unacceptable, as it failed to match the house style of *Starblazer*'s other artists – a point with which I could only agree, as it was actually far superior!

Realising that we were wasting our time, Phil and I abandoned any further attempt to promote Ron's strip work to McLoughlin. However, I still held out some hope that cover work might prove a different matter. There were only a few cover artists that D C Thomson used on *Starblazer*, and although the excellent Ian Kennedy was amongst them, he also did cover work for *Commando*, and it seemed to me that Ron could easily fill in for him when other, less talented artists might otherwise be called upon.

In view of McLoughlin's earlier request for examples of 'recent work' and his emphasis on 'house style', I arranged for Ron to produce a spec colour cover based on elements taken from an issue of *Starblazer* itself, thinking this might be more likely to find favour than examples of his old cover work or a piece based on one of the Fearn stories. The resultant painting was, in my eyes, superb, and easily on a par with any of Kennedy's. I felt sure that if Ron were to be given regular *Starblazer* cover work, not only would he be in his element but he would also help to boost the comic's profile, just as Kennedy was doing on *Commando*. But when I submitted the piece to McLoughlin, he didn't agree. In a brief note of reply, he stated that Ron's style was dated and lacked impact, and was therefore totally unsuited to D C Thomson's requirements.

That Ron, a highly respected artist who had made his name in the SF genre, and whose expertise with colour was second to none, should be passed over in favour of inferior newcomers, was absolutely unbelievable to me, and an insult to his talent. But clearly D C Thomson were not an easy company to deal with, and whether their repeated rejections were a legacy of Hall's disagreement with them a few years earlier or a consequence of their known bias against using artists from south of the border, Phil and I were left in no doubt that if we wanted Ron to be able to continue working, and in the SF genre, we would have to find some way of achieving this ourselves.

Phil had many more Fearn booklets he intended to publish privately, all of which would need covers, but these alone would not be enough to give Ron the volume of work he'd need. Then it dawned on us: if, instead of simply reprinting Fearn's stories, he were to commission Ron to illustrate comic-strip reinterpretations of them, with two or three frames to the page, this would be far more substantial and should enable Ron to continue his career – provided the idea met with his approval, of course.

Phil searched through his vast collection of Fearn stories to try to find one with enough futuristic hardware and action to appeal to Ron. Most were either unsuitable or would require a considerable amount of rewriting. However, we soon realised that what we were looking for was right under our noses: the *Special Agent to Venus* tale we had tried to sell to D C Thomson. Although this would run to almost double the length of the 32-page booklet we had planned, a possible solution would be to split it into two volumes, published very close together. But, of course, this was all academic unless we had Ron's agreement.

A few days later, I paid Ron a visit. On entering his houseboat studio, I was intrigued to see his scratchpad covered in drawings of prehistoric creatures. Initially I assumed these were just doodles, but then he explained that David Hunt, the IPC editor who had always admired his work, was looking for an artist to take over from Jim Baikie on the *Eagle*'s *Bloodfang* strip, set mainly in prehistoric times, and he was amongst those in the frame for it. How this opportunity had arisen I was not quite sure – possibly my earlier efforts on Ron's behalf had finally borne fruit, or possibly Greg Hall was still making efforts of his own – but, in any event, the strip required only three pages of artwork per week, and Ron reckoned he could cope with it. That said, he was in two minds about it, as the storyline would involve him drawing page after page of dinosaurs fighting, and while on the one hand that repetition would make his task easier, on the other it would make it quite a tedious assignment. But in light of the bad news regarding *Starblazer*, he felt he had no choice but to try for it, if he still wanted regular well-paid work.

Then, though, I told Ron of the plans Phil and I had for a *Dan Dare/Rick Random*-style SF comic strip we would like him to illustrate, and this seemed to interest him a lot more than the idea of drawing endless scenes of battling dinosaurs. I gave him a synopsis of the story for consideration, emphasising that if he were to take it on there would be no deadline pressures, and adding that while sadly we could not match IPC's rate of pay, we hoped that, as it would be in a small, digest-size format, similar to the War Picture Library, he would be willing to accept around 50% of his usual fee for this type of work. Before leaving, I also explained that Phil would like if possible to commission him for a series of full colour, unlettered recreations of some of his best Vargo Statten covers, and handed him original paperback copies of the first two: *Annihilation!* (1950) and *The Inner Cosmos* (1952).

Ron later phoned to confirm that he was interested in taking on both Phil's vintage cover recreations and, perhaps more significantly, our proposed comic strip, though he did have a concern about the fee for the latter: it was not so much that he was unhappy with the amount on offer – Phil and I having agreed to share the cost between us – as that he was worried we might not actually come through with payment! I assured him we would, and said that we could even pay in advance if he would prefer. Noting my sincerity, he declined the offer of advance payment and agreed to our terms. This was his type of story, he said, and he would be pleased to be back working on a decent script at last, after all the repetitive juvenile material he'd had to contend with in recent years. I suspect he may also have seen in us something of himself 30 years earlier, when he had been in a similar position – full of enthusiasm to produce his own comics. Nothing had come of the possible *Bloodfang* assignment, and while I never learned if this was because he had turned it down or because Hunt, possibly influenced by Tomlinson, had removed him from the shortlist, I'd like to think it was Ron's genuine desire to work with us that had swayed the outcome. Either way, Phil and I were delighted. From that point on, Greg Hall's health issues having forced him to retire, I became Ron's new agent; and over the years that followed, I would keep him almost continuously supplied with work, whether Phil's Vargo Statten cover recreations or completely new commissions.

Fired by Ron's acceptance, Phil set about preparing a script for the first instalment of *Special Agent to Venus*. Comic strips had been a large part of his life as a child, and even into his teens, when his enthusiasm for Frank Hampson's *Dan Dare* had led him to write and draw his own versions of the character's exploits, many of them adapted from Radio Luxembourg's *The Adventures of Dan Dare* serials of the '50s. More recently, he had also produced comic-strip adaptations of some of Fearn's novelettes and even full-length novels. So he knew how to structure a story and could clearly visualise each panel he wanted. Moreover, he had picked up how to format a script professionally back in 1982, when writer and artist David Lloyd, having gained his permission to serialise a Fearn novel, *The Golden Amazon*, for Dez Skinn's *Warrior* magazine, had sent him the drafts for approval. Consequently Phil had all the skills he needed.

Keen to create a new space hero in the grand tradition of Dan Dare and Rick Random, Phil and I decided to rename the story's main character Nick Hazard – coincidentally also the name of a professional footballer, though neither of us knew that at the time! – and whereas in Fearn's original he had been confined to our solar system we chose to make him an Interstellar Agent, emphasising this by retitling the story *Mission to Vorga*. Also in the classic tradition, we gave Hazard a sidekick, Viona Kenyon, a strong female who would become his regular companion. If the publication proved successful, the pair could then feature in further Fearn adaptations set anywhere in the universe.

In plot terms, *Mission to Vorga* tells of a war between Earth and Vorga. The human forces on Vorga are being decimated by a deadly plague, and Hazard has to get an antidote formula through to their scientists, crossing a barrier of armed satellites and the Vorgan space fleet on the way. When Phil sent me the first part of the script a few days before Christmas 1984, I was delighted with how it was shaping up. Over the holidays I added some ideas of my own, then the phone line between us became red-hot as we discussed each other's amendments, refining the story until we were satisfied it would do full justice both to Fearn's original and to Ron's talents. We also decided that, to give Ron more time to produce the artwork, we would split it over not two but three monthly booklets, rounding out the contents with reprints of some of his original *Space Ace* strips – the first time any of these had seen print since the '50s!

As the New Year approached, we were both excited at the prospect of what lay ahead. 1984 had been the year that Ron Turner finally returned to his first love – science fiction. 1985, we hoped, would see our *Nick Hazard* collaboration go from strength to strength. However, plans don't always work out.

Painted early in 1985 as a private commission for Philip Harbottle, Turner's recreation of his cover for *Annihilation!* (Scion, 1950).

Painted early in 1985 as a private commission for Philip Harbottle, Turner's recreation of his cover for *The Inner Cosmos* (Scion, 1952).

19: HAZARDS AHEAD

During January and February 1985, Phil compiled the scripts for the second and third parts of our new *Nick Hazard* strip. Once more we supplemented Fearn's original story with fresh elements of our own, including a sequence of Hazard's ship crash-landing on Vorga's moon, exposing him to the dangers of an alien jungle replete with carnivorous vegetation! Again, we spent a great deal of time thrashing out action scenes and revising narrative and dialogue until we felt they were good enough to inspire Ron to produce his best work. I then set about choosing two cliffhanger points and proceeded to lay out the frames for the three issues, leaving Ron with scope to make alterations wherever he felt necessary. Finally, we had a full set of three scripts we felt satisfied with, and in March, I delivered the first of them to Ron.

In the meantime, Ron had not been idle. Ironically, while we had been creating a *Dan Dare*-type strip for him, he had at last been offered an opportunity to contribute to the real thing – or at least, the nearest IPC would ever get to it. The commission was for a story in the 1985 *Eagle Holiday Special*, and although Ron had been keen to take on Hampson's creation, he was unprepared to discover, on receiving the script, the travesty it had become. Having always associated *Dan Dare* with mature storylines and strong scientific content, he found this puerile entry involving a giant, rampaging, one-eyed alien gorilla distinctly uninspiring. However, the opportunity to produce a full-colour double-page centre-spread and six pages of black-and-white line-and-wash was ample compensation for the script's shortcomings.

Below: Turner's full-page centre-spread for the *Dan Dare* story 'The Mighty Colossus' in 1985's *Eagle Holiday Special*. A section of this artwork was also reused as the main illustration on the special's front cover.

This *Dan Dare* strip was followed by a few other one-offs for that year's IPC annuals and for World Distributors' *The A-Team Annual 1986*, and Phil and I were pleased to see Ron receiving these new professional commissions, as the income he gained from them would at least supplement the comparatively meagre amount we were paying for our own work. That work included further recreations, for both of us, of vintage Vargo Statten and Volsted Gridban paperback covers, such as those for *Exit Life* (1953), *Scourge of the Atom* (1953) and one of Phil's – and Fearn's – favourites, *The Genial Dinosaur* (1954). But it was our new *Nick Hazard* strip that was uppermost in our minds, and as Ron started in on the illustrations, we were anxious to see the results. This being a low-paid semi-professional commission, my concern was that Ron might not give it his best efforts. However, I needn't have worried. When the first few pages were completed, it was obvious that he was totally committed to the project; not only was the overall standard excellent but, under Ron's expert hand, various unscripted enhancements had been made and some wordy two-frame sequences had been transformed into dynamic single frames.

I sent Phil photocopies of the pages for him to check, and over these he pasted the scripted narrative and dialogue balloons, adjusted as necessary to allow for Ron's modifications. Unfortunately, though, some of the changes Ron had made were inconsistent with basic plot requirements. For instance, he had depicted Vorga with a cratered surface, whereas it should have had Earth-like continents. He had also shown only a couple of space forts orbiting the planet, whereas it should have been ringed by them. Years before, when I'd had an opportunity to view some of Ron's original *Rick Random* artwork, I'd been annoyed to see that certain parts of it had been amended by way of editorial paste-overs. Now, though, when I was in the position of editor myself, I could well understand why those changes might have been necessary; and in view of the warnings I'd had from Hall about the highly negative way Ron would react if ever his work was questioned or criticised, I realised I was left with no choice but to make similar amendments of my own.

Above: the title page of a story Turner illustrated for the boxing-themed series *The Fists of Danny Pyke*; this saw print in the *Eagle Annual 1986*, published in the autumn of 1985.

Thankfully, it wasn't too difficult for me to paste over the craters and add a few lines to suggest continents; and the space forts Ron had drawn could be photocopied several times at different sizes and the copies added to the scene. Once this operation had been successfully carried out and Phil and I were satisfied with the quality of the work, in both literary and artistic terms, I took on the chore of lettering the pages; and although this proved to be not as easy as I'd imagined, I felt the outcome was quite adequate.

In the meantime, we kept Ron busy with yet more full-colour recreations of his classic SF paperback covers; and Phil now decided to take this a step further by commissioning him to produce a 'what might have been' piece based on the Vargo Statten novel *Cataclysm* (1951), one of Fearn's very best stories set in a futuristic utopia, which he had been denied the opportunity to interpret before, as

Turner's 1985 recreation of his original cover for the Volsted Gridban novel *The Genial Dinosaur* (Scion, 1954).

The 1985 Philip Harbottle-commissioned Turner illustration based on the 1951 Vargo Statten novel *Cataclysm*.

another artist had been assigned to provide the cover on its original publication. Was Ron's old magic still there? It certainly was! His gorgeous, colourful composition, showing the decadent lifestyle of a populace waited on hand and foot by both slave girls and robots, was a perfect distillation of the story's central theme – and it became just the first of many such originals that Phil would commission from Ron over the next couple of years, alongside additional vintage cover reproductions and in between work on our comic-strip magazine.

But although producing the magazine was something we could do ourselves, marketing it would be more challenging. We first approached Nick Landau of Titan Magazines in the hope that he would agree to handle the distribution, but on seeing the completed pages, he raised several concerns. First, he felt that my lettering, while it might be quite adequate for a fanzine, lacked the professionalism needed to do Ron's artwork full justice. Secondly, the A5 format we had chosen for the magazine was again more typical of a fanzine than a professional publication, and meant that it would not match other titles on the sales racks. Thirdly, as its cover would be in black-and-white – colour printing being unaffordable for us – this would only reinforce the impression of it being a fanzine, deterring many potential buyers from even picking it up. In short, in its current format, this was not a publication that Titan would be prepared to take on.

While Landau's points were all undeniably valid, this dealt us quite a blow. To address the first issue, Landau offered to contact a professional letterer for us; but cost considerations again ruled this out. Our project appeared doomed, until suddenly I realised we had the answer all along: all I had to do was arrange for Ron to letter the artwork himself! After all, he had handled the lettering on all his early comic strips, up to and including *Space Ace*, so who better to do it? When asked, Ron readily agreed, and the next time I visited him to collect the latest batch of cover art, I found that he had actually taken the trouble to prepare samples of his lettering – including straight and italic and upper- and lower-case characters – as if to prove that his skills in this regard hadn't flagged over the years – not that I had ever had any doubts, of course.

Landau's other two objections, however, were ones we could not overcome. The artwork had already been prepared for an A5 format, and our limited budget restricted our printing options. So, having come this far, and wanting to keep Ron motivated, we decided we had no choice but to change tack and distribute the magazine ourselves, through outlets such as comic-mart dealers, science-fiction bookshops, and mail-order adverts in comic fanzines. Optimistic about our prospects, we agreed that for each issue we would print the highest number of copies we could, using the cheapest method we could, until the quality began to deteriorate – which we later discovered would happen around the 400 copy mark.

By this time, we had decided to call the magazine *JRF Presents: Nick Hazard, Interstellar Agent* – the *JRF* of course standing for John Russell Fearn – so that if our new space hero character failed to find favour with the readership we could simply drop the *Nick Hazard* part and switch to presenting other Fearn stories instead. Ron then produced some striking title logos, while Phil prepared an editorial and I photocopied the artwork and got the pages camera-ready; and although full-colour printing remained beyond our means, I was at least able to add a splash of red spot-colour to the cover, in the hope that this would help to make the magazine stand out.

One thing Phil and I were very keen to do with this endeavour was to ensure that Ron received further long-overdue public recognition. Over the years, his reluctance to sign any of his work had left a legion of fans not even knowing who he was. With *Nick Hazard*, we decided, all that should change. Consequently, we not only featured his name on the cover but also used the editorial to highlight his involvement and detail some of the huge contributions he had already made to the SF genre during the course of his career.

With the first issue assembled and printed, bearing a September/October 1985 cover date, we proceeded as planned by distributing copies to various comic-mart dealers and suitable bookshops throughout the country and placing adverts in comic fanzines such as Denis Gifford's *Ace* and Martin Lock's *Fantasy Advertiser*. The orders we received in response were reasonable rather than

Above: the covers of the first two issues of *JRF Presents: Nick Hazard, Interstellar Agent*; and the title pages of their respective instalments of *Mission to Vorga*. For extra impact, the covers were printed on coloured paper.

HAZARDS AHEAD

Above: the front cover of the third issue of *JRF Presents: Nick Hazard, Interstellar Agent*, published in January 1986; and the title page of the corresponding third and final part of the *Mission to Vorga* strip story.

spectacular, but nevertheless sufficient for us to press on and produce the second and third issues, completing the *Mission to Vorga* story. Sadly, though, sales had not increased across the six-month run, and we were barely breaking even. We realised that if we were to boost our circulation we would need to heed Nick Landau's words and move to the larger American comic format, with around 32 pages per issue and a full-colour cover. This would also benefit Ron by giving him more creative freedom than the current limit of two or three frames per page allowed. While the cost of making these changes would still be prohibitive for us alone, fortunately Titan were now satisfied that their initial concerns had been addressed, and they provisionally agreed to back us by publishing and distributing the next issue.

In view of the format change, we decided to dispense with the *Space Ace* back-up strip and in future have each issue present a complete one-off story. For the first of these, Phil chose to adapt a 1951 Scion-published Vargo Statten novel called *The Red Insects*, which had itself been adapted by Fearn from a 1938 *Thrilling Wonder Stories* novelette called *Lords of 9016*. In his script, Phil cleverly took elements from both of Fearn's earlier versions, making judicious changes to accommodate the Nick Hazard character, expand the action from an Earth-based setting to an interstellar one and introduce additional 22nd Century elements that he knew would bring out the best in Ron's work, such as an underground alien city and an asteroid-like spacecraft.

The result was a better-developed story than *Mission to Vorga*, with far more visual potential, and we felt that we at last had a chance of cracking the US market. However, in early 1986, just as Ron was about to start work on the illustrations, from out of the blue he received a commission from IPC to tackle another *Dan Dare* strip, to appear in that year's *Eagle Holiday Special*. Phil and I greeted this news with mixed feelings: while on the one hand we were delighted for Ron that he was getting more fully-professional work, on the other we were frustrated by the inconvenient timing. We had no choice but to wait; but within a week of Ron delivering the *Holiday Special* artwork, he was asked by IPC to produce three more one-off strips – one for the *Eagle Annual 1987* and two for the *Dan Dare Annual 1987*. These assignments would take him at least two months to complete and push our project back even further – making our planned June publication date no longer achievable.

One of Turner's exciting page layouts for the *Nick Hazard* story *Mission to Vorga*, taken in this case from the debut instalment.

One of two Turner pieces commissioned by Philip Harbottle in 1985 for a planned but unpublished reissue of John Russell Fearn's short story 'The Last Secret Weapon', which he wrote under the pseudonym Polton Cross for the April 1941 issue of the US pulp *Marvel Stories*. This was the story Fearn later expanded into the Vargo Statten novel *The G-Bomb* (Scion, 1952).

Turner's 1985 recreation of his original cover for the Alvin Westwood novel *Sinister Forces* (Brown Watson, 1953).

Turner's 1985 recreation of his original cover for the J M Walsh novel *Vanguard to Neptune* (Cherry Tree, 1952).

Turner's 1985 recreation of his original cover for the Volsted Gridban novel *Exit Life* (Scion, 1953).

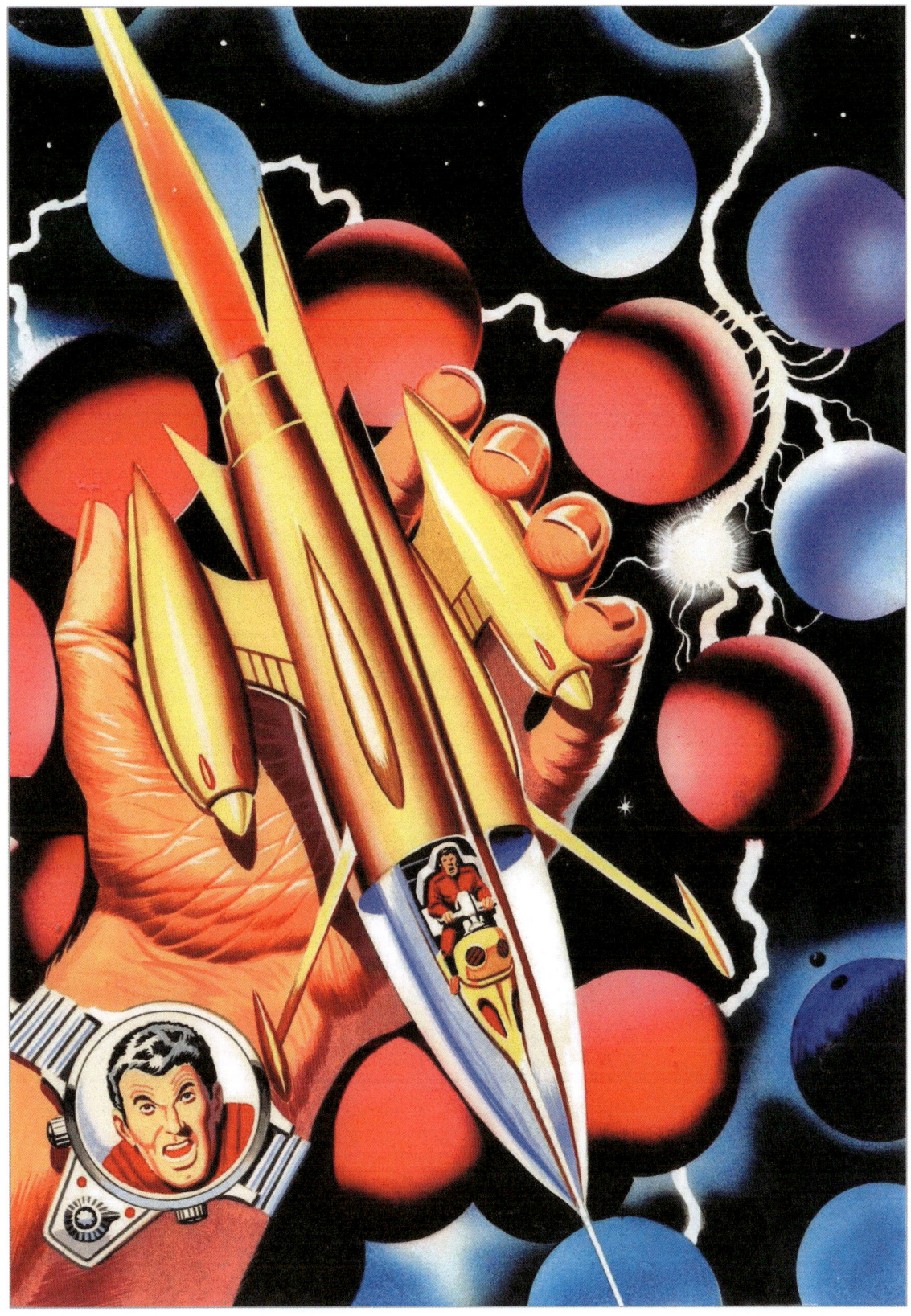

Turner's 1985 recreation of his original cover for the Volsted Gridban novel *Scourge of the Atom* (Scion, 1953).

Turner's 1985 recreation of his original cover for the Vargo Statten novel *Wealth of the Void* (Scion, 1954).

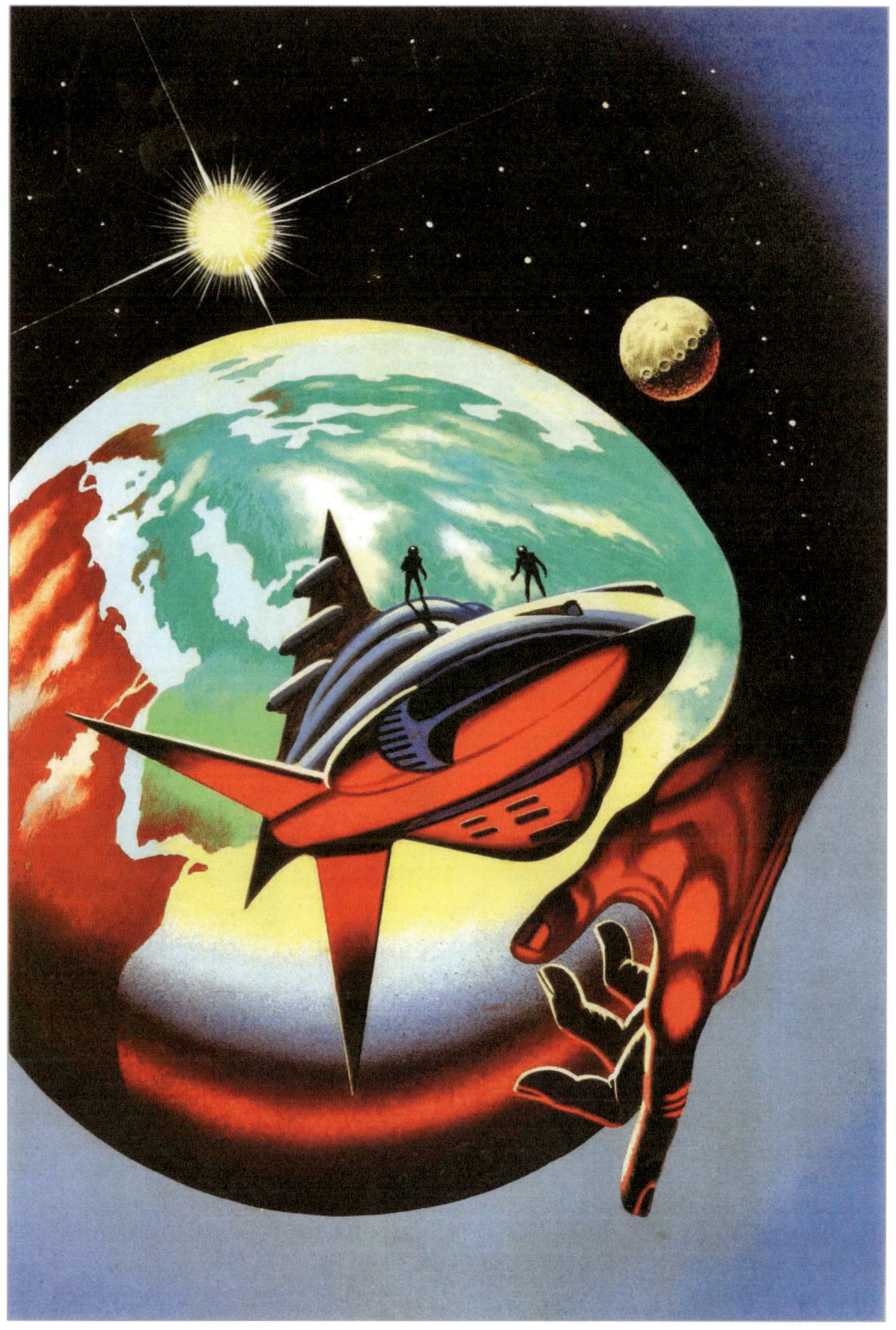

Turner's 1985 recreation of his original cover for the Vargo Statten novel *Black Bargain* (Scion, 1953).

Turner's 1985 recreation of his original cover for the Vargo Statten novel *The Space Warp* (Scion, 1952).

Turner's 1985 recreation of his original cover for the John Rackham novel *Alien Virus* (*Tit-Bits* Science Fiction Library, 1955).

The opening page of the first of the two *Dan Dare* stories that Turner illustrated for the *Dan Dare Annual 1987*.

20: A GOLDEN OPPORTUNITY

It took Ron, in the end, nearly three months to complete his new IPC assignments. These would prove to be his last for the company, and it is perhaps ironic that he bowed out illustrating stories for Frank Hampson's *Dan Dare*, the very series that had so inspired him as a young man. Having been less than impressed with the *Dan Dare* scripts he had already worked on for the *Eagle Holiday Special*, he expected little of the two he was tasked with for the *Dan Dare Annual 1987*; but, while hardly exceptional, they did at least give him his first and only opportunity to draw Dare's classic adversary the Mekon – a character he had longed to take on – and, unlike the *Holiday Special* stories, they included plenty of action scenes, hardware and aliens on which he could exercise his imagination. The first story's alien space raider villain, Zazak, particularly amused him. The character being essentially a futuristic pirate, Ron took great delight in giving him cybernetic equivalents of the stereotypical hook, peg-leg and eyepatch; on sketching out the details, he jokingly dubbed him 'Max Unipart – the ultimate in spare part surgery!'

But finally Ron was able to return to *Nick Hazard* and start work on *The Red Insects* – or, as we had now retitled it, *Invaders from Time*. Phil had produced a very detailed script for the story, to which I had added many ideas of my own, but we had still left scope for Ron's own input, and he came up with some very effective amendments. As originally scripted, a captive Hazard and his companions were to be marched into an alien city miles below the surface of the featured planet. Ron, however, saw a marvellous opportunity to enliven

Below: Turner's original sketchpad designs for the character he dubbed 'Max Unipart'.

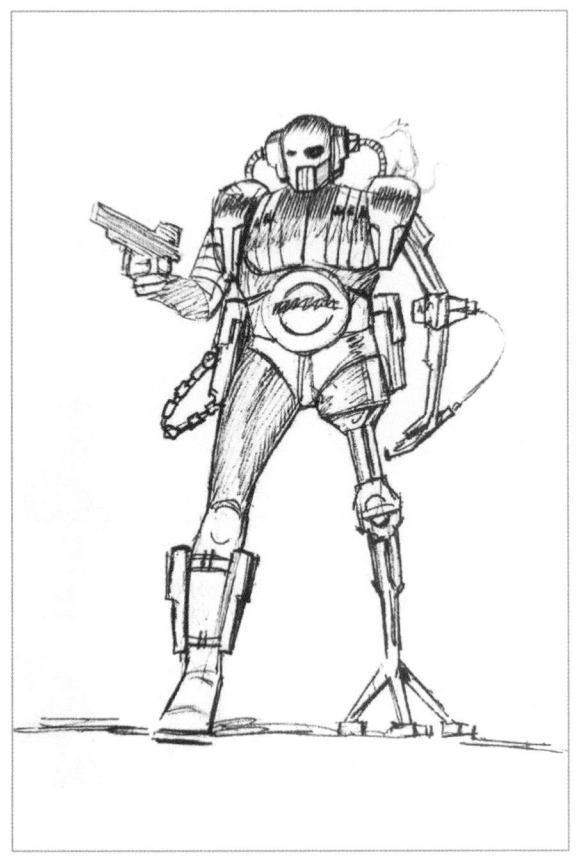 

the visuals by instead having them whisked to their destination on a magnetic vehicle passing through a network of tunnels. Similarly, the script's suggestion that the aliens' science had advanced beyond conventional, computer-based systems inspired Ron to think that their instruments would be sensitive enough to respond to telepathic impulses if they were powered by crystal technology, and so to give their whole civilisation a crystalline appearance, quite unlike anything he'd devised before. Only Frank Hampson, some 30 years earlier, had gone to as much trouble to give his comic-strip alien cultures an individual 'designer' look, and Ron's attention to detail clearly showed the enthusiasm he had for *Nick Hazard* and the effort he was prepared to put into it.

When we saw the completed artwork, Phil and I both agreed that it was easily the best Ron had produced in years, and fully deserving of the polished presentation Titan's involvement would give it. However, as weeks went by without any positive response from Titan, we began to doubt their commitment. It soon became clear that during the hiatus when our work had been held up by Ron's unavailability they had taken on other projects that now rated more highly with them. We realised that the delay had cost us dearly, and it could be months before they again turned their attention to us.

Phil was keen to begin scripting the next *Nick Hazard* adventure, but there seemed little point when *Invaders from Time* had yet to be published. Feeling let down at the eleventh hour, we were devastated. We considered seeking another publisher, but felt we wouldn't be able find one that offered us the same level of financial support and professional advice as Titan. It seemed we had no choice but to go on waiting. But, at the same time, we wanted to keep Ron active, and although he was still producing vintage cover reproductions for us, these were only fill-ins, and he would really prefer to be creating brand new work. Then I had an idea.

A few months earlier I had been contacted by one of Ron's European fans, Jean-Pierre Dupont, with whom I'd been in touch ever since my original article about Ron had appeared in *Golden Fun* magazine in 1980. He had told me he was planning a book presenting artists' impressions of ultramodern architecture and, remembering Ron's *Rick Random* designs, wanted to commission him to produce some paintings depicting futuristic cities. At the time, Ron had been so busy that I'd had to turn Dupont down. Now, though, the situation had changed, and Ron was free to accept the work – something he readily agreed to do.

Starting in 1986, Ron went on to produce over a dozen paintings for Dupont. Most of these presented variations on terrestrial constructions, but some were more fanciful, including scenes of cities on other planets. Particularly impressive were some 'Atlantis' compositions, which allowed him to indulge his interest in marine biology by showing various forms of strange aquatic life swimming outside an underwater city.

Ron was thoroughly enjoying creating these original pieces, but still looked forward to our next collaboration – for, although painting was his preferred medium, he liked to ring the changes, and some new strip work would make a welcome break. For the time being, though, *Nick Hazard* remained in limbo, with Phil and I still awaiting word from Titan and rapidly losing faith in their support. The non-appearance of *Invaders from Time* was starting to prompt queries from people who had subscribed to the magazine, and we decided that the only way to keep them on board was to publish an unplanned stop-gap issue. From the letters we'd received, it appeared that many readers had liked the previous issues' inclusion of *Space Ace* back-up strips, while others had wanted to see articles on both Fearn and Ron. We therefore decided that our stop-gap issue should be a *Space Ace* special. It would consist mainly of reprints of two of the series' best stories, 'Blasco's Revenge' and 'The Guided Missile', while the remaining pages would be given over to an article about Fearn's Vargo Statten and Volsted Gridban novels, illustrated with many examples of Ron's original covers – and, for the first time anywhere, a photograph of Ron himself.

But although this stratagem succeeded in keeping the magazine going, there was still the problem of finding Ron a new strip assignment. Suddenly it hit us that perhaps we *could* test the waters with another publisher – but with something other than *Nick Hazard*. That way, we could all keep busy while still leaving the door open for our prospective deal with Titan. But what new strip could we come up with?

Phil was a long-time fan not only of John

A GOLDEN OPPORTUNITY

A 'City of Tomorrow' painting produced by Turner in 1986 for Jean-Pierre Dupont.

A *'Rick Random* Science City' painting produced by Turner in 1987 for Jean-Pierre Dupont.

Above: the fourth issue of *JRF Presents*, published in August 1986, this time with *Space Ace* reprints as its main feature.

Russell Fearn but also of E C 'Ted' Tubb, another of the authors behind Scion's classic Volsted Gridban titles. Back in 1964, Phil had written a bibliography of Tubb's work and presented it to him at a big SF convention, and the pair had kept in touch ever since. One of Phil's favourite Tubb stories was *Kalgan the Golden*, a tale I'd also read some years earlier and had always felt would make a great comic strip for Ron; so this quickly became our preferred option. Luckily, when asked, Tubb was more than happy for Phil to adapt the story – especially as the artwork would be by Ron, whose covers had graced a number of his '50s novels.

The next step was to find a suitable publisher, and one who came immediately to mind was Martin Lock. Not only was he one of those comic-mart dealers who had distributed copies of *JRF Presents* for us, but under his Harrier Comics banner he was already issuing a string of comics, using amateur artists who had previously contributed to his long-running *Fantasy Advertiser* fanzine. The chance to sign up a strip by Ron, a professional whose work he admired, was one he couldn't resist; so, having read a copy of Tubb's story, he agreed to publish our adaptation of *Kalgan the Golden* as a US-format title, for distribution on both sides of the Atlantic.

At that time, British comics had gained a cult following in America, courtesy of *2000 AD*'s black-and-white reprint albums of strips by artists such as Dave Gibbons and Brian Bolland, so we were hopeful that this new outlet for Ron's work might give him a foothold in that lucrative market. However, Phil still needed to write his script for the story, and it would then have to be run past both Tubb and Lock, and possibly amended, before Ron could even start work on it, all of which would take weeks. So, what was Ron to do in the meantime?

Phil had many more Fearn stories he wanted to reissue in booklet form, and planned to commission Ron to produce a pair of illustrations for one titled *Climate Incorporated*. But it was really comic-strip work that Ron wanted to get back to, to give him some respite from his arduous run of

Below: the cover illustration produced by Turner for Philip Harbottle's reissue of John Russell Fearn's *Climate Incorporated*.

The second illustration that Turner produced for Philip Harbottle's 1987 reissue of John Russell Fearn's *Climate Incorporated*.

Above: an 'Atlantis' painting produced by Turner in 1988 for Jean-Pierre Dupont.

'futuristic city' paintings for Jean-Pierre Dupont. There was just one possibility I could think of.

Having always been disappointed that, back in 1978, Ron had failed to illustrate the sixth and final instalment of *2000 AD*'s last *Rick Random* story, 'The Riddle of the Astral Assassin', I realised I now had the opportunity to commission him to do just that. While this was mainly for my own benefit, I also had in mind that if IPC were ever to reprint the story, this would give them the option of presenting it as it really should have been seen, with Ron's pages substituted for those originally supplied by fill-in artist Carlos Ezquerra.

Some years earlier, I been in touch with the story's writer, Steve Moore, and he had kindly sent me all of his scripts and production notes for it. This meant I was now in a position to give Ron a copy of the original script for the last part, so that he could approach it without having to refer to or be in any way influenced by what Ezquerra had done. The outcome, though, was not as I had expected. The relatively relaxed circumstances under which he was now working meant that Ron was able to give the script a far more detailed interpretation than he would have done for *2000 AD*, and the result was a sixth instalment almost as different from the first five as Ezquerra's version had been. However, at least I had finally seen Ron finish the story.

In the meantime, Phil had now completed the script for *Kalgan the Golden*. With an enthusiastic publisher on board, we felt sure this would at last give us the break we'd been looking for and pave the way for many other projects we had in mind. But then, just when everything seemed so positive, we were dealt another blow. The next stage in the process was for Ron to produce sketches of the characters and hardware for our and Tubb's approval, but when I phoned to let him know the script was on its way, I learnt to my dismay that he was ill and, worse, would need to go into hospital.

The title page of Turner's unpublished 1986 version of the final instalment of the *Rick Random* story 'The Riddle of the Astral Assassin', produced as a private commission for author John Lawrence.

Turner's 1986 recreation of his original cover for the Vargo Statten novel *Deadline to Pluto* (Scion, 1951).

The title page of the finished artwork for the *Nick Hazard* story *Invaders from Time*.

21: CUT-UPS AND SETBACKS

Unbeknown to us, Ron had for some time been suffering with a prostate problem, and now the condition had become worse and would require an operation. This caused us a certain amount of concern, for although the procedure was regarded as routine, and should put Ron out of action for no more than a few weeks, there was no telling how it might affect his work. Would he remain just as active as before, or would it leave him weak and slow him down? Either way, the publication of *Kalgan the Golden* would clearly be delayed, and we feared that Harrier might give us the 'Titan treatment', putting us out in the cold once again. But there was a glimmer of hope. We still had the unpublished *Nick Hazard* story *Invaders from Time*, in which Titan had seemingly lost all interest. Would Harrier be prepared to accept this as a substitute for *Kalgan the Golden*, on the same kind of deal …?

E C Tubb was a well-known author in the States, on the strength of his classic, long-running *Dumarest* saga, and currently John Russell Fearn wasn't, so it would have made better marketing sense to publish Tubb's *Kalgan the Golden* first. Nevertheless, with that project now unavoidably delayed, and needing to get something into print, Martin Lock agreed to make *Invaders from Time* a Harrier publication. There was, though, a problem. We had persuaded Titan to let the story run to 36 pages, slightly longer than the standard 32 pages for an American comic book, as we had thought that necessary to do it full justice. Now, though, with Titan out of the picture and all of Lock's publications adhering to the 32-page norm, we were faced with the prospect of having to cut four pages. And considering how meticulously plotted and laid out the story had been, that wouldn't be easy!

Over the next few days, Phil and I discussed how we might reduce the page count by eliminating certain frames and reducing others in size, with extra narrative added to bridge the missing scenes. We realised that three pages was actually all we could remove without disastrously affecting the story; but fortunately Lock agreed to accept this, generously allowing the conclusion to appear on the comic's inside back cover, where he would normally have run a full-page advert.

Over Christmas 1986, I photocopied six of the original artwork pages and cut and pasted the selected frames to create three new ones as replacements. This sadly meant that some of Ron's superb full-page pieces, which had been designed to be revealed on the turn of a page for greater reader enjoyment, would now be printed on a facing page instead, and their 'wow factor' would be partly lost. However, if the book was to be published, sacrifices had to be made.

Now that the wheels were finally turning, with *Invaders from Time* accepted by Harrier and Ron poised to begin work on *Kalgan the Golden* as soon as his health permitted, we realised that another *Nick Hazard* script would then be needed to continue the series. Phil had sent me several outlines some months earlier, but I'd considered all of them unsuitable. We really wanted something a little different from the humans-versus-aliens 'shoot 'em ups' that featured heavily in *Invaders from Time* – though still with plenty of action sequences and enough good material for Ron to get his teeth into.

Confident that he'd now found the ideal Fearn story in 'Chameleon Planet', first published in the February 1940 issue of *Astonishing Stories*, Phil scripted it direct from the original novelette, then sent the results to me to pass on to Ron. It was, though, a pity he had chosen to do this rather than show us a synopsis first, as in the event we found we couldn't share his enthusiasm, judging the story a poor follow-up to *Invaders from Time*. The plot involved Nick and Viona landing on a strange planet with an unusual orbit that takes it past a black hole, causing its native lifeforms to evolve at a furious pace. In the time they are on the planet, the pair observe the transition from single-cell amoebae, through insects, dinosaurs, birds and apes into men and supermen, before the whole process starts all over again. Our heroes find themselves in danger from fast-growing trees, rapidly-forming mountains and huge tidal waves, and have to fight for survival against the planet's rapidly evolving creatures.

This was certainly a very different type of story from *Invaders from Time*, relying more on a 'sense of wonder' than on pulp science-fiction trappings, and would have worked beautifully as a piece of animation – but not, Ron and I felt, as a printed comic strip. Moreover, it lacked any opportunities for Ron to demonstrate his ingenuity in depicting new kinds of alien hardware, which would at least have compensated for the story's surfeit of animal life and natural disasters. Added to this, Nick and Viona acted more as explorers than as investigators, and therefore failed to fulfil their established roles.

However, on the plus side, reading 'Chameleon Planet', in which the adversary is essentially the planet itself, reminded me of another Fearn story, 'A Time Appointed', which Phil had loaned me some time before. This had captured my imagination immediately, and seemed to have all the elements needed for a *Nick Hazard* tale. It too had the idea of a planet working against our heroes, but here the dangers were booby-traps deliberately engineered by a long-dead alien civilisation. So, not only did the story feature weird creatures, it also had fantastic alien technology and, as an added bonus, a nice line in dialogue that wouldn't need much revising.

When I suggested the story to Phil, he too felt it had great potential; it had action, but also a touch of mystery and menace, raising it above the hackneyed 'shoot-'em-ups in space' format we wanted to avoid. It wouldn't be an easy story to adapt, as Fearn had written more than one version, and Phil would need to take elements from each, and make some additions of his own, before it would work as a *Nick Hazard* adventure. Nevertheless, he agreed to tackle the task.

Meanwhile, in early January 1987, Ron had been admitted to hospital for his operation. Fortunately, all had gone well and he had been discharged two weeks later. However, he was still unable to start illustrating *Kalgan the Golden*, because he always worked standing up, and this was something he couldn't do at present, as he had to take things easy for a while. There was, though, nothing to prevent him doodling on a pad, so while he was recuperating we arranged for him to produce some preliminary sketches of Kalgan and other significant characters, spacecraft and other hardware from the story, for our prior

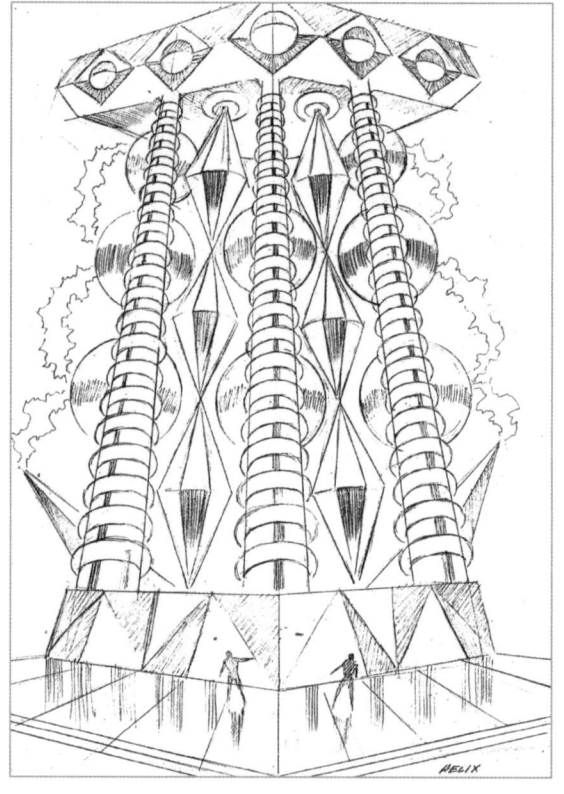

Right: three of Turner's preliminary sketches for *Kalgan the Golden*, drawn during his recuperation from his prostate operation.

CUT-UPS AND SETBACKS

approval. The alterations we had previously made to reduce the length of *Invaders from Time* also required some re-lettering, which Ron could easily do while sitting down, and this all helped to keep him busy until, at last, he was able to resume work in earnest.

The plot of *Kalgan the Golden* centres around an adventurer named Kalgan who gains the secret of immortality on a strange, machine-like alien world, only to regret it as his lover grows old and dies. Tharg, a young spaceman, learns of Kalgan's secret, wants the same immortality and gets it – but must fight Kalgan to the death in order to keep it. However, if both men are immortal, who can win? A fine Tubb tale, this was more cerebral than the *Nick Hazard* adventures we were trying to promote, but Ron rose to the challenge, and when I visited him to collect the completed artwork for the first half, I could see that he had produced some magnificent visuals. His keen sense of design and adept characterisation were obvious right from the very first page, where he had enlivened a virtually static auction scene with a corner vignette of a lawman arresting a pickpocket, oblivious to the fact that his own wallet is at that very moment being lifted by another miscreant!

Unscripted embellishments such as this, of which there were several, delighted Phil and me, and reassured us that Ron was prepared to give us his full commitment. The story's relatively few action scenes – featuring a monstrous mutant on the loose, a barroom brawl between different alien races and Tharg's attempts to kill Kalgan – were also superbly executed.

At this point, Phil and I were still uncertain how the main female character, Leedora, who appeared only in the second half of the story, should be dressed, for although Ron had presented us with some ideas in his preparatory sketches, neither of us were really happy with them. However, Ron wasn't going to let our

Above: the opening page of Turner's completed artwork for *Kalgan the Golden*.

procrastinations hold him up, so he pressed ahead and drew Leedora completely naked, explaining that he would 'dress her' later, when we had finally made up our minds!

The one thing about Ron's work that never failed to surprise us was, ironically, his ability to surprise. In one scripted scene, Tharg stands inside a huge machine while a helix of power swirls around him, turning him into an immortal. I felt this really ought to be presented as a full-page piece for maximum impact, but space constraints ruled that out, and I imagined Ron would have to confine it to either the top or the bottom half of a page – but no. He did indeed divide the page into two, but vertically from top to bottom rather than from side to side. The narrowness of the frames in fact served only to intensify the drama in a way that a full-page piece never could have done. Simple, but highly effective.

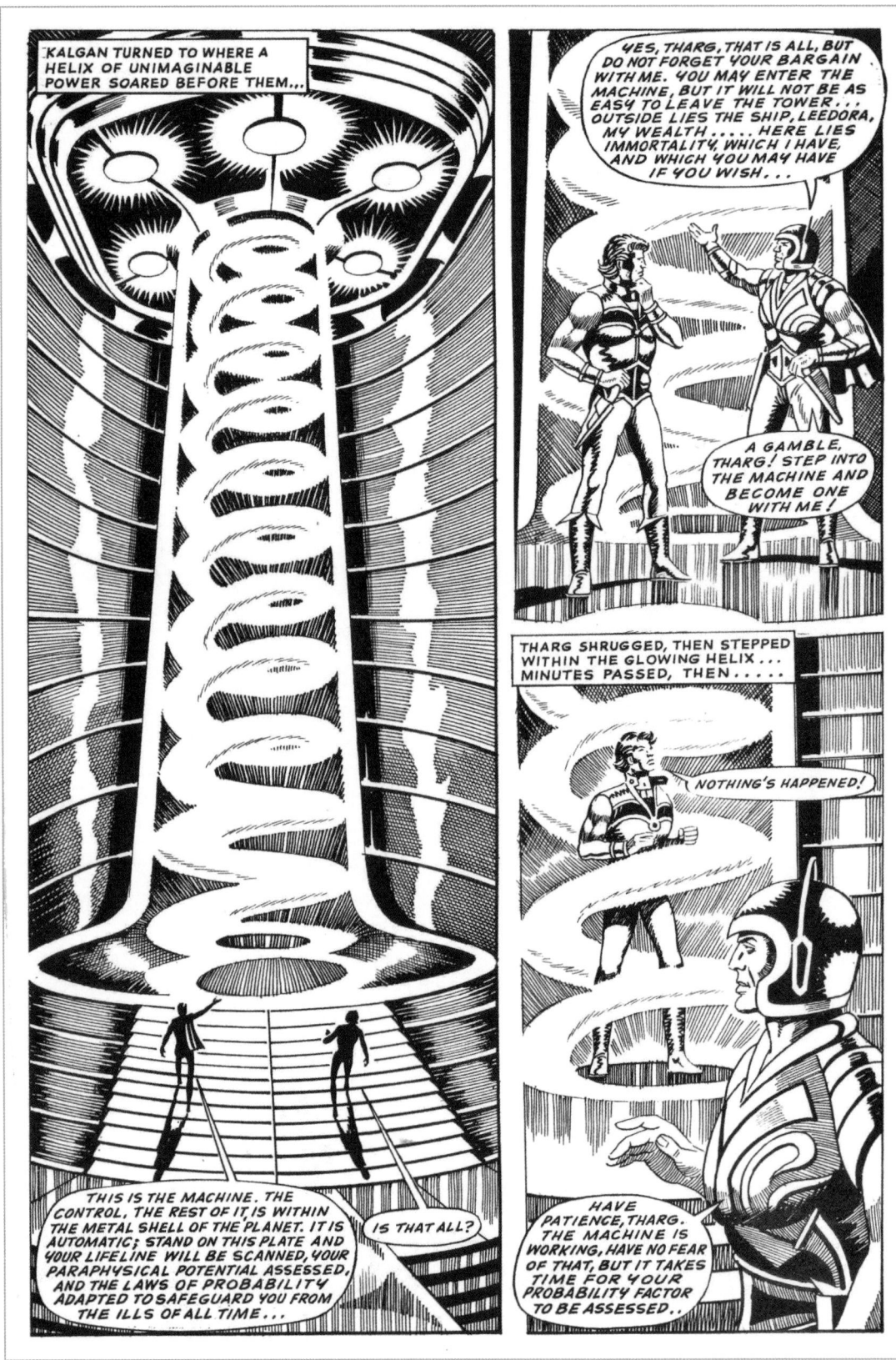

Tharg gains immortality, as ingeniously depicted by Turner in *Kalgan the Golden*.

Two months later, Ron had completed the illustrations for the story, and copies were sent to Ted Tubb for approval. Fortunately, Tubb was delighted – so much so, in fact, that he then gave us the option to adapt several other short stories of his. Consequently, although we had initially seen it as only a 'fill-in' while we were waiting to launch *Invaders from Time*, now that we had this excellent opportunity we decided to make *Kalgan the Golden* the debut entry in a new anthology line – another string to our entrepreneurial bow – which we would call *SF Classics*.

The idea here was to alternate strip adaptations of some of Tubb's finest SF short stories of the '50s with further *Nick Hazard* tales, all illustrated by Ron. And now, although Ron was still taking on the occasional private commission, we could be sure that he would be able to focus on our work, free of any other distractions. His last IPC project, the strip completed the previous year for the *Eagle Annual 1987*, had been another uninspiring juvenile subject, 'Jamie', about a boy in the Scottish Highlands encountering an eagle, and – whether at his decision or theirs – this had finally marked the end of his long association with the company.

Above right: the title page of 'Jamie', Turner's final IPC strip project. Below: *The Red Baron*, a spectacular private commission from 1987.

Private commissions completed by Turner in 1987, showing asteroid mining in space (top) and two spaceship pilots (bottom).

More private commissions circa 1987, showing an astronaut tempted by space sirens (top) and a planetary colony (bottom).

Turner's original artwork for the cover of *Invaders from Time*, the first *Nick Hazard* comic-book.

22: ALL THAT GLITTERS

Events were now moving quickly toward publication of *Invaders from Time* as the first *Nick Hazard* comic-book. Martin Lock indicated that cover artwork would soon be required for it, so Ron duly set about producing a suitable painting. As Lock would be making direct sales to specialist shops in the US and the UK, he had first to prepare and distribute solicitation copies – half-size mock-ups of the comic – in order to gauge interest and establish the print-run. We were fairly confident that it would be well-received – but realised that having a very different type of story in *Kalgan the Golden* as a follow-up might prove fortuitous, should our optimism turn out to be misplaced.

Lock, for his part, felt that we should already be looking for other characters to try out, and threw a suggestion our way. In a mid-1980s Michael Parry-edited anthology called *Superheroes*, he had come across a story about the Golden Amazon, a heroine in the style of Wonder Woman but created two years earlier, and felt that she would have a far more immediate appeal than Nick Hazard to the American market. And, as luck would have it, the story's author was none other than John Russell Fearn! Would Phil be interested in adapting the Golden Amazon's adventures for a future strip? *Would he!* Phil didn't need asking twice – the Golden Amazon was his favourite Fearn character. She was also the most famous and successful, having featured in 24 published novels.

An amazingly powerful woman in every sense of the word, the Amazon was as vicious as she was beautiful. With superior strength and a highly developed intellect, she saw herself both as a contributor to the Earth's advancement and as the planet's defender, battling a wide variety of menaces. She was also, though, something of an antihero, her fixation on scientific experimentation almost leading to disaster.

Phil had first come across the character as a teenager in 1955, when as a fan of Fearn's Vargo Statten paperbacks he had been surprised to find the author's work in hardback in the local library. The hardback in question was *The Golden Amazon's*

Above: the printed version of the *Invaders from Time* cover, as prepared by publishers Harrier Comics.

Diamond Quest, and after reading this, Phil was hooked. He spent the next two years tracking down and eagerly devouring the five other Golden Amazon books published to that date. Later he learned that the character had originated in a Canadian magazine, the Toronto *Star Weekly*, which continued to run her adventures. Through mail order, he was able to follow the series in the publisher's *Star Weekly* novels range, until this came to an abrupt end with Fearn's death in 1960.

The Amazon had already been the subject of one comic-strip adaptation, in Dez Skinn's *Warrior* magazine in 1982, in a story approved by Phil and adapted and drawn by David Lloyd (as mentioned on page 226). However, this had never been fully developed, as Lloyd had become preoccupied with the successful *V for Vendetta* strip on which he was also working. But the idea of an Amazon strip had stayed at the back of Phil's mind, and he couldn't have been happier when Lock suggested that we consider this as a new project for Ron to illustrate.

The particular Amazon story that had first attracted Lock featured an early version of the character, with dated concepts unsuited to a modern interpretation. Consequently, Phil proposed that we instead 'jump forward' and adapt *Conquest of the Amazon*, the seventh novel in the character's second series, which had begun a new phase in her development and established her as a superheroine. Like the original *Nick Hazard* adventure in *JRF Presents*, this was far too long to be retold within just a single issue, so we decided to serialise it over three consecutive ones.

Lock was keen to get this new project up and running straight away, so although we already had 'A Time Appointed' lined up for adaptation as the next *Nick Hazard* issue, he asked that Phil defer this and instead script the first part of the Amazon story and send it off to Ron as soon as possible.

In this tale, the Amazon is accused and found guilty of her scientific activities in outer space having caused a rapid decline in the Sun's power. With the Earth slowly freezing over, she is sentenced to die in a 'coffin-ship' and blasted into orbit around the planet. Her subsequent escape and attempts to restore the Sun's power make for a tremendous story, including undersea action, a battle to halt the progress of a giant glacier, and finally a showdown on the planet Mercury. This all gave Ron plenty of scope for his imagination. The story's length also allowed for the inclusion of subplots and a greater degree of characterisation than in our previous efforts, adding a certain degree of depth to it.

With the 'superwoman' heroine likely to appeal to US readers and the hard SF edge sure to bring out the best in Ron, we felt confident of success on both sides of the Atlantic. However, Ron's predilection for drawing scantily-clad women meant that we had to reject his initial designs for the Amazon's outfit. A brief, revealing costume was not only out of character for this type of woman but also implausible, given the freezing temperatures she would be encountering during the action! But, that aside, Ron's advance sketches were soon approved by all concerned, and he set to work on illustrating the story.

By now, we had several irons in the fire and were quite pleased with the way all our projects were shaping up. Having fulfilled Lock's request to get *The Golden Amazon* under way, Phil was at last able to return his attention to *Nick Hazard* and the adaptation of 'A Time Appointed', which he retitled *Planet of Doom*. This we felt to be a tremendous tale, which when graced with Ron's marvellous artwork would make a great follow-up to *Invaders from Time*. Everything seemed to be coming together nicely – but then, in October 1987, we were hit with bad news. The advance order figures for *Nick Hazard* # 1 had now come in, and they weren't good; nowhere near what we had expected, and in fact needed in order to make the series a viable one. Determined to go ahead and publish anyway, we consoled ourselves with the thought that once the issue was actually on the stands, it might generate additional sales and prompt reorders. If not, we still had *Kalgan the Golden* and *The Golden Amazon* to fall back on.

By the turn of the year, Ron had completed his illustrations for the first of the three planned issues of *The Golden Amazon* and begun work on those for *Planet of Doom*. However, when *Nick Hazard* # 1 finally reached the shops in early 1988, the pessimistic forecast was borne out, with only 1,600 copies sold in the US, where our core readership had to be. Disappointed, we still held out hope that *SF Classics* # 1, featuring *Kalgan the Golden*, would do much better when it went on sale the following month. Sadly, this wasn't to be, as in the event it performed equally poorly.

Had we been able to launch six months earlier, when the 'Brit invasion' of the US comic-book scene was in full swing, we could have expected orders of at least 10,000. Since then, though, other publishers had jumped on the bandwagon, flooding the market with a glut of inferior UK-style material in the hope of making a killing while they could. This had understandably resulted in buyers becoming more discriminating, and the downturn in demand had left wholesalers and distributors with large quantities of unsold stock. Now, shops were much

Turner's artwork graces the cover of *SF Classics* #1, *Kalgan the Golden*, published by Harrier Comics in early 1988.

warier of taking British offerings, and in order for a new title to succeed it had to be actively promoted on its own merits, not automatically assumed to have a market ready and waiting for it. And in our case, that simply hadn't happened.

Ultimately, our pitiable sales figures had been due not to any lack of interest from US readers but to poor publicity by the distributors. Martin Lock, for his part, had also been unable to promote the new titles as much as he might have done in his own and other UK comics fanzines, as his advertising budget was dependent on his profits, and after printing and distribution costs were taken into account, these were virtually non-existent.

Phil and I were devastated by this turn of events, but decided to persevere with Harrier Comics and pin all our hopes on *The Golden Amazon* being properly promoted with a strong advertising campaign in both the US and the UK. We had been looking forward to seeing Ron's finished pages for *Planet of Doom*, but after the poor sales of the first *Nick Hazard* issue we had serious doubts as to whether or not we should proceed with it. After a lot of deliberation, we decided to remain positive and allow Ron to complete the commission in the hope that, if *The Golden Amazon* proved successful, new orders for *Invaders from Time* and *Kalgan the Golden* might be picked up along the way.

When Ron delivered the completed *Planet of Doom* artwork, we both considered it superb, and quite possibly the best he had yet produced for *Nick Hazard*. We always had our own expectations of how he would interpret the scripts we gave him, but he never failed to surprise and delight us by including extra elements we hadn't even thought of. In this case, certain scenes, especially those set in the story's fantastic Hall of Machines, recalled the superlative imagery of his best *Rick Random* work. Surely this story couldn't fail to be well-received!

But then Martin Lock gave us the bad news that *The Golden Amazon* #1 had received no greater advance orders than our previous two titles. Disillusioned with the sales prospects of British comics, American dealers were apparently now interested only in those that were already well-established; and of course ours didn't meet that criterion. We could still press ahead with publication of *The Golden Amazon*, but clearly the US dalliance with UK-style black-and-white comics was well and truly over, and despite the quality of our work, any profits we might make would be extremely low. In fact, we had still to receive any payment at all for our first two Harrier titles, and were starting to have grave misgivings about the whole operation.

At the eleventh hour, Phil and I decided to pull *The Golden Amazon* from publication. We were sure we had a saleable property, but it seemed the time wasn't right, with US and UK publishers alike currently preferring to take the shortsighted approach of relying on old, tried-and-tested material such as *2000 AD* reprints. We didn't rule out the possibility of having Ron complete the full story for publication elsewhere at some later point, but for the time being it seemed we had reached the end of our attempts to launch our own comic-book series.

This, though, didn't stop us undertaking any commissions we might receive from other sources. Consequently, when Phil learned of *Ground Zero*, a new digest-size SF anthology due to be launched in mid-1988, he immediately contacted its editor, Carlton Campbell, to suggest that he consider including a short strip illustrated by Ron. Campbell agreed, and Phil offered him a tale called 'No Greater Love', written by Sydney J Bounds, a contemporary of Fearn and Tubb, whose work Phil was now promoting through his agency. Running to eight pages, the story told of a prospector mining asteroids with the assistance of the loyal and dependable Bea – a Bio-Electrical Analogue computer that is also a sentient creature grown from human brain cells. Initially the prospector is cold and disparaging toward his bio-electrical companion, but when he gets trapped in a cave by a deadly creature and Bea saves him at the last moment in an act of great personal sacrifice, he finally realises the true extent of its devotion to him. No greater love, indeed.

Ron's illustrations for the story, produced in the small Picture Library format we'd previously used for the initial *Nick Hazard* strips in *JRF Presents*, were excellent – worthy of being accorded more than eight pages – and Campbell was sufficiently impressed to commission from Phil a further eight-page story for *Ground Zero*'s second issue. This was

Turner's 1988 cover page illustration for the then-unpublished *Nick Hazard* story *Planet of Doom*.

More starry vistas adorn Turner's title pages for the prospective *Ground Zero* contributions 'No Greater Love' and 'The Ghost Sun'.

'The Ghost Sun', a Fearn and Bounds collaboration of sorts, in that Fearn had written the opening pages pre-war, when it had originally been intended as the first part of a 'round robin' series to which various writers would contribute, and Bounds had finished it off much more recently, when Phil had passed him the surviving fragment. The tale told of a dying spaceman issuing a warning to avoid the lethal radiations of a mysterious sun, little realising that this last, selfless act will be the salvation of a whole alien race for generations to come.

While Ron was working on his artwork for 'The Ghost Sun', we waited for the first issue of *Ground Zero* to be published – and waited, and waited … In the end, it never appeared, and all our attempts to query this with the editor were met with total silence. We could only conclude that the magazine was a non-starter; and although Campbell had paid for the artwork for 'No Greater Love', that was not the case for 'The Ghost Sun'. It seemed that even when we were *approached* for work, we were doomed to be let down.

Martin Lock then offered us a crumb of comfort: he was considering publishing an album of short SF strips, the *Harrier SF Comics Special*, and suggested we might like to contribute. Despite our recent disappointments, Phil agreed. However, he was unable to offer Lock either of the two unused *Ground Zero* strips, as Lock's project was to have the larger, standard comic-book page format. Thus Phil came up instead with a script adapted from a Fearn short story entitled 'Thoughts That Kill', first published in the October 1939 issue of the pulp magazine *Science Fiction*. This I gave to Ron to illustrate over the Christmas period. It was the tale of an advanced but dying race planning to conquer the lowlier life-forms of Venus. There, however, any similarity to the usual hackneyed alien invasion yarn ended, the twist being that the aliens were so advanced that their own telepathic sensibilities were ultimately their downfall.

At the beginning of 1989, I collected from Ron the six pages of artwork required for 'Thoughts That Kill'. As expected, Phil and I were both very pleased with the results; the story was intelligently told, with some interesting concepts, and Ron had responded be rendering it with a considerable amount of detail. He hadn't let us down. Sadly, however, Martin Lock had. It turned out that he'd overspent his budget, and the *Harrier SF Comics Special* would not now appear!

In an attempt to make amends, Lock suggested we try Fleetway – recently sold by IPC and now under new ownership – as a possible client for Ron's work. He'd heard that a couple of new SF-themed comics were in the pipeline, and thought we could perhaps test the waters there. Co-manager Steve McManus had vowed never to use Ron again after the antagonism over *2000 AD*'s *Rick Random* revival, but that had been ten years earlier. Much had changed since then, and we could now ensure that any new work McManus might sanction for Ron would actually be delivered. It was worth a try.

Phil sent McManus various script and artwork samples, together with a complete copy of 'Thoughts That Kill'. However, as time went by and no response was forthcoming, we began to doubt the veracity of Lock's information. Over the past few years, I had been in touch with one of Fleetway's managing editors, Gil Page, when I had been attempting to reclaim some of Ron's old artwork from the company vaults, and he had always replied to my letters – and promptly – so I decided to approach him for clarification. True to form, Page came through with an answer. However, while he confirmed that two new comics were indeed in preparation, he went on to say that the art would be produced to an in-house specification, for which Ron's work was considered unsuitable!

Phil and I found these continual knock-backs hard to take. We had produced with Ron some truly excellent comic-strip stories, but it seemed there was simply no outlet for them! Although all of the unpublished material would eventually see print elsewhere, we were not to know that at the time. We had received not a penny in royalties from the two titles that Harrier had published, and as we had mostly paid Ron up-front out of our own pockets for those and the subsequent projects, we had suffered a devastating financial loss.

Somewhat dejected, we continued to keep Ron busy by commissioning him to produce further recreations of his vintage Vargo Statten and Volsted Gridban paperback covers, including those for *The Eclipse Express* (1952), *The Multi-Man* (1954) and *Frozen Limit* (1954). Phil also expanded on this

Above: Turner's impressive title page for the initially unpublished story 'Thoughts That Kill'.

by asking him to produce entirely new pieces for titles that, back in the '50's, had been handled by other artists, such as *The Last Martian* (1952), *Across the Ages* (1952) and *A Thing of the Past* (1953) – the prequel to *The Genial Dinosaur*, the cover of which had elicited praise from John Russell Fearn himself. These novels all included scenes Phil knew would inspire Ron to produce highly imaginative compositions, and he was not wrong. Perhaps best of all was the one Ron painted for *The Time Trap* (1952), which equalled some of his finest vintage work. The story featured weird alien 'flying tortoises', and Ron captured the essence of it perfectly, in a symbolic piece that emphasised the creatures' carnivorous nature by showing them looming over a pile of skeletons. It was brilliantly realised, making the scene seem totally believable.

But despite Ron producing these magnificent cover pieces, they were still only private commissions to keep him occupied. As far as his strip work was concerned, we would need to find other outlets for it, or else accept that we'd now reached the end of the line.

Turner's 1988 recreation of his original cover for the Vargo Statten paperback *The Eclipse Express* (Scion, 1952).

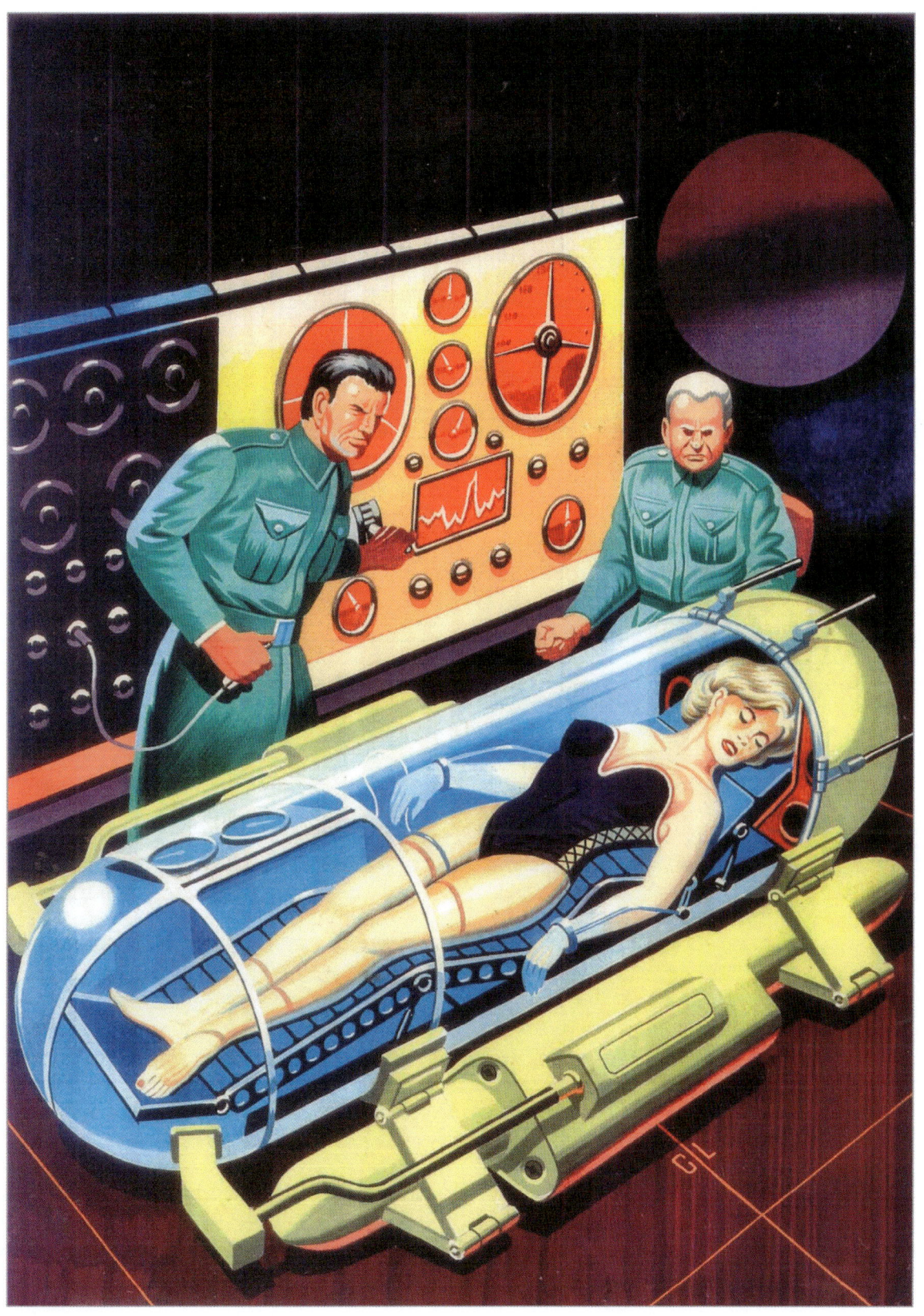
Turner's 1989 recreation of his cover for Volsted Gridban's *Frozen Limit* (Scion, 1954), incorporating a likeness of film star Marilyn Monroe.

Painted in 1989 as a commission for Philip Harbottle, Turner's new cover piece for the Vargo Statten novel *The Time Trap* (Scion, 1952).

23: A DALLIANCE WITH THE DALEKS

Over the next few months, while Ron was busy working on our vintage cover commissions, I continued to approach any publishers I felt might be interested in the type of strip work that Phil and I wanted to produce with him. Acme Press and Hawk Books were both offered *The Golden Amazon* as a graphic novel project, but neither responded positively. Publishers at that time seemed to want nothing but scratchy, sketchy, unappealing artwork, coupled with nonsensical storylines. Nevertheless, I persevered.

In a recent issue of Marvel UK's *Doctor Who Magazine*, I happened to read of plans to feature the Daleks in a new eight-page comic-strip. Marvel was another publisher that Ron had fallen out with in the past, but again, that was some years earlier, and in the meantime the magazine's whole editorial team had changed. I felt this could be a fresh opportunity for Ron to get his foot in the door, on subject matter he enjoyed and with which he was totally familiar. I immediately contacted editor John Freeman. Freeman knew of Ron's work, but unfortunately was already committed to using one of his regular artists for the upcoming Dalek strip. By coincidence, though, he also had plans to run a series on the history of the Daleks' appearances in *TV Century 21*, and I quickly realised that a new illustration by Ron would be ideal to introduce this.

Freeman soon confirmed his interest in commissioning a piece by Ron, and made a few suggestions regarding the type of scene he was looking for, the basic idea being to show a man and a woman running away from a couple of Daleks. This was quickly amended when Ron took on the work: the man and woman remained, but instead of just a couple of Daleks, Ron drew a spacecraft dispensing a whole line of them under the command of their Emperor, all suitably framed against a futuristic city skyline.

Freeman was very impressed with the results, and asked if Ron would care to be interviewed for the upcoming series. I knew that Ron would have no interest in being interviewed in person, but not wanting to lose this chance of extra publicity for his work, I offered to pass some written questions on to him and return his replies in time to tie in with the feature – an idea that Freeman readily accepted.

During the course of the ensuing discussion, I learned that a new strip featuring the Doctor's perennial adversaries the Cybermen was under consideration for a forthcoming issue of the magazine. Hoping to persuade Freeman that this would be a suitable commission for Ron, I prepared a six-frame sequence featuring the current Doctor, as played by Sylvester McCoy, and arranged for Ron to illustrate it. Ron tried his best, but he was always the first to admit his weakness at capturing a likeness, and although he pulled off his long-shot depictions of the character, in close-up the Doctor looked more like Sylvester *Stallone* than Sylvester McCoy! Needless to say, Ron wasn't selected for the Cyberman strip, or any other in the near future. However, he had at least managed to re-establish himself with Marvel – an achievement that would eventually bring dividends.

Toward the end of 1989, Ron asked Phil and me if we were intending to finish the Golden Amazon story. He had already illustrated the first 25 pages, and we estimated that it would need around 75 to 80 to complete it. So far, we had found no publisher willing to take it on. However, knowing that Ron was keen to alternate between our private commissions and new comic-strip work, to give him a more balanced output, we decided to go ahead in the hope that a suitable publisher might eventually be found. Phil, though, felt that we should now consider finishing the story in 60 pages rather than 80. Initially I was unhappy with the idea of reducing the page-count, but upon reflection I realised it made economic sense. We were, after all, taking another gamble with our own money, and if the story could be told effectively in fewer pages than we had originally envisaged, then why risk more? The costs involved in producing an 80-page graphic novel might also deter some potential publishers, whereas a 60-page one would be more affordable.

So, over the last few weeks of 1989, Phil

Above: Turner's new Dalek illustration, published in *Doctor Who Magazine* # 153, dated October 1989.
Below: the artist's unsuccessful pitch for illustrating a Cyberman comic-strip in the magazine.

set to work tightening up the remainder of the scripts until we had a story that could be effectively told in 61 pages – which, with a title page and a short introduction, would give us the 64 pages we felt would be ideal (given that printers generally work in multiples of 16 pages).

Consequently, during the first half of 1990, Ron again became heavily occupied with *The Golden Amazon*, injecting a lot of his own ideas into the story. The results were excellent. Whenever Phil and I got depressed about all the rejections we'd suffered and felt like giving up, seeing Ron's latest work would raise our spirits and give us the confidence to continue.

Meanwhile, we were still seeking a publisher for the story, and Phil sounded out Bryon Whitworth, editor of the semi-pro UK fanzine *The Comic Journal*. Whitworth greatly admired Ron's work and had already agreed to pick up both 'The Ghost Sun' and 'Thoughts That Kill'. It turned out that, with the Amazon story now complete, he was very interested in either serialising it in his fanzine or else publishing it complete as a single issue. So, although not our original intention, we decided that in order to do some kind of justice to the tremendous amount of effort Ron had put into the project, we would allow it to be published in an A5-size limited edition, via Whitworth's fanzine outlet.

Whitworth may well have been interested in publishing the second *Nick Hazard* story, *Planet of Doom*, on the same basis, but around this time I came across an advert in the UK comics fanzine *Speakeasy*, seeking contributions for a new line of SF comics to be professionally published by a company called Farpoint Publishing. Phil immediately contacted Farpoint, offering to supply them with strips based on classic Fearn and Tubb SF stories and arranging to send them samples of Ron's recent work on *Planet of Doom*, *Kalgan the Golden* and *The Golden Amazon*. The response was extremely enthusiastic, Farpoint agreeing to all our terms and expressing particular interest in the *Nick Hazard* story – which was fine by us, as we had already found a home for *The Golden Amazon*.

Having been let down so often in recent years, we remained apprehensive, but were much reassured when Farpoint sent us a mock-up of an advert they intended to place in publications such as *Speakeasy*, *NME*, *Melody Maker* and a new magazine of their own, *View*, presenting several frames from *Planet of Doom* and stating that the first two thousand copies of the comic would be individually numbered for collectors. This clearly demonstrated a great deal of commitment, and we felt that at last we'd found a publisher sympathetic to our cause. Easy to deal with and responsive to our wishes, they were now keen to finalise the project. Moreover, impressed by *Kalgan the*

Below left and centre: advance cover designs for the planned but ultimately unpublished Harrier Comics editions of *Nick Hazard* # 2 and *The Golden Amazon* # 1. Below right: the cover of Whitworth's complete graphic novel edition of *The Golden Amazon*, published in 1990.

Golden, they also intimated an interest in publishing a Tubb story. Liking their enthusiasm, and keen to foster further collaborations, Phil offered them *Sword in the Snow*, a fantasy tale for which he had already prepared a script some years earlier. Sword-and-sorcery artist Jim Cawthorn had originally been lined up to illustrate this, but had been unable to take it on, so I had persuaded Phil to let Ron tackle it instead. I knew that Ron liked a break from SF occasionally, and also relished a challenge, so this seemed a good opportunity to find out how he would take to a genre he'd never attempted before.

However, Ron didn't get off to a very good start. His initial design for the story's main character, Malkar, was let down by an enormous belt buckle that, as Phil observed, would have given him an appendicitis if he tried to bend over! Fortunately, this was quickly amended, and having approved the revised version, and the look of a few other key characters, we let Ron loose to produce the work.

But when the twenty finished pages came in, although the presentation was up to Ron's usual standard, the content wasn't, and I realised he hadn't quite got the feel for the subject in the way we had hoped he would. A particular issue was his depiction of the horrific dragon-like creature that played a key role in the story. This was an element we hadn't felt the need to approve in advance, as we had expected Ron to come up with a creation just as weird and imaginative as the alien beings in his SF pieces. Sadly, though, in trying to produce something more fantastical than usual, he had missed the mark. Phil was particularly upset with the look of the creature, likening it to the friendly children's character Puff the Magic Dragon!

There were other aspects of the work that also needed tweaking to suit the genre, and I now realised it had been a big mistake to expect Ron to master straight away a type of illustration in which he had little experience. I tried to salvage the situation, sketching an idea I'd had myself for the creature's appearance and making notes of other amendments I thought necessary to bring the work up to scratch, gaining Tubb's approval for these via Phil. However, when I approached Ron to make the changes, he was clearly very unhappy at the prospect.

Years earlier, Greg Hall had warned me how temperamental Ron could be if asked to make alterations to his work, and I was now seeing that first-hand. Once he had finished with a piece, he would rather redraw it from scratch than make smaller adjustments to it. Nevertheless, on this occasion, he did reluctantly agree to do just that, and the revised pages were eventually approved by all concerned.

Ironically, though, all this effort proved to be for nothing. As enthusiastic and helpful as Farpoint had been, one thing they clearly lacked was business acumen, for the next thing we knew, they had gone into liquidation! Sales of their *View* magazine, although initially strong, had subsequently taken a nosedive, and as they had been relying on that income stream to finance their comics line, they had been trying to run before they could walk! Consequently, with the company's collapse, neither *Planet of Doom* nor *Sword in the Snow* reached publication. Yet again, Phil and I had been let down, and although we knew Farpoint had been sincere in their dealings with us, this was still a crushing blow. It was now 1991, and by this point we had to accept that all our efforts to market Ron's comic-strip work had been unsuccessful. We would have to change tack.

On learning that Hawk Books, who had been publishing a highly successful series of *Dan Dare* reprints, were planning to issue a fact-filled tome entitled *The Dan Dare Dossier*, Phil realised he had something unique he could contribute. Like Ron, he had been an avid follower of the good Colonel's adventures since the character's inception in the 1950s, when (as mentioned on page 226) he had even been inspired to fill exercise books with his own comic-strip stories based on transcripts he had made of Radio Luxembourg's *The Adventures of Dan Dare* serials. While some of those stories had been left unfinished, due to a fluctuating radio signal that at times had made the broadcasts almost impossible to hear, four had been completed, and it seemed these were now the sole surviving record of those serials. Phil consequently offered them to Hawk for possible inclusion in *The Dan Dare Dossier*, to afford completist fans a glimpse of a little-known aspect of the *Dan Dare* canon, with the option of having them redrawn by Ron, if so desired, to give them a more professional presentation.

Remarkably, Hawk showed no interest in this

Turner's finalised title page for the E C Tubb story adaptation *Sword in the Snow*.

exclusive. However, not to be completely outdone, Phil then turned to the *Dan Dare*-related fanzine *Eagle Times* and offered them an article entitled *The Unknown Dan Dare*, describing how he had come to draw the four stories. Editor Howard Corn, amazed to learn that a 14-year old schoolboy had had the patience and ability to make a visual record of some of those now long-lost radio shows, readily accepted Phil's article as a worthy contribution. This then prompted Phil to commission Ron to redraw one of his favourite sequences from a story called 'The Sirillium Stealers', to use as an illustration for the article. Ron was only too happy to oblige, for although he had been given the opportunity to draw *Dan Dare* a few years earlier, as one of his last IPC assignments, that was their 'remodelled' version of the character, rather than the original Frank Hampson version that Phil was now asking him to interpret.

Meanwhile, Phil had decided to resurrect another of his pet projects: the John Russell Fearn short story reprints he had begun producing privately in digest-size booklet form even before Ron became involved in our work. He now decided to commission Ron to produce new black-and-white cover and interior illustrations for reprints of further stories by Fearn, and also by Ted Tubb and Syd Bounds amongst others, the idea being that these could be sold alongside his previous endeavours through specialist shops and mail order.

These *Fantasy Booklet* publications soon attracted the attention of a Wiltshire-based pulp-fiction enthusiast named Maurice Flanagan. On learning that Phil was also an authority on vintage pulp novels, Flanagan was encouraged to contact him for advice on setting up his own semi-pro magazine: *Paperback, Pulp and Comic Collector*. Phil was only too pleased to assist, realising this would serve as an opportunity to promote his own publications and also our work with Ron. The strong sales that Flanagan's first issue achieved were a real eye-opener for him, showing him just how much interest there was in '50s pulp fiction and leaving him in no doubt as to the viability of his idea. The magazine went from strength to strength; and Phil followed up by providing articles on Fearn and Ron for subsequent issues.

Aside from publishing his magazine, Flanagan also began trading as a vintage book dealer under the name Zardoz Books, selling second-hand SF pulps and paperbacks. In due course, encouraged by Phil, he then added another string to his bow and became a publisher too. Phil immediately proposed that his first release should be *Lord of Atlantis*, the eighth Golden Amazon novel, following on from the six originally published in the UK in the '40s and '50s and the seventh in 1976. Flanagan happily agreed – especially when Phil suggested that Ron could produce the cover. Consequently, in the summer of 1991, *Lord of Atlantis* appeared as a limited edition with a superb 'dinosaur' cover scene by Ron, under Flanagan's new imprint Zeon Books – a name inspired by that of vintage publishers Scion (pronounced 'Skee-on').

Below: Turner's cover for the Zeon Books edition of *Lord of Atlantis*.

Ron's work received further promotion in the third issue of *Paperback, Pulp and Comic Collector*, published in July 1991. Gracing the front of the issue was a new 'what might have been' cover Phil had commissioned for the vintage Volsted Gridban novel *A Thing of the Past* (1953), while inside could be found the previously completed but unpublished comic-strip adaptation of Syd Bounds' 'No Greater Love' plus a feature by Phil on Ron's six *Tit-Bits* Science Fiction Comics entries. Rounding things off was a back-cover advert for *Lord of Atlantis*.

By the fourth issue, published that November, Flanagan was offering postcard reproductions of 24 classic SF covers, mostly by Ron; so if the new generation of pulp-fiction fans and collectors hadn't previously been aware of Ron's work, they certainly were now.

Meanwhile, Ron continued to undertake further private commissions for Phil, producing new cover pieces mostly for other Vargo Statten novels he had not worked on back in the '50s, such as *Born of Luna* (1951), *To the Ultimate* (1952), *Black Wing of Mars* (1953), *Man in Duplicate* (1953) and the classic film novelisation *The Creature from the Black Lagoon* (1954) – a spectacular composition that would later appear on the cover of the eighth issue of Flanagan's magazine. For each of these pieces, Phil and I would first read the selected novel and agree on a scene we thought suitable for Ron to illustrate, then I would send Ron a copy of the book along with my description of the chosen scene, to which he could add or improve if he so wished – and the results were never less than impressive.

Having grown up on Ron's comic-strip work rather than his paperback pieces, I myself also commissioned him to produce reproductions of all of his *Tit-Bits* Science Fiction Comics covers. In this way, we kept him busy throughout most of 1991. However, conscious that these were still only private commissions, I was continually on the look-out for any commercial assignments that might be suitable for Ron, and from which he might also earn more money than we could afford to pay him. Then, toward the end of the year, I believed I'd finally found one.

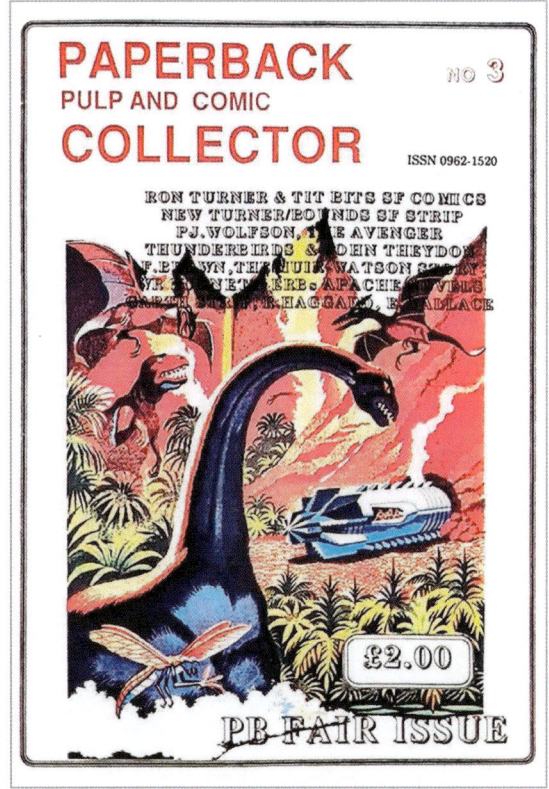

Top right: Turner's work graces the cover of the third issue of *Paperback, Pulp and Comic Collector*, published in 1991.

Bottom right: a 1991 private commission based on the John Russell Fearn novel *Liners of Time*, published by World's Work in 1947.

Turner's illustration based on the Vargo Statten hardback novelisation of *The Creature from the Black Lagoon* (Dragon, 1954).

A DALLIANCE WITH THE DALEKS

Completed in 1990 and 1991, Turner's new covers inspired by the mid-1950s Scion-published Vargo Statten novels *Across the Ages* (top left), *The Red Insects* (top right), *Black Wing of Wars* (bottom left) and *Man in Duplicate* (bottom right).

A jungle fantasy scene privately commissioned from Turner in 1991 on behalf of the editor of the fanzine *Ungawa!*.

24: THUNDERBIRDS ARE GO, AGAIN?

October 1991 saw the debut of a new fortnightly Fleetway publication called *Thunderbirds – The Comic*. Recent television repeats had led to a resurgence of public interest in the classic Gerry and Sylvia Anderson puppet show, and that in turn had prompted Fleetway to launch this new title. In the editor's chair was Alan Fennell, a former *Thunderbirds* scriptwriter who had also edited *TV21* and *Countdown*. The comic initially majored on reprints of old *TV21* strips drawn by Frank Bellamy, but these were soon joined by adaptations of some of Fennell's fondly-remembered TV episodes such as 'Pit of Peril' and 'Sun Probe', illustrated by a fresh generation of artists including Steve Kyte, Keith Page and Malcolm Stokes. Ron had always been a fan of *Thunderbirds*, and had really enjoyed the work he'd carried out for the various tie-in annuals and specials he'd been asked to contribute to in the late '60s and early '70s. It seemed to me that if Phil and I couldn't come up with a successful strip of our own for Ron to illustrate, then getting him involved in this already popular one might be our best bet.

Undeterred by the brush-offs I'd previously had from Fleetway, I got in touch with Fennell, who remembered Ron's work and was surprised to learn he was still active. I replied that not only was he still active, but he was as good as ever, and would be keen to contribute to the new comic. Fennell was interested, but needed some reassurance regarding the quality of Ron's current work, so he suggested that I arrange for him to produce some sketches of the Thunderbirds craft and crew. This I did, and Ron drew action scenes of the vehicles accompanied by close-ups of the relevant team members.

Below: three of the 'try-out' sketches Turner produced in 1991 for Alan Fennell, editor of Fleetway's new *Thunderbirds – The Comic*.

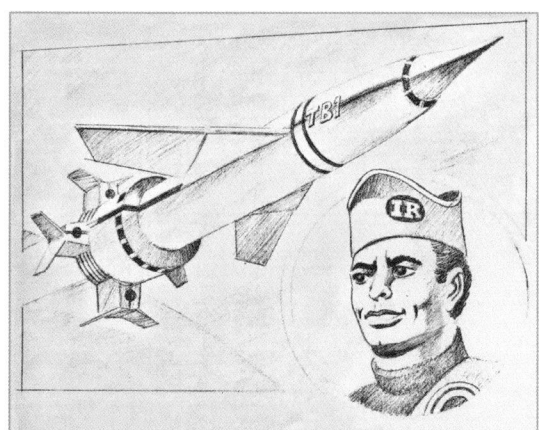

Above: the other three sketches that Turner prepared in 1991 for consideration by Alan Fennell, editor of *Thunderbirds – The Comic*.

I had planned to send these sketches in to Fennell, but he asked if I would instead bring them along to the Fleetway offices in person, so that he could explain to me in greater detail what would be required, should he decide to commission Ron. So, on a very dark and miserable November morning, I visited the new Fleetway offices in North London, managing to get caught in a sudden downpour and arrive at the premises looking like a drowned rat.

Once I had dried off in reception, Fennell came out to greet me and showed me into his office, which was lined with *Thunderbirds* illustrations, both photographic and painted. He began by querying the arrangement I had with Ron, as on *TV21* he'd always dealt with Greg Hall. I explained how Hall had retired and I had encouraged Ron to keep working by providing him with a continuous supply of private commissions and various comic-strip projects. On reviewing the sketches Ron had produced, Fennell agreed that he certainly hadn't lost his touch. He said that provided the standard could be maintained, and the work came in on time, then he would be keen to use Ron. He added that although he had previously encountered problems with him meeting deadlines, he had never been sure if that was down to Ron himself or to Hall – and that at one time he had even suspected they were one and the same person! At least I had now been able to set him straight on *that* point!

Fennell then explained that if Ron wanted a commission, he would be required to operate in a quite different way than he was used to, as there would be no script provided for him to follow. The comic's current strips were adaptations of TV adventures, and therefore he would instead be given videos of the episodes he was assigned, along with an indication of the amount of artwork required. It would then be up to him to choose which scenes to illustrate, and when the pages were completed, Fennell would add the appropriate captions and dialogue.

My heart sank when I heard this, as I immediately suspected it would cause problems. For one thing, I knew that Ron didn't even own a VCR: not being an avid TV viewer, he had no need of one. Admittedly, that hurdle could be quite easily overcome, as I had a spare machine I could loan him. However, whether or not he would be happy to work in this novel way was another matter entirely … Nevertheless, I kept a positive attitude, told Fennell I would be in touch, and left to brave the elements once again.

To my surprise, when I explained the situation to Ron, he initially agreed to accept the assignment – though, as I later came to believe, this was probably more out of a feeling of moral obligation toward me for all the effort I'd gone to, than out of any great enthusiasm on his part. The first episode to be tackled was one called 'Martian Invasion', and when I had the recording to hand, I decided to check that it would play properly before I set out to deliver it to Ron. It was lucky I did this, because I found there was a problem: the VCR wouldn't co-operate, even though it had worked fine the night before. Realising it might take some time to identify the issue, I rang Ron to explain that I might be late arriving. Half an hour later, Ron rang me back, sounding more than a little agitated. He said that although he was keen to draw the strip, he was concerned that if the VCR were to fail while he was working, he would be unable to finish it. Recalling the previous problems with Fennell over deadlines, he had been anxious and uncertain about committing himself anyway, and this latest turn of events had made up his mind for him: he was sorry, but he felt he just couldn't work this way, and would therefore have to turn the commission down.

Although a big disappointment, this decision was understandable, so I reluctantly informed Fennell that, due to unforeseen circumstances, Ron would be unable to complete the commission. Naturally Fennell was not best pleased to learn this. In retrospect, however, it was perhaps fortunate that fate *had* stepped in. As lucrative as the assignment would have been, the unfamiliar working method might well have led to problems later on. Ron might have chosen to interpret scenes in a way Fennell was unhappy with – giving too much emphasis to the Thunderbirds machines rather than the characters, for instance – or failed to allow enough room for dialogue; and if he had been asked to make amendments, that would doubtless have resulted in disagreements and delays, causing a great deal of stress all round – the very reason Ron had given up professional commissions in the '80's! I decided that, for the time being, it was best that he continue to focus on our private commissions.

In the meantime, though, I had been contacted by Andy Darlington, a knowledgeable SF enthusiast and occasional writer of magazine articles about various '50's comic-strip characters. He told me he was currently planning a feature called *The Rivals of Dan Dare*, which would include pieces on Captain Condor, Space Ace, Rick Random and his particular favourite, Jet-Ace Logan. An experienced comic-strip writer, having produced work for D C Thomson, he had also scripted a new Jet-Ace Logan story for publication in one of the many semi-pro magazines to which he'd previously contributed, and wondered if there was any chance Ron might be willing to illustrate it. He added that he had always been hugely impressed by Ron's work on Jet-Ace's Thriller Picture Library exploits, and to acquire his services for this latest adventure would be the icing on the cake.

If all had gone according to plan with the *Thunderbirds* strips, I would have had to turn down this request, but as it was, there was now a gap in Ron's schedule, and he was both free and willing to take on Darlington's assignment. Consequently, early in 1992, Ron provided the artwork for the new six-page Jet-Ace Logan adventure 'Terror from Moon 33'. The story included plenty of intriguing ideas and space visuals for him to get his teeth into, including a crashed spacecraft, pest-control robots that create havoc on a colonised moon of Jupiter, and the final discovery on the titular moon of a fearsome alien creature – Ron's depiction of which was one of his finest. For Darlington, this project fulfilled a dream to collaborate with Ron on a strip character dear to his heart, and he was delighted with the results, which were far better than he could have hoped for. Approval having been obtained from Fleetway, the strip finally appeared in *Mentor*, an Australian semi-pro magazine, in 1993.

At around this time, Ron also produced for Phil a three-page strip called 'The World That Dissolved'. Based on a Fearn short story originally published in a 1939 issue of *Amazing Stories*, this told of a couple of crooks who steal a shipment of precious ore and think they're set up for life, but who reckon without the intervention of celestial phenomena and ultimate cosmic retribution. Phil and I had previously offered this story to *Eagle*, back when we had been attempting to secure work for Ron on the comic's *Amstor Computer* series, and Phil had even pencilled a detailed layout for it, to give an idea of how it might be presented. However, it had been rejected by editor David Hunt on the grounds that it was 'too advanced' for the comic's young readership. With the current lull in activity, I had now persuaded Phil to have Ron do his own version of the story. Naturally Ron was free to interpret it as he saw fit, using Phil's earlier work purely as a guide. However, to Phil's surprise, the final layout was so close to his own that if he had ever feared he might have queered the pitch with his first attempt, that doubt was now well and truly dispelled.

At the time, we had no particular home in mind for 'The World That Dissolved', and although – like 'The Ghost Sun' and 'Thoughts That Kill' – it would eventually appear in an issue of Bryon Whitworth's fanzine *The Comic Journal*, it was our hope that all these one-off stories would one day find a fully professional outlet, perhaps in a Ron Turner anthology, if a sufficiently perceptive publisher could be found.

Throughout 1992, Ron continued to work mainly on our private commissions, including new illustrations for further vintage Fearn short stories and novels such as *The Dust Destroyer* (1953), *The Conqueror's Voice* (1954) and *Here and Now* (1955). Another piece came about as an indirect result of my discovery, through having for several years been in contact with a Belgian collector, that Ron's mid-1950s *Tit-Bits* Science Fiction Comics series had run not to six entries, as Phil and I had always believed, but to

Right: the first and last pages of the new Jet-Ace Logan tale 'Terror from Moon 33'.

The title page of 'The World That Dissolved', as illustrated by Turner in 1992.

seven, with the seventh, 'The Diamonds of Death', having appeared only in translation in the French publication *Aventures de Demain!...* (see page 81). I decided to send details of this 'lost' entry to Maurice Flanagan for publication in his *Paperback, Pulp and Comic Collector* magazine as a postscript to Phil's article on the comics, three issues earlier. Flanagan responded positively, and suggested that maybe Ron could provide a '*Tit-Bits* style' cover to accompany the piece. I already had Ron reproducing some of the original *Tit-Bits* covers, but in looking for something a little different, I realised that the double-page endpaper piece he had supplied for *Laurie's Space Annual* (see page 69) dated from the same time and had a similar style about it, and would make a great wraparound cover. The original having been produced only in line and wash, this would also be an opportunity for Ron to bring the piece to life in glowing colour – which he certainly did!

Ron later suggested that if we wanted to reprint 'The Diamonds of Death' and could arrange for the text to be translated back into English, he was quite prepared to re-letter the pages and provide a cover for it. At that point, though, we had abandoned all thought of producing further comic-strip publications of our own, and so didn't take up his offer – a decision I now regret, as although 'The Diamonds of Death' wasn't one of his better stories, I realise he might have quite liked to see it finally published in the UK. Had he suggested the idea earlier, I might at least have agreed that he should produce a brand new cover piece for the *Paperback, Pulp and Comic Collector* issue – but, as it was, the reproduction of the *Laurie's Space Annual* endpaper was tremendously effective, and enthusiastically received by many readers as the best cover the magazine had yet featured.

Meanwhile, Phil had another invasion-themed commission for Ron, except that on this occasion the invaders weren't weird aliens from another planet but of a more down-to-earth variety – Vikings! Phil's late father, James Harbottle, had privately squirreled away many poems and short stories about the history of his local north-east area, written either for his own amusement or at most to share with his wife and friends at a local amateur writers' club. Having discovered these after his father's death, Phil felt it would help him to come to terms with his loss if he could create something positive from them, that would form a lasting memory. Consequently, he decided to publish a small collection under the title *Viking Blood*, and wanted Ron to provide a cover and some interior illustrations for this. I was uncertain if Ron would even be interested in taking on such an assignment, but in fact he seemed quite keen to accept the challenge of something so different from our usual commissions and showed an amazing knowledge of the period – he even asked me if he should draw the Viking helmets with the clichéd horns, or more accurately without that feature, ultimately deciding on the latter. The result was an excellent colour wraparound cover and three black-and-white illustrations, which were just as thoughtfully and creatively produced as his more popular SF works.

As much as Ron enjoyed his cover assignments, he still craved the respite that occasional comic-strip work would give him. With no opportunities for such on the horizon, it was

Below: the front of Turner's wraparound cover for the sixth issue of Maurice Flanagan's *Paperback, Pulp and Comic Collector*.

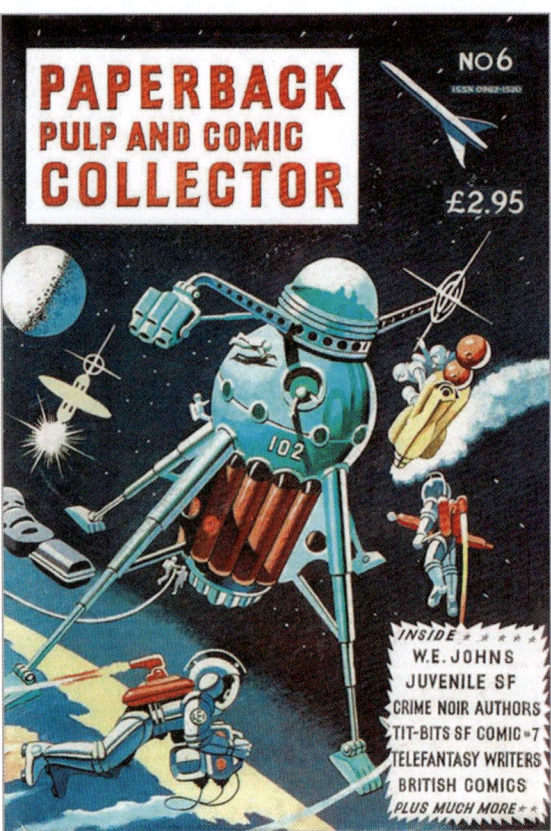

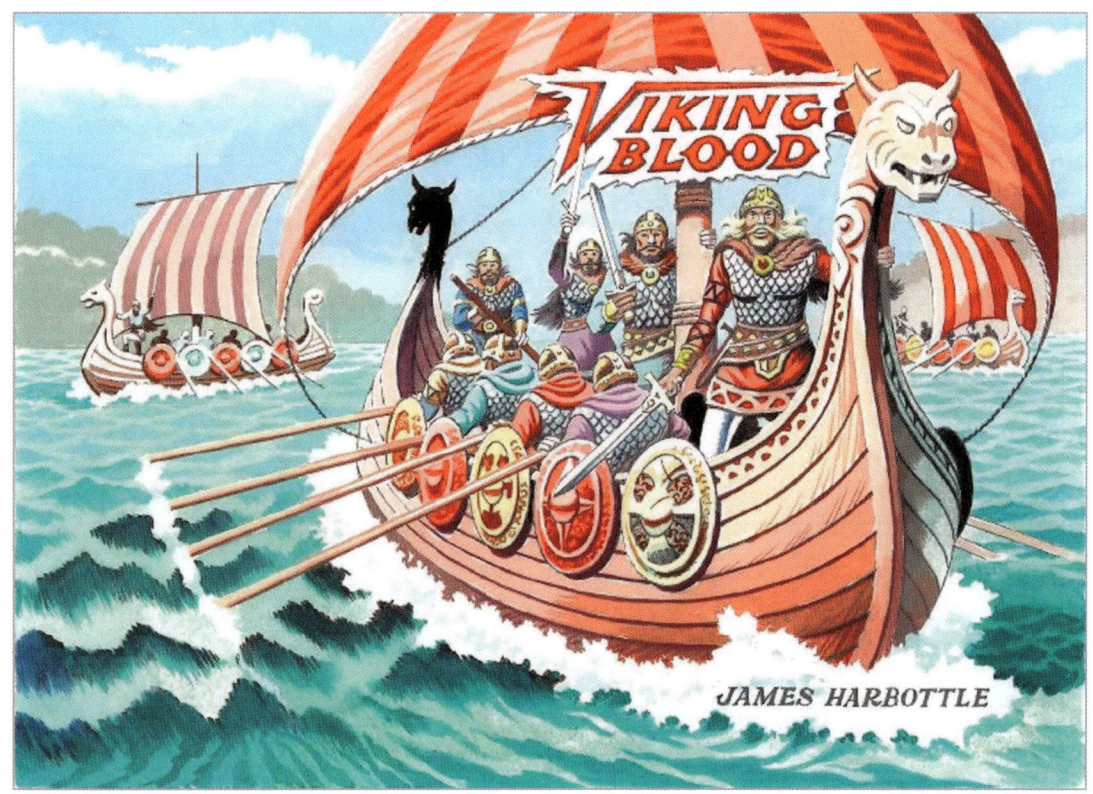

The cover and one of the internal illustrations produced by Turner for the James Harbottle collection *Viking Blood* (Cosmos, 1993).

difficult to know what to suggest. At the time, though, I had already started thinking of compiling a book like *The Fantastic Art of Ron Turner*, and had been building up quite a lot of information about Ron's life. He would sometimes tell me anecdotes about his wartime experiences, and it occurred to me that there could be no better way of recording these than to have Ron illustrate them himself. Thus it was that he began to draw a short series of biographical episodes in comic-strip form (see Chapter 1 for some of these), turning to this activity whenever he needed a break from painting covers or had a little time to fill.

I also suggested to Ron that he might consider writing a new Space Ace adventure, and while he preferred not to revisit that classic character, he did agree to devise a new strip in the same style – something he'd done only once before in recent years, in the form of the dot-to-dot filler, 'The Cosmic Key!', that he'd both written and drawn for the *Whoopee! Annual 1983*. His new offering was a seven-page story, 'The Killing Zone', set thousands of years in the future, when the Earth has died and its surviving races have colonised other worlds. A dictator arises on one of those worlds, set on invading and subjugating all the others, but finds his attempts resisted by a small band of guerrilla fighters. The fighters discover that all the power to operate the dictator's spacecraft and equipment is beamed from a central transmitter, and that by putting that out of action they can stop the invasion force. The plot was a fairly basic one, but Ron's excellent visuals more than compensated for that, and showed that his storytelling, like his artwork, was still well up to par. Again, we had no immediate outlet in mind for this story, but it kept Ron busy and was another we could hold 'in the bank' until such time as we found a ready market for his work.

Toward the end of 1993, Ron phoned me with the good news that he had completed another batch of our private commissions, including reproductions of his vintage covers for the Tubb novel *The Wall* and for the *Tit-Bits* Science Fiction Library editions of Fearn's *The Hell Fruit* and *Cosmic Exodus*. But he also had some very bad news: he was in imminent danger of losing his home!

Life on the houseboat, *Sagittarius*, had always been a little precarious. During the great storm of 1987, one of the mooring ropes had come loose and the boat had been swept out into the middle of a raging current – though luckily the phone line had remained intact and Ron had been able to make an emergency call. There had been other occasions, too, when the river level had risen and threatened to swamp the craft. This time, Ron had awoken in the night to discover that the hull had sprung a leak and there was water about a foot high lapping round his bed! Fortunately, he had prepared for such an eventuality by rigging up a pump, and by morning the water had all been expelled. However, the leak still had to be investigated and dealt with.

On having the boat inspected, Ron was told that the hull needed a complete refit. Age had weakened it to the extent that if any river debris, such as a loose branch, were to strike it, it could be badly damaged – and Ron mightn't be so lucky next time. When he approached his insurance company, though, he was informed that the cost of a refit would exceed the value of the boat. In short, it was a write-off! Ron was devastated. He didn't even have the option of taking a chance and simply having the current leak fixed, as mooring legislation precluded an unsafe vessel being kept on the river. There was no choice. The boat would have to be scrapped and Ron would have to find a new home. He talked of maybe buying another boat, but his financial situation was such that he was worried he might not be able to afford one big enough to allow him to continue painting, forcing him to retire for good. For the moment, though, he just had to deal with the problem at hand: he would consider his future later on.

So, on a cold, damp, November morning, I called round to see Ron, knowing that this would be the last time I would visit him on his boat. It was a very sad occasion. Ron had been in the middle of creating a reproduction of another of his classic Milestone covers, for the Volsted Gridban novel *Fugitive of Time*, which wouldn't now be completed until after his move – a strange quirk of fate, given that the original had also suffered a delay back in 1953 (see page 61). As I gathered up the latest batch of finished artwork and said goodbye, I couldn't help but wonder if this would prove to be the end of a great collaboration. I desperately hoped not – a feeling that was only heightened a couple of months later when, in the midst of all the uncertainty, I received an offer of a commission for Ron that would be more lucrative than anything else he had taken on over the past decade.

Turner's 1993 recreation of his cover for *The Wall* (Milestone, 1953), written by E C Tubb as Charles Grey.

THE FANTASTIC ART OF RON TURNER

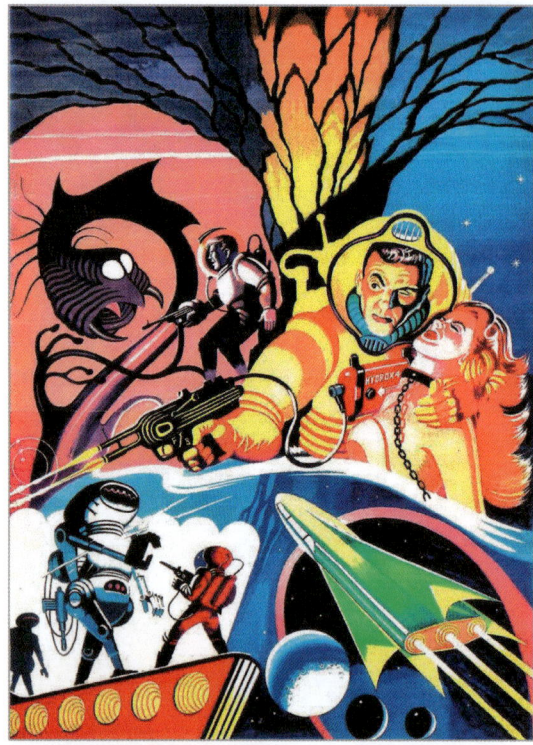

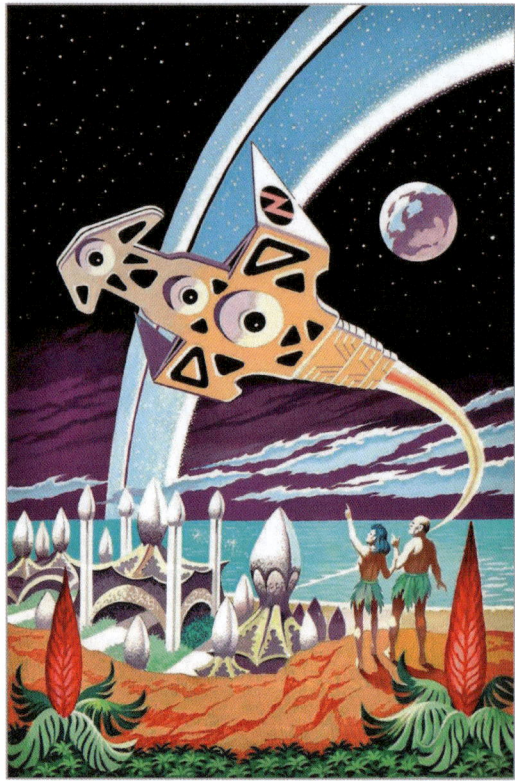

Turner's 1993 paintings recreating his original covers for *Vargo Statten Science Fiction Magazine* # 1 (Scion, 1954) (top left) and *The Hell Fruit* (C Arthur Pearson, 1953) (top right); and his new cover pieces for *Z Formations* (Curtis Warren, 1953) (bottom left) and *The Intelligence Gigantic* (World's Work, 1943) (bottom right), all written by John Russell Fearn.

Turner's 1993 recreation of his cover for *The Cosmic Exodus* (C Arthur Pearson, 1953), written by John Russell Fearn as Conrad G Holt.

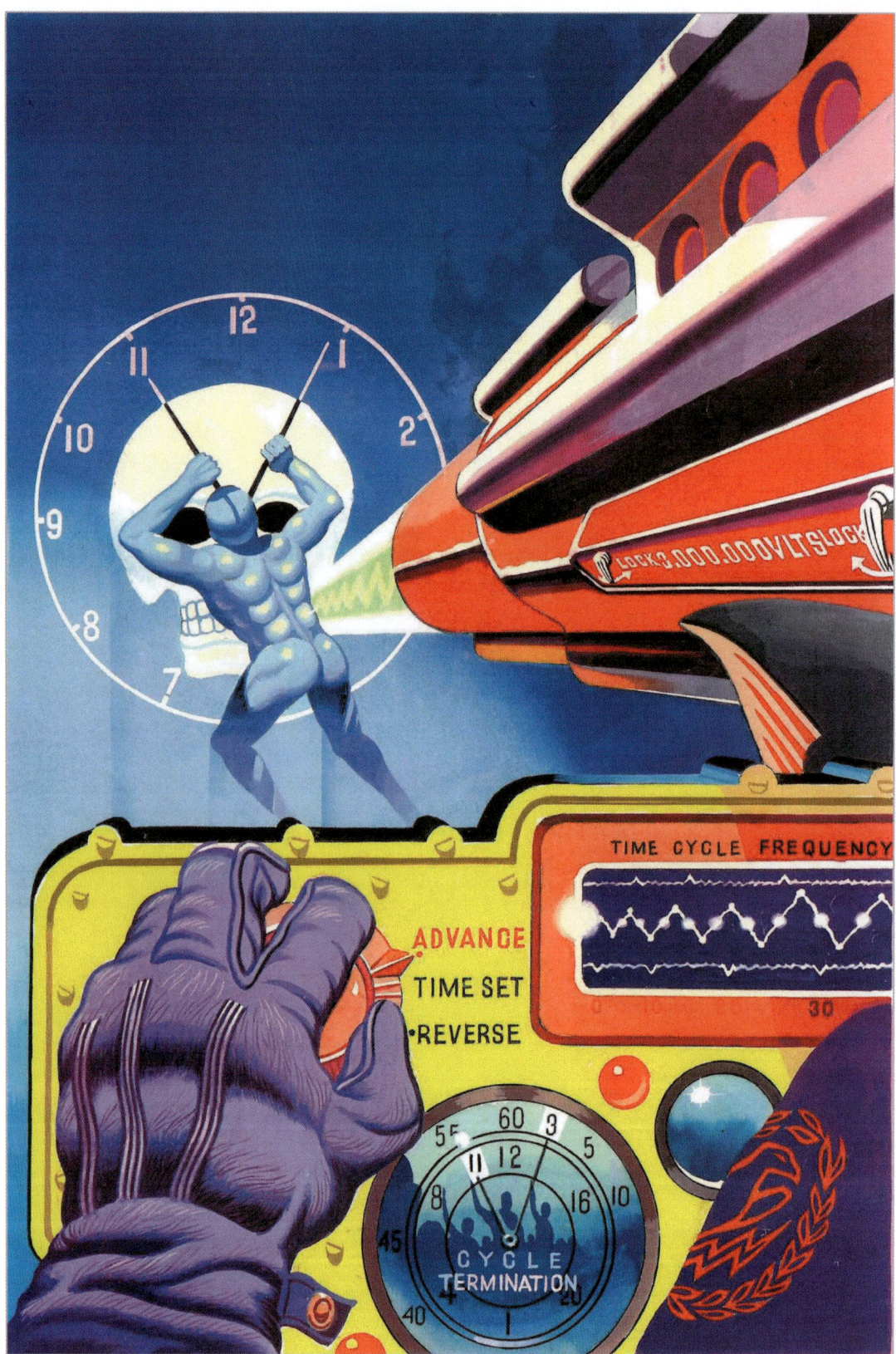

Turner's 1994 recreation of his cover for *Fugitive of Time* (Milestone, 1953), written by John Russell Fearn as Volsted Gridban.

25: BACK ON FAMILIAR GROUND

It was not until February 1994 that I heard from Ron again. He explained that, having finally given up on the idea of continuing to live a life on the river, he had found himself a small place in Sunningdale and would be spending the next few weeks making it habitable. After that, he could settle down to producing more work for Phil and me. This came as a great relief, not least because a couple of weeks earlier I'd received a phone call from Gary Russell, the new editor of Marvel UK's *Doctor Who Magazine*, with an invitation for Ron to provide a cover for *The Dalek Chronicles*, a summer special collecting together the whole of *The Daleks* comic-strip as originally published in *TV Century 21*.

Six months prior to this, having noticed that selected stories from *The Daleks* were being reprinted in *Doctor Who Magazine*'s sister title, *Doctor Who Classic Comics*, I had approached Russell, suggesting that Ron might provide a cover for one of the issues, or better still for a complete collection, should Marvel ever decide to publish one. There had been no interest at that time, but obviously my idea had not been forgotten, and now a firm professional commission was awaiting Ron. The irony was that, until I heard from him, I had no idea if he would, or could, take it on!

Russell was unaware of the recent change in Ron's living circumstances. As far as he was concerned, Ron was simply very busy – which was of course true. I had been reluctant to tell him the full story, for fear the commission might be lost. But now that Ron and I were back in touch again, and he had confirmed his interest, the only question was whether or not he could meet the deadline. Luckily the cover wasn't needed until May 1994, which meant that he would just about have time to set up his new studio before he needed to start work.

The cover required was of the wraparound variety, and Russell's initial suggestion was that it should show a couple of Daleks on the right-hand side, looking across to a huge bank of monitor screens on the left, with those screens showing significant characters or elements from stories throughout the series. Thus, when the cover was folded, the Daleks would appear on the front, and the bank of monitor screens on the back. I wasn't particularly happy with this idea, and neither was Ron, who suggested that a montage showing some sort of interaction between all the different elements would be more dynamic. This put me in mind of the covers of vintage *Rupert* annuals, which often showed characters from various different stories in one composite wraparound scene, and I agreed that a similar approach would work best for *The Dalek Chronicles*.

Between us, Ron and I came up with several ideas for scenes featuring the two-headed dinosaur-like Terrorkon creatures, the flying robot K2, plus the Daleks' blue-skinned humanoid ancestors (not the Kaleds in this version of their history). Ron produced a few sketches for approval, but I still felt that something more was needed. Then I remembered the black-and-white illustration Ron had produced for *Doctor Who Magazine* some five years earlier, showing a line of Daleks disembarking from their spaceship and advancing toward their Emperor (see page 276). Agreeing that this was a powerful piece of imagery that would give the scene the edge it needed, Ron proceeded to produce some revised sketches.

Eventually the composition was finalised. The Dalek spaceship appeared on the front, blending almost seamlessly into an action-packed vista on the back, showing the Terrorkons attempting to attack the flying form of K2 as he swoops down to observe the small, blue-skinned figures of the original Daleks. When I saw the end result, I felt sure that Russell would be happy with it. The piece amply fulfilled his brief to include elements from throughout the series, forming an exciting action scene when opened out flat and two equally effective standalone ones when folded and viewed individually as front and back covers.

Russell's response was just as positive as I had expected. He was already delighted to be publishing such a great collection of strips, but to have them presented under so stunning a cover was the icing on the cake for him. In fact, so impressed was he with Ron's cover that he even asked if he could buy

Above: Turner's full, unlettered wraparound cover for *The Dalek Chronicles* (Marvel UK, 1994).

the original artwork! And if Ron thought this would be a one-off, he was much mistaken, for once it became known that he had produced a new piece of Dalek art, he began to receive private commissions from various Dalek fans and collectors; and this kept him busy for most of the rest of 1994.

Other professional commissions were on the horizon, too. Back in late 1991, while attending the first Maurice Flanagan-organised London Book Fair, Phil had met Gary Lovisi, an American book dealer who published a collectors' magazine, *Paperback Parade*, and was also establishing his own small press, Gryphon Books. A collector of vintage British paperbacks, Lovisi had invited Phil to write articles for *Paperback Parade* about John Russell Fearn and Ted Tubb, and this had led to Phil becoming a regular contributor. Amongst the pieces Phil supplied during 1994 was one about a series of Fearn novels often dubbed the Martian Quartet, which had parallels to *John Carter of Mars* and the other SF fantasy epics of Edgar Rice Burroughs – an author much admired by the American SF fraternity. The four novels had all received a UK publication in 1950, but had never been reprinted, and so were now quite rare. Phil's article created considerable interest amongst US readers, and when news of this reached him, he quickly spotted an opportunity: if, in his capacity as Fearn's literary executor, he could sell Lovisi on the idea of reissuing the Martian Quartet through his Gryphon Books imprint, with new covers by Ron, then this could give all their fortunes a boost. Gryphon's early titles had been rather poorly-produced black-and-white booklets, and Phil could see that the proficiency of their cover artwork left a lot to be desired. So, who better than Ron to remedy that?

It didn't take Phil long to convince Lovisi of the merits of his idea. His thought was to create an immediate impact with US readers by putting out all four Martian Quartet titles simultaneously; then, if that proved successful, they could consider issuing further publications with the same classic author/artist combination, to improve and promote

Two paintings produced by Turner circa 1994 as private commissions for a Dalek fan.

Another spectacular Dalek painting produced by Turner as a private commission.

Gryphon's output.

Up until this point, when Phil had commissioned Ron to produce new cover paintings for Fearn novels that he hadn't had the chance to illustrate back in the '50s, this had been mainly for his own enjoyment, to see 'what might have been'. There was the incidental thought that if those novels were ever to be reprinted, then Ron's new cover pieces could be used for them. However, with no specific plans for that to happen, our general approach had been simply to decide on a suitable cover scene for each novel and brief Ron with a description for him to work from. Now, though, with a firm commitment from Gryphon to reissue the Martian Quartet, and a professional commission for Ron to supply the covers, we realised that a lot more thought and consideration would have to go into the presentation. Consequently, we adopted a new approach whereby we would send Ron a copy of each novel to read, along with suggestions for several sequences we thought might work well for the cover, then leave it to him to decide which of those had the most potential and sketch them out for our approval.

As 1995 began, Phil and I came up with several cover ideas for the first book, *Emperor of Mars*, but none of them appealed to Ron. He felt that as Mars was mentioned in the title then the planet should feature, large and imposing, somewhere in the illustration – perhaps as seen from the observation deck of the spaceship carrying the abducted hero, Clay Drew, to the Red Planet. This immediately reminded me of one of the first private black-and-white commissions Ron had produced for me back in 1984. It was a fantastic scene reminiscent of a *Rick Random* page, set aboard a starship with the captain looking out of a large observation window at a distant galaxy, while small figures in the background operated equipment. All that was needed, I felt, was to replace the galaxy with the planet Mars, and it would be ideal. Phil and Ron both agreed.

The end result, now rendered in colour, made for an outstanding cover for the first entry in the series. Lovisi also wanted Ron to provide a black-and-white frontispiece for each book, so our time spent coming up with different cover ideas would not be wasted, as any deemed unsuitable for the cover could be used instead for the internal illustration.

Right: the front cover and internal frontispiece for John Russell Fearn's *Emperor of Mars* (Gryphon, 1995).

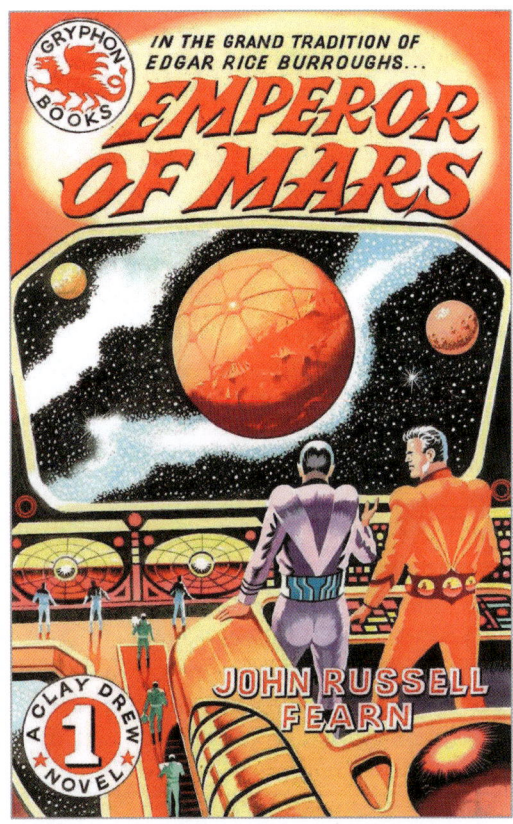

Ron's idea that the title should be reflected in some way in the cover illustration was carried through into the series' second entry, *Warrior of Mars*, with an action scene of Drew knocking a Martian guard from the top of a tower to prevent him from using a disintegrator cannon – the design of which Ron based on an element from one of his classic Dalek strips. For the third, *Red Men of Mars*, he reworked an element from a *Rick Random* adventure, showing the characters gripped in the writhing tentacles of a carnivorous plant. For the fourth, *Goddess of Mars*, he devised a scene featuring a spacecraft, robots and the pretty heroine; a composition that was right up his street, and would surely serve to attract readers to the series.

When Lovisi saw the finished paintings he was astounded by their quality – and absolutely delighted. They were certainly a big step up from the substandard pieces his previous contributors had supplied. He didn't even need to concern himself with the title lettering, as Ron had developed a standard font running across and unifying all four books, plus a new Gryphon Books logo.

It was obvious from the degree of commitment Ron had shown that he was greatly enjoying being gainfully employed once more on the type of work closest to his heart, knowing that it would be seen by a much larger audience than the private commissions he had been producing for us. Lovisi, for his part, was sufficiently enthused to adopt Phil's suggestion of following up the Mars Quartet with a succession of further reissues. It seemed that Ron had reached another turning point in his career, and was about to embark on his first regular run of commissions for a US publisher.

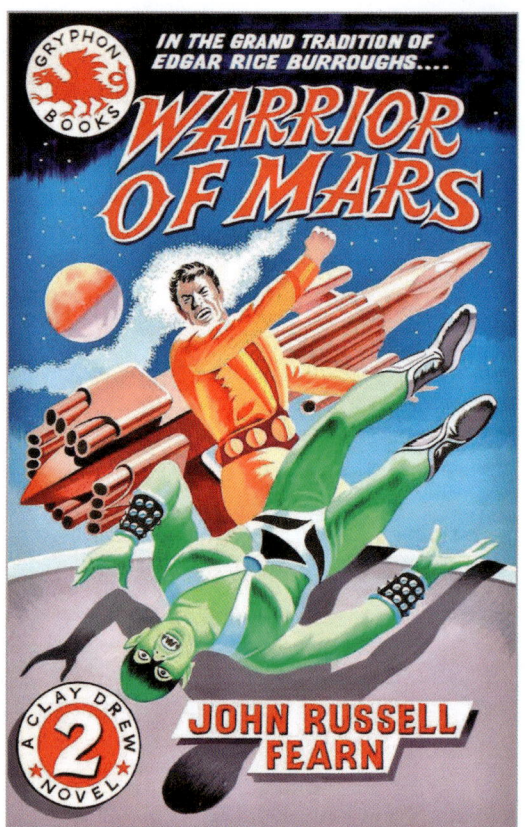

Above: Turner's cover illustration for John Russell Fearn's *Warrior of Mars* (Gryphon Books, 1995).

Below: the black-and-white frontispiece illustrations for (left to right) *Warrior of Mars*, *Red Men of Mars* and *Goddess of Mars* (all Gryphon Books, 1995).

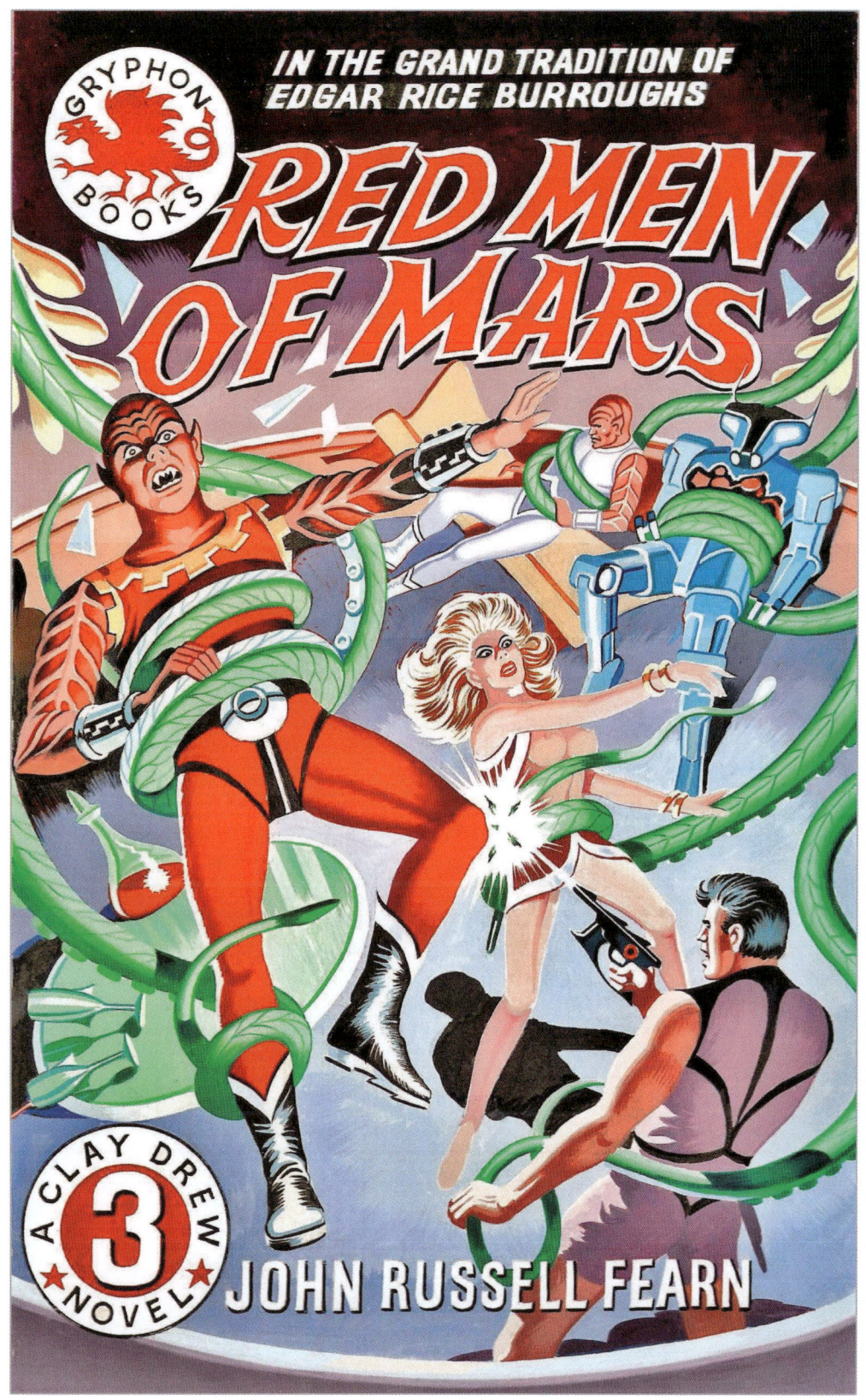

Turner's cover painting for John Russell Fearn's *Red Men of Mars* (Gryphon Books, 1995).

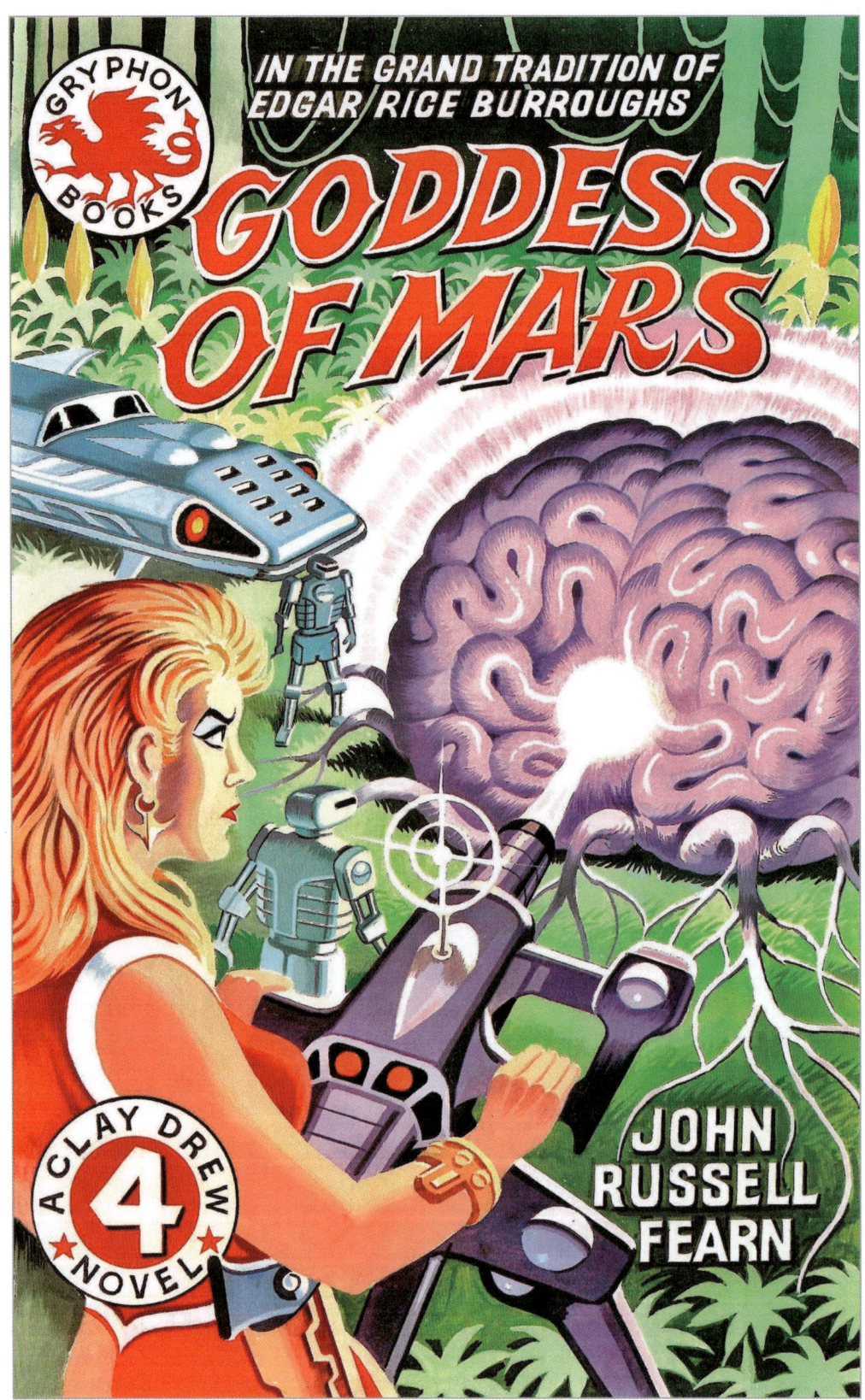

Turner's cover painting for John Russell Fearn's *Goddess of Mars* (Gryphon Books, 1995).

26: CRIME DOES PAY!

In the summer of 1995, while on a trip to the US with his daughter Claire to celebrate her gaining her Master of Arts degree, Phil took the opportunity to call in on Gary Lovisi at his Brooklyn, New York home. The reissue of the Martian Quartet novels having been successfully accomplished, Lovisi had hinted that he might next like to publish something by Ted Tubb, so Phil had judiciously taken along with him the manuscripts of two unpublished Tubb novels, *The Spore Menace* and *The Temple of Dra Vheera*, which had fallen back into the author's hands when the boom in SF paperbacks had ended in 1954. On being offered these two 'lost' stories, with the prospect of Ron supplying the covers, Lovisi was immediately receptive. In fact, as the conversation continued, he indicated that he would be prepared to accept *any* Fearn or Tubb stories with covers by Ron. It was at this point that Phil decided to play his trump card by offering him Fearn's 'magnum opus', the adventures of the Golden Amazon.

We had already secured the first UK publication of the series' eighth entry, *Lord of Atlantis*, a few years earlier via Maurice Flanagan's Zeon Books (see page 280), but that had been just a one-off. Now, in light of Lovisi's enthusiasm, Phil felt this was an ideal opportunity to relaunch the series from the start – though the possibility of republishing all 26 of Fearn's series entries was something not even contemplated at the time. Lovisi agreed to take the first book, *The Golden Amazon*, and Ron was duly tasked with providing the cover. Phil suggested depicting the Amazon as a baby, undergoing the operation through which she gains her super-strength. My feeling, though, was that she should be shown fully mature, tackling a thug, to emphasise her power. We finally settled on my suggestion of presenting both of these ideas in a split scene, with the Amazon's speeding spaceship, the *Ultra*, acting as a divider and adding a more obvious SF aspect.

Ron set to work on the painting, but unfortunately failed to stick to the brief we had given him. The 'origin of the Amazon' section of the composition was supposed to be set in the 1940s, and Phil had wanted the *Ultra* to be drawn as a cigar-shaped spaceship typical of the SF of that era. Ron, however, had given it the same, more modern design he had devised for our earlier comic-strip adaptation of the Amazon's exploits. Moreover, instead of showing the Amazon being operated on as a baby, he had drawn her as a grown woman!

At our request, Ron produced a second version – but he still declined to draw the Amazon as a baby on the operating table, arguing that this was completely inappropriate subject matter for an SF cover! Instead, he compromised by depicting her as a young girl.

Fortunately, although it was not quite as we had intended, the revised cover was accepted by Lovisi, and when published in the spring of 1996,

Below: Turner's revised cover painting for *The Golden Amazon* (Gryphon Books, 1996).

the book sold well, securing his commitment to continuing with further volumes in the series. The success of these would indeed encourage him to expand his publishing operations and issue a whole new line of SF paperbacks that, at Phil's suggestion, he would call the Gryphon SF Rediscovery Series.

As the series progressed, Lovisi was delighted with the consistently high quality of Ron's work on the covers, to the extent that he was even moved to send him a personal letter declaring just how much he appreciated his efforts (just as Fearn himself had done more than forty years previously). Considering that Lovisi was a real cover-art aficionado, this was some tribute!

But SF was not Lovisi's only interest. He also had a passion for classic detective fiction, and was now considering publishing a line of crime novel reprints. For the covers of these, he first planned to commission British artist Denis McLoughlin, who back in the '50s had been responsible for the majority of Boardman Books' cover art. In fact, in many ways, McLoughlin was to the crime genre what Ron was to the SF one. Both had similar dedicated working methods: complete familiarity with the subject matter; use of both realistic and symbolic interpretation; stylised lettering; and an intuitive feel for colour. When he approached McLoughlin, however, Lovisi was disappointed to learn that, although he was still working, he had retired from cover illustration and had no desire to return to it.

Lovisi had other artists in mind, but having been so impressed with Ron's work on the SF titles, he wondered if he might now be interested in tackling the crime series as well. The general cover theme for these books would be what Lovisi called 'the three Gs' – Guys, Gals and Guns – with the female subjects being either damsels in distress, menaced, held at gunpoint or tied up, or else self-assured she-devil types, in control and packing guns themselves. Having previously produced only a handful of crime covers for Scion, prior to his run of SF commissions back in the '50's, Ron saw this as an opportunity to flex his artistic talents in an unfamiliar direction, and eagerly accepted the challenge.

The first title in the new series was *Get Me Headquarters*, written by Hank Janson creator and author Stephen Frances under his Ace Capelli pseudonym. Phil's initial suggestion of a cover depicting a detective climbing into a room through a window and shooting at the hoodlum inside was rejected by Ron. Although unfamiliar with McLoughlin's work, Ron shared his view that showing a violent deed being done was less effective than simply suggesting it by depicting the situation either directly before or directly after, thereby heightening readers' anticipation. Blazing guns, he felt, were more suitable for comic covers. Consequently, he modified Phil's idea to achieve a more mature and successful presentation, showing the lawman kicking open the door rather than entering through the window, and having him and the hoodlum wielding guns at each other, emphasising the tension in their confrontation.

Keen to demonstrate his proficiency in this genre, Ron also produced four other highly-detailed crime-scene sketches for Lovisi's approval, adding a literal title to each to show also his various lettering styles. The first, *Spectacle*, consisted of a close-up of a dead man's glasses lying on the floor, reflecting an image of his female assassin. The second, *Process of Elimination*, featured another 'tough dame', concealing a gun in her stocking top after disposing of a recent victim. The third, *Rainman*, presented an atmospheric scene of a girl with murderous intent, stalking her victim during a downpour. Finally, *Body of Evidence* showed the naked body of a dead girl surrounded by handcuffs, coins, bullets and a gun.

Lovisi was delighted with all these ideas, and again wrote to Ron to tell him how superb he thought they were: not only matching McLoughlin's standards but in some cases even surpassing them. The only minor shortcoming to be addressed was that, in trying to emphasise the women's murderous nature, Ron had made them a little too hard-faced, rather than the lushly beautiful 'cover girls' usually designed to sell books.

Lovisi confirmed that a run of crime cover commissions would now be forthcoming – although the SF assignments would not be forgotten either. Sure enough, Ron soon found himself being asked to provide covers for crime novels not only by UK writers such as Norman Lazenby and Syd Bounds, but also by leading US ones including Howard

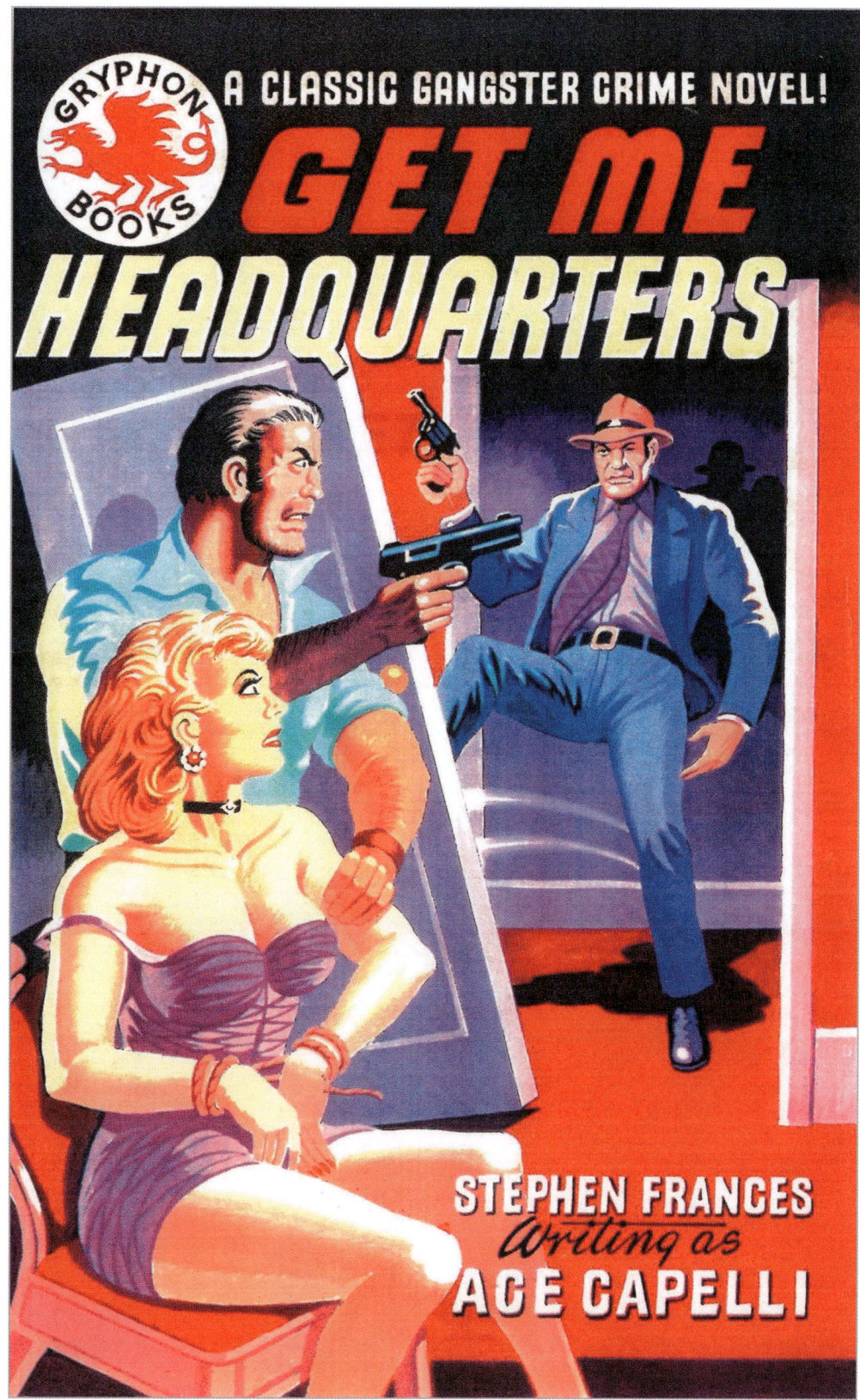

Turner's 1996 cover for the debut Gryphon Books crime reissue, *Get Me Headquarters* by Stephen Frances.

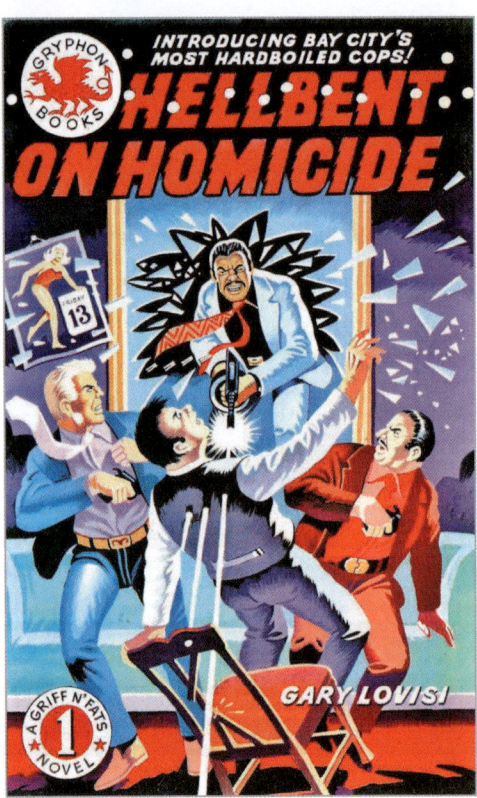
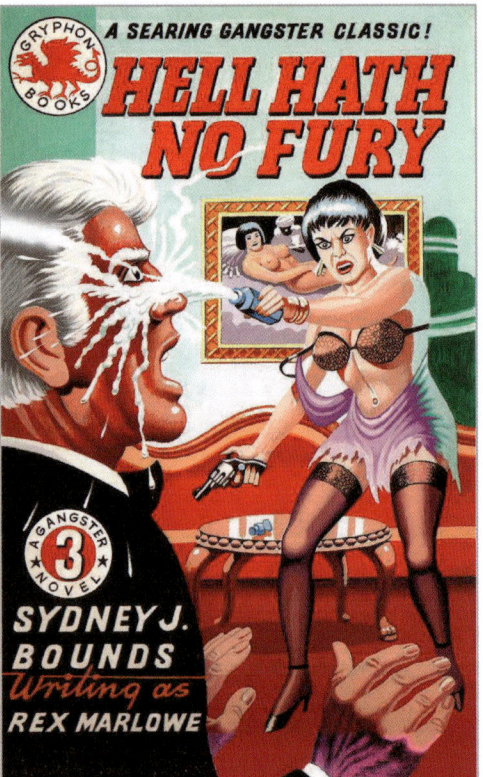

More 1996 Gryphon crime covers: *Assignment New York* by E C Tubb (top left); *She Wanted a Guy* by Norman Lazenby (top right); *Hellbent on Homicide* by Gary Lovisi (bottom left); and *Hell Hath No Fury* by Sydney J Bounds (bottom right).

CRIME DOES PAY!

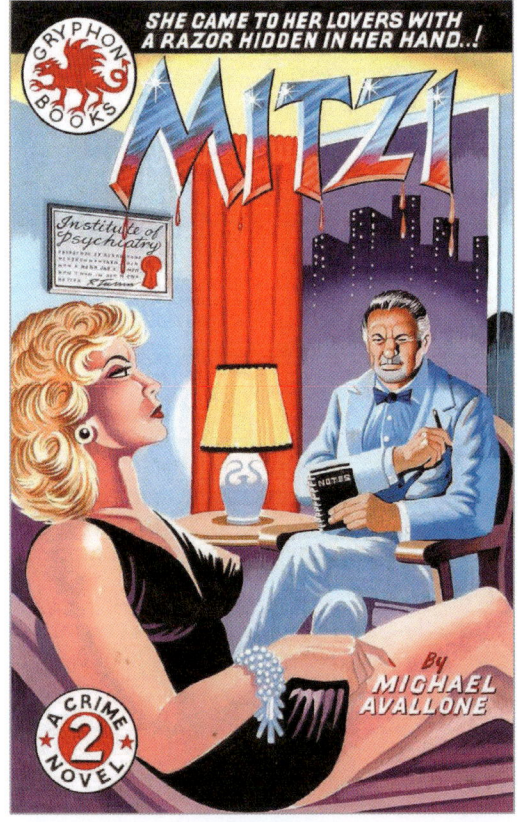

Browne and Michael Avallone. The piece that graced Avallone's novel *Mitzi* is of particular interest, as the psychiatrist shown interviewing a murderous blonde was based by Ron on his former agent, Greg Hall, while the certificate on the wall bears the signature 'R Turner'!

With Ron's cover-artist credentials now firmly established in the US, I had meanwhile returned to the idea of trying to launch his comic-strip work in that market, reasoning that the failure of our earlier Harrier Comics project had been due more to bad timing than to anything else. Fired by Phil's success with Gryphon, I felt I might now have better luck, particularly as there seemed to be few if any opportunities in the UK. Phil was far too busy to write a new script himself, but I had a few ideas of my own, and this would be my chance to explore the possibilities.

I started by noting down all the elements I knew Ron liked to see in an SF story: spacecraft, machines, aliens, weird creatures and action scenes of some description. I also knew that he enjoyed drawing beautiful women; one look at his original *Rick Random* artwork was enough to see that, and there had indeed been several occasions when he had been asked to redraw his female characters to give them less revealing attire. This time, I was keen to let Ron depict his women however he wanted, with no restrictions.

As far as a publisher was concerned, I intended to try approaching *Heavy Metal*, the US magazine run by Kevin Eastman. This featured a lot of nudity, and the strip I had in mind for Ron was actually less risqué than those they usually ran, so I didn't see how there could be any objections on grounds of taste. The tale I had devised was titled 'Blonde Bombshell' and concerned a businessman dealing in androids. When a swindling ex-partner who double-crossed him years earlier orders a love-droid from the businessman's new company, an ironic opportunity for revenge presents itself. The love-droid is primed to react to body heat, but is activated prematurely by a photon storm on board the space-freighter taking it to its destination. Then the freighter is attacked by a gang of marauders – and that's when things really begin to heat up!

This fast-paced story was right up Ron's street, but he still produced numerous sheets of roughs showing all the characters and spacecraft, to check that I was happy

Left: Turner's covers for the crime novels *Mitzi* by Michael Avallone and *Kidnapped!* by Morris Hershman, both published by Gryphon Books in 1997.

Above: two of Turner's pages for the 'Blonde Bombshell' strip.

with how he intended to approach it. The majority of *Heavy Metal*'s content was in colour, so to leave open the possibility of this being a fully painted strip, should it be accepted, I asked Ron to draw it in pencil only at this stage.

Four weeks later, Ron had finished the 13-page strip, and I was more than satisfied with the results. He had given it his best shot, and had clearly enjoyed drawing the love-droid and the few alien women I'd thrown in for good measure. As in the best of his earlier work, he had also shown the action from a variety of different angles – high, low, close, distant – to make the presentation as interesting as possible. It was a fantastic piece of work, which I felt sure would be well received. Consequently, I proceeded to send a copy to Phil, and he agreed to submit it via his agency to the *Heavy Metal* offices in New York.

Several weeks passed without any response, but I wasn't too concerned. *Heavy Metal* was a monthly title with many established contributors, so I assumed it would take some time for the editors to find space for 'Blonde Bombshell'. It therefore came as something of a shock to me that when a reply did at last arrive, it was in the form of a rejection slip, indicating that the editors found the story unsuitable for their magazine! Judging by the content of previous issues, I knew it certainly couldn't have been the semi-nudity that had put them off. More likely, it hadn't gone far enough!

Disappointed but not defeated, I next submitted the story to the London operations office of *Omni*, a US science-fiction magazine published by Bob Guccione of *Penthouse* notoriety. After a week or so had gone by without any response, I was beginning to feel that this was the *Heavy Metal* situation all over again, so I decided to phone up and ask what was happening. My call was answered by a woman who thanked me for the samples but described them as 'pulpy' and not in the magazine's required style. Unwilling to give up straight away, I began to explain that Ron was flexible, and could if necessary adjust his style to suit the circumstances. I was in full flow when suddenly the woman interrupted me, announcing that she had to ring off as 'a man has arrived to read my meter'. Although initially annoyed at this rather abrupt end to the call, I had to smile, as given the *Penthouse* association, I couldn't help but wonder if this was some sort of euphemism! Probably not; but, either way, I was left in no doubt that 'Blonde Bombshell' would not be appearing in *Omni*.

Feeling very deflated, I nevertheless asked Ron to ink the strip, confident that one day I would find a place for it, either in another magazine or as part of a collection of Ron's work. When he later delivered the finished pages, I noticed that he'd adopted a new shading technique. Along with his usual hatching and cross-hatching, he'd also used what is sometimes known as 'basket-weave'. This I immediately recognised as a technique favoured by Denis McLoughlin, and realised that Ron must have picked it up when I had sent him some examples of McLoughlin's work before he started producing his crime covers. Ever keen to try different things, he had obviously wanted to see if he could incorporate this approach into his own work. That was fine – except when applied to a half-page frame showing the space-freighter almost engulfed by writhing tendrils of energy as it encountered the photon storm. This could have been a stunning illustration – if only Ron hadn't used basket-weave for the starfield! I recalled that he had actually tried something similar on his very first *Space Ace* story back in 1954, but that had been on a much smaller scale than here. In this half-page scene, it just didn't work – especially as in the following frames he had reverted to representing space as the standard black wash with white dots for the stars!

Sadly, Ron sometimes got carried away with his experimentation at the expense of the story. I was put in mind of when, back in the '80s, I had been lucky enough to see some books of his original *Rick Random* artwork, and had been appalled to note how the editors had 'whited out' or modified certain sections, only later coming to understand why that had been necessary, due to Ron's resistance to amending his own work. Now I found myself resorting to a black felt-tip pen to correct the problem with that half-page space-freighter scene. Other than that, though, Ron had done full justice to my script, and overall the strip was truly excellent.

In the meantime, Gary Lovisi remained keen to publish some of Ted Tubb's SF books, now holding them in the same high regard he had previously reserved for Fearn's. The first to appear, at the start of 1996, preceding *The Golden Amazon* by a couple of months, was *The Spore*

Right: Turner's covers for *You Take the Rap* by John Russell Fearn and *Kill and Desire* by Stephen Frances, both published by Gryphon Books in 1997.

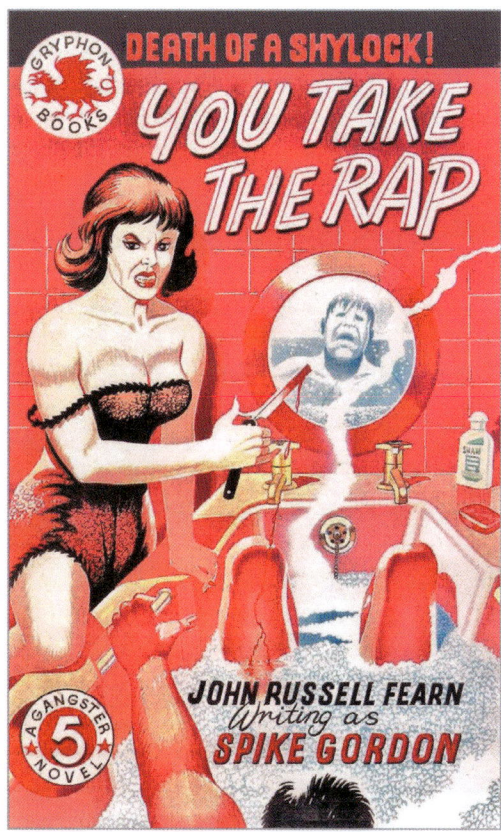

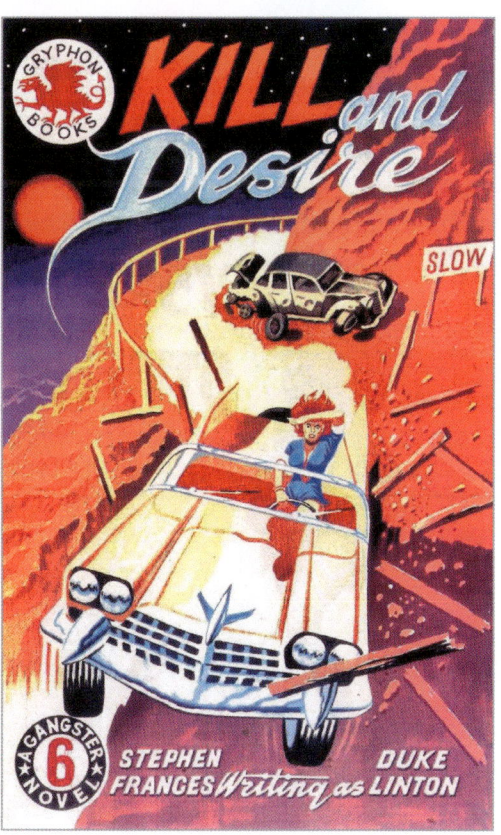

Menace, now retitled *Pandora's Box*. This was soon followed by *Saturn Patrol*, Tubb's very first SF novel, for which Ron painted a *Star Wars*-style dogfight in space, and *The Temple of Dra Vheera*, now retitled *Temple of Death*. The latter had originally been written for the mid-1950s *Tit-Bits* Science Fiction Library range, and would almost certainly have had a Turner cover back then, had it been published, so it was entirely fitting that Ron should now illustrate the Gryphon edition. He produced not only a beautiful colour cover for the book, but also an excellent black-and-white frontispiece, showing hundreds of small figures gathering outside the titular temple. I had actually given Ron two suggestions for this piece, indicating that although the crowd scene was my favourite, I would quite understand it if he preferred to go for the easier alternative. However, Ron always liked a challenge, and knowing that the crowd scene would be more impressive, he had taken the time and trouble to present it in all the detail it required. He later told me that drawing the scene hadn't really been a chore, but an exercise to see if it could be effectively achieved. The tiresome aspect had been having to repeat the process when he came to ink over the initial pencils.

Throughout this period, Ron continued to accept private commissions, including reproductions of more of his vintage paperback covers and further Dalek-themed paintings. However, it was Lovisi's Gryphon assignments that earned him his main professional income. The crime titles made up the majority of these, with the SF ones generally taking a back seat. There were, though, notable exceptions, including the cover for the second Amazon novel, *The Golden Amazon Returns*, and that for Ted Tubb's *The Return*, the thirty-second and last book in the classic *Dumarest* saga, telling of Earl Dumarest, abducted as a child and taken to a far-off world where he grows into a tough adventurer determined to find his way back to his home planet, Earth. Although previously published in France, *The Return* had never had an English edition, and both Phil and Tubb himself had been keen to remedy that. Consequently they had approached Lovisi, and he had agreed to take it on.

Meanwhile, though, Ron was about to experience a 'return' of his own.

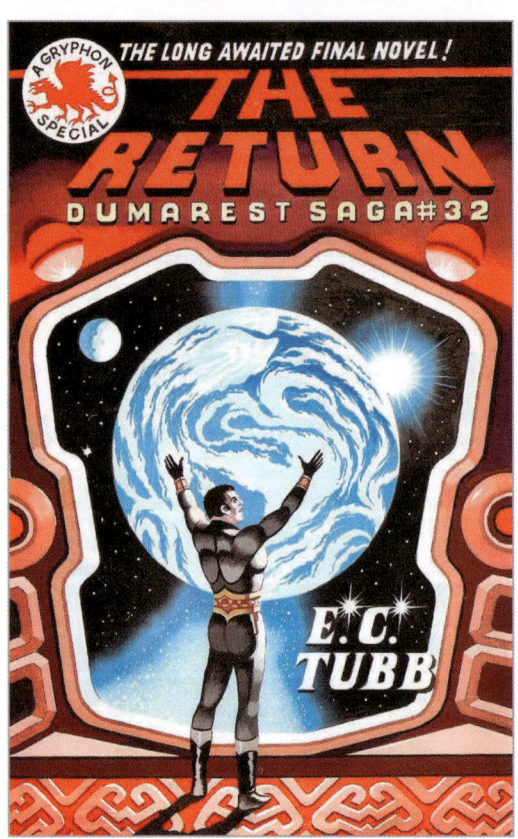

Right: Turner's dramatic covers for the Gryphon Books editions of John Russell Fearn's *The Golden Amazon Returns* and E C Tubb's *The Return*, both published in 1997.

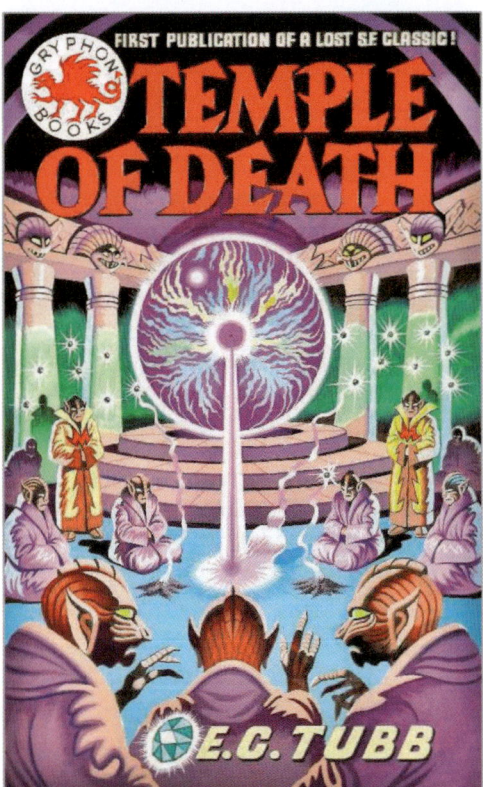 

Turner's colour covers and accompanying black-and-white frontispieces for the E C Tubb novels *Pandora's Box* (top row) and *Temple of Death* (bottom row), both published by Gryphon Books in 1996.

Above: a 1996-painted piece used by Gryphon Books for a 2004 *Hardboiled* magazine cover; and covers for Gryphon Books editions of John Russell Fearn's *Aftermath* (1996) and E C Tubb's *Saturn Patrol* (1996) and *Murder in Space* (1997).

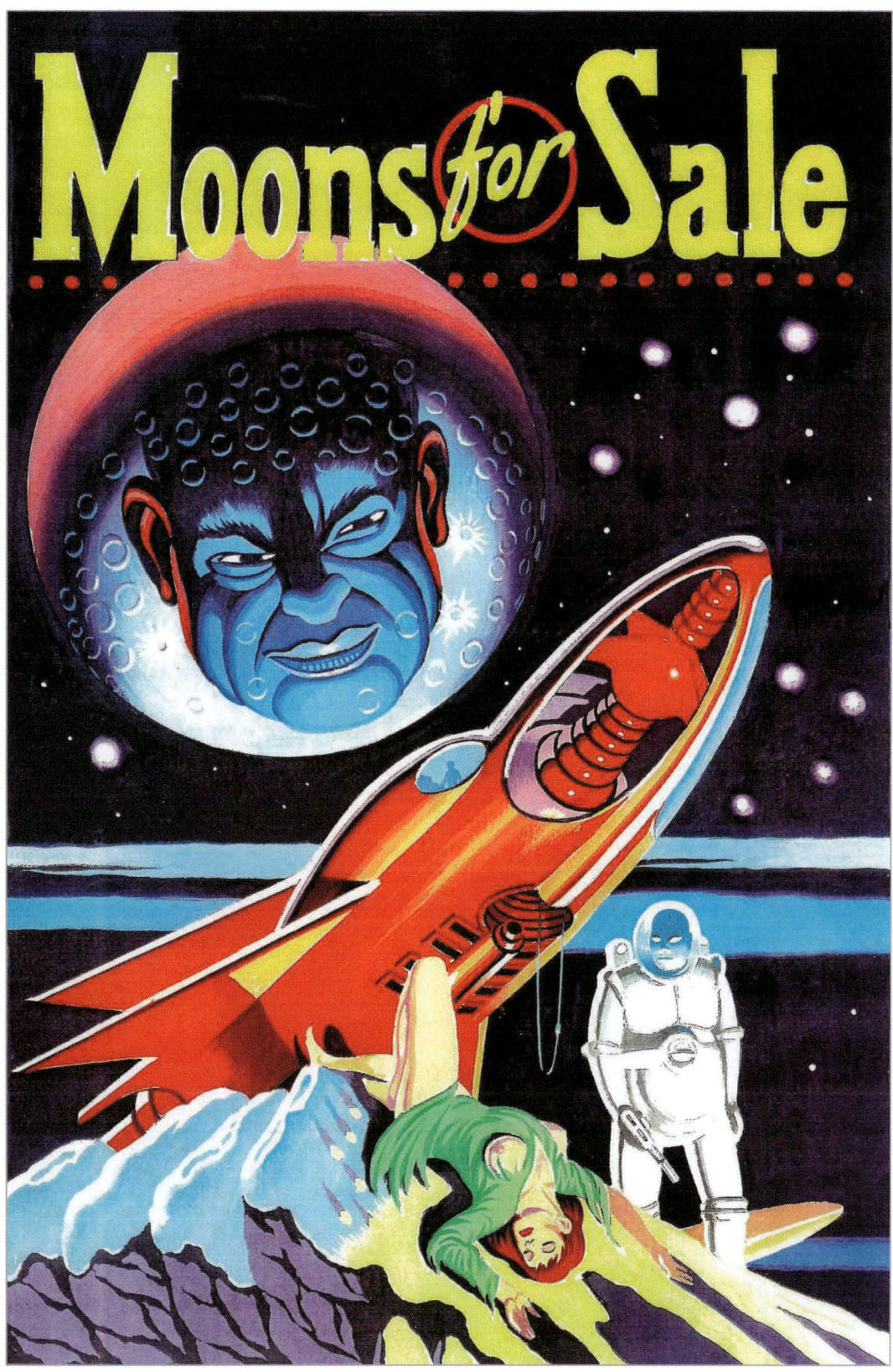

Turner's 1996 recreation of his original cover for the Volsted Gridban novel *Moons for Sale* (Scion, 1953).

A 1995 private commission painting based on the 1994 Philip Harbottle story 'Twilight World' in the *Daily Mirror*'s *Garth* series.

Turner's 1996 recreation of his original cover for the Vargo Statten novel *The G-Bomb* (Scion, 1952).

A Dalek-themed piece painted by Turner as a private commission in 1997.

27: A RETURN TO SKARO

Still receiving a regular stream of private commissions for scenes featuring the Daleks, Ron was prompted to ask me if I thought a revival of the *TV Century 21* comic-strip would ever be considered by *Doctor Who Magazine*. I personally had been so pleased with Ron's cover for *The Dalek Chronicles* that I had planned to commission him myself to paint a reproduction of one of his best *TV Century 21* pages. However, as they had all been so good, I had found it difficult to choose just one, and so had taken the idea no further. But now, Ron's query caused me to speculate as to how a revived Dalek strip might evolve. Had it not ended in January 1967, what would the next page have looked like? The story had concluded with the Emperor Dalek declaring war on Earth, as a lead-in to the invasion seen on TV in the 1964 serial 'The Dalek Invasion of Earth'. It could therefore be argued to have reached a natural conclusion, with no scope for continuation. However, I figured that it could still be extended, without impinging on the TV show's continuity, if a storyline could be devised concerning events on the Daleks' journey between Skaro and Earth. Then, it could become just a previously untold chapter of Dalek history.

The more I considered it, the more thoughts occurred to me as to how such a story might be developed, and the more convinced I became that a revival would indeed be feasible. It then dawned on me that instead of having Ron reproduce one of his old pages, I should commission him to paint a fresh one, based upon my suggestions. If he could recapture the mood of the original series, then that might possibly encourage Panini, the new owners of *Doctor Who Magazine*, to give serious consideration to publishing a new run. I discussed the matter with

Below: another of the numerous Dalek scenes painted by Turner in the mid-1990s as private commissions.

Ron, who thought it was a tremendous idea and offered me his full support.

Ron and I both felt that the opening page should feature the Dalek invasion fleet, plus the intervention of some adversary to provide an action element. I worked out and scripted a nine-frame sequence, adopting the brief caption technique of the original series, and sent it to Ron, who then applied similarly vintage layout ideas. I reasoned that if Panini weren't prepared to accept our proposal, at least I would have a nice piece of artwork to add to my collection. But when Ron showed me the finished page, I knew it was too good simply to hang on my wall – it just had to be published!

A panoramic view of the Dalek fleet crossing the orbit of Saturn on its way to Earth made for a great opening frame, before cutting to the Daleks themselves. The alien adversaries' craft, which I had described as organic rather than metallic, Ron had designed to resemble huge pods with seed nodules that could be fired as projectiles, and these featured magnificently in the final two frames, as the aliens defend themselves against a Dalek attack. But it was Ron's clever colour choices that really made the work so outstanding. With oranges, yellows and blues predominating, he had used shades that complemented each other incredibly well, producing a really vibrant piece of art.

Fired with the prospect of seeing Ron's Daleks back in print, I knuckled down and developed a complete story outline for a six-part serial I called 'Return of the Elders'. I then submitted this, along with Ron's sample artwork page, to the new *Doctor Who Magazine* editor, Gary Gillatt. Not being a professional writer, I was uncertain if my story would be considered acceptable; but the idea was there, and Ron was ready and willing to tackle the illustration. If Gillatt felt that the story needed amending, or that someone else should be asked to write a new one entirely, that would be fine with me – provided that Ron got the commission. As it turned out, though, Gillatt quickly approved my story, and commissioned us to go ahead and complete the serial. The timing couldn't have been better, as he and his team had already been mulling over ideas to mark the thirtieth anniversary of the end of the original *TV Century 21* strip. To publish a follow-up, illustrated by one of the original artists, was the perfect solution.

The next step was for me to write a detailed script for all six parts. First I checked with Ron to see if he was happy with the story, or if he had any improvements to suggest. His response, that he thought it 'worthy of a TV episode', was all the encouragement I needed.

The action begins as the Daleks, on course to conquer Earth, discover another alien fleet on the same heading and suspect that they also intend to invade. They attack the strangers but find them a formidable foe and have to retreat. Coming across a mining colony on Titan, they overpower it, forcing the base commander and his men to pilot three of their ships to attack the strangers, thus drawing their fire and giving the Daleks the chance to destroy them. But the plan goes wrong, as the strange craft are not conventional ships but organic ones, operated by benevolent beings responsible for safeguarding the Earth, returning after millennia to save and purify the planet from mankind's abuse and neglect. Disabling the commander's ship with a powerful beam, the aliens direct a mind-ray against the Daleks, causing a madness that results in their self-destruction. Only the Emperor's ship survives to witness the vanquishing of the invasion force, before it turns and flees. The human commander, now back in control, gives chase, but loses the Emperor's ship in the rings of Saturn. The Emperor escapes, vowing to return with a new fleet and conquer the Earth.

This idea had been sparked by a remark Ron had made to me in one of his reflective moments, when he had observed that humans were destroying the Earth and that things would have been better if they had never set foot on the planet. Picking up on his 'green' sentiments, years before these became fashionable, I conceived the notion of 'the gardeners of Earth' returning to correct the damage that man has caused. Their interaction with the Daleks – who, having no concept of love or beauty, are totally unable to comprehend the situation – provided the necessary conflict.

I was reasonably satisfied with the script, but sent a copy to Phil Harbottle for his comments, and he provided some helpful input. Then I submitted it to Panini, who made a few tweaks of their own. By

Turner's opening page for the new series of *The Daleks* comic strip.

Another of the Dalek scenes painted by Turner as private commissions.

the beginning of December 1996, I had their full approval for Ron to start illustrating the remaining pages, resuming work on a strip that had seemingly ended almost thirty years earlier.

Although Ron had told me he could see no room for improvement in my script, he did come up with a few ideas of his own as he worked his way through it – though one these was ultimately vetoed. As written, the second part of the story ended with the Daleks attacking Titan, causing one of the mining towers to topple over, while the third part opened with them turning their firepower on the pressurised dome of the living quarters. Ron suggested that the toppling tower could instead be shown hitting and fracturing the dome, resulting in its occupants being blasted out into the moon's thin atmosphere. This was a time-honoured approach of his, going back to his *Rick Random* days, of routinely combining two separate incidents into a single, more dramatic one. He offered me four pencilled versions of the proposed scene for approval, and although I was happy with the revision, I felt I should run it past Panini first. Unfortunately, their opinion differed from mine. Although Ron's idea made for a more spectacular sequence, it tended to suggest that the dome's occupants had been killed by accident rather than by design, detracting from the Daleks' ruthlessness. So, the dome would have to come under direct fire after all.

The work took Ron five weeks to complete, and Panini were delighted with the end result, their only reservation being that he had shown an increasing tendency to alter the Daleks' design. For example, he had generally given them one or two neck rings, when to match their TV appearance they should really have had three; and in some cases he had omitted the shoulder-section slats or altered the arrangement of the skirt-section hemispheres. This was nothing new, as discrepancies such as these had also occurred on the original strip, when Ron had got so carried away with designing new story details that he had failed to replicate established ones. Some of the changes, though, were deliberate. In his Dalek makeover, Ron had again substituted a more practical claw for the traditional 'sink-plunger' appendage, and given the 'egg-whisk' armament a more stylised look. Although these departures from the standard Dalek form were not entirely appreciated by Panini, with printing deadlines to meet, there was no time for changes to be made, so they accepted them, hoping that there weren't too many Dalek purists out there who would complain!

Under a new series masthead, the first of the story's six parts was published in *Doctor Who Magazine* # 249, cover dated 12 March 1997. By that time, anticipating that Dalek fans would enjoy the story and want to see the strip continue, I was already working on a sequel. Having completed an outline for this, under the title 'Deadline to Doomsday', I sent it in to Gary Gillatt for his approval. However, although he personally agreed that a second story was a great idea, he told me he would need to await reader response to the first before committing himself. This strip was the single most expensive aspect of the magazine's contents, so he had to be cautious.

As weeks went by, with 'Return of the Elders' having apparently been well-received but still no positive word from Gillatt, I arranged for Ron to illustrate the first page of 'Deadline to Doomsday' as a sample for me to submit. Emphasising that whether or not the story was commissioned might well depend on this, I urged him to take his time and do the best job he could.

To my mind, the sequel was a far superior story to the first, as it dealt with a threat to the Daleks' very existence. Returning to Skaro, the Daleks find it strangely unfamiliar and deduce that their ship's instruments must have been affected by a mysterious cloud of coalescent matter they passed through in space; therefore this isn't their home planet after all. Suddenly their ship is fired upon, causing it to crash-land, whereupon it is immediately attacked by natives. The Daleks soon repel the natives and discover that they are a band of primitive scavengers caught up in a battle for supremacy between the planet's two ruling races, the Tarls and the K'laats. Needing equipment to repair their damaged ship, the Daleks force the natives to lead them to one of the Tarl workshops. The Tarl leader, however, refuses to help unless the Daleks in turn give them 'burrowing bombs' that will dig their way under the K'laat city and destroy it. As agreement is reached, the bombs are made and sent in motion and the Dalek ship is repaired.

By nightfall, the Daleks are ready to leave, but suddenly they notice nearby the wreckage of a downed K'laat vessel, the dead pilot of which closely resembles their own progenitor race, the Kaleds. With rising concern, they compare the planet's star patterns against their own astro-charts. Finding them to be identical, they realise that the mysterious cloud their ship passed through was not a spatial disturbance but a temporal one; they are in fact on Skaro, but thousands of years in the past, when the Thals were called the Tarls and the Kaleds were the K'laats. Realising that the bombs they have launched will soon destroy their own ancestors, and that they themselves will then cease to exist, the Daleks take off in their ship and blast a huge crater between the bombs and the K'laat city. The bombs emerge from the crater, fall and explode harmlessly. The Daleks then pass back through the temporal disturbance and return to the Skaro of their own time.

Ron's first suggestion was that he should come up with a new design for the Dalek ship. Bored with the current one, he wanted to devise another that would make for an impressive opening frame to the new story. However, as much as I hated to stifle his enthusiasm, I had to rule this out, as the action was supposed to follow on directly from the end of 'Return of the Elders' and feature the same ship. Thankfully, Ron was able to work out a compromise that satisfied both himself and the story requirements, drawing the ship from an oblique perspective that showed its underside and thus gave it an altogether different appearance.

The final page, left unlettered, was extremely impressive. Whereas for 'Return of the Elders' Ron had used mainly bright, solid colours, creating a very vibrant effect, on this occasion, relieved of the time pressure of a firm deadline, he had added subtler tones, producing a truly striking piece of work. We felt sure its undeniable quality would tip the balance in our favour. However, although the artwork was indeed well-received by Gary Gillatt, his disappointing response was that the story had been judged too expensive for the magazine to run. We offered to renegotiate our price – I was willing to waive my own writer's fee if it would help matters – but to no avail Doubtless there were clearance costs involved in the use of the Daleks; besides which, it seemed that under Panini, budgets were less flexible than they had been under Marvel UK. This was a great shame – especially as Ron was currently experiencing a lull in his Gryphon Books commissions.

The past few months had seen Gary Lovisi put a considerable amount of additional cover work Ron's way, for titles to be published in late 1997 and early 1998. These had included two more of Tubb's SF novels, *Alien Life* and *I Fight for Mars*; Fearn's jungle adventures *The Gold of Akada* and *Anjani the Mighty*; a third Amazon series entry, *The Golden Amazon's Triumph*; and two horror novels by Lovisi himself, *The Gargoyle* and *The Winged Men*. However, Lovisi had overspent, and was now having to reduce his schedule. *The Gargoyle* would ultimately not appear until 2000, and *The Winged Men* would remain unpublished (until years later, when a revised version would be issued with a different cover). For Ron, coming at the same time as Panini declined to take 'Deadline to Doomsday', this downturn was a real blow. All I could do was offer him a couple more private commissions and hope that something else would soon surface – but, unfortunately, it wouldn't.

Below: Turner's cover for Gary Lovisi's *The Gargoyle*.

Turner's cover for the 1998 Gryphon Books edition of E C Tubb's *Alien Life*.

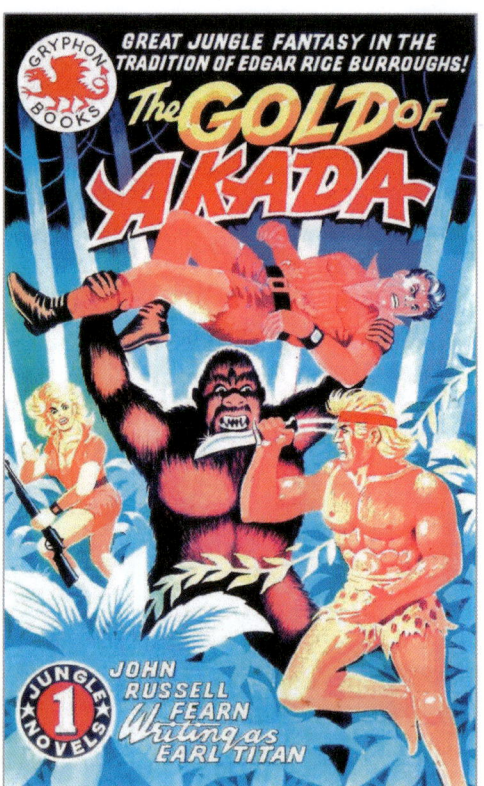
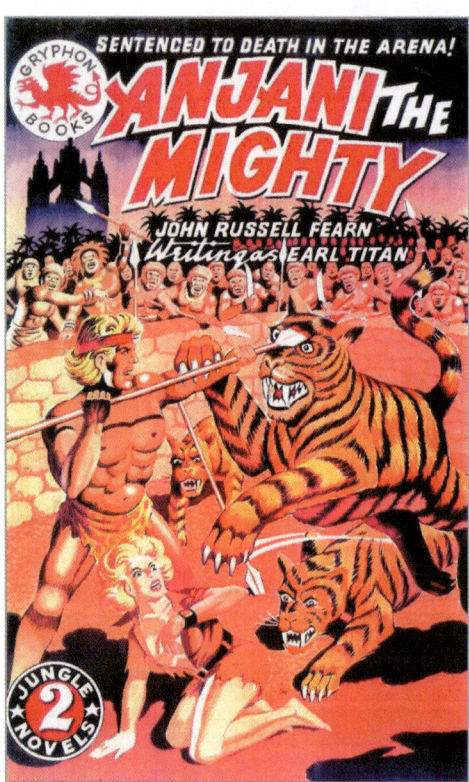
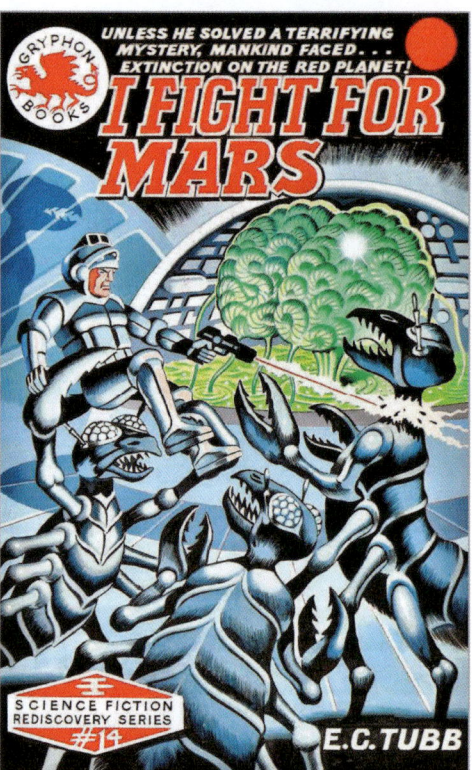

Above: Turner's colourful covers for the Gryphon Books editions of John Russell Fearn's *The Golden Amazon's Triumph* (1997), *The Gold of Akada* (1998) and *Anjani the Mighty* (1998) and E C Tubb's *I Fight for Mars* (1998).

28: CARVING OUT NEW INTERESTS

When I next saw Ron, a couple of months later, I found that in addition to the private commissions I'd given him he had painted a couple of other SF scenes, purely for his own amusement. But aside from these, he had also embarked on a totally different and quite remarkable pastime – he had begun sculpting, from wood, life-size carvings of fish! As mentioned in Chapter 1, Ron had always been fascinated by aquatic life, and during his formative years had even entertained ideas of becoming a marine biologist. During his post-war travels through South-East Asia, he'd seen several examples of exquisitely-carved fish, and one that he'd brought back with him had been on his wall ever since I'd known him. On a recent visit, I had remarked upon this, and my interest must have sparked within him the enthusiasm to attempt some creations of his own. To this end, he had constructed a large metal frame to hold the wood, which could be rotated while he worked on it, using power tools to establish the basic shape and form before finally finishing it off with a sander. The pieces he'd made were typical of his work: finely detailed, colourfully painted and beautifully presented. He'd evidently taken this on as a challenge to his creative abilities, and I could see that the results pleased him. It was gratifying to me to know that, should new artwork commissions remain elusive, this newfound endeavour would be something Ron could turn to, to keep him busy. The thought even crossed my mind that there might be the makings of a small business here, for fans intrigued at the thought of owning a Ron Turner *sculpture*. But that was maybe something for

Below: Ron Turner at home, with some of his fish carvings proudly displayed on his wall. The cross-stitch tapestry immediately behind him was the work of his daughter Dianne.

another day. For the moment, I was preoccupied with the need to find more artwork projects.

By the end of 1997, the only Gryphon commissions Ron was working on were the covers for the next two Amazon titles, *The Amazon's Diamond Quest* and *The Amazon Strikes Again*. I consequently decided to make a renewed attempt to interest Panini in publishing our second Dalek story, 'Deadline to Doomsday', in the hope that they might find the money for this from their 1998 *Doctor Who Magazine* budget.

Thinking that it could help to seal the deal, I arranged for Ron to illustrate the story's second instalment. Again, he produced a tremendous page of work, opening with the crashed Dalek ship, continuing with a panoramic panel of the natives astride huge, lumbering, prehistoric-looking steeds, and ending with the natives' attack on the ship, all beautifully drawn and sensitively coloured. But it was only when I'd finished admiring the layout that I noticed something wrong: it looked too square! On measuring it, I confirmed that it was indeed the wrong shape. And when I checked the first page, I found that too had the same literal shortcoming. Clearly there had been some miscommunication over the required page dimensions. Should the strip be accepted by Panini, this would necessitate extra detail being added to the top or bottom of each page, or possibly both, to bring them up to the acceptable size for publication.

This was annoying, especially knowing how Ron hated making alterations to his own work. However, I reasoned that it wasn't crucial at this stage, and could be addressed later on if the strip were commissioned. At

Above: Turner's two unlettered sample pages for the ultimately unfinished Dalek comic-strip story 'Deadline to Doomsday'.

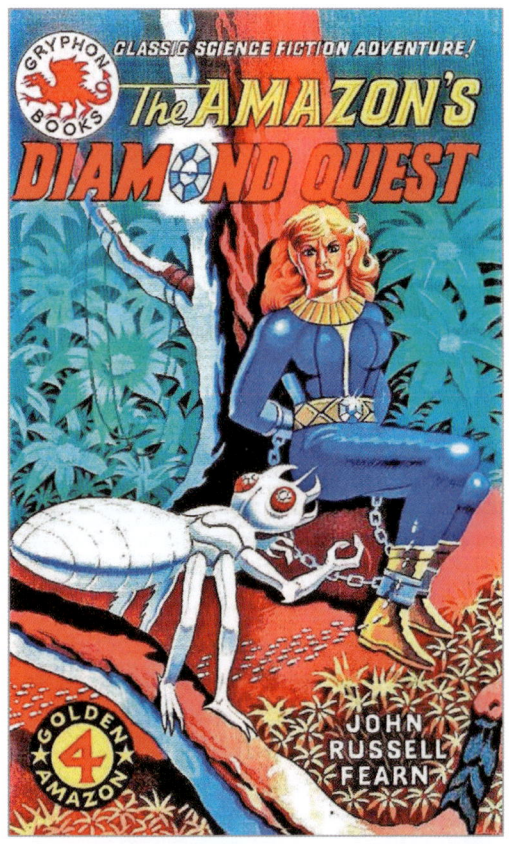

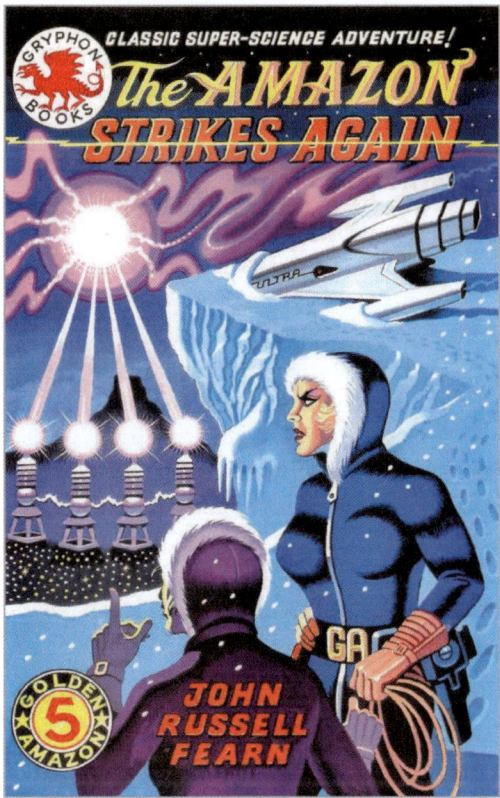

least then Ron would know that the changes were worthwhile, and would hopefully find them less of a chore.

Consequently I went ahead and submitted the second instalment to Panini, to see if they would now feel able to accept the story. At the same time, having given the matter some further thought, I also put forward an alternative proposal. It had occurred to me that if Panini's budget still wouldn't stretch to printing the strip in *Doctor Who Magazine* itself, a more financially viable option for them might be to produce a follow-up to *The Dalek Chronicles*, collecting together 'Return of the Elders', 'Deadline to Doomsday' and perhaps other relevant material, such as articles, interviews or even additional strip stories – Phil certainly having enough talent within his agency to supply any scripts that might be required. Published several years earlier, the original *The Dalek Chronicles* had sold out very quickly, and dealers had told me they could have charged three times the cover price and still seen copies fly off the shelves. While that might have been a slight exaggeration, clearly the venture had been a success, and I felt sure that a follow-up would do equally well. Yet, although my pitch was a strong one, Panini still weren't prepared to commit to anything. It seemed our only remaining hope was to wait until later in 1998, when the results of *Doctor Who Magazine*'s latest readers' poll came in, showing how 'Return of the Elders' had rated relative to other contents published over the past year.

In the meantime, Ron was still picking up occasional work illustrating the booklets of Fearn and Tubb short stories that Phil continued to publish from time to time under his own Cosmos imprint. Thankfully, a few further Gryphon cover commissions were also coming in, the latest being for the sixth Amazon story, *Twin of the Amazon*, and for a Jack Williamson novel, *The Fortress of Utopia*. When I called round to collect the finished paintings for these, I found that Ron had again done an outstanding job on them – the one for *The Fortress of Utopia*, showing an observatory on a Bonestell-like moonscape, being particularly impressive. But, in addition, I saw that Ron had also produced more of his wood sculptures, which now encompassed not only fish but also birds, all affixed to plaques and mounted on his walls. It was as if taking up this unusual hobby had given

Left: Turner's covers for the Gryphon Books editions of John Russell Fearn's *The Amazon's Diamond Quest* and *The Amazon Strikes Again*, both published in 1998.

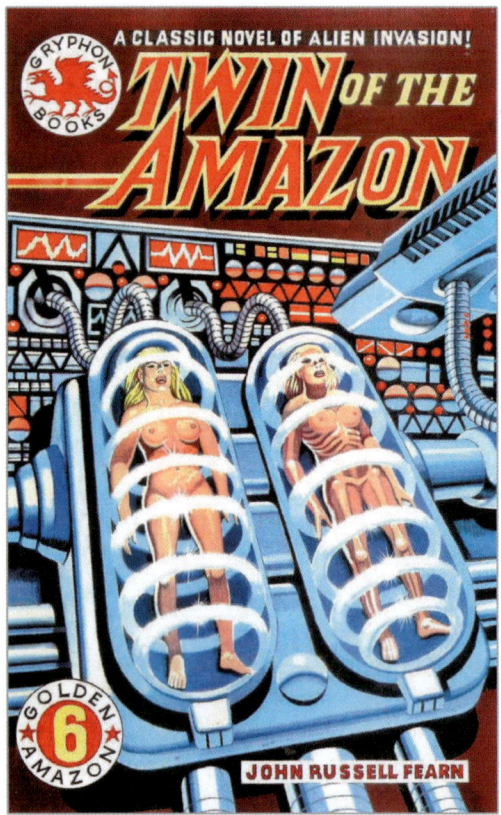

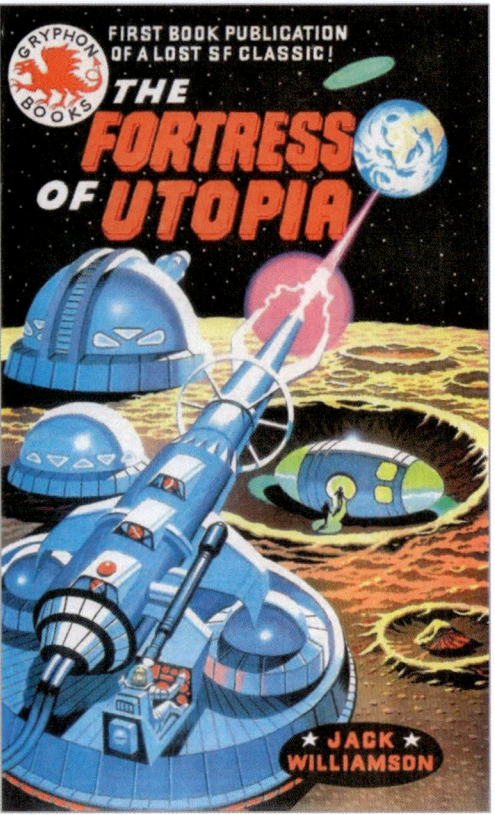

him a new lease of life; and rather than detract from his artwork, it had only increased his enthusiasm and heightened his creativity. The thought crossed my mind that he might perhaps even be interested in producing sculptures of some of his vintage *Rick Random* and *Space Ace* spacecraft and hardware – although again I said nothing about this at the time.

Ron's next commissions were a private one for a black-and-white *Dan Dare* scene, and a better-paying professional one for the cover of Gryphon's next Amazon reissue, *Conquest of the Amazon*. As the latter was the same novel for which we had previously produced a comic-strip adaptation, published only semi-professionally by Bryon Whitworth back in 1990 (see page 277), we sent a copy of that earlier version to Gary Lovisi to help him decide on cover suggestions. To our delight, so impressed with Lovisi with the strip that he asked if he could publish it in its entirety, as a separate graphic novel. The problem was, it ran to only 60 pages and so was too short to fill the standard page-count of one of his paperbacks. But we had another unpublished strip available: *Planet of Doom*, the second full-length *Nick Hazard* adventure, superbly illustrated by Ron. At Phil's suggestion, Lovisi agreed to publish both stories in one volume, together with the text of the original Golden Amazon tale from 1939 and an in-depth history of the series. This would make up enough material for a full, 140-page book.

When I next called on Ron, I found that he had made a grand job of the *Conquest of the Amazon* reissue cover, combining several different images suggested by the comic-strip version to form a very effective montage. His *Dan Dare* piece was equally tremendous; another montage, showing a giant Dan in space, straddling the Earth and advancing with blaster in hand, while Treen ships zoom by and the Mekon looks on. The only odd thing about this was that the Mekon's head had obviously been drawn on a separate piece of card, cut out and pasted onto the scene. When I queried this, Ron explained that he had had a slight accident with the artwork, but hoped the client wouldn't mind the repair, as it saved him having to redo the whole thing.

Clearly Ron was also still pursuing his new passion, as I noticed even more wood carvings on display; and now he had progressed beyond fish and birds to various other

Left: Turner's covers for the Gryphon Books editions of John Russell Fearn's *Twin of the Amazon* and Jack Williamson's *The Fortress of Utopia*, both published in 1998.

subjects, including a bust of a helmeted Roman centurion and one of Tutankhamen's death mask! I thought now might be a good opportunity for me to mention my idea of him producing SF-inspired sculptures; but, before I could do so, I spotted something less pleasing: Ron was sporting a nasty bruise on the side of his head. When I asked about this, he explained that he had got so carried away with a recent carving that he had tripped and fallen over the lead of the electric sander he was using to finish it off. This accounted for the accident he had had with the *Dan Dare* illustration – it had been damaged when he had fallen. I suggested that Ron ought to get the injury checked out, but he dismissed my concerns, assuring me that he was fine. However, this had opened my eyes to a less positive aspect of his new hobby: involving the heavy use of power tools, it carried the ever-present risk of him suffering another mishap.

Now with renewed determination to keep Ron busy on artwork projects, I decided to pursue a notion I had been toying with for some time, of writing a new, but old-style, *Rick Random* comic-strip for him to illustrate. A few ideas came to mind, and I began to prepare a story. However, I realised it would take me some time to complete this, and what I really needed was something ready-scripted for Ron to work on straight away. Then I recalled that when I had first met Ron, he had given me the initial dozen or so pages of pencils he had prepared for a subsequently-cancelled War Picture Library story, *Whiplash* (see page 218). I also had the original script for the story, and knew that if I could persuade Ron to take on the task of completing the full artwork, this would keep him occupied for a few months, especially if I got him to do the lettering as well. As this would involve him illustrating small black-and-white pages, which attracted a much lower fee than large, full-colour ones, I realised I could afford to pay him in dribs and drabs as the work progressed. It also occurred to me that I might even be able to arrange for the finished story to be published, as although the War Picture Library had long since ended as an ongoing title, there had in recent years been some holiday special reprint collections issued.

Ron had not been too happy with *Whiplash* when first presented with it, but that had been 14 years ago,

Right: the two Gryphon Books editions of John Russell Fearn's *Conquest of the Amazon*: the graphic novel version (top), the cover of which Turner based on his black-and-white piece for the original fanzine publication (see page 277); and the text reissue version (bottom).

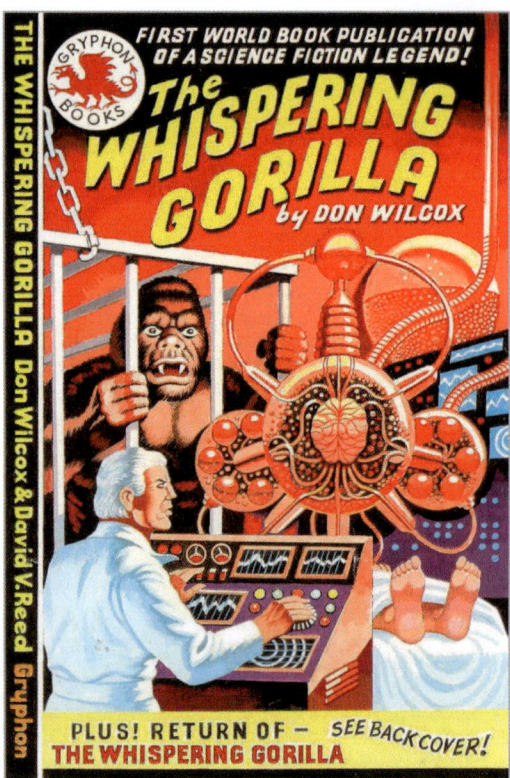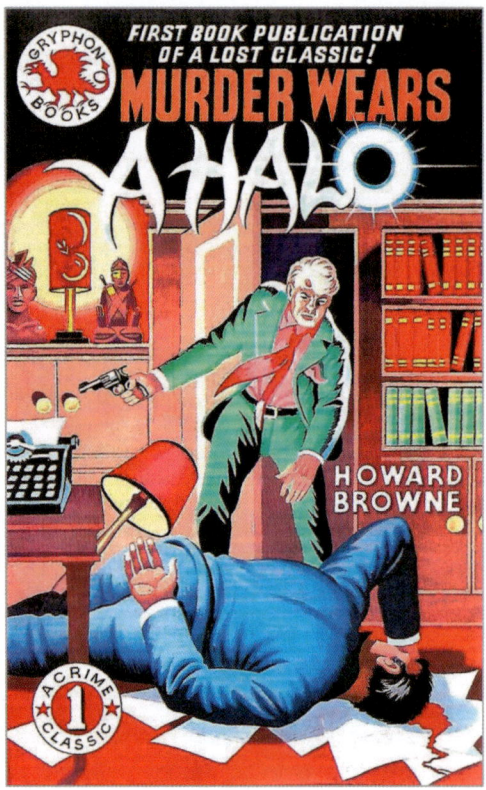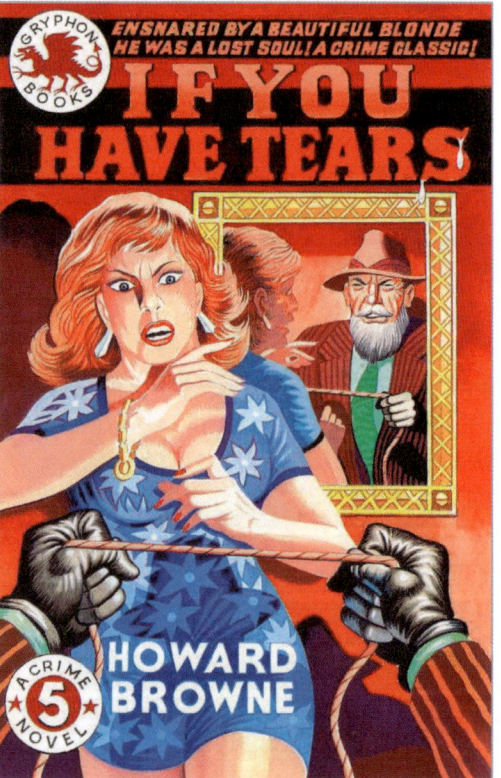

Above: Turner's covers for the Gryphon Books editions of Don Wilcox's *The Whispering Gorilla* (1999), John Russell Fearn's *The Slitherers* (1999) and Howard Browne's *Murder Wears a Halo* (1997) and *If You Have Tears* (1998).

and he had since mellowed. Therefore, in view of his current situation, he agreed to accept the commission, on the understanding that he would fit his work on this 64-page war story around any further cover assignments that might come in.

Two of the next three Gryphon cover pieces were for SF titles: a Don Wilcox-authored American pulp tale, *The Whispering Gorilla*, and a new edition of John Russell Fearn's *The Slitherers*, for which Ron had already supplied a black-and-white cover some years earlier (see page 224). The third, however, was for another Howard Browne crime novel, *If You Have Tears*, and this proved to be the subject of some contention. When Ron had first started taking on work for Gryphon, he had often put his own ideas into the cover scenes. As time had gone by, however, and the sketches Phil had provided him with had become increasingly detailed, he had tended to follow these more precisely. Here, though, that certainly wasn't the case. Phil's basic brief had been for him to depict a girl being violently strangled in her home, with another lying unconscious at her feet, the contents of her purse scattered on the floor around her. Fantasy violence was one thing, but this was just a little too realistic for Ron, so he had simply dashed the piece off as quickly as possible, paying scant attention to the room decor, the view from the window or the various other details Phil had described. The end result was unacceptable to Gary Lovisi – not least because he was expecting Browne to play a large part in Gryphon's future, and so was particularly keen to ensure that the author was happy with this cover.

While understanding Lovisi's point of view, I also sympathised with Ron's, and agreed with him when he pointed out that we had gradually drifted away from his preferred approach to the crime covers, of merely suggesting rather than actually showing violent incidents occurring. I also recognised that Phil having provided Ron with increasingly precise instructions had curtailed his scope for using his own compositional skills and imagination.

Ron suggested a different approach to the *If You Have Tears* cover. His idea was that the assault need only be suggested by way of a close-up of the girl fearfully regarding a length of rope held taut between a pair of gloved hands in the foreground, with the attacker's face shown reflected in a wall-mirror in the background. This would dispense with the need for all the additional details Phil had requested, while still retaining the essence of the scene, in a more subtle and menacing way. This new concept was approved by Lovisi, and Ron duly completed a second painting – though, just to show willing, he also submitted a revised version of the first, with all of Phil's original requirements now added in, leaving Lovisi to make the final choice as to which to use. After all, Lovisi still called the shots, and Ron didn't want to run the risk of losing any future commissions. In the end, though, Lovisi agreed with Ron that the second painting was the more effective of the two, and went with that one for the book.

At around this time, Phil decided he wanted to publish a new bibliography chronicling the extraordinary writing career of his long-time friend and client Ted Tubb. Having compiled the text in collaboration with an American colleague, Sean Wallace, he felt that a cover by Ron would add the finishing touch. But what should it portray? Thinking back, he remembered that before Tubb had turned to writing for a living he had been a salesman, and that his voluble nature was always in evidence at the many SF conventions he attended, especially during the auction events, when he would often act as the auctioneer, dispensing appropriate patter as copies of classic SF works went under the hammer. When he recalled that the very first page of our comic-strip adaptation of Tubb's *Kalgan the Golden* had also depicted an auction scene (see page 259), Phil knew he had found the cover idea he was seeking: he commissioned Ron to duplicate that page, in full colour this time, but with Tubb's face substituted for the auctioneer's. The bibliography eventually saw print in August 1998.

Meanwhile, I was still keen to see how 'Return of the Elders' had fared in the latest *Doctor Who Magazine* readers' poll. When the results finally appeared, they were very encouraging: our Dalek story had been one of the most popular items published over the past year, gaining far more votes than the regular *Doctor Who* comic strip. I felt sure this would finally convince Panini to commission the 'Deadline to Doomsday' sequel. When I contacted

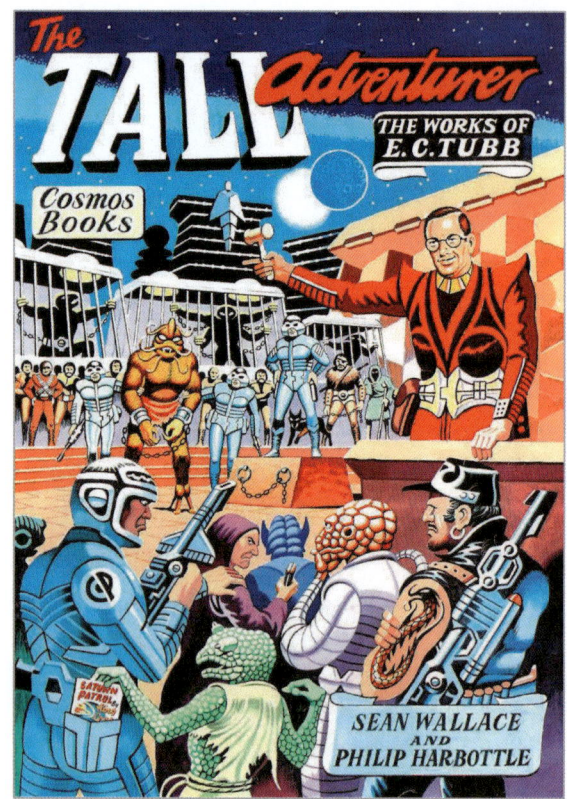

Above: Turner's cover for *The Tall Adventurer*, the Sean Wallace and Philip Harbottle-written E C Tubb bibliography from 1998.

different as the Daleks. There was also the fact that the two already-completed pages for 'Deadline to Doomsday' would have to be resized to correct the previous error; and, in view of the recent upset over the crime cover, this wasn't a good time for me to be requesting alterations. Besides, the Gryphon commissions were now starting to pick up again – covers were needed for two more Ted Tubb novels, *The Wall* and *Earth Set Free*; for a Jack Williamson double novel, *The Ruler of Fate* and *Xandulu*; and for the next two Amazon titles, *Lord of Atlantis* and *Triangle of Power* – and a private commission had just come in that looked likely to be only the first of many from a new fan. Consequently I felt it best to wait until *Whiplash* was finished before deciding whether to ask Ron to complete the Dalek story, or else to start work on my new *Rick Random* script, if that was ready by then. Little did I know that any such decision would soon be taken out of my hands.

Below: Turner's cover for the Gryphon Books edition of E C Tubb's *The Wall* (1999).

them, however, the response was still negative, with budgetary restrictions again being cited as the reason. I could only conclude that I had been simply fobbed off before, and that Panini had never had any real intention of commissioning the story. Devastated, I had to accept that all our efforts to secure the series' continuation had been in vain.

I was strongly inclined to have Ron illustrate the remaining instalments of 'Deadline to Doomsday' regardless, on the off-chance I might one day find another home for it somewhere. At present, though, he was devoting all his spare time to illustrating the War Picture Library story, *Whiplash*; and, moreover, he was showing genuine enthusiasm for the work, pointing out and addressing any inconsistencies he spotted in the script and clarifying any sections he found unclear, resulting in some very impressive pages. War, as a genre, had always rated second only to SF in Ron's estimation, and I realised it would be churlish of me to drag him away at this point and possibly destroy his feel for the story by having him switch back to illustrating something as

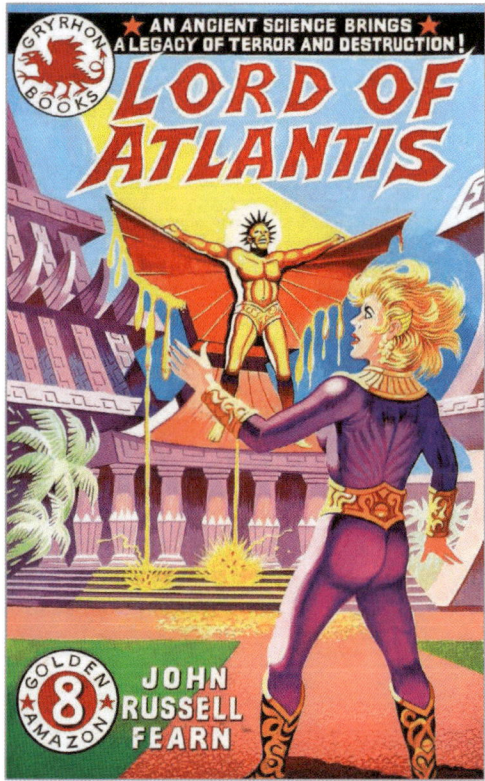
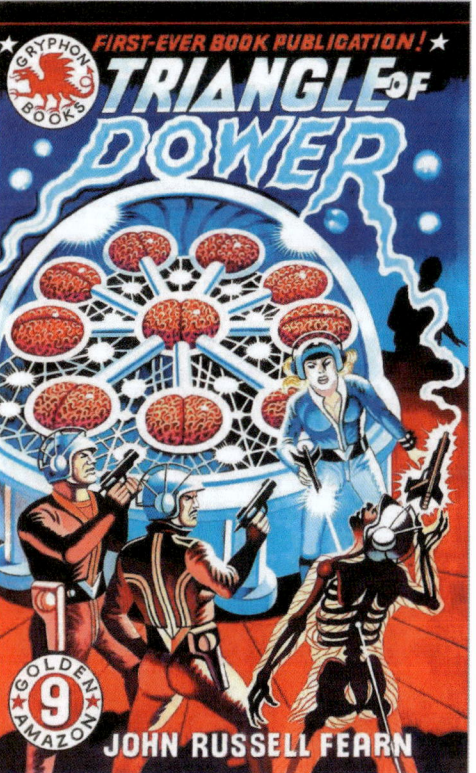

Above: Turner's covers for the Gryphon Books editions of E C Tubb's *Earth Set Free*, Jack Williamson's *The Ruler of Fate* and *Xandulu* and John Russell Fearn's Amazon series entries *Lord of Atlantis* and *Triangle of Power*, all published in 1999.

Completed in 1998, the very last of Turner's vintage cover recreations, for the Vargo Statten novel *The Time Bridge* (Scion, 1952).

29: FAREWELL TO THE MASTER

The next time I saw Ron was six weeks later, in August 1998, a few days after his seventy-sixth birthday. I had called to collect the latest Gryphon cover artwork and the War Picture Library story, which he had finally completed. However, I was concerned by what I saw – not in the artwork, which was fine, but in Ron himself. He looked ill, and had cuts and bruises about his face and neck! He told me he'd been experiencing some dizzy spells that had resulted in a couple of nasty falls. However, he assured me he'd seen his doctor, been prescribed some medication, and was now feeling better and keen to do more work.

On studying the *Whiplash* pages, I noticed a few mistakes in the lettering and a few captions that had been overlooked, so I agreed to leave the relevant boards with him for correction. The mistakes were not surprising, given his recent health problems, but they did convince me he was not currently up to working on anything as involved as the Dalek strip. So, as there were no new commissions to give him at present, we instead discussed a possible cover for *Whiplash* – something that was not necessarily required, but would keep him busy without being too demanding.

A few days later, I received a letter from Ron, requesting a favour. Apparently his usual art supplier had closed down, and he had a list of materials he hoped I could source for him from one of my own local shops. On making enquiries, I discovered there were no shops in my area that stocked all the listed items, so some would have to be ordered in. However, I did manage to find a couple of the fine-tipped brushes and three of the colours Ron required. I told him I would bring them along on my next visit.

However, when I returned to collect the *Whiplash* cover – for which Ron had produced two different versions – he told me he had had another fall. Even more worryingly, he had developed a pain in his side, which I noticed he was clutching in some discomfort. He intended to see his doctor again as soon as possible. This was all distressing news, and

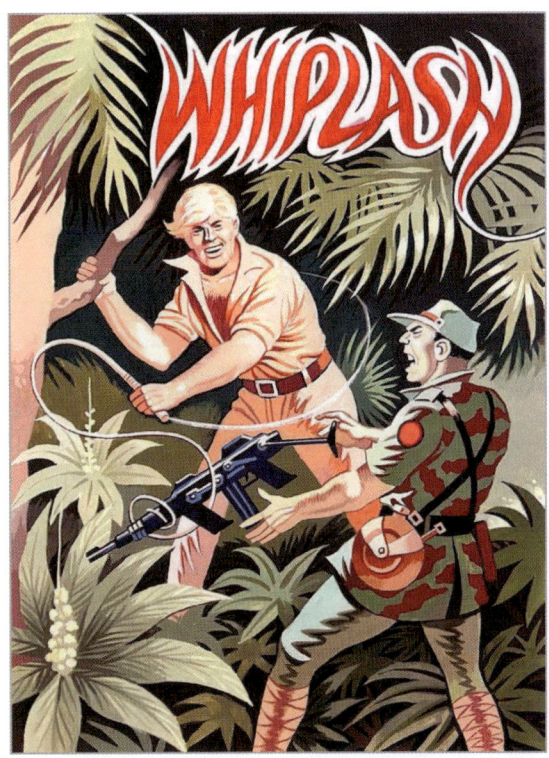

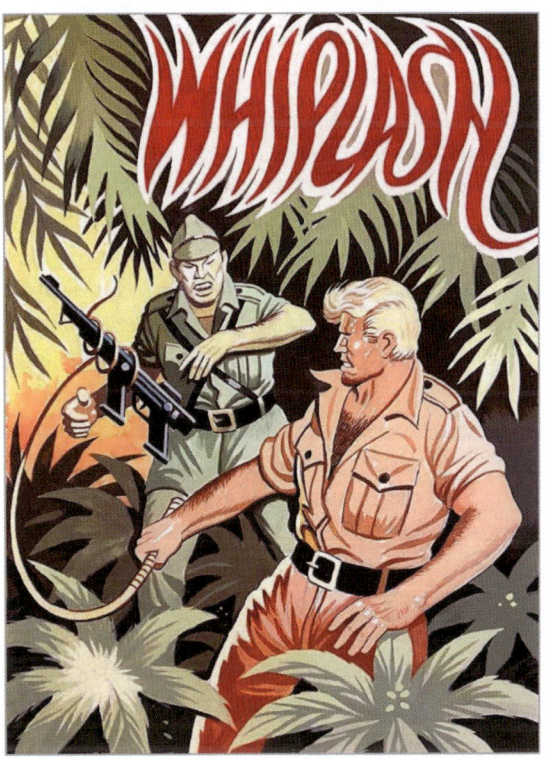

Right: Turner's alternative cover designs for the 64-page illustrated war story *Whiplash* – two of the last pieces he ever produced.

although Ron seemed very pleased I'd managed to get some of the materials he wanted, I couldn't help but wonder if his regular shop really had closed down, or if he had simply felt too poorly to drive over there. It would have been typical of him to play down just how ill he was – although, by the time of my visit, that was patently clear.

I phoned Ron later, and again over the next few days, to check on his condition, and he told me that further medication seemed to have stabilised the problem. I still had no new commissions to give him – and doubted he would be well enough to complete them even if I had – but it occurred to me that, although I hadn't yet finished the script, he might perhaps be interested in producing some pencil roughs for the *Rick Random* story I was working on. Ron agreed, so I sent him a synopsis of the story, titled *Mystery on the Paradise Planet*, plus suggestions for the characters, spacecraft, aliens and various other elements that would need to be designed, giving him the option of producing several alternative versions of each. I was about to take a short break, so this seemed an ideal time for him to sketch whatever he wanted, to his heart's content. Hopefully by the time I got back, his health would be a lot better.

On my return, I phoned Ron. He told me he was indeed feeling better, and that the sketches I'd requested were now finished. But would I be collecting them, or should he post them to me? Having prior commitments, and with no particular reason to visit him just then, I asked him to post them. The package arrived the following Saturday, and when opened revealed some truly marvellous work that Ron had produced for me. Especially in view of his condition, he had done tremendously well, suggesting ideas and designs that fitted my story perfectly. His depiction of Rick Random himself was spot-on – remarkably so, considering that, barring the *2000 AD* travesty, he hadn't drawn the character for nearly forty years. However, the piece of board he'd used to reinforce the package posed a mystery. It had on the back of it a superb picture of a three-masted schooner, with masses of rigging and billowing sails, painted by Ron with the very fine-tipped brushes I'd managed to find for him and the only three colours I'd given him: blue for the sky and sea, pink for the sails and clouds and black for the ship itself. But why on earth had he gone to all the trouble of painting such a lovely, detailed scene, only to use it as packaging material? It was later I sadly realised that the whole exercise had probably been just a way for him to distract himself from his illness: once he had completed it, it had served its purpose and was considered disposable.

But Ron's parcel was only one of three that arrived that day. From Phil I received the next two Gryphon cover commissions – one for another Jack Williamson double novel, *The Blue Spot* and *Entropy Reversed*, the other for a Ted Tubb tale, *Malkar* – with the promise of more to come. I also received a private commission from a client seeking a recreation of one of Ron's best *Tit-Bits* Science Fiction Library covers, *The Dissentizens*. So, with new work coming in and Ron's health apparently improving, things seemed to be looking up. Before I could send Ron anything, though, I first needed to clarify a few points with Phil about the Gryphon assignments, and also get an enlarged colour

Below: the schooner painting used by Turner as packaging material.

photocopy made of the original *The Dissentizens* cover, for Ron to work from more easily. This meant that he wouldn't actually receive the commissions until early the following week. I reasoned that a couple of days' delay wouldn't make much difference and would give him a chance to take things easy for a bit. But it seemed there was only so much reading and television that Ron could stand before he became restless, so instead he returned to the new passion he'd acquired in recent months – his wood sculptures.

On the day the new commissions were due to arrive with Ron, I received a call from his son Clive – whom I'd never spoken to before – and immediately realised something must be terribly wrong. It was. Ron had been taken ill on the Sunday and was now in Ascot General Hospital. He'd had a stroke as a result of a blood clot evidently caused by all the falls he'd suffered recently. Whether the crisis had come because of his resumption of the physically demanding work of sculpting, or whether it had been simply inevitable, was unknown. However, it appeared that the medication Ron had been taking hadn't helped at all; more likely, it had just masked his symptoms. Now, his condition was such that he'd lost the ability to walk or even talk.

This was shocking news, especially as Ron had seemed to be making such good progress when I last spoke to him. However, I was heartened to learn that the long-term prognosis was favourable; with good therapy and proper care and attention, there was every chance he would regain his faculties and make a full recovery.

Over the next few weeks, I made several visits to see Ron in hospital, and as he slowly improved, regained his speech and became a little more active, I took to providing him with a pad and drawing materials to help him pass the time. On one occasion, looking through a pile of hospital magazines, I discovered a copy of *2000 AD*, and when this prompted a young male orderly to comment that *Judge Dredd* was a particular favourite of his, I impressed him by explaining that the man he was caring for was one of the artists who had actually drawn the character. Ron would entertain some of his fellow patients with little drawings, and he told me the nurses were always asking him to do some for them too – though he added with a suggestive wink that he wouldn't expect them to pay in *cash*. Whatever else had been affected, it certainly wasn't his libido!

Ron also continued sketching ideas for my *Rick Random* story, drawing frames that he recalled from the script, even though he'd already done as much as was needed. This was good therapy for him, and talking about the project seemed to be aiding his recovery. One thing that concerned him was the quality of the work he was producing, which admittedly wasn't as tight as that he'd completed before his stroke. However, being in a hospital bed wasn't exactly conducive to him achieving his best results, so I felt sure that, given time, things would improve.

Ron continued to make good progress, and after a couple of months the doctors decided he was well enough to return home. This, though, was a mixed blessing. Ron was still weak in the legs, and was likely to remain so for the foreseeable future. He would be unable to stand for any length of time, or return to driving, and would need care-workers to call on him regularly to attend to his needs. I knew he would find all this deeply frustrating. As a very private person, he preferred his own company, and would not take well to strangers dropping by throughout the day, even if it was for his own benefit. He had loved tinkering with his car, too, and the independence it had given him – and now, he would be reduced to using a mobility scooter!

Worst of all, as he had always worked standing up, he would no longer be able to paint. The most he would be able to manage, sitting down, was comic-strip illustration – and while that would be fine for my *Rick Random* assignment, it would mean the end of his cover commissions. As far as the doctors were concerned, Ron had made a satisfactory recovery; but, when he got home, these drastic lifestyle changes would clearly restrict him in ways he would find very hard to take.

Hoping the situation might improve at a later date, I encouraged Ron to focus for the time being on the *Rick Random* work. He told me that if he were to take it on, he'd need to use some tonal aid such as Zip-A-Tone to relieve him of the laborious manual chore of hatching and cross-hatching. I reminded him that this wouldn't in fact be an issue, as I wanted the new strip to be faithful to the style of the 1950s originals – of which I'd already sent him a few example pages for reference. These all featured the classic high-contrast look characteristic of his early work, with little or no shading applied, and so would be quicker and easier for him to replicate. Strangely, though, Ron now seemed to think that the work he'd produced back then looked rushed; he claimed that he'd used that technique simply to ensure that he could meet his deadlines. Now with more time at his disposal, he wanted to produce 'finished' work. To emphasise the point, he brought out one of the example pages I'd sent him, sections of which he had shaded over in pencil to show how he felt the strip should now be presented. I wasn't very happy to hear this, and wasn't even sure how to go about obtaining the tonal aids he felt he needed, but decided it was not the time to discuss such matters; we could cross that bridge when we came to it. The important thing was for Ron to get back home and try to adjust to a new working routine.

Clive, however, wasn't entirely happy with my plan. He felt that Ron should avoid doing too much initially, and that although there would be no time pressure on him to complete the *Rick Random* strip, the fact that it ran to 64 pages, and that he would doubtless be keen to make progress on it, could lead to him overdoing things. So, to start with, something less demanding would have to be found for him to do. But what else could I give him? It would have to be something he could work on sitting down, which ruled out any of the commissions he had recently been offered, all of which were for colour paintings. I couldn't help but think it somewhat ironic that when, for the first time in ages, Ron had plenty of work available, he couldn't do any of it! Instead, any task I gave him would have to be purely recreational.

In the end, it occurred to me that if I were to ask Ron simply to produce a copy of one of the best of his vintage full-page *Rick Random* scenes, that would be a much gentler way to ease him back into illustration work. It would also hopefully put him in the right frame of mind to tackle my new story, when the time came. Searching through my collection of original *Rick Random* issues, I finally found a suitable scene in one called *The Space Pirates*. I then sent off my mini-commission in the expectation that Ron would find it waiting for him on his return home. In the event, though, Ron arrived before my package did, and waiting for him instead was a part-carved sculpture of a bird, staring at him, begging to be completed. He knew he shouldn't do it, but – whether out of frustration at his situation, or simply a determination to try to finish what he had started – he resumed work on the sculpture, with the perhaps inevitable result that he suffered another attack. Luckily he had been fitted with a Careline alarm bracelet, and the emergency services were quick to respond. However, Ron was now back in hospital, and in very different circumstances than before.

This time, Ron realised there was no prospect of him ever regaining his full strength or being able to return to the activities he loved. Certainly there would be no more colour painting, and his artistic prowess had in any case been severely diminished by the effects of the stroke. In short, his life would never be the same again; and, to him, this was unacceptable. Over the next few days, he gradually lost the will to recover, and although I tried to encourage him, he had obviously made up his mind that, with his quality of life gone, there was no point carrying on.

My last memories of Ron are of his final days in hospital, when he was attended by his sons Rodney and Clive and we sat around his bed, sharing reminiscences of our times with him. But on my last visit, Ron was very weak, and could hardly speak. Before I left, I shook his hand – the hand that over the years had produced such amazing and memorable images – and thanked him again for all the marvellous work he'd done for Phil and me. This was the last time I saw him. Two days later, on 19 December 1998, Clive phoned to tell me that Ron had passed away.

Ron had suffered during his last few weeks, but at least his final years had been happy ones. For, through our many attempts to obtain commissions for him, he had finally found his niche and been able to return to producing the type of work he really enjoyed and with which he had originally established himself all those years ago at the start of his career – SF cover art. And, ironically, his work had come full circle: the last SF cover he had produced had been for *Triangle of Power* by John

Russell Fearn, the very author whose work he had graced with his first SF cover, *Operation Venus*, in 1950.

The funeral took place on 30 December 1998 at Bracknell Crematorium, and I was invited by Ron's family to deliver a eulogy. I remarked not only on Ron's incredible talents as an artist, but also on his kind and generous nature in working with Phil and me, turning out such high quality work for such low returns. It was something we would always appreciate.

Fittingly, there was a song in the charts that month called 'Goodbye', by the Spice Girls. Although it concerned simply the departure of one of their group members, the sentiments had a certain poignancy that reflected my feelings at the time, and hearing it will always bring back memories for me of that sad occasion. A line in the lyrics ran, 'Goodbye my friend, it's not the end'. And, sure enough, it was not the end, for although Ron died in 1998, his artwork has continued to appear in print into the 21st Century.

Without Ron to produce his covers, Gary Lovisi initially feared he would have to end his Gryphon Books imprint. However, Phil was quick to reassure him. Over the past decade and a half, Ron had produced so many private commissions and other unpublished pieces that it would be quite easy to find appropriate examples to use as covers for further titles.

In the end, Lovisi issued numerous additional books with covers by Ron, even completing the whole 31-volume Golden Amazon saga – the 24 novels published during Fearn's lifetime, the two originally unpublished ones that Phil had later found amongst Fearn's effects, another that Phil wrote himself based on Fearn's notes for an uncompleted entry, and four follow-ups by another author, John Glasby.

Phil had always believed he would eventually find publishers willing to reissue all of Fearn's novels – and when that happened, he was determined they should all have Ron Turner covers! Phil's belief was well-founded, as a great many of Ron's wonderful covers have continued to appear posthumously, not only on the Gryphon titles but also on the Fantasy Adventures series of books published by Wildside Press, demonstrating quite emphatically the enduring appeal of his work. But Ron's legacy doesn't end there.

Right: two Gryphon Books with posthumously-published Turner covers: Jack Williamson's *The Stone from the Green Star* (1999) and John Russell Fearn's tenth Amazon novel, *The Amethyst City* (2000).

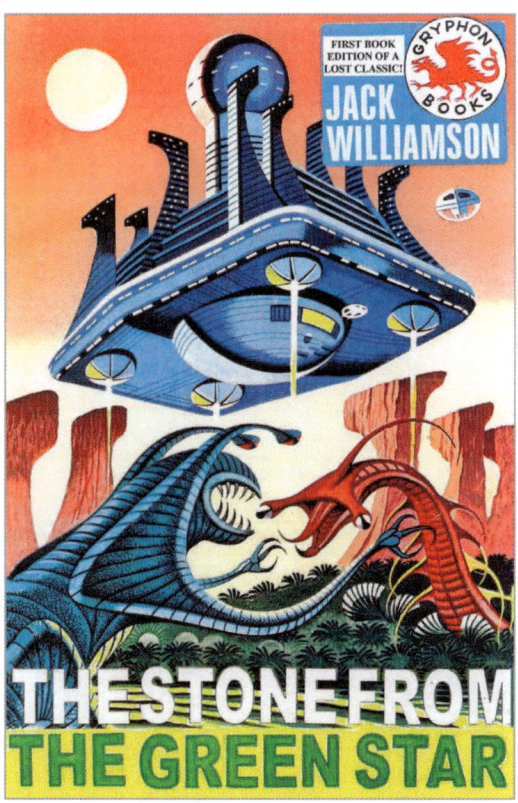

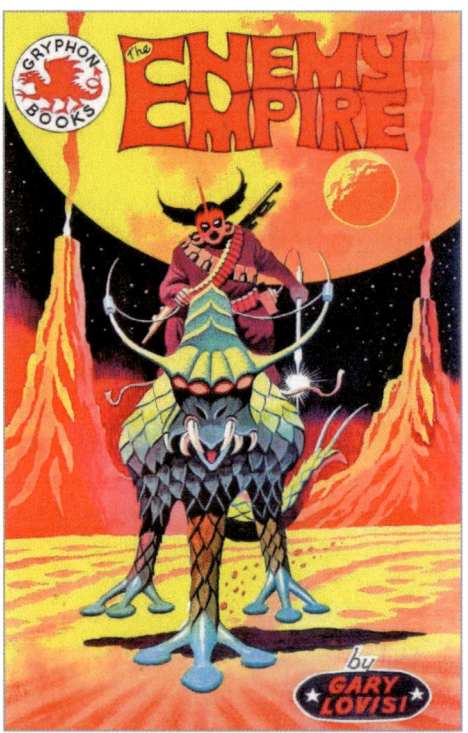

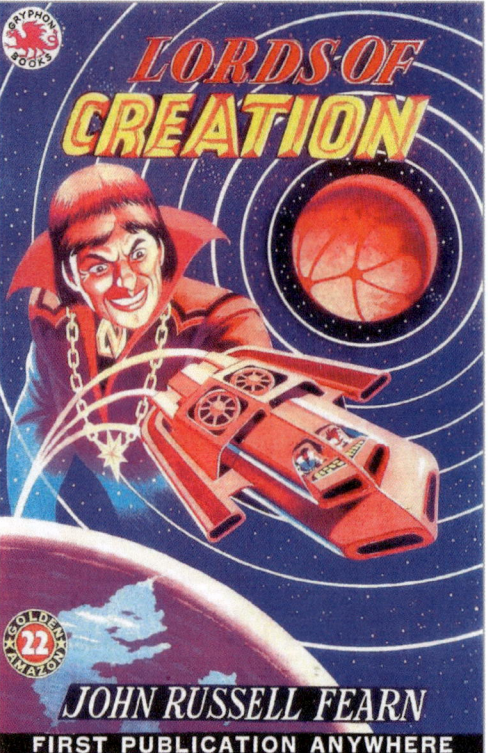

Above: more Turner pieces used posthumously by Gryphon Books: a recreation of the cover of the 1950 Vargo Statten novel *Annihilation!*, repurposed for a 2004 edition of John Russell Fearn's *Kingpin Planet*; an *Alien Warrior* private commission from 1993, used as a draft cover for Gary Lovisi's *The Enemy Empire* (ultimately published with different artwork); the rejected first attempt at *The Golden Amazon* cover in 1996 (see page 305), used for Fearn's *Daughter of the Golden Amazon* in 2001; and a 1990 private commission based on the 1952 Vargo Statten novel *The Last Martian*, used for Fearn's *Lords of Creation* in 2005.

30: INTO THE FUTURE

In early 2013, Rod Barzilay, founder and publisher of the *Dan Dare* tribute magazine *Spaceship Away*, was looking for similarly-themed strips to run alongside his new adventures of the Pilot of the Future. Reprints of Ron's *Rick Random* series had been considered, but the hefty licensing fee wanted by Fleetway had been unaffordable for what was essentially a small, fan-run magazine. Then Barzilay had come across a copy of our first *Nick Hazard* comic, *Invaders from Time*, published by Harrier in 1988. He contacted me, explained that he thought a reissue of this would be ideal back-up material for his magazine, and sought my approval. Ever keen to see Ron's work promoted, I agreed.

But then Barzilay told me that as the original strip was in black-and-white, for the purposes of his magazine he would need to have it coloured. At this point, I became apprehensive, for I recalled how some of Ron's beautiful black-and-white artwork had been ruined by slipshod third-party colouring in the past, particularly in the *TV21* annuals, and had no wish to see that happen again. Barzilay, however, assured me that the work would be treated with the utmost consideration, as it would be undertaken by respected British artist John Ridgway. I remained concerned, as although I knew of Ridgway's black-and-white work, I had no idea of his colouring style or techniques. Again, though, Barzilay assured me that the results would be sympathetic to Ron's style, adding that he had already arranged for Ridgway to colour a few *Rick Random* and *Nick Hazard* frames as test pieces and was more than happy to send them to me for approval. Still unconvinced, I agreed to take a look.

When the test pieces arrived, I was very pleasantly surprised – the results were superb! Ridgway had indeed given Ron's work the care and respect it deserved, and rather than detract from it in any way, his treatment served only to enhance it. In fact, it was almost as if Ron had coloured it himself! Consequently, I was more than happy to give Barzilay my full approval for *Invaders from Time* to appear in *Spaceship Away*; and when I informed him that there was in fact a second *Nick Hazard* story, *Planet of Doom*, he indicated that he might well consider printing that also, at a later date, if *Invaders from Time* proved popular. This made me think that an even better idea would be for him to start from the very beginning with *Mission to Vorga*, the original *Nick Hazard* story that Phil Harbottle and I had launched in our own self-published series of booklets in the mid-'80s.

Barzilay was happy with this idea – but there was a stumbling block. The original *Mission to Vorga* artwork, printed at relatively small size in our A5 booklets, was in the Picture Library format, with only two rows of three or at most four panels per page; but *Spaceship Away*, a larger A4 title, was in the *Eagle* format, typically with three rows of three panels per page. While the original pages could in theory have been left as they were and simply enlarged, that would have left them looking inconsistent with the rest of the magazine's contents, and the story, although serialised, would have extended over too many instalments. Consequently the decision was taken to reformat the strip by combining up to four of the original pages into one. This would entail certain frames being rearranged or lost, and captions and speech bubbles being readjusted, and consequently I asked to be put in contact with Ridgway so that we could work together on the project. Ridgway was only too happy to have me on board, and I found we had much in common – he was also a great admirer of Ron's work and determined to do it full justice. From that point on, I knew we would get along well.

So began an association whereby John Ridgway would combine the original pages into new composites, while I would suggest amendments and amend the dialogue and narrative as necessary to preserve the story continuity. John would then take my changes on board and finally colour the pages. I found this a very easy working relationship – John was amenable to my suggestions and I to his – and over the course of the next couple of months we succeeded in condensing the original 58 pages of the story into the 20 new ones that would run over the next five issues of *Spaceship Away*: they eventually appeared in Issues 16 to 20, published from 2008 through to 2010.

With *Mission to Vorga* completed, I anticipated that *Invaders from Time* and *Planet of Doom* would follow straight on, again with colours supplied by John; and as those stories were already in a suitable format, this time there would be no rejigging required. As things transpired, though, Rod Barzilay had now decided to leave *Spaceship Away*, and incoming new editor Des Shaw had plans of his own, so the *Nick Hazard* reissues were abandoned.

Fortunately, the hiatus was only a temporary one: remembering that *Mission to Vorga* had been well-received by the magazine's readers, Shaw later agreed to serialise several more of our strips: Phil's Fearn short story adaptations (Issues 28 to 31, published from 2012 to 2013); *Planet of Doom* (Issues 35 to 40, published from 2015 to 2016); *The Golden Amazon* (Issues 42 to 50, published from 2017 to 2020); and *Invaders from Time* (Issues 54 to 61, published from 2021 to 2023). This time, the stories were all splendidly coloured by Martin Baines.

Back in 2010, I had feared that Shaw's decision to drop *Nick Hazard* from *Spaceship Away* would mean the end of the good working relationship I had developed with John Ridgway. So keen was I for that association to continue that I looked into the possibility of republishing Ron's *Rick Random* stories myself. However, when I found out how much the licensing fees would cost, I could well understand why Barzilay had shied away from the idea! As Shaw at that time had no plans to pick up *Invaders from Time* and *Planet of Doom*, I then considered seeking Phil Harbottle's agreement to republish those instead. In the end, though, I concluded that would be too risky a venture, given that *Nick Hazard* was a much less well-known series than *Rick Random*.

There was, though, another series Ron had produced concurrently with *Rick Random* that might just be accessible: *Space Ace*. I had in my collection every single *Space Ace* story published between 1954 and 1963, and very few of these had ever been reprinted. I felt they deserved to be rescued from obscurity and enjoyed anew by fans of Ron's *Rick Random* era, and moreover had the potential to be very popular. Buoyed by this realisation, I conceived the idea of publishing a collection of vintage *Space Ace* strips in a magazine of the same size and quality as *Spaceship Away*. However, I was concerned about copyright, for although Atlas, the original publishers, had gone out of business in the late '60s, the rights could have passed to another company. I scoured the internet and various other sources, looking for possible current copyright-holders, but could find none. Ultimately, I decided that if copyright did rest with another company, and they actually recognised the series as one of their properties, they would get in touch with me soon enough – in which case I would either have to come to some arrangement with them or else scrap the project.

Consequently, I decided to take a chance, and in 2012, having chosen four of Ron's best *Space Ace* stories, sufficient to fill a 40-page magazine, I arranged for John to colour them – or, as I later termed it, 'colourise' them, which I thought better expressed the aim of treating the original artwork with consideration and respect, and in a way that reflected Ron's own production values. Waiting to see each page as John completed it, I felt a sense of excitement similar to that I had experienced when Ron had produced the original artwork back in the day.

Optimistically marking the finished magazine 'Vol 1' – for in truth I had no idea at that point if it would sell well enough to warrant a follow-up – I found a suitable printer and placed an order for just over 100 copies. I then proceeded to secure as much publicity as I could through various SF and comic-based websites, such as Steve Holland's popular Bear Alley.

In the event, Vol 1 was a sell-out, generating more orders than I could fulfil. This left me in no doubt that a follow-up was indeed a viable proposition. So, six months later, I issued another collection of four stories, again colourised by John, alongside which I was able to publish some of the many letters of support I'd received; and I was still getting so many enquiries about the first issue that I had to arrange for a reprint in order to satisfy demand.

Vol 2 also proved to be a sell-out, as did Vol 3 when I went on to publish that. I now knew without

A page of Turner's artwork for *The Golden Amazon*, as colourised by Martin Baines for *Spaceship Away* Issue 42, published in 2017.

A page of Turner's artwork for the *Space Ace* story 'The Hunter of Hankora', as coloured by John Ridgway for *Space Ace* Vol 1.

question that I had a successful venture on my hands. Therefore I decided to continue putting out further issues at six-monthly intervals, provided John was free to undertake the colouring work.

Up till now, I had selected each issue's contents from amongst the short, seven-page stories that had made up the main *Space Ace* run, and I began to wish that Ron had written some longer tales with more scope, as he had for the *Tit-Bits* Science Fiction Comics range. Then I remembered that in fact he had! When *Space Ace* had first begun, it had presented four serialised adventures published at the rate of four pages per issue over six monthly issues. Running to 24 pages in total, these stories were almost book-length, and would be ideal to reprint in the magazine.

Each of the original instalments had opened with a title and, except for the first of each story, a recap of the plot so far, whereas for a collected edition, only an initial title would be needed for each story. However, I reasoned that, between us, John and I should be able to modify the artwork and dialogue to remove the superfluous intermediate titles and recaps; the changes needed would, after all, be less extensive than those we'd made before on *Mission to Vorga*. John was in full agreement: it would be a challenging but worthwhile project, and we could pull it off. Thus it was that we began preparing a revised version of 'The Island Universe'. It took a lot of work, but eventually we were satisfied with the results, and the story duly appeared in Vol 4 in March 2015, along with an article recalling the chats I'd had with Ron about its creation. Feedback indicated that we'd made the right decision, so we proceeded to give the other three serialised *Space Ace* stories the same treatment for Vols 5, 6 and 7, before returning to collections of shorter stories.

I was pleased when the magazine's issue-count reached double figures, but nevertheless decided to make Vol 12 the last. I initially planned to move on next to reprinting Ron's *Tit-Bits* comics, but had to drop that idea when I discovered that in this instance there was still an active copyright-holder. As I was working essentially on a non-profit basis, even a small licence fee was something I couldn't afford to pay. Consequently, I instead chose to publish *Beyond: A Ron Turner Special*, a collection of some of Ron's very last strips, again colourised by John: 'The Killing Zone'; 'Terror From Moon 33'; a war story, 'Lone Eagle'; and my own 'Blonde Bombshell'. Originally intended for April 2020, and cover-dated November 2020, this eventually appeared in February 2021.

Although I had billed Vol 12 as the final *Space Ace* collection, feeling that the remaining stories weren't strong enough to justify another, I soon began to receive correspondence asking for more. I then realised that a further volume might be possible if I were to repeat an idea I had tried once before, of combining several different stories into one entirely new one. The main difficulty with this was that, although I could create a flowing narrative, the fact that Ron's style had changed quite a bit over the years meant that there was a danger of different parts of the composite story looking so different from each other that they jarred awkwardly. In this case, though, I was able successfully to weave together a new 21-page adventure that I called 'The Search'. This I published in November 2021 as *Space Ace – Special Edition*, along with two back-up strips: 'The Plot', one of Ron's very last *Space Ace* stories, in which Ace meets aliens who appear to be descended from the Metharons of 'The Island Universe'; and 'The Kidnappers', one of his very first, which had no aliens but much charm and good characterisation.

This I followed up in October 2022 with *Ron Turner's Steve Larabee*, a Western special collecting together two stories: 'The Apache Pass Viaduct', written by Ron and first published in *Lone Star Magazine* # 12 in December 1958, and the much longer *Red Revolt*, originally included earlier in 1958 in the fourth *Lone Star Annual*.

If Ron were around today, I feel sure he would be both amazed and delighted to see his work still appearing in print, and still being warmly appreciated by his many admirers – perhaps even more so than back in the 1950s. Not only are there further comic-strip collections still in prospect, but Phil Harbottle continues to promote Ron's cover work on new reissues of John Russell Fearn and E C Tubb novels from Wildside Press and others. And with Ron's life and career now also chronicled in *The Fantastic Art of Ron Turner*, his marvellous legacy seems set to endure well into the future.

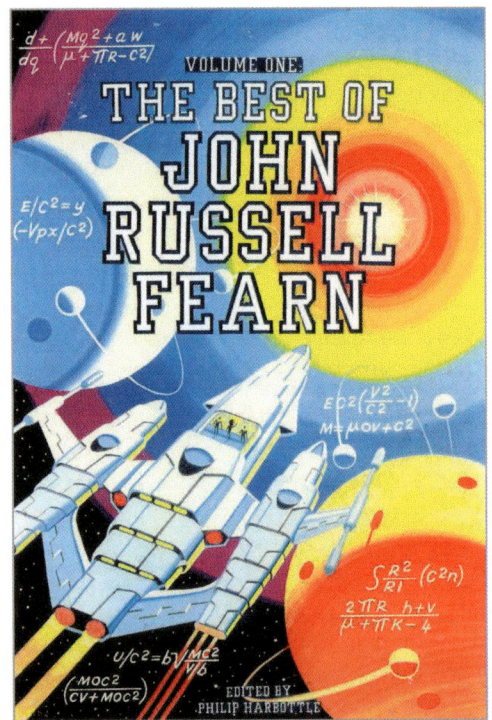
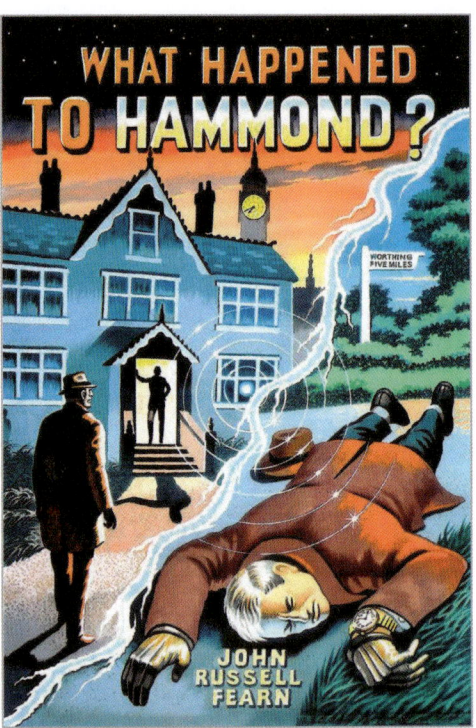

Above: *The Best of John Russell Fearn* Volume 1 (Cosmos/Wildside, 2001), using a 1991 private commission painting based on the 1952 Vargo Statten novel *To the Ultimate*; *What Happened to Hammond?* by John Russell Fearn (Borgo/Wildside, 2011), using a 1996 private commission painting for that novel (with a small correction: Turner painted the first word of the title as 'Whatever'); *The Dust Destroyer* by John Russell Fearn (Borgo/Wildside, 2016), using a 1992 private commission painting based on that novel; and *Secret of the Towers* by E C Tubb (Wildside, 2025), a retitled edition of *Space Hunger*, using Turner's vintage cover originally intended for that novel but mistakenly used by publishers Milestone on the same author's *Tormented City* (see page 73).

CONCLUSION

A 1994 private commission painted for Philip Harbottle, based on the 1949 John Russell Fearn novel *The Trembling World*.

TRIBUTES

JOHN FREEMAN

There are several distinctive artists in every decade of British comics – creators whose work has a distinct, unforgettable individuality that leaves an indelible memory on the reader. Ron Turner was, for me, one such creator, whose work on *The Daleks* for *TV Century 21* thrilled me as a child growing up in the 1960s, and whose later contributions to comics such as *2000 AD* still entertained. It's fair to say his work has had a lasting influence on many other British comic artists, the interest revived thanks to John Lawrence and John Ridgway through the *Space Ace* title in recent years. A singular talent, deserving of accolade.

ALAN CLARK

Back in the 1970s, I wasn't a fan of Ron Turner's work. That was because I had barely seen any of it. It had been done mainly for somewhat obscure books that then weren't so easy to find, as they had been issued post-war by the small publisher Scion. Turner did covers for the firm's science fiction paperbacks. It was a 1980 article by John Lawrence that converted me. Turner's work was outstanding. And different. It stood out, even from that of his (excellent) contemporaries. His pen-and-ink work was impressive: he knew what not to ink in, and the white spaces he left gave his drawings an even bigger impact. It also made his work instantly recognisable. After Scion, Turner moved on to Super Detective Library and *Rick Random* in the 1950s and gained a new legion of fans. John Lawrence's article linked him up with Philip Harbottle, literary agent of the late John Russell Fearn, and those two enthusiastic fans persuaded Turner to produce complete drawn adventures of a space-age hero named Nick Hazard, based on stories written by Fearn; the *Nick Hazard* title also reprinted *Space Ace* adventures from 1958. To my mind, Turner's work became even better when he began to realise that it was appreciated. And, astonishingly, his work in colour was equally impressive as it had been in black-and-white and often spectacular; his drawings often appearing to explode off the page. We lost a great science fiction artist when we lost Ron Turner.

GARETH KAVANAGH

Ron Turner is as much responsible for the image of the Daleks as writer Terry Nation and designer Ray Cusick. I wasn't old enough to enjoy *TV Century 21* the first time around, but the reprinted strips in *Doctor Who Weekly* and, better still, the '70s Dalek annuals were mind-blowing. The sheer imagination on display in those pages was breathtaking. These were Daleks with a culture and a confident Ron Turner aesthetic. Starships that gleamed. Technology built for Daleks, from hoverbouts through to the elegance of Agent 2K. And colour. All that colour. Bold, brash primary colour as befitted the arrogance of the Daleks. Ron Turner may not have created the Daleks, but for me he undoubtedly made them.

We were approached by John Lawrence not long after issue two of our fanzine *Vworp Vworp!* launched, with an intriguing idea. Would we be interested in finishing Ron's final Dalek strip from 1993? It was a chance we leapt at. Oddly cancelled by *Doctor Who Magazine*, those strips were part of the rich and vibrant Wilderness Years of *Doctor Who*, where invention walked hand in hand with nostalgia. Thanks to John, we were able to access the pages Ron had finished before putting his brushes down, and the baton was passed to Lee Sullivan to complete the story. Getting those pages published in *Vworp Vworp!*, alongside a comprehensive appreciation of Ron, his work and the *TV Century 21* Daleks phenomenon remains one of my proudest moments. An eight year old's dream made real. Thank you John.

KEITH PAGE

I first came across Ron Turner's work on *Space Ace* in *Lone Star Magazine*. He had an extremely original style, very strong black-and-white work faultlessly rendered. Dramatic lighting effects were much enhanced in his colour pages, and everything had an 'untouched by human hand' air about it. A true craftsman who would obviously never let anything in any way second rate leave his drawing board.

I would say my favourite pieces are the ferocious 'Vargo Statten' covers (rather before my time).

JOHN RIDGWAY

I knew Ron's work primarily as a science-fiction artist and writer. As a young man, I collected the stories he produced for *Tit-Bits* Science Fiction Comics – short black-and-white stories with dazzling colour covers. I also knew his work from the tremendous number of covers he produced for Scion science fiction novels by 'Vargo Statten' and E C Tubb. Later I followed his *Rick Random* comics, in which his line work took on a beautiful flowing style similar in some respects to that of Mac Raboy. At the same time, he was working on *Space Ace*, again in black-and-white, making it very much his own. Best of all, I remember his work on *The Daleks*, in full colour, for *TV Century 21*. His colour work is outstanding and his designs powerful and elegant.

ALAN LANGFORD

I never actually met Ron Turner; being thirty years his junior, our careers and our paths never coincided. However, I first became aware of his carefully-crafted artwork as a teenager while reading *TV Century 21*, the weekly comic that featured mainly Gerry and Sylvia Anderson's Supermarionation TV serials. On the reverse cover there was depicted a history of the origin of the terrifying Daleks, that had most of my generation enthralled when we first saw them on *Doctor Who*, way back in the 1960s. Two artists were the main contributors to this series, Richard Jennings and Ron Turner, and both gave very different but equally talented colourful interpretations of the Daleks and the world they inhabited. I personally remember being impressed by the two-headed reptilian monstrosities that inhabited the lakes of Skaro. Also I admired Turner's technically believable designs for his spacecraft, and his accurate designs of the Dalek city interiors.

He was a very accomplished illustrator, and his contribution to comic art should be fondly remembered by everyone who enjoyed his work.

DAVE GIBBONS

Some of the best British comic treasures published in the '50s and '60s were the pocket-size Picture Libraries. They were 64 pages in black-and-white and are best remembered for the series focused on the Second World War, such as the War, Battle, Air War at Sea and Commando Picture Libraries. Alongside these, Fleetway also published titles in other genres: Cowboy Picture Library, featuring versions of Kit Carson, Davy Crockett and Buck Jones, amongst others; Thriller Picture Library, with its odd mishmash of spy, historical adventure, and science fiction; and Super Detective Picture Library, featuring amongst others *Rip Kirby* reprints, *The Saint*, *Dick Barton* and my runaway favourite, *Rick Random*.

Where most science-fiction strips of those days had a slightly clunky, sketchy feel, *Rick Random* shone with both elegant futuristic design and smooth, bold drawing. As with most of my favourites of the time, it was years before I learnt the identity of the artist, but I eventually discovered that this master of the future was prosaically enough called Ron Turner. His work evoked the feel of the best American SF illustrators of the time, people like Ed Emshwiller and Edd Cartier, who sounded more the part. As I understand it, Turner had started as an engineering draftsman, but soon became the quintessential artist for many of the SF pulps and comics of the '50s and '60s. His work was admittedly

Below: the John Ridgway-colourised title page of Turner's artwork for the *Space Ace* story 'The Asteroid'.

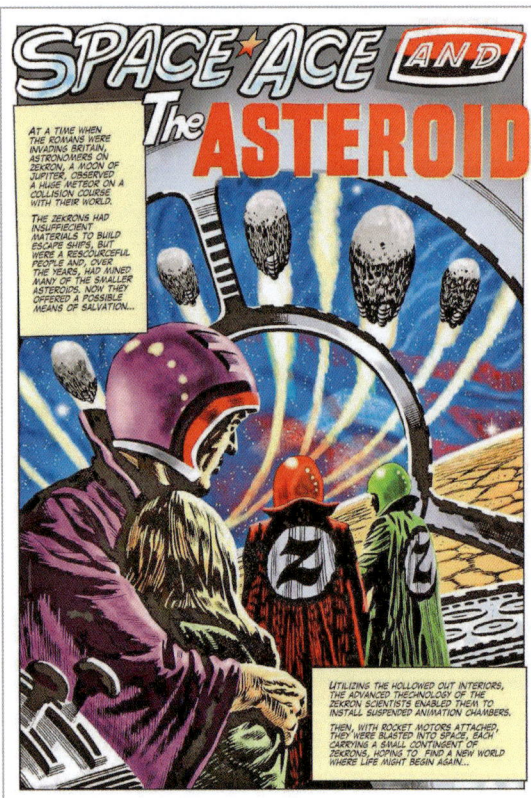

Above: a previously unpublished 1990 undersea kingdom painting.

tightly focused, and his occasional forays into genres like sport or war never quite rang true, being too polished and idealised. But give him a fleet of space cruisers or an army of alien soldiers and there was no-one better. His powers of invention were stunning, with a new design of spacecraft or weird beast on every other page, it seemed. Rick Random himself had the languid air of a futuristic James Bond, charming elegant women or merely lounging on an anti-grav couch, suavely smoking a cigarette or drinking an extraterrestrial cocktail. This was aspirational science fiction, sexy and dreamlike.

Turner often got wonderful scripts to draw, some of them written by the ubiquitous Harry Harrison, who'd started as an inker in American comics with Wally Wood before setting off to roam Europe while writing the Flash Gordon newspaper strip for Dan Barry. It was with Turner, though, that the future was best realised; you can always tell when an artist is enjoying a script and, time after time, the joy of graphic invention jumps off his pages.

Some of Turner's best work was on Space Ace, with many episodes also written by him. These appeared in Lone Star Magazine, in a standard comic-book format. Ace and his sidekick Bill Crag were space cops, which meant plenty of gun-shooting and space chases. The Lone Star company made children's toys, and the comic largely served as publicity for their ranges of revolvers and ray-guns.

I was heartbroken when the Super Detective Picture Library ceased publication, and even wrote to Fleetway to complain. I got a kind and polite note back, containing a couple of copies of the Thriller Picture Library, one of them featuring Jet Ace Logan, another space character, by way of consolation. Strangely, the note was probably written by Barry Coker, who was then on staff at Fleetway and years later would be my art agent. He tells me he even helped write one of the Rick Random stories.

Turner went on to draw some strips for Fleetway weeklies, which didn't make the best use of his talents, before finding his way to illustrating The Daleks strip in glorious painted colour for TV Century 21. This was a heaven-made match, and Turner's graphic élan added incredible excitement to the frankly stolid world of the Daleks, who were essentially trashcans on castors.

I understand that Turner went on to doing the art for painting-by-numbers kits, which his clean and vibrant style fitted well. There was a last hurrah for Rick Random and Turner in a short serial for 2000 AD, written by Steve Moore, but the elegant space detective was already strangely anachronistic and quickly faded away for good.

There was a mystery attached to Ron Turner that might have taken a super detective to unravel: apparently, no-one at Fleetway had ever met or spoken to him in all the time he worked for them. All his business was conducted through a Mr Hall, apparently his art agent, although as far as I know he represented no other clients. It was believed, therefore, that Hall might have been Turner himself.

A final, though distant, resonance with Turner later occurred for me. I got my start on 2000 AD by successfully visualising Harlem Heroes, the comic's requisite sports story, following several rejected attempts by a variety of artists, both British and European. Many years later, my early Harlem Heroes original art pages were returned to me, and I was interested to find a number of other artists' audition sketches and partial pages included in one package. Amongst them, to my excitement, was Ron Turner's version of the first page that I'd also drawn for my attempt (see page 178). It was wonderful to see that we'd both worked on the same script in our own way, even if my way bore the clear influence of my 'competitor.'

Turner had sadly passed away by that time, so I still have the page in safe-keeping. I like to think that he, and the mysterious Mr Hall, would be happy to know it is treasured by a grateful acolyte.

A 1993 private commission painting produced for Philip Harbottle, based on the 1946 John Russell Fearn novel *Other Eyes Watching*.

AFTERWORD
by John Lawrence

As a child, reading the adventures of Space Ace and Rick Random and marvelling at their incredible artwork, I never in all my wildest dreams expected that I'd actually come to meet the artist who drew them, let alone have the opportunity to get to know and work with him. Initially, therefore, I felt a little in awe of Ron. But not for long, as I soon found him to be a modest, unassuming kind of person, with a generosity and a willingness to tackle any project I gave him, large or small.

Ron was also very articulate and had an extremely cultured and distinguished manner of speaking – though what impressed the listener was not so much how he spoke as what he said. Whether he was remarking on some technical problem with his car or pontificating on the nature of the universe, the discourse became so involved at times that, being in the presence of this highly intelligent and knowledgeable man, I felt a little out of my depth. But this was leavened by a very self-deprecating manner that made him seem more down-to-earth. Once, I asked him to recall why he'd produced a piece of his earlier work in a particular way, and he replied, 'I'm afraid I can't remember. Some people have the gift of almost total recall. In my case, it's a blank – situation normal!' This, in addition to a very dry sense of humour.

Shortly after I met him, he told me how much he enjoyed life on the river – but hadn't expected to experience it quite as closely as he had. He explained how he'd recently seen a small boy slip off the towpath and into the water, and had had to jump in and drag him to safety. He then went on to state that the experience had taught him something that up till that moment he'd never realised. I presumed he was about to reveal some profound truth; that we're never aware of our true capabilities until faced with a sudden crisis, perhaps. But no. His revelation was that he'd discovered his watch was waterproof!

Ron was also generous in an almost altruistic way, even with regard to the planet. On one of my visits, he pointed out to me some new technological marvel that had caught his eye. He remarked on how 'Man's capacity for invention seems never-ending,' but then went on to decry the mindless violence in the world and add, 'I sometimes wonder, the way events are heading, if the world wouldn't have been a far better place if Man had never appeared at all!'

Ron was fascinated by new technology and always interested in learning about the latest scientific discoveries and developments. Despite this, he preferred to observe from afar rather than actually acquire any of the latest gadgets and gizmos that were beginning to dominate domestic life. His only concession to modern appliances was a 12-inch portable colour TV. When I first met him, he had no radio, just an old gramophone that had seen better days, on which he played the few classical LP records he owned. This changed only when his sons bought him a midi hi-fi system for a birthday present – although he seemed to derive more pleasure from seeing how the remote control operated the CD player than from being able to listen to and enjoy the music!

Ron's selflessness also showed in his lack of material things, for he led an extremely Spartan existence. No paintings graced his walls and no books occupied his shelves – he had no books! None, that is, except for one, which was his bible. Not the Bible itself, but a special book he kept in a drawer; one that had been his inspiration for years: *The Solar System*, with planetary illustrations by Chesley Bonestell. He led a relatively clutter-free life, and any books that did happen to come his way would soon be disposed of, together with his newspapers and magazines. On one occasion, I took along a vintage *Thunderbirds* annual for him to use as reference material for the roughs he was preparing as a try-out for a new comic. In the end, the idea was abandoned, but when I asked for the return of my annual, he couldn't find it! Apparently it had been dumped along with a load of other stuff he had been clearing out in the interim. From then on, I made sure that I sent him only photocopies.

Even Ron's furniture – his table, chairs and so on – was handmade. Not of the flatpack self-assembly type, either, but of the old-fashioned DIY type. He was an intensely practical man whose creativity didn't stop at the drawing board. And it wasn't only through the wood carvings of his final years that he demonstrated this.

Working at a printing firm, I often took advantage of situations where surplus or redundant card stock was about to be thrown away, securing this for Ron to save him extra expense. One day when I arrived to collect some work from him, I was greeted with the statement, 'I'm afraid I owe you for four pieces of art card!' On entering his living room, I saw what he meant: in the corner were four wine bottles he had adapted into table-lamps, with shades made from my card! One he had decorated with a picture of a snake coiling around to rear up threateningly; another he had adorned with an image of an eagle, its wings encircling the lamp; a third he had given a depiction of a jewelled Arabian scabbard. But it was the fourth that was the most impressive. On this, he had created a night scene of New York harbour, with a view of the Statue of Liberty against the Manhattan skyline, made all the more striking by cut-outs he had put in the flame of the Statue's torch and in the windows of the skyscrapers, allowing the light to shine through and achieve an amazing effect.

On another occasion, I arrived at Ron's gate to hear the sound of running water. Thinking at first that he must be emptying a bath, I soon discovered that he had actually constructed in his front garden a small waterwheel, ringed with little buckets that filled and emptied sequentially to propel it forward.

Ron always liked to be busy, and if he wasn't working on projects such as these, he would be doodling ideas on the backs of envelopes or bills or in the margins of newspapers. Though these would consist mainly of spacecraft and aliens, they would never turn up later in any of our stories: they were complete originals, quickly sketched and then forgotten about. I would always ask him to save them for me, but unless I happened to visit at the right time, I'd get the answer, 'Sorry – must have thrown them out.' The enjoyment for him was in the creation. Once a drawing had been committed to paper, he lost interest in it. I enquired once how he managed to dream up such convincing aliens and spacecraft. His reply was: 'I've never had a problem with imagination. I see every line and simply copy it onto my drawing board.' It was only when I thought about it later that I realised this hadn't really told me anything!

On another occasion when I visited Ron, I noticed two tremendous SF paintings propped up in a corner. At first I assumed these must have been created for someone else, as I hadn't commissioned them, but then he told me: 'Just something I did in my spare time. You can have them if you like.' When I asked how much he wanted paying for them, he replied, 'Oh, just take them away – I'm sick of looking at them!' I can only suppose that if I hadn't called when I did, these would have ended up in the bin as well!

Another time, I found Ron working on a painting inspired by the then recent Galileo mission to Jupiter. This showed the main spacecraft in orbit, sending a smaller probe down toward the planet, and had been built up in thick layers with the addition of a filler compound to the paint, expertly applied so that the surface had a three-dimensional quality. The work was only part done, with the background and spacecraft still to be completed, so I was keen to see how it would turn out. However, when on my next visit I asked to view the end result, Ron told me, 'Oh, that's gone – I wasn't really satisfied with it.'. If I'd realised he might dispose of it, I would have asked him to keep it for me – though, knowing how he took against any of his work he wasn't entirely happy with, it would probably still have gone the way of all the rest.

It was this perfectionism that drove Ron forward. A low boredom threshold meant that he didn't suffer third-rate scripts gladly; but, while he would treat shoddy work with all the disdain it deserved, if he could see that a writer had at least made an effort, and there was an opportunity for improving a story, then he would often introduce elements of his own to brighten it up. Some editors were astute enough to recognise the merit of what he had done, and flexible enough to accept the

AFTERWORD

A *Rick Random* scene painted by Turner as a private commission in 1989.

changes; others, though, were less enamoured, their main requirement being that an artist stick to the script. Being a conscientious type, Ron found it hard to accept that some editors really weren't looking for high-quality and innovative artwork. Provided it told the story and came in on time, that was all they were concerned about. Keen to avoid any hassle, they preferred to deal with artists they found amenable, or could even socialise with. Consequently, over the years, Ron had fallen foul of a number who found him so difficult to work with that they ultimately decided to stop using him. Unaware just how many admirers he had amongst science-fiction fans, he had thus been left with a very jaundiced view of how his work was regarded.

But to be rejected by an editor was one thing; to be asked to make alterations was quite another, and something he detested. He had produced the work the way he felt was right, and when it was finished, he had no wish to see it again. If someone else amended it later on, so be it, but it took a lot of persuasion to get him to do it himself. On past occasions when he had refused, it had sometimes fallen to his agent Greg Hall to make the changes, aided by his artist wife, for fear of losing future work.

The only time I fully experienced this situation myself arose when alterations were needed to a piece of artwork that Ron had produced for Phil Harbottle and me, the requirements for which I had probably failed to make sufficiently clear. I had considered making the changes myself, but they were quite involved and I had lacked the confidence. So, I felt I had no choice but to ask Ron. As expected, he was very resistant to changing anything, and although he did eventually agree, he made it quite clear that he was doing so under strong protest. 'What about this?' he demanded, pointing to another piece he was working on. 'Anything wrong there?' Realising I had crossed a line, I quickly replied, 'No, no, that's fine.' Still angry, Ron insisted, 'Are you sure? I might as well alter that as well, while I'm at it!' I decided never to ask him again.

So, although Ron was a brilliant artist, keeping editors at arms' length and rubbing them up the wrong way was not the best way to promote his work. He was also someone who disliked deadlines. This was why he had enjoyed working on the Picture Library titles, with their less critical editors and looser schedules. Whether the genre was SF, where he could use his imagination to create fantastical images, or war, where he could call on a certain amount of personal experience to embellish the story, this Picture Library format was the only area of comic-strips in which he could be totally satisfied with what he produced. Otherwise, he wasn't happy working for the mass market, where everything was wanted yesterday. He needed time to produce his best work and refine it to a state where he was pleased with it and it could be fully appreciated; which is why, when Phil and I came along, Ron finally got that time, along with the credit, respect and consideration he truly deserved.

As I write, it has been nearly 14 years since Ron passed away – almost the same amount of time for which I knew him – but I still miss him and the journey I used to make to his Sunningdale home on a Sunday morning, eager to see how a particular piece of work had turned out. Although I would have a pretty good idea how he would interpret any given brief, he would always surprise me with that little unexpected touch – that little extra element he'd added – that little bit of Ron Turner magic that made the work so unique.

But he was someone who always downplayed his own achievements, and seemed never fully to believe that he had a following. When I told him in hospital that I planned to write a book about his life and work he said, 'Oh really? Do you think anyone will be interested?' 'Yes, of course,' I replied. His rather self-deprecating rejoinder, as he shook his head, was, 'I can't think why!'

I believe, deep down, he did know why: he realised he was good at what he did; he just couldn't bring himself to acknowledge it. But that didn't mean he didn't want to hear it. Ron liked to be appreciated as much as anyone would, given how much thought and effort he always put into his work – in some cases, far more than was needed. And that is why this book has been written; to show my appreciation and give credit where credit is unquestionably due, for all the marvellous work Ron produced over the years.

Ron Turner was indeed a remarkable talent – a bit of a genius, I would say – and I doubt we will see his like again. It was a pleasure and a privilege to know him.

John Lawrence, Dunstable, 2023

BIBLIOGRAPHY

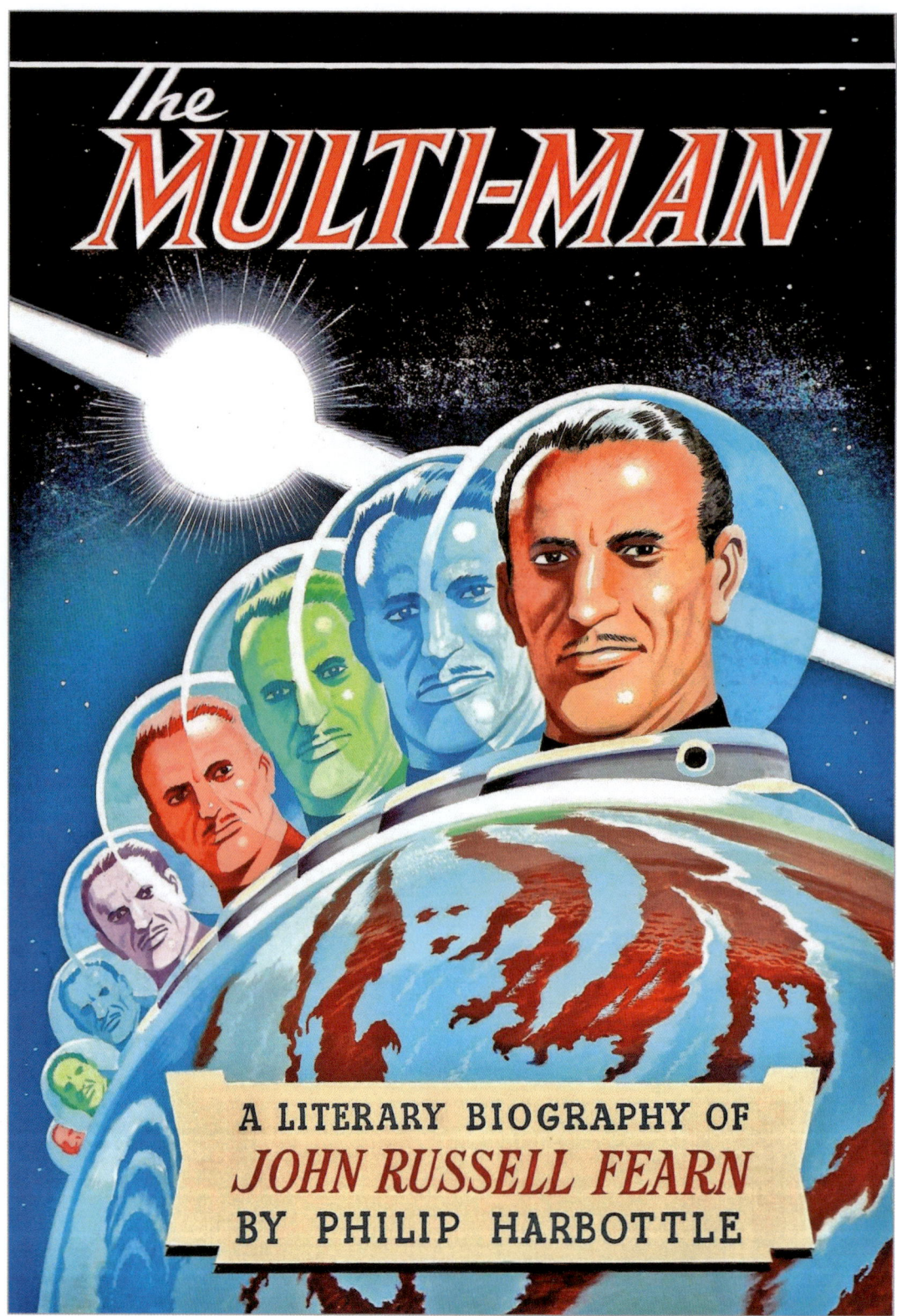

Above: previously unpublished, Turner's cover for a planned but ultimately abandoned late 1980s reissue of a Philip Harbottle-written literary biography of John Russell Fearn, originally issued in 1968 with a cover by Harbottle himself. This new cover was a pastiche of that for the 1954 Vargo Statten novel *The Multi-Man* (see page 88).

BIBLIOGRAPHY

This bibliography lists all the artwork known to have been produced professionally by Ron Turner, subdivided by year and then alphabetically by publisher, with any private commissions listed at the end of each year. Private commissions are sometimes identified with a descriptor rather than a title. Where a publication date is known, this is given in brackets. Where an entry is followed by an asterisk, this denotes the publication of a piece previously used elsewhere or originally painted as a private commission (although some reissues of previously published artwork are omitted). Except where otherwise indicated, published pieces were covers in full colour.

1941

Odhams

Modern War: 'Bucking Bronco of the Air' (1 spot illustration, line and wash) (22 March)

1947

Odhams

Kinematograph Weekly: various illustrations (line and wash)

1949

Muir-Watson

The Avenger by Cal Hogan

Scion

Big Scoop: *Scoop Grainger* (line and red/blue overlay cover, and 2 pages b/w) / *The Atomic Mole* (3 pages b/w)

Big Ranch: *The Atomic Mole* (3 pages b/w)

Big Atlantis: *The Atomic Mole* (line and red/blue overlay cover and 2 pages b/w)

Big Combat: *The Atomic Mole* (line and red/blue overlay cover and 2 pages b/w) / *Track to Fame* (3 pages b/w)

Big Mounty: *Big Mounty* (line and red/blue overlay cover and 2 pages b/w)

Mystery At Vellum by R J Finney (cover)

Find The Lady by R J Finney (cover)

1950

Odhams

Marvels Of Modern Science: Radio Valves / Structure of the Atom / Reflecting Radio Waves / Spark Jumping / The 'Skip' Effect in Broadcasting / Atmosphere Control in Aircraft (illustrations, line and wash)

How And Why It Works: Watch / Sewing Machine / Electric Iron / Ratchet Screwdriver (illustrations, line and wash)

Things The Handyman Can Make For The Home: numerous pieces (illustrations, line and wash)

Scion

Heartbreak by June Carole (two-tone red/blue cover)

Take Your Happiness by June Carole (two-tone red/blue cover)

Cupid Wears Emeralds by Vivienne Carne (two-tone red/blue cover)

Mountain Madonna by Fe Wendel (two-tone red/blue cover)

Dance to Heaven by Vivienne Carne (two-tone red/blue cover)

Between Two Loves by Barbara Ransome (two-tone red/blue cover)

Forget Me Not by Vivienne Carne (two-tone red/blue cover)

Poison Ivy by Vivienne Carne (two-tone red/blue cover)

Death In The Stars by Norman Lazenby

Operation Venus by John Russell Fearn (May)

Vargo Statten novels: *Annihilation!* (May) / *The Micro Men* (June) / *Wanderer of Space* (August) / *2000 Years On!* (September) / *The Cosmic Flame* (October) / *Nebula X* (November) / *Inferno!* (December) *The Sun Makers* (December)

1951

Edwin Self

Destination Mars by George Sheldon Brown (December)

John Spencer

Tales of Tomorrow No 3 (March)

Scion

Vargo Statten novels: *The Avenging Martian* (January) / *Deadline to Pluto* (March) / *The Petrified Planet* (August) / *The Devouring Fire* (September) / *The New Satellite* (October) / *The Renegade Star* (December) / *The Catalyst* (December)

The Gold of Akada by Earl Titan (May)

Anjani the Mighty by Earl Titan (July)

Victor Norwood novels: *The Untamed* (August) / *The Caves of Death* (September) / *The Temple of the Dead* (November) / *The Skull of Kanaima* (December)

Spawn of Space by Franz Harkon (November)

Commando Craig No 1: *The Adventures of Jack Hawkins* (2 pages line and red/blue overlay and 1 page b/w) / *Valley of Death* (2 pages line and red/blue overlay and 2 pages b/w)

Commando Craig No 2: *Sons of Darkness* (2 pages line and red/blue overlay and 2 pages b/w)

Commando Craig No 3: *The Red Devil* (2 pages line and red/blue overlay cover and 2 pages b/w)

1952

Cherry Tree

Vanguard to Neptune by J M Walsh (July)

John Spencer

Futuristic Science Stories No 7

Tales of Tomorrow No 4

Wonders of the Spaceways No 3 (May)

Worlds of Fantasy No 6 (4 interior illustrations, b/w) (September)

Worlds of Fantasy No 7

Kaye

Tremor by Frank Lederman (May)

Panther

Two Days of Terror by Roy Sheldon (May)

Scion

Vargo Statten novels: *The Inner Cosmos* (January) / *The Space Warp* (February) / *The Time Bridge* (March) / *The Man from Tomorrow* (April) / *The Eclipse Express* (April) / *Laughter in Space* (May) / *The G-Bomb* (June)

1953

Brown Watson

Sinister Forces by Alvin Westwood (February)

C Arthur Pearson

Tit-Bits Science Fiction Library: *Cosmic Exodus* by Conrad G Holt (August) / *The Hell Fruit* by Lawrence F Rose (September) / *Doomed Nation of the Skies* by Steve Future (November) / *The Star Seekers* by Francis G Rayer (December)

Tit-Bits Science Fiction Comics: No 1: *Planet XI* (31 pages b/w) / *Giants of the Second World* (33 pages b/w and colour cover) (October); No 2: *The Terror of Titan* (32 pages b/w) / *The Planetoid Plague* (32 pages b/w and colour cover) (November); No 3: *Captain Diamond and the Space Pirates* (34 pages b/w and colour cover) (December)

Comyns

Star-Rocket No 1: *Captain Sciento*: 'The Solar Condenser' (11 pages b/w)

Star-Rocket No 3: *Space Pirates* (17 pages b/w) / *Captain Sciento*: 'The Missing Levitanium' (10 pages b/w)

Zhorani by Karl Maras (December)

Edwin Self

Conquerors of Venus by Edgar Rees Kennedy (June)

Fawcett

Masterman # 14: 'The Caverns of Doom' (6 pages b/w) (February)

Milestone

Volsted Gridban novesls: *Planetoid Disposals Ltd* (January) / *Fugitive of Time* (February)

Charles Grey novels: *The Wall* (April) / *Dynasty of Doom* (May) / *Tormented City* (July) / *Space Hunger* (August) / *I Fight for Mars* (October)

Scion

Vargo Statten novels: *Ultra Spectrum* (January) / *Zero Hour* (May) / *The Black Avengers* (June) / *Odyssey of Nine* (July) / *Pioneer, 1990* (August) / *Man of Two Worlds* (October) / *The Lie Destroyer* (November) / *Black Bargain* (December)

Volsted Gridban novels: *Moons for Sale* (May) / *The Dyno-Depressant* (June) / *The Magnetic Brain* (July) / *Scourge of the Atom* (September) / *Exit Life* (October) *The Master Must Die* (November)

Odhams

Picturegoer: Coronation scene and map of route (line and wash)

Panther

The Great Ones by Jon J Deegan (May)

Top Fiction

The Unseen Assassin by Hank Janson (with Reginald Heade) (October)

T Werner Laurie

Laurie's Space Annual: Endpapers (line and wash with two-tone red/blue) / *Death of a Planet!* (8 pages b/w)

1954

Amalgamated Press

Super-Detective Library: No 44: *Rick Random: Kidnappers from Space* (64 pages b/w) (December)

Birn Brothers

Into Space With Ace Brave (pop-up book) (4 pop-ups and 8 pages colour)

Boardman

Project Jupiter by Fredric Brown (August)

C Arthur Pearson

Tit-Bits Science Fiction Library: *Before the Beginning* by Marx Reisen (January) / *The Living World* by Carl Maddox (February) / *Menace from the Past* by Carl Maddox (March) / *Mission to the Stars* by Philip Kent (April) / *Vassals of Venus* by Philip Kent (May) / *Space Puppet* by John Rackham (June) / *Slaves of the Spectrum* by Philip Kent (July) / *The Master Weed* by John Rackham (August) / *Jupiter Equilateral* by John Rackham (September) / *The Dissentizens* by Bruno G Condray (October) / *Home is the Martian* by Philip Kent (November) / *Slave Traders of the Skies* by Steve Future (December)

Tit-Bits Science Fiction Comics: No 4: *Scourge of the Carbon Belt* (32 pages b/w and colour cover) (January) / No 5: *The Dome of Survival* (21 pages b/w) (February) / *The Inner World* (21 pages b/w) / No 6: *The Diemos Deadline* (21 pages b/w and colour cover) (March)

Tit-Bits: *Daughter of the Sea* Pt 1 (2 spot illustrations, line and wash) (26 June) / *Daughter of the Sea* Pt 2 (title illustration, line and wash) (3 July)

City Magazines

Blighty Xmas Extra: 'The Ghost of Limbo' (1 page b/w)

Comyns

Peril from Space by Karl Maras (December)

Dakers

Journey to the Centre of the Earth by Jules Verne (full colour frontispiece plus colour cover) (November)

DCMT

Lone Star Magazine: Nos 17-22: *Space Ace*: 'The Island Universe (4 pages per issue, b/w) (July to December)/ No 19: *Steve Larrabee*: 'War Drum' (September)

Dragon

1000 Year Voyage by Vargo Statten (November)

Edwin Self

Voyage into Space by Erle Van Loden (May)

The Yellow Planet by George Sheldon Browne (May)

John Spencer

Out of this World No 2 (Winter)

Merit

Charles Grey novels: *The Hand of Havoc* (July) / *Enterprise 2115* (September)

Milestone

The Extra Man by Charles Grey (February)

Newnes

Practical Mechanics: Lunar Spaceship (March) / Fishing Tackle (September)

Paladin

Alien Life by E C Tubb (January)

The Plant from Infinity by Karl Maras (July)

Turner's 1991 recreation of his cover for the *Tit-Bits* Science Fiction Library entry *Scourge of the Carbon Belt* (C Arthur Pearson, 1953).

Turner's 1994 recreation of his cover for *Wonders of the Spaceways* No 3 (John Spencer, 1952).

Scion

Vargo Statten novels: *The Grand Illusion* (January)/ *Wealth of the Void* (February) / *A Time Appointed* (March) / *I Spy* (April) / *The Multi-Man* (June)

Volsted Gridban novels: *The Purple Wizard* (January) / *The Genial Dinosaur* (February) / *Frozen Limit* (March) / *I Came – I Saw – I Wondered* (April) / *The Lonely Astronomer* (May)

E C Tubb novels: *City of No Return* (April) / *The Hell Planet* (May) * / *The Resurrected Man* (May)

Vargo Statten Science Fiction Magazine Vol 1 No 1 (January)

Vargo Statten British Science Fiction Magazine Vol 1 No 4 (May) / Vol 1 No 5 (June)

1955

Amalgamated Press

Super-Detective Library: No 49: *Rick Random: The Man Who Owned the Moon* (64 pages b/w) (March) / No 51: *Mystery of Table 13* (cover) (April) / No 53: *Rick Random: The Space Bubble* (cover) (May) / No 55: *The Mystery of Peril Island* (64 pages b/w) (June) / No 64: *Rick Random: The Five Lives of Mr Quex* (64 pages b/w) (September) / No 66: *Rick Random: The Gold-Rush Planet* (64 pages b/w) (October) / No 70: *Rick Random: The Moving Planet* (64 pages b/w) (December)

C Arthur Pearson

Tit-Bits Science Fiction Library: *Exile from Jupiter* by Bruno G Condray (January) / *Alien Virus* by John Rackham (February) / *Dimension of Ilion* by Irving Heine (March)

City Magazines

Blighty Summer Extra: 'The Venus Lady' (1 page b/w)

DCMT

Lone Star Magazine: Nos 23-28: *Space Ace*: untitled story (4 pages per issue, b/w) (January to June) / Nos 29-34: *Space Ace*: untitled story (4 pages per issue, b/w) (July to December)

Lone Star Annual No 1: Endpapers (line with red/blue overlay) / *Space Ace*: 'The Pallasium Pirates' (13 pages, b/w)

Dragon

British Science Fiction Magazine: Vol 1 No 10 (February) / Vol 1 No 11 (March) / Vol 1 No 12 (April) / Vol 2 No 1 (June) / Vol 2 No 2 (July) * / Vol 2 No 3 (August) * / Vol 2 No 4 (September) * / Vol 2 No 5 (October) * / Vol 2 No 6 (November) *

John Spencer

Supernatural Stories No 6 (March)

Newnes

Practical Mechanics: Aircraft Carrier (April) / Planetarium (September) / Space Station, and Earth Satellite (spot illustration, b/w) (November)

Practical Householder: Building Your Own Bungalow (spot illustration, b/w) (November)

Panther

Deep Freeze by Jonathan Burke (March)

Rich & Cowan

The Man with Absolute Motion by Silas Water (June)

1956

Amalgamated Press

Cowboy Comics Library: No 174: *Buck Jones: Apache Uprising* (40 pages b/w) (July)

Super-Detective Library: No 79: *Rick Random: The Planet of Lost Men* (64 pages b/w) (June) / No 83: *Rick Random: Invaders from the Ocean Planet* (64 pages b/w) (July) / No 90: *Rick Random: Manhunt Through Space* (64 pages b/w) (October) / No 91: *Rick Random: Mystery in the Milky Way* (title page and few frames only, b/w) (November)

Beaverbrook

Express Weekly: No 101: 'Sentries of the Sea' (half page, colour) (25 August) / No 105: 'Skimming the Waves' (half page, colour) (22 September) / No 113: 'Here Come the Jet-Cars' (half page, full colour) (17 November)

DCMT

Lone Star Magazine: Vol 2 Nos 1-6: *Space Ace*: untitled story (4 pages per issue, b/w) (January to June) / Vol 2 No 8: *Space Ace*: untitled story (aborted serial – 4 pages b/w)

Lone Star Annual No 2: Front endpaper (b/w)

Dragon

British Science Fiction Magazine: Vol 2 No 7 (January) *.

John Spencer

Vengeance Trail by James S Farrow

Newnes

Practical Mechanics: Watch Repairing (June)

Practical Householder: Installing a Service Hatch (spot illustration, b/w), and How to Renovate Books (spot illustration, b/w) (November) / Papering a Ceiling (spot illustration, b/w), and Making Stained Glass Windows (spot illustration, b/w) (December)

Practical Motorist: A Pair of Handlebar Muffs (spot illustration, line and wash), and A Folding Steering Wheel (spot illustration, line and wash) (November)

1957

Amalgamated Press

Super-Detective Library: No 97: *Rick Random: The Time Travellers* (64 pages b/w) (February) / No 101: *Rick Random: The Riddle of the Vanishing People* (64 pages b/w) (April) / No 109: *The Oasis of Mystery* (64 pages b/w) (August) / No 111: *Rick Random: Sabotage from Space* (64 pages b/w) (September) / No 115: *Rick Random: SOS from Space* (64 pages b/w) (November)

Atlas

Lone Star Magazine: Vol 3 No 1: *Space Ace*: 'The Raiders from Space' (7 pages b/w) (January) / Vol 3 No 2: *Space Ace*: 'Renegade from Rathan' (7 pages b/w) (February) / Vol 3 No 3: *Space Ace*: 'The Hunter of Hankora' (7 pages b/w) (March) / Vol 3 No 5: *Space Ace*: 'The Slave Runners' (7 pages b/w) (May) / Vol 3 No 6: *Space Ace*: 'The Kidnappers' (7 pages b/w) (June) / Vol 3 No 8: *Space Ace*: 'The Fishmen of Formonda' (7 pages b/w) (August) / Vol 3 No 10: *Space Ace*: 'The Fire Ship' (7 pages b/w) (October) / Vol 3 No 11: *Space Ace*: 'The Tower of Tongaylor' (7 pages b/w) (November) / No 12: *Space Ace*: 'The Magnetic Meteor' (7 pages b/w) (December)

Lone Star Annual No 3: Front endpaper (b/w) / *Space Ace*: 'The Black Pirate' (12 pages b/w) / *Space Ace*: 'The Tyrant of Trathane' (12 pages b/w)

Mireillo

Aventures de Demain! ...: No 21: *Les Diamants de la Mort* (*The Diamonds of Death*) (24 pages b/w) (November)

Newnes

Practical Mechanics: Tea Maker (February) / Earth Satellite (April) / Silk Screen Printing (June) / Russian Satellite (December)

Practical Householder: Two-Way Switching Made Easy (spot illustration b/w) (February)

THE FANTASTIC ART OF RON TURNER

1958

Amalgamated Press

Super-Detective Library: No 123: *Rick Random*: *The Planet of Terror* (64 pages b/w) (March) / No 127: *Rick Random*: *The Space Pirates* (64 pages b/w) (May) / No 129: *Rick Random*: *Perilous Mission* (64 pages b/w) (June) / No 133: *Rick Random*: *The Frozen Planet* (64 pages b/w) (August) / No 137: *Rick Random*: *The Robot World* (64 pages b/w) (October)

Atlas

Lone Star Magazine: Vol 4 No 1: *Space Ace*: 'The Robot Ruler' (7 pages b/w) (January) / Vol 4 No 2: *Space Ace*: 'The Guided Missile' (7 pages b/w) (February) / Vol 4 No 3: *Space Ace*: 'Scourge of Saturn' (7 pages b/w) (March) / Vol 4 No 4: *Space Ace*: 'Looters of Loomar' (7 pages b/w) (April) / Vol 4 No 6: *Space Ace*: 'Blasco's Revenge' (8 page b/w) (June) / Vol 4 No 7: *Space Ace*: 'The Exiles' (7 pages b/w) (July) / Vol 4 No 8: 'The Wreckers' (7 pages b/w) (August) / Vol 4 No 9: *Space Ace*: 'The Blood Stones' (7 pages b/w) (September) / Vol 4 No 10: *Space Ace*: 'The Weed of Death' (7 pages b/w) (October) / Vol 4 No 11: *Space Ace*: 'The Enemy Beneath' (7 pages b/w) (November) / Vol 4 No 12: *Steve Larrabee*: 'The Apache Pass Aqueduct' (8 pages b/w) (December)

Lone Star Annual No 4: Front endpaper (line with red/blue overlay) / *Space Ace*: 'The Sphere of Doom' (8 pages b/w) / *Steve Larrabee*: The Red Revolt (16 pages sepia/green overlay) / *Space Ace*: The Creeping Death (8 pages b/w)

Newnes

Practical Mechanics: London Planetarium (April) / Film Slide Viewer, and Electric Motor (spot illustration, b/w) (October) / Metal Casting (December)

Practical Householder: Brick Incinerators (spot illustration, b/w) (July) / Operating Costs of Electrical Appliances (two spot illustrations, b/w) (August)

Practical Motorist: Preparing to Lay Up the Car (spot illustration, line and wash) (November)

Pedigree

A Mirror Of Witchcraft by Christina Hole

1959

Amalgamated Press

Comet: *Island of Peril* (serialised version of the Super-Detective Library No 55 story *The Mystery of Peril Island*) (3 pages per issue, b/w) (January to June) *

Super-Detective Library: No 143: *Rick Random*: *The Terror from Space* (64 pages b/w) (January) / No 153: *Rick Random*: *The Threat from Space* (64 pages b/w)) (June) / No 163: *Rick Random*: *The Kidnapped Planet* (64 pages, b/w) (December)

Atlas

Lone Star Comics: Vol 5 No 1: *Space Ace* 'The Wanderers' (7 pages b/w) (January) / Vol 5 No 2: *Space Ace*: 'The Menace from Minos' (7 pages b/w) (February) / Vol 5 No 3: *Space Ace*: 'The Battle on X3' (7 pages b/w) (March) / Volume 5 No 4: 'The Magic Circle' (8 pages b/w) (April) / Vol 5 No 5: *Space Ace*: 'The Plunderers' (7 pages b/w) (May) / Vol 5 No 6: *Space Ace*: 'The Sleeping Egyptian' (7 page b/w) (June) / Vol 5 No 7: *Space Ace*: 'Race with Death' (7 pages b/w) (July) / Vol 5 No 9: *Space Ace*: 'Robbers of Rakkor' (7 pages b/w) (September) / Vol 5 No 10: *Space Ace*: 'The Seed' (7 pages b/w) (October) / Vol 5 No 12: *Space Ace*: 'Station XO4' (7 pages b/w) (December)

Lone Star Annual No 5: Front endpaper (line with red/blue overlay) / *Space Ace*: 'Jet Black and his Merry Men' (10 pages b/w) / *Space Ace*: 'Terror on Titan' (10 pages b/w)

Dakers

Ace Carew by Edward R Home-Gall

Newnes

Practical Mechanics: Spot Welding (red/grey two-tone cover) (March)/ Reflecting Telescope (orange/blue two-tone cover), and Workbench (spot illustration, b/w) (May) / Battery Charger (orange/blue two-tone cover), and Giro Compass (spot illustration, b/w) (June) / Light Aircraft (orange/blue two-tone cover) (September) / Tape Recorder (red/blue two-tone cover) (October) / Space Flyer (spot illustration, b/w), and Hover Car (spot illustration, b/w) (November) / Marionette Theatre (orange/ blue two-tone cover) (December)

Practical Householder: Beginners Guide to Tools and Materials (supplement) (colour front colour and line-and-wash back cover) (February) / Sharpening Woodworking Tools (spot illustration, b/w), and *Pictorial Reference Guide* (supplement) (March) / *Pictorial Guide to Outside Jobs* (yellow/white two-tone cover) (May) / Concrete Plinths for Garden Sheds (spot illustration, b/w) (July)

1960

Atlas

Lone Star Magazine: Vol 6 No 1: *Space Ace*: 'The Acid Test' (7 pages b/w) (January) / Vol 6 No 2: *Space Ace*: 'The Scourge from Zambara' (7 pages b/w) (February) / Vol 6 No 4: *Space Ace*: 'The Hunters' (7 pages b/w) (April) / Vol 6 No 6: 'Make a Model P40 "Flying Tiger"' (featue) (1 page b/w)

Lone Star Annual No 6: Front endpaper (b/w) / *Space Ace*: 'The Time Transistor' (10 pages b/w) / *Space Ace*: 'The Molten Menace' (10 pages b/w)

Space Ace

No 1: 'The Barrier' (7 pages b/w), and 'Man in Space' (feature) (1 page b/w) (August) / No 2: 'The Two Enemies' (9 pages b/w), and 'The Hovercraft' (feature) (1 page b/w) (September) / No 3: 'The Race with Death' (9 pages b/w), and 'The Man-made Universe' (feature) (1 page b/w) (October) / No 4: 'The Enslaved Planet' (9 pages b/w), and 'Unusual Aircraft' (feature) (1 page b/w) (November) / No 5: 'The Hollow World' (9 pages b/w), and 'Pry-Out and Tear-Away (feature) (1 page b/w) (December)

Fleetway

Super-Detective Library: No 169: *John Steel*: *Gateway to Glory* (64 pages b/w) (March) / No 177: *John Steel*: *Operation Tina* (64 pages b/w) (July) / No 183: *John Steel*: *The Hidden War* (64 pages b/w) (October)

Thriller Picture Library: *Dogfight Dixon* (20+ pages for uncompleted/unpublished story)

Newnes

Practical Householder: Keeping Electrical Appliances Safe (spot illustration, b/w) (January)

Practical Mechanics: Building a Caravan (orange/blue two-tone cover), and Electroplating (spot illustration, b/w) (January) / Radio Control Receiver (orange/blue two-tone cover and spot illustration, b/w) (February) / Baby Alarm (orange/blue two-tone cover) (March) / Go-Karts (red/blue two-tone cover) (April) / Cabin Cruiser (red/blue two-tone cover), Bering Dam Project (spot illustration, b/w), and 'Exposure Measurement (spot illustration, b/w) (May) / Remote Control Aircraft (red/blue two-tone cover), and Life-Spheres (spot illustration, b/w) (July) / Mini-Golf (red/green two-tone cover), and Elevated Railways (spot illustration b/w) (August) /

Lab Apparatus (red/blue two-tone cover) (September) / Solar Power (spot illustration, b/w) (October)

1961

Atlas

Space Ace: No 6: 'The Plot' (9 pages b/w), and 'Undersea Exploration' (1 page feature, b/w) (January) / No 7: 'The Lost City' (9 pages b/w), and 'Super-Seaway' (1 page feature, b/w) (February) / No 8: 'The Colossus of Rhodes' (8 pages b/w), and 'Giants of the Rails' (1 page feature, b/w) (March) / No 9: 'The Robots' (8 pages b/w) (April) / No 10: 'The Magic Circle' (8 pages b/w) (May) * / No 11: 'The Messenger' (8 pages b/w) (June) / No 13: 'The Arizona Crater' (8 pages b/w) (July)

Lone Star Annual No 7: Front and back endpapers (line and colour overlay) / *Space Ace*: 'The Lens' (8 pages b/w) / *Space Ace*: 'The Asteroid' (8 pages line and colour overlay); 'The Racing Car' (1 page feature, b/w)

Fleetway

Super-Detective Library: No 188: *The Shadow*: *School for Spies* (64 pages b/w) (January)

Film Fun: *Scoop Donovan*: untitled story (2 to 2½ pages per issue, b/w) (7 January to 6 May) / untitled story (2 pages per issue, b/w) (20 May to 8 July) / untitled story (2 pages per issue, b/w) (22 July to 2 September) / untitled story (2 pages per issue, b/w) (16 September to 7 October) / untitled story (2 pages per issue, b/w) (21 October to 4 November) / untitled story (2 pages per issue, b/w) (18 to 25 November) / untitled story (2 pages per issue, b/w) (9 to 16 December)

Tiger: *Jet-Ace Logan* (sample page, b/w)

Buster: *Dan Dare*-type strip (sample page, b/w)

Newnes

Practical Mechanics: Nuclear Sub (January) / Solar-Powered Spaceships (spot illustration, b/w) (February) / The Short SCI, Prototype Plane of the Future (March) / Hovercraft (April) / Oil Rigs, and Drilling Rig (spot illustration, b/w) (May) / Man in Space (June) / Nuclear Aircraft (July) / Space Observatory (September) / Wave-Power, and Saturn Rocket (spot illustration, b/w) (October) / Jet-Packs (November) / Hover-Rail (December)

1962

Atlas

Book of Space Adventures aka *Boys' Book of Space*: *Space Ace*: 'The Rain of Death' (8 pages, line and colour overlay) / *Space Ace*: 'The Revolt' (7 pages, line and red overlay) / *Space Ace*: 'The Conjuror' (eight pages, line and red overlay) / *Space Ace*: 'The Rescue' (8 pages, line and colour overlay)

Fleetway

Film Fun: *Scoop Donovan*: untitled story (2 pages b/w) (27 January) / untitled story (2 pages b/w) (17 February) / untitled story (2 pages b/w) (12 May)

Thriller Picture Library: No 418: *Jet-Ace Logan*: *Times 5* (64 pages b/w) (July)

Buster Book of Thrills: Rick Random and the Terror from Space (16 pages b/w; heavily edited, abridged and resized from Super Detective Library 143) *

Newnes

Practical Mechanics: Rocket Power (January) / Radio-Telescopes (February) / Thames Heliport, and Heliport Transport (two spot illustrations, b/w) (March) / Economy Flying (April) / Two-Man Spacecraft (colour cover, and two spot illustrations, line and wash) (May) / One-Man Auto-Gyro (June) / Giant Excavator (July) / Channel Tunnel (August) / Solar Telescope (half-page spot illustration, line and wash)

1963

Craft Master

Painting-by-numbers kits: Veteran cars / Eagles in flight / Poodle portraits / Little girls: Samantha and Joanna / Winter mantle (2 scenes of each)

Fleetway

Thriller Picture Library: No 442: *Jet-Ace Logan*: *Power from Beyond* (56 pages b/w) (January)

Air Ace Picture Library: No 141: *The Claws of the Cat* (56 pages b/w) (March)

Newnes

Practical Mechanics: Atomic Reactor (half-page illustration, line and wash) (January) / Rocket Flight (6 spot illustrations, line and wash) (March)

1964

Craft Master

Painting-by-numbers kits: Harbour lights / London landmarks: Big Ben and Tower of London / Majestic mountains: Matterhorn and Blumsalp / Horse racing / Angling by sea and river / Antelopes in Africa / Mares and foals / Italian lakes / Jungle big cats (2 scenes of each)

Odhams

Today: Tunguska meteorite (spot illustration, line and wash with red overlay) (11 January) / Roberta the Robot (spot illustration, line and wash) (28 March)

1965

City Magazines

TV Century 21 International Extra: *Stingray*: 'The Delta Computer' (7 pages b/w and wash)

Stingray Special: 'Double Trap' (2 pages colour, 2 pages b/w and wash)

Craft Master

Painting-by-numbers kits: Wild horses / Sailing ships (2 scenes of each)

1966

City Magazines

TV Century 21: Nos 50-51: *The Daleks*: untitled story (1 page colour per issue) (1 to 8 January) / No 52: 'The Electrode 909 Space Fighter' (spot illustration, line and wash) (15 January) / Nos 59-102 *The Daleks*: untitled story (1 page colour per issue) (5 March to 31 December) / No 73: News feature: 'The Magnacar' (spot illustration, line and wash) / No 76: News feature: 'Moonbase' (spot illustration, line and wash) (2 July) / No 83: News feature: 'Forest Clearer' (full page, line and wash) (20 August) / No 86: News feature: 'Futuristic City' (spot illustration, line and wash) (10 September)

Thunderbirds Extra: untitled story (6 pages, b/w line and wash)

Stingray Annual: 'The Collector' (8 pages, line and colour overlay) / 'The Sunken City' (6 pages, line and colour overlay) / 'Death Ray' (eight pages, line and colour overlay) / 'History of Titanica' (2 pages, line and colour overlay) / Aquatraz Cutaway (centrespread, line and colour overlay)

Thunderbirds Annual: 'The Hood Makes a Strike' (8 pages, line and colour overlay)

THE FANTASTIC ART OF RON TURNER

The title page of the two-page 'Operation "Rescue"' strip drawn by Turner for IPC's *Valiant Summer Special* in 1966.

BIBLIOGRAPHY

Fireball XL5 Annual: 'The Drifting Coffin' (6 pages b/w)

Craft Master

Thunderbirds Oil Painting by Numbers Sets: Lady Penelope / Control Centre / Thunderbird 1 / Thunderbird 2/ Thunderbird 3 / Thunderbird 4 (2 scenes in each set)

IPC

Valiant Summer Special: 'Operation "Rescue"' (2 pages, colour)

J Rosenthal Toys Ltd

Thunderbirds 3D Painting Sets: 'Thunderbird 1 Blasts Off' / 'Virgil and Tin-Tin Foil the Hood' / 'Thunderbird 4 to the Rescue' / 'Lady Penelope Scores a Hit'

1967

City Magazines

TV Century 21: Nos 103-104: *The Daleks*: untitled story (1 page colour per issue) (7 January to 14 January)

Tv Century 21 Spring Extra: *Thunderbirds*: untitled story (4 pages b/w, and colour centrespread)

Thunderbirds Annual: 'Bridge of Fear' (4 pages, line and colour overlay)

Captain Scarlet Annual: untitled story (5 pages, line and colour overlay)

TV Century 21 Annual: *Thunderbirds*: 'Volcano Alert' (7 pages, line and colour overlay) / *Zero X*: 'Conflict on Mars' (6 pages, line and colour overlay)

Craft Master

Captain Scarlet Oil Painting By Numbers Sets: Captain Scarlet / Colonel White / Destiny Angel (2 scenes in each set)

Fleetway

Tiger and Hurricane: 4 to 18 March issues: *The Robot Builders*: untitled story (2 pages per issue b/w) / 25 March issue: *The Robot Builders*: untitled story (line and colour overlay cover, and 2 pages b/w) / 1 to 15 April issues: *The Robot Builders*: untitled story (2 pages per issue b/w) / 22 April issue: *The Robot Builders*: untitled story (line and colour overlay cover, and 2 pages b/w) / 29 April to 27 May issues: *The Robot Builders*: untitled story (2 pages b/w per issue) / 3 June issue: *The Robot Builders*: untitled story (line and colour overlay colour, and 2 pages b/w) / 10 June to 1 July issues: *The Robot Builders*: untitled story (2 pages per issued b/w) / 8 July issue: *The Robot Builders*: untitled story (line and colour overlay cover, and 2 pages b/w) / 15 July to 7 October issues: *The Robot Builders*: untitled story (2 pages per issue b/w)

1968

City Magazines

Joe 90 Puzzle Book (80 pages b/w)

Joe 90 Dot-to-Dot Book (80 pages b/w)

Joe 90 Sticker Fun Book (8 pages b/w, and 4 pages of colour stickers)

The Champions Dot-to-Dot Book (80 pages b/w)

Captain Scarlet Annual: untitled story (single spot illustration opening panel, and 5 pages, line and colour overlay)

Thunderbirds Annual: 'Day Return from Death' (4 pages, line and colour overlay) / 'Curse of the Elastos' (8 pages, line and colour overlay)

TV21 Annual: *Zero X*: 'Brink of Disaster' (6 pages, line and colour overlay) / *Captain Scarlet*: untitled story (6 pages, line and colour overlay)

Joe 90 Annual: 'The Deadly Toy' (4 pages, line and colour overlay) / 'Rat Trap' (6 pages, line and colour overlay) / 'Ambush' (4 pages, line and colour overlay) / 'Doctor Fawkes' (6 pages, line and colour overlay) / 'Checkmate' (5 pages, line and colour overlay)

1969

City Magazines

TV21 Annual: *Captain Scarlet*: 'Destroy San Francisco' (6 pages, line and colour overlay) / *Zero X*: 'Breakout' (5 pages, line and colour overlay) / *Captain Scarlet*: 'Lost in Time' (8 pages, line and colour overlay)

Captain Scarlet / Thunderbirds Annual: *Thunderbirds*: 'Fire Lords' (4 pages, line and colour overlay) / *Thunderbirds*: 'Crash Down' (8 pages, line and colour overlay)

Joe 90 Annual: 'Breakdown' (4 pages, line and colour overlay) / 'The Deadly Swarm' (8 pages, line and colour overlay)

Joe 90: Top Secret Annual: *The Champions*: 'Error of Judgement' (7 pages, line and colour overlay) / *Star Trek*: untitled story (6 pages, line and colour overlay) / *Land of the Giants*: untitled story (7 pages, line and colour overlay)

IPC

Air Ace Picture Library: No 450: *Fighter Ace* (56 pages b/w) (August)

Whizzer and Chips: 18 October to 27 December issues: *The Space Accident* (2 pages per issue, line and red overlay)

Unpublished

Interplanetary Rescue Service: four-frame sample newspaper strip (b/w)

1970

City Magazines

TV21: Nos 58-61: *Star Trek* (3 pages colour per issue) (31 October to 21 November)

IPC

Whizzer and Chips: 3 to 31 January issues: 'The Space Accident' (2 pages per issue, line and red overlay) / 7 February to 26 December issues: *Wonder-Car*: untitled stories (2 pages per issue, line and blue overlay)

Cor!!: 21 November to 26 December issues: *Robby Hood and his One Man Band*: untitled stories (2 pages per issue, b/w)

Scorcher Summer Special: *Billy's Boots* (7 pages b/w)

Smash Annual 1971: Tri-Man (5 pages colour)

Whizzer and Chips Holiday Special 1971: Wondercar (6 pages, line and wash)

Whizzer and Chips Annual 1971: 'It Came on Firework Night' (8 pages colour)

1971

Hamlyn

Daily Mirror Book For Boys 1972: 'Calamity Rose' (5 pages colour)

IPC

Cor!!: 2 January to 24 April issues: *Robby Hood and his One Man Band*: untitled stories (2 pages per issue, b/w)

Tiger: 16 October to 25 December issues: *The Tigers*: untitled stories (2 pages per issue, line and wash)

Whizzer and Chips: 2 January to 25 December issues: *Wonder-Car*: untitled stories (2 pages per issue, line and blue overlay)

Scorcher Summer Special: *Billy's Boots* (6 pages b/w)

Whizzer and Chips Holiday Special: *Wonder-Car* (6 pages, line and wash)

Scorcher Annual 1972: *Billy's Boots* (8 pages, line and colour overlay)

Whizzer and Chips Annual 1972: *Wonder-Car* (1 page colour, and 6 pages, line and wash) / 'Old Mac' (2 pages b/w) / 'William the Tele Fanatic' (2 pages b/w) / 'Hugo Furst' (2 pages b/w)

Polystyle

Thunderbirds Annual: 'Invisible Invader' (8 pages colour) / 'The Law Breakers' (8 pages colour)

1972

IPC

Tiger: 1 January to 30 December issues: *The Tigers*: untitled stories (2 pages per issue, line and wash)

Whizzer and Chips: 1 January to 22 July issues: *The Castaways*: untitled stories (2 pages per issue, line and blue overlay) / 29 July to 30 December issues: *Archie's Angels*: untitled stories (2 pages per issue, b/w)

Scorcher Annual 1973: *Billy's Boots* (8 pages, line and wash)

Tiger Annual 1973: *The Barbed Wire XI* (8 pages, line and wash)

Whizzer and Chips Annual 1973: *Wonder-Car* (6 pages, line and wash)

Polystyle

Countdown Annual: *Thunderbirds*: 'The Collector' (7 pages, line and wash and green overlay)

1973

IPC

Tiger: 6 January to 29 December issues: *The Tigers*: untitled stories (2 pages per issue, line and wash)

Shiver and Shake: 13 October to 15 December issues: 'Malice in Wonderland' (2 pages per issue, b/w)

Whizzer and Chips: 6 January to 23 June issues: *Archie's Angels*: untitled stories (2 pages per issue, b/w)

Tiger Annual 1974: *The Tigers*: untitled story (6 pages, line and wash)

Whizzer and Chips Annual 1974: *Archie's Angels*: untitled story (6 pages, line and wash)

Williams

Quizzer No 1: 'The Mystery of Grimm Grange' (puzzle strip) (5 pages b/w)

1974

IPC

Tiger: 5 January to 5 October issues: *The Tigers*: untitled stories (2 pages per issue, line and wash)

Whizzer and Chips: 29 June to 21 December issues: *Danny Drew's Dialling Man*: untitled stories (2 pages per issue, line and blue overlay)

Battle Picture Library: No 789: 'Only a Number' (back-up to *Opposite Sides*) (8 pages b/w) (February) / No 869: 'Combined Operation' (back-up to *Broken Jinx*) (8 pages b/w) (December) / No 871: 'Driving Force' (back-up to *Sixth Sense*) (8 pages b/w) (December)

War Picture Library: No 1018: 'A Debt Repaid' (back-up to *False Start*) (8 pages b/w) (December)

Cor!! Summer Special: *Young Macdonald & His Farm*: untitled story (8 pages, line and wash)

Knockout Annual 1975: 'Jim Smiley versus The Brothers Grimm' (8 pages, line and orange overlay)

Scorcher Annual 1975: 'The Substitute' (4 spot illustration, line and wash)

Shiver and Shake Annual 1975: 'Eagle Eye' (8 pages, line and wash) / 'The Phantom Piper' (8 pages, line and wash)

Tiger Annual 1975: *The Tigers*: untitled story (6 pages, line and wash)

Whoopee! Holiday Special: *The Space Accident* (untitled story) (13 pages b/w)

Whoopee! Annual 1975: 'The Lone Ranger' (6 pages, line and wash)

Whizzer and Chips Annual 1975: *Archie's Angels*: untitled story (6 pages, line and wash)

1975

Byblos Productions

Junior Quizzer: 'Dice with Death' (2 pages, line with red overlay, and half-page b/w)

IPC

Whizzer and Chips: 18 January to 27 December issues: *Danny Drew's Dialling Man*: untitled stories (2 pages per issue, line and blue overlay)

Battle Picture Library: No 875: 'Close-Up' (back-up to *Shoulder to Shoulder*) (8 pages b/w) (January) / No 876 'Flying Visit' (back-up to *Four of a Kind*) (8 pages b/w) (January) / No 886: 'Death's Head' (back-up to *A Deadly Sting*) (8 pages b/w) (February) / No 893: 'The Fuehrer' (back-up to *Who Dares Wins*) (8 pages b/w) (March) / No 896: 'Armed Raider' (back-up to *Fight With Honour*) (8 pages b/w) (March) / No 950: 'The Phoenix' (back-up to *Tide of Conquest*) (8 pages b/w) (April)

War Picture Library: No 1038: 'A Good Friend' (back-up to *Codeword – Jupiter*) (8 pages b/w) (February) / No 1047: 'The Prisoner' (back-up to *Blood Feud*) (8 pages b/w) (March) / No 1147: *Walk Tall* (64 pages b/w) (December)

Top Secret Picture Library: No 25: *Secret Enemy* (64 pages b/w) (April)

Whoopee! Holiday Special: *Wonder-Car* (reprinted from *Whizzer and Chips*) (9 pages b/w) *

Scorcher Holiday Special: *Billy's Boots* (6 pages b/w)

Scorcher Annual 1976: *Billy's Boots* (8 pages, line and wash)

Tiger Annual 1976: *The Tigers* (6 pages, line and wash)

1976

IPC

Whizzer and Chips: 3 January to 22 May issues: *Danny Drew's Dialling Man*: untitled stories (2 pages per issue, line and blue overlay)

Monster Fun: Nos 63-73: 'March of the Mighty Ones': (2 pages per issue, b/w) (21 August to 30 October) / Nos 65-68: 'Land of the Monsters' (wall chart with centrespread cut-outs) (line and colour overlay) (4 September to 25 September)

Battle Picture Library: No 987: 'The Mutineers' (back-up to *Final Objective*) (8 pages b/w) (March) / No 1002: 'Larkin's Luck' (back-up to *Rough Justice*) (8 pages b/w) (May) / No 1041: *Theirs the Glory* (64 pages b/w) (October)

War Picture Library: No 1166: 'No Mercy' (back-up to *Teeth of the Shark*) (8 pages b/w) (January) / No 1196: 'Living Target' (back-up to *The Blood of Heroes*) (8 pages b/w) (April) / No 1206: *No Hiding Place* (64 pages b/w) (May) / No 1208: 'Strange Allies' (back-up to *Murder Mission*) (8 pages b/w) (May) / No 1209: 'Flint Hard' (back-up to *Brink of Danger*) (8 pages b/w) (May) / No 1211: 'Fog of War' (back-up to *The Jungle Has Eyes*) (8 pages b/w) / No 1218: *Hell's Gates* (64 pages b/w) (June) / No 1231: *Gunfire* (64 pages b/w) (July) / No 1243: *Fighting Retreat* (64 pages b/w) (August) / No 1291: *Regan's Revenge* (64 pages b/w) (December)

Whizzer and Chips Holiday Special: *Danny Drew's Dialling Man* (5 pages, line and wash)

Scorcher Holiday Special: *Billy's Boots* (4 pages b/w)

Scorcher Annual 1977: *Billy's Boots* (8 pages, line and wash)

Vulcan Annual 1977: *Billy's Boots* (7 pages b/w)

Whoopee Annual 1977: *Wonder-Car* (7 pages b/w)

Whizzer and Chips Annual 1977: *Danny Drew's Dialling Man* (8 pages, line and wash)

Harlem Heroes: sample page for *2000 AD* (b/w)

1977

War Picture Library: No 1338: *Appointment with the Devil* (64 pages b/w) (April) / No 1362: *Hellfire Hill* (64 pages b/w) (June) / No 1399: *The Last Judgement* (64 pages b/w) (September)

Whizzer and Chips: 22 January to 5 February issues: *Thingamajig* (2 pages per issue, b/w)

2000 AD: No 9: *Judge Dredd*: 'The Robot Wars' (5 pages b/w) (23 April) / No 11: *Judge Dredd*: 'The Robot Wars' (4 pages b/w, and 1 page line and colour overlay) (7 May) / No 13: *Judge Dredd*: 'The Robot Wars' (4½ pages b/w) (21 May) / No 16: *Judge Dredd*: 'The Robot Wars' (4 pages b/w, and 1 page line and colour overlay) (11 June) / No 21: *Judge Dredd*: 'The Solar Sniper' (4 pages b/w, and 1 page line and colour overlay) (16 July) / No 29: *Tharg's Future Shocks*: 'Just like Home!' (3 pages b/w) (10 September) / No 30: *Tharg's Future Shocks*: untitled story (2½ pages, b/w) (17 September)

Action: 17 September to 12 November issues: *The Spinball Slaves*: 'The Black Gladiators' (for 17 September issue: line with colour overlay cover, and 3 pages b/w; for other issues: 4 pages per issue b/w)

Battle-Action: 19 November to 31 December issues: *The Spinball Wars*: 'Tower of Doom' (4 pages per issue, b/w)

Buster/Monster Fun Holiday Special: *Pete's Pocket Army* (4 pages b/w)

Scorcher Holiday Special: *Billy's Boots* (4 pages b/w)

Whizzer and Chips Holiday Special: 'Whizz' Wheels (4 pages, line and wash) / *Thingamajig* (6 pages, line and wash)

Cor!! Annual 1978: *Super Spook* (9 pages b/w)

Knockout Annual 1978: *Junior Detective*: three untitled stories (first story: 3 pages, line and blue overlay; second story: 3 pages, line and red overlay; third story: 4 pages, line and red overlay)

Scorcher Annual 1978: *Billy's Boots* (6 pages, line and wash)

Shiver and Shake Annual 1978: 'Revolt of the Robomen' (6 pages, line and blue overlay)

Whizzer and Chips Annual 1978: *Danny Drew's Dialling Man* (6 pages, line and blue overlay)

Whoopee! Annual 1978: 'The Missile Mystery' (adapting unused 31-page *Joe 90* dot-to-dot artwork) (8 pages b/w)

World Distributors

Terry Nation's Dalek Annual 1978: 'Rogue Planet' (newly-titled reprint of pages from 1966 *TV Century 21* strip *The Daleks*) (11 pages colour)

1978

IPC

Battle Picture Library: No 1161: *The Screw Guns* (64 pages b/w) (January)

Battle-Action: 7 January issue: *The Spinball Wars*: 'Tower of Doom' (cont) (4 pages b/w) / 21 January to 18 March issues: *The Spinball Wars*: 'Death Squad' (4 pages per issue, b/w) / 25 March to 20 May issues: *The Spinball Wars*: 'Duel of the Dictators' (4 pages per issue, b/w) / 27 May to 10 June issues: *The Spinball Wars*: 'The Mole' (3 pages per issue, b/w) / 17 June to 8 July issues: *The Spinball Wars*: 'The War Monger' (4 pages per issue, b/w) / 15 July to 26 August issues: *The Spinball Wars*: 'Revenge of the Mutants' (4 pages per issue, b/w) / 9 September to 30 September issues: *The Spinball Wars*: 'Assassin' (4 pages per issue, b/w) / 7 October to 25 November issues: *The Spinball Wars*: 'The Megathon Menace' (4 pages per issue, b/w) / 9 December to 23 December issues: *The Spinball Wars*: 'The Hostage' (3½ pages per issue, b/w)

Whizzer and Chips Annual 1979: 'Whiz' Wheels (8 pages, line and red overlay)

Whoopee! Annual 1979: 'The Mountain Menace' (dot to dot) (6 pages b/w)

Cheeky: 12 August to 16 September issues: *Archie's Angels*: untitled stories (reprinted from *Whizzer and Chips*) (3 pages per issue, b/w)

2000 AD Sci-Fi Special: *Rick Random and the SOS from Space* (resized reprint from Super Detective Library) 6 pages b/w

1979

IPC

Battle-Action: 6 January to 17 March issues: *The Spinball Wars*: 'The Agron Plague' (3 pages per issue, b/w) / 24 March to 26 May issues: *The Spinball Wars*: title unknown (3 pages per issue, b/w) / 2 June to 16 June issues: *The Spinball Wars*: 'Desert Hijack' (3 pages per issue, b/w) / 23 June to 7 July issues: *The Spinball Wars*: 'Peril from the Past' (3 pages per issue, b/w) / 14 July to 28 July issues: *The Spinball Wars*: 'Arena of Death' (3 pages per issue, b/w) / 4 August to 18 August issues: *The Spinball Wars*: 'The Zombie Master' (3 pages per issue, b/w) / 25 August to 8 September issues: *The Spinball Wars*: 'Meltdown' (3 pages per issue, b/w) / 15 September to 6 October issues: *The Spinball Wars*: 'The Island' (3 pages per issue, b/w) / 13 October to 3 November issues: *The Spinball Wars*: 'Town of Terror' (3 pages per issue, b/w) / 14 October issue: *The Spinball Wars*: 'The General Dies at Dawn' (line and colour overlay cover only) / 8 December issue: *The Spinball Wars*: 'The Challenge' (4 pages b/w)

2000 AD: Nos 113-117: *Rick Random*: *The Astral Assassin* (6 pages b/w) (19 May to 16 June)

1980

D C Thomson

Scoop: 27 December issue: *Stark*: untitled story (3 pages, line and wash)

IPC

Speed: 23 February to 16 August issues: *Journey to the Stars*: untitled stories (for 12 April, 10 May, 12 July and 9 August issues: colour cover, and 2 pages colour; for all other issues: 2 pages colour) / 23 August to 25 October issues: *Winner!*: untitled stories (for 6 September and 4 October issues: colour cover, and 2 pages colour; for all other issues: 2 pages, line and colour overlay) / 23 August issue: *Special Request*: 'Whittle – Jet Pioneer' (1 page, line and colour overlay) / 30 August issue: *Special Request*: 'Fangio – Grand Prix Ace' (1 page, line and colour overlay) / 6 September issue: *Special Request*: 'Twiss – Supersonic Test Pilot' (1 page, line and colour overlay) / 13 September issue: *Special Request*: 'Cobb – Land Speed King' (1 page, line and colour overlay) / 20 September issue: *Special Request*: 'Cockerell – Hover Power Genius' (1 page, line and colour overlay) / 27 September issue: *Special Request*: 'Gagarin – First Cosmonaut' (1 page, line and colour overlay) / 4 October issue: *Special Request*: 'Brian Jacks – King of Judo' (1 page, line and colour overlay) / 11 October issue: *Special Request*: 'El Cordobes – King of Bullfighters' (1 page b/w) (11 October) / 18 October issue: *Special Request*: 'Holland – Submarine

Pioneer' (1 page b/w) / 25 October issue: *Special Request*: 'Mitchell – Aircraft Designer Extraordinaire' (1 page, line and colour overlay) / 20 August issue: '£1,000,000 Challenge' (3 pages b/w)

Battle-Action: 12 July issue: 'Freedom Fighters' (4 pages b/w) / 19 July issue: 'Escape!' (4 pages b/w) / 20 September issue: 'Two-Man Force' (3 pages b/w) / 4 October issue: 'Runaway Bomber!' (3 pages b/w) / 29 November issue: 'Shotgun Slade' (3 pages b/w)

Action Annual 1981: *Spinball* (8 pages, line and colour overlay)

Knockout Annual 1981: 'The Speed Family in Space' (12 pages, line and blue overlay)

Speed Annual 1981: *Journey to the Stars* (4 spot illustrations, colour)

Cheeky Summer Special: 'Malice in Wonderland' (reprinted 1973 *Shiver and Shake* serial) (13 pages b/w) *

Space Picture Library Holiday Special: *The Vortex* (retitled reprint of *Rick Random* story *Kidnappers from Space* from *Super-Detective Library* No 44) (64 pages b/w) / *Power from Beyond* (reprint of *Jet-Ace Logan* story from *Thriller Picture Library* No 448, with 8 previously unpublished pages) (64 pages b/w) / *The Tenth Planet* (retitled reprint of *Rick Random* story *Mystery of the Moving Planet* from *Super-Detective Library* No 70) (64 pages b/w) (July) *

Battle Picture Library: No 1415: *Death Ride* (64 pages b/w) (October)

Shiver And Shake Annual 1981: *Robby Hood* (reprinted from *Whizzer and Chips* 1973) (18 pages, line and blue/yellow colour overlay) *

Monster Fun Annual 1981: *The Castaways* (resized and reprinted from *Whizzer and Chips*) (23 pages b/w) *

1981

D C Thomson

Scoop: 3 January to 14 March issues: *Stark*: untitled stories (3 pages per issue, line and wash) / 21 to 28 March issues: *The Losers*: untitled stories (3 pages per issue, line and wash)

IPC

Battle-Action: 21 February issue: *Train Raid* (3 pages b/w) / 28 March issue: *Ghosts!* (3 pages b/w) / 25 April issue: *Imposter!* (2½ pages b/w) / 2 May issue: *The Skeleton* (2½ pages b/w) / 6 June issue: *Grenadier Attack!* (2½ pages b/w) / 13 June issue: *Air-Raid* (2½ pages b/w) /

Above: a drawing of the pop group Bucks Fizz, produced by Turner in 1981 as a try-out – in the end unsuccessful – for the ITV comic *Look-In*.

18 July issue: *Red Dog* (2½ pages b/w) / 15 August issue: *Well of Death* (2½ pages b/w) / 29 August issue: *War Horse* (2½ pages b/w) / 19 September issue: *Flag of Treachery* (2½ pages b/w) / 31 October issue: *A Fighting Chance* (2½ pages b/w) / 14 November issue: *Medic Morgan* (2½ pages b/w)/ 12 December issue: *The Maze* (2½ pages b/w)

Battle-Action Holiday Special: *Charley's War* (4 pages b/w)

Speed Annual 1982: *Topps on Two Wheels* (8 pages, line and colour overlay)

Battle Picture Library: No 1487: *Yellow Peril* (64 pages b/w) (October)

Unpublished

Sample page for *Blake's 7 Magazine* (b/w)

Sample illustrations of Bucks Fizz for *Look-In* (line & wash)

Samples *Spiderman* pages for Marvel Comic: (2 pages, pencil only)

1982

Attack Picture Library Holiday Special: 'Grand Larceny' (8 pages b/w) (April)

War Picture Library: No 1950: *Cold Courage* (64 pages b/w) (September) / No 1962: *Fire Trap* (64 pages b/w) (November)

Battle Holiday Special: *The Fists of Jimmy Chang* (4 pages, line and wash)

Cor!! Holiday Special: *Young Macdonald & his Farm* (4 pages, line and wash) / *Young Macdonald & His Farm* (4 pages, line and wash) / 'If you Go Down to The Woods Today' (dot-to-dot colour centrespread)

Buster Book 1983: *The Leopard from Lime St.* (12 pages b/w)

Cheeky Annual 1983: 'Lee's Amazing Secret' (12 pages b/w)

Cor!! Annual 1983: *Young Macdonald & his Farm* (8 pages, line and orange overlay)

Eagle Annual 1983: *The Collector*: 'Tall Story' (5 pages, line and colour overlay)

Whoopee Annual 1983: 'The Cosmic Key!' (6 pages dot-to-dot b/w)

Polystyle

Thunderbirds Special: 'The Fire Trap' (reprint from 1971) (8 pages b/w, line and wash) * / 'Thunderbirds and the Space Pirates' (reprint from 1971) (8 pages, b/w line and wash) *

1983

IPC

War Picture Library: No 1974: *Tokyo Joe* (64 pages b/w) (January) / No 2010: *Jungle Ambush* (64 pages b/w) (July)

Battle Holiday Special: *The Hunters* (4 pages, line and wash)

BIBLIOGRAPHY

Above: two *Journey to the Stars* illustrations that Turner produced for the *Speed Annual 1981*. The top one had the title overlaid.

Buster Holiday Special: *The Leopard from Lime St* (5 pages, line and wash)

Cor!! Holiday Special: Young Macdonald & his Farm (5 pages, line and wash)

Eagle Holiday Special: *The Collector*: 'The Eyes of Harry Eden' (4 pages, line and wash)

Battle Annual 1984: *The Fists of Jimmy Chang* (5 pages b/w)

Buster Book 1984: *The Leopard from Lime St* (12 pages, line & wash)

Cor!! Annual 1984: Young Macdonald & his Farm (6 pages, line and orange overlay)

Eagle Annual 1984: *The Collector*: 'Yellow Fever' (4 pages, line and wash)

Shiver and Shake Annual 1984: *Toby's Timepiece* (5 pages, line and wash)

Whoopee! Annual 1984: 'Captain Neptune's Secret' (6 pages dot-to-dot b/w)

Eagle: No 84: *Amstor Computer*: 'Second Time Lucky' (3 pages b/w) (29 October) / No 92: *Amstor Computer*: 'A Modern Christmas ...' (3 pages b/w) (24 December)

Battle: 16 July issue: Mini-Book No 1 (supplement): *Action Force*: 'Ironblood's Revenge!' (6 pages, line and colour overlay) / 10 September issue: Mini-Book No 5 (supplement): *Action Force*: Space Battle (cover, and 6 pages, line and colour overlay)

Battle Action Force: 3 December to 31 December issues: *Action Force*: 'Codename – Sky Raider' (4 pages per issue, b/w)

1984

Cosmos

The Slitherers by John Russell Fearn (front and back covers b/w)

IPC

Battle Picture Library: No 1655: *Bulldog Courage* (64 pages b/w) (February)

War Picture Library: No 2056: *Pirate Guns* (64 pages b/w) (March) / Unpublished: *Whiplash* (12 pages b/w)

Battle Action Force: 7 January issue: *Action Force*: 'Codename – Sky Raider' (cont) (4 pages b/w) / 28 January issue: *Action Force*: 'The Bull' (3 pages b/w) / 24 March to 21 April issues: *Action Force*: 'Sea Fury' (for 24 March issue: cover, and 2 pages line and colour overlay, and 2 pages b/w; for all other issues: 2 pages line and colour overlay, and 2 pages b/w) / 30 June to 4 August issues: *Action Force*: 'Death Castle' (for 4 August issue: cover, and 2 pages line and colour overlay, and 2 pages b/w; for all other issues: 2 pages line and colour overlay, and 2 pages b/w)

Eagle: 21 July issue: *Amstor Computer*: 'Tomorrow's World' (3 pages b/w) / 4 August issue: *Amstor Computer*: 'Dead Reckoning' (3 pages b/w) / 22 December issue: ''Into Oblivion'' (1 page b/w)

Battle Action Force Holiday Special: *Johnny Red* (6 pages, line and wash)

Eagle Holiday Special: *The Collector*: 'Fool's Gold' (4 pages, line and wash) / *Crowe St Comp* (6 pages, line and wash)

Action Man Annual 1985: *Battle Honours*: 'Hunting Tigers' (2 pages, line and colour overlay) / *Battle Honours*: 'The Undefeated' (2 pages, line and colour overlay)

Battle Action Force Annual 1985: *Action Force*: 'Ambush!' (8 pages b/w)

Buster Book 1985: *The Leopard from Lime St* (12 pages b/w)

Eagle Annual 1985: *The Collector*: 'Samurai's Vengeance' (4 pages/line & wash)

Whoopee! Annual 1985: 'The Prehistoric Peril' (5 pages dot-to-dot b/w) / *Drew's Dialling Man* (6 pages, line and blue overlay)

Unpublished

Sample colour cover illustration for D C Thomson's *Starblazer*.

Private Commissions

Heroes Tableaux / Attack on Moonbase One (b/w originals)

Mining on Titan / Repairing a Space Station / View from a Starship / Futuristic City (2 versions) / (line and wash originals)

The Hand of Havoc (colour cover reproduction)

1985

Cosmos

JRF Presents: No 1: *Nick Hazard*: 'Mission to Vorga' (cover and 19 pages, all b/w) / No 2: *Nick Hazard*: 'Mission to Vorga' (cover and 19 pages, all b/w)

IPC

Eagle Holiday Special: *Dan Dare*: 'The Mighty Colossus' (6 pages, line & wash, and colour centrespread)

Cor!! Annual 1986: Young Macdonald & his Farm (6 pages/blue overlay)

Eagle Annual 1986: The Fists of Danny Pyke (7 pages, line and wash)

World International

A-Team Annual 1986: 'The Night the Face Turned Traitor' (6 pages colour)

Private Commissions

Annihilation! / The Inner Cosmos / Sinister Forces / Exit Life / The Genial Dinosaur / Scourge of the Atom / Black Bargain / Wealth of the Void / The Space Warp / Vanguard to Neptune / The Petrified Planet / Alien Virus / Renegade Star (colour cover reproductions)

Alien City / Attack on Titan / Forbidden Planet / Cataclysm (colour originals)

The Last Secret Weapon (2 illustrations b/w) / *Sargasso Sea of Space / Mining the Asteroids* (b/w originals)

The Shadow (line and wash original)

1986

Cosmos

JRF Presents: No 3: *Nick Hazard*: 'Mission to Vorga' (cover and 20 pages, all b/w)

IPC

Eagle Holiday Special: *Dan Dare*: 'The Man-Ape Mutants' (7 pages, line and wash, and colour centrespread)

Dan Dare Annual 1987: 'The Vargan Raiders' (8 pages, line and wash) / 'Last of the Thought Warriors' (8 pages, line and wash)

Eagle Annual 1987: 'Jamie' (5 pages, line and wash)

Judge Dredd: The Early Cases: No 1: 'The Robot Wars' (reprinted from *2000 AD*) (14½ pages, colour overlay) (February) * / No 2: 'The Robot Wars' (reprinted from *2000 AD*) (cover, and 5 pages, colour overlay) (March) * / No 3: 'Solar Sniper' (reprinted from *2000 AD*) (5 pages, colour overlay) (April) *

Private Commissions

Deadline to Pluto (colour cover reproduction)

City of Tomorrow (2 versions) / Dead Planet / Cities in Space / Wild World / Government City (Rick Random) / City of Domes (colour originals)

Rick Random: The Astral Assassin Part 6 (6 pages b/w)

1987

Cosmos

Climate Incorporated by John Russell Fearn (cover and interior illustration, all b/w)

A 1985 private commission painting by Turner, based on a classic poster for the movie *Forbidden Planet*.

Above: spectacular futuristic city scenes painted by Turner as private commissions in 1986.

BIBLIOGRAPHY

Private Commissions

Pleasure Planet / Science City (*Rick Random*) / Flyover Patrol / Sub-Marine Observatory / Space Sirens / The Red Baron (colour originals)

1988

Fleetway

The Best of Eagle Monthly: No 1: *Amstor Computer*: 'Second Time Lucky' (reprint from *Eagle*, 1983) (3 pages b/w) (1 May) * / No 4: *Amstor Computer*: 'Dead Reckoning' (reprinted from *Eagle*, 1984) (3 pages b/w) (8 October) *

Harrier

Nick Hazard: No 1: *Invaders from Time* (colour cover, and 33 pages b/w) / No 2: *Planet of Doom* (colour cover, and 28 pages b/w) (advertised but unpublished)

SF Classics: No 1: *Kalgan the Golden* (colour cover, and 24 pages b/w)

Quality Comics / Fleetway

No 25 (US): *2000 AD Showcase*: *Rick Random and the Riddle of the Astral Assassin* (reprinted from *2000 AD*, 1978) (11 pages, line with colour overlay) * / No 26 (US): *2000 AD Showcase*: *Rick Random and the Riddle of the Astral Assassin* (cont) (reprinted from *2000 AD*, 1978) (10 pages, line with colour overlay) * / No 27 (US): *2000 AD Showcase*: *Rick Random and the Riddle of the Astral Assassin* (cont) (reprinted from 2000 AD, 1978) (11 pages, line with colour overlay) * / No 15: *Time Twisters*: 'Just Like Home!' (reprinted from *2000 AD, Tharg's Future Shocks*, 1977) (2½ pages b/w) (November) *

Private Commissions

The Multi-Man / Eclipse Express (colour cover reproductions)

Atlantis (two versions) (full colour originals)

'No Greater Love' (8 pages b/w) / 'The Ghost Sun' (8 pages b/w)

1989

Marvel UK

Doctor Who Magazine: No 153: *The Daleks* (2 b/w illustrations – one new, one reprinted from *TV Century 21*)

Unpublished

Cyberman strip try-out for Marvel UK's *Doctor Who Magazine* (1 illustration b/w)

Private Commissions

The Frozen Limit / Thing of the Past (colour cover reproductions)

Worlds to Conquer / The Time Trap (colour cover originals)

Lunaport (*Rick Random*) / The Banquet (*Rick Random*) (colour illustration reproductions)

1990

Fleetway

The Best of Billy's Boots Holiday Special: Billy's Boots (reprint) (8 pages, with new colour added by publisher) *

Whitworth

The Comic Journal: 'The Ghost Sun' (8 pages b/w)

The Golden Amazon: 'Conquest of the Amazon' (cover and 60 pages, all in b/w)

Private Commissions

The Golden Amazon / The Last Martian / Across the Ages / Earth 2 / The Undersea Kingdom / The Interloper / The Red Insects (colour cover originals)

'Thoughts That Kill' (8 pages b/w)

1991

Eagle Society

Eagle Times: Spring issue: *Dan Dare* (1 page b/w)

Cosmos

Fantasy Booklet No 1: 'He Walked On Air' by John Russell Fearn (cover and 3 internal illustrations, all b/w) (March) / *Fantasy Booklet No 2*: 'Sorcerer' by Leslie J Johnson (cover and 2 internal illustrations, all b/w) (June)

Whitworth

The Comic Journal: 'Thoughts that Kill' (6 pages b/w)

Zardoz

Lord of Atlantis by John Russell Fearn (colour cover, and 1 illustration b/w)

Private Commissions

The Diemos Deadline / Scourge of the Carbon Belt (colour cover reproductions)

Black Wing of Mars / Born of Luna / Creature from the Black Lagoon / Ungawa! / Man in Duplicate / To the Ultimate / Liners of Time (colour cover originals)

'The Sword in the Snow' (20 pages b/w)

Illustrated invitation (commissioned by John Lawrence for his daughter's eighteenth birthday party)

1992

Fleetway

The Complete Judge Dredd: No 1: 'The Robot Wars' (reprinted from *2000 AD*, 1977) (15 pages b/w) (February) * / No 2: 'The Robot Wars' (cont) (reprinted from *2000 AD*, 1977) (10 pages b/w) (March) *

Zardoz

Paperback, Pulp and Comic Collector: No 6 (wraparound colour cover reproduction of 1953 *Laurie's Space Annual* frontispiece, and title lettering)

Private Commissions

Planet X1 / Captain Diamond and the Space Pirates / The Terror of Titan (colour cover reproductions)

Science Metropolis / The Dust Destroyer / Decreation / Here and Now / The Conquerors Voice / Dark Boundaries (colour cover originals)

'The World That Dissolved' (3 pages b/w)

1993

Clark

The Mentor: *Jet Ace Logan*: 'Terror from Moon 33' (6 pages b/w)

Cosmos

Viking Blood by James Harbottle (wraparound colour cover, and 3 illustrations b/w)

Below: the invitation specially commissioned from Turner by author John Lawrence, for his daughter's eighteenth birthday party.

Painted for Philip Harbottle in 1992, Turner's new cover for John Russell Fearn's 1955 magazine story 'Here and Now'.

Fleetway

Roy Of The Rovers Holiday Special: *Billy's Boots* (reprint) (6 pages, b/w and wash)

Private Commissions

Vargo Statten Science Fiction Magazine No 1 / *The Hell Fruit* / *Cosmic Exodus* / *The Wall* (colour cover reproductions)

Z Formations / *Slaves of Ijax* / *The Intelligence Gigantic* / *Other Eyes Watching* / *Alien Warrior* (colour cover originals)

'The Killing Zone' (7 pages b/w) / 'Lone Eagle' (3 pages b/w)

1994

Marvel UK

The Dalek Chronicles (colour wraparound cover, plus reprints of *The Daleks* strip from *TV Century 21*)

Whitworth

The Comic Journal: 'The World That Dissolved' (first publication of 1992 private commission) (3 pages b/w) *

Private Commissions

Fugitive of Time / *Wonders of the Spaceways* No 3 / *The Micro Men* / *The New Satellite* / *Futuristic Science Stories* No 7 / *The Sun Makers* / *The Black Avengers* (colour cover reproductions)

Skaro City / Dalek Control Centre / *The Trembling World* (colour originals)

Rick Random Spacecraft / *Scourge of the Carbon Belt* (b/w originals)

1995

Gryphon

Emperor of Mars by John Russell Fearn (colour cover, and 1 illustration b/w) (July)

Warrior of Mars by John Russell Fearn (colour cover, and 1 illustration b/w) (July)

Red Men of Mars by John Russell Fearn (colour cover, and 1 illustration b/w) (July)

Goddess of Mars by John Russell Fearn (colour cover, and 1 illustration b/w) (July)

Private Commissions

The Purple Wizard / *The Lie Destroyer* / *The Unseen Assassin* (colour cover reproductions)

Garth: 'Twilight World' / Daleks Airlift / Captives of the Daleks / Dalek Scouter / Liquid Death / Whatever Happened to Hammond? / *The Golden Amazon* (colour originals)

'Blonde Bombshell' (13 pages b/w)

1996

Gryphon

Pandora's Box by E C Tubb (colour cover, and 1 illustration b/w) (January)

The Golden Amazon by John Russell Fearn (colour cover, and 1 illustration b/w) (March)

Get Me Headquarters by Stephen Frances (March)

Saturn Patrol by E C Tubb (April)

Temple of Death by E C Tubb (colour cover, and 1 illustration b/w) (April)

Assignment New York by E C Tubb (September)

Hell Hath no Fury by Sydney J Bounds (September)

She Wanted a Guy by Norman Lazenby (October)

You Take the Rap by John Russell Fearn (October)

Aftermath by John Russell Fearn (November)

Private Commissions

Moons for Sale / *The Grand Illusion* / *The G-Bomb* / *Wealth of the Void* / *The Magnetic Brain* (colour cover reproductions)

Hardboiled / *Hell-Bent on Homicide* (colour cover originals)

First World War Dogfight (line and wash centrespread) / Second World War (line and wash centrespread)

1997

Cosmos

Fantasy Annual No 1: 'Time and Again' by E C Tubb (cover illustration b/w) / 'The Long Journey' by Sydney J Bounds (1 illustration b/w) / 'Ron Turner's War Years' (8 pages b/w) (April)

Gryphon

The Golden Amazon Returns by John Russell Fearn (March)

Murder Wears a Halo by Howard Browne (April)

The Return by E C Tubb (May)

Mitzi by Michael Avallone (June)

Kill and Desire by Stephen Frances (June)

Kidnapped by Morris Hershman (August)

Murder in Space by E C Tubb (August_

The Golden Amazon's Triumph by John Russell Fearn (November)

Panini

Doctor Who Magazine: Nos 249-254: *The Daleks*: 'Return of the Elders' (1 page per issue, colour) (cover-dated 12 March to 30 July)

Private Commissions

British Science Fiction Magazine No 12 / *Alien Virus* (colour repros)

Daleks – Invasion Earth / Dalek Attack / Martian Probe / Saturn Fireball / Seascape (colour originals)

1998

Beccon Publications

The Tall Adventurer – The Works of E C Tubb (colour cover, printed as two-tone) (August)

Cosmos

Fantasy Annual No 2: 'Mirror of the Night' by E C Tubb (b/w cover illustration) / 'The Silver Disc' by John Russell Fearn and Sydney J Bounds (1 illustration, b/w) / 'Meet the Author: Ron Turner' (8 pages b/w) (April)

Gryphon

The Gold of Akada by John Russell Fearn (January)

The Amazon's Diamond Quest by John Russell Fearn (January)

Anjani the Mighty by John Russell Fearn (February)

I Fight for Mars by E. C. Tubb (March)

Alien Life by E C Tubb (March)

The Fortress of Utopia by Jack Williamson (May)

The Amazon Strikes Again by John Russell Fearn (July)

Twin of the Amazon by John Russell Fearn (July)

Conquest of the Amazon by John Russell Fearn (August)

If You Have Tears by Howard Browne (September)

The Golden Amazon (includes *Nick Hazard*: *Planet of Doom*) (graphic novel reprint) (28 pages b/w) *

Woods

Phoenix: No 1: *Dan Dare* montage (1 page b/w)

Unpublished

If You Have Tears by Howard Browne (unused alternative colour cover)

Whiplash (completed work for unpublished War Picture Library title) (two colour cover variants, and 52 pages b/w)

Three-Masted Schooner (colour original)

Private Commissions

The Time Bridge (colour cover reproduction)

1999

Cosmos

Death God's Doom by E C Tubb (March) *

The Sleeping City by E C Tubb (June) *

Fantasy Annual No 3: 'Manton's World' by John Russell Fearn (December) *

Gryphon

The Whispering Gorilla by Don Wilcox (March)

The Wall by E C Tubb (April)

Earth Set Free by E C Tubb (April)

The Ruler of Fate / Xandulu by Jack Williamson (May)

The Slitherers by John Russell Fearn (June)

Lord of Atlantis by John Russell Fearn (August)

Triangle of Power by John Russell Fearn (August)

The Stone from the Green Star by Jack Williamson (September)

Panini

Doctor Who Magazine: No 276: *The Daleks*: 'Deadline to Doomsday' (unfinished strip story) (2 pages colour)

Woods

Phoenix: No 2: (cover illustration, b/w) *

2000

Cosmos / Wildside Press

The Extra Man by E C Tubb *

Invader on My Back by Philip E High (December) *

These Savage Futurians by Philip E High (December) *

Gryphon

The Amethyst City by John Russell Fearn (March) *

The Blue Spot / Entropy Reversed by Jack Williamson (May) *

The Gargoyle by Gary Lovisi (October)

2001

Cosmos / Wildside Press

Fantasy Annual No 4 (January) *

The Best of John Russell Fearn Vol 1 (April) *

The Best of John Russell Fearn Vol 2 (April) *

Fantasy Quarterly (April) *

Gryphon

Daughter of the Golden Amazon by John Russell Fearn (June) *

Quorne Returns by John Russell Fearn (June) *

The Central Intelligence by John Russell Fearn (August) *

2002

Cosmos / Wildside Press

Fantasy Adventures # 1 (January) *

The Best of Philip E High (January) *

The Space Born by E.C. Tubb (May) *

'Liquid Death' and Other Stories by John Russell Fearn (July) *

Fantasy Adventures # 2 (August) *

Gryphon

The Cosmic Crusaders by John Russell Fearn (December) *

Parasite Planet by John Russell Fearn (December) *

2003

Cosmos / Wildside Press

Stardeath by E C Tubb (February) *

Fantasy Adventures # 3 (May) *

Fantasy Annual 5 (May) *

Fantasy Adventures #4 (July) *

Fantasy Adventures #5 (July) *

Fantasy Adventures #6 (September) *

Fantasy Adventures #7 (December) *

The Best of Sydney J Bounds # 1 *

The Best of Sydney J Bounds #2 *

The Voice of the Conqueror by John Russell Fearn *

The Intelligence Gigantic by John Russell Fearn *

Liners of Time by John Russell Fearn *

Gryphon

A Thing of the Past by John Russell Fearn (January) *

The Genial Dinosaur by John Russell Fearn (January) *

World out of Step by John Russell Fearn (October) *

The Shadow People by John Russell Fearn (October) *

2004

Cosmos / Wildside Press

Fantasy Adventures # 8 *

Fantasy Adventures #11 (October) *

Step to the Stars by Philip E High (October) *

Gryphon

Kingpin Planet by John Russell Fearn (February) *

World in Reverse by John Russell Fearn (February) *

Dwellers in Darkness by John Russell Fearn (February) *

Dark Centauri by John Glasby (February) *

2005

Gryphon

World in Duplicate by John Russell Fearn (January) *

Lords of Creation by John Russell Fearn (January) *

Duel with Colossus by John Russell Fearn (January) *

Standstill Planet by John Russell Fearn (September) *

Ghostworld by John Russell Fearn (September) *

Earth Divided by John Russell Fearn (September) *

2006

Gryphon

Chameleon Planet by John Russell Fearn and Philip Harbottle *

The Golden Amazon of Venus by John Russell Fearn *

2007

Gryphon

Seetee Sun by John Glasby (May) *

The Crimson Peril by John Glasby (May) *

The Sun Movers by John Glasby (July) *

2008

Battered Silicon Dispatch Box

Eight Problems in Space by Arthur Porges *

Cosmos / Wildside Press

Fantasy Adventures # 13 (January) *

Prion

Rick Random – Space Detective (9 Super-Detective Library stories reprinted, b/w) *

BIBLIOGRAPHY

2011

Borgo / Wildside Press

1000 Year Voyage by John Russell Fearn *

What Happened to Hammond? by John Russell Fearn (May) *

The G-Bomb by John Russell Fearn (November) *

Space Warp by John Russell Fearn (November) *

2012

Borgo / Wildside Press

The Wonderful Day by E C Tubb (January) *

Star Haven by E.C. Tubb (May)

Fugitive of Time by John Russell Fearn (November) *

2013

Borgo / Wildside Press

Voice of the Conqueror by John Russell Fearn (January) *

The Gold of Akada by John Russell Fearn (January) *

Anjani The Mighty by John Russell Fearn (January) *

Legacy From Sirius by John Russell Fearn (January) *

A Thing of the Past by John Russell Fearn (January) *

The Genial Dinosaur by John Russell Fearn (January) *

World Beneath Ice by John Russell Fearn (January) *

Triangle of Power by John Russell Fearn (February) *

Quorne Returns by John Russell Fearn (February) *

World Without Chance by John Russell Fearn (March) *

Daughter of the Amazon by John Russell Fearn (May) *

The Amethyst City by John Russell Fearn (May) *

The Central Intelligence by John Russell Fearn (May) *

The Shadow People by John Russell Fearn (July) *

World Out of Step by John Russell Fearn (July) *

Kingpin Planet by John Russell Fearn (July) *

World in Reverse by John Russell Fearn (July) *

Only One Winner by E C Tubb (August) *

Dwellers in Darkness by John Russell Fearn (December) *

Lords of Creation by John Russell Fearn (December) *

2014

Borgo / Wildside Press

Fool's Paradise by John Russell Fearn (January) *

World in Duplicate by John Russell Fearn (January) *

The Master Must Die by John Russell Fearn (September) *

Before Earth Came by John Russell Fearn (October) *

2015

Borgo / Wildside Press

Glimpse by John Russell Fearn (January) *

The Lonely Astronomer by John Russell Fearn (February) *

The Red Insects by John Russell Fearn (March) *

The Intelligence Gigantic by John Russell Fearn (September) *

2016

Borgo / Wildside Press

The Dust Destroyer by John Russell Fearn (May) *

Liners of Time by John Russell Fearn (November) *

2017

Book Palace

Jet-Ace Logan (reprinting *Times 5* and *Power From Beyond* from Thriller Picture Library, b/w) *

Borgo / Wildside Press

Lord of Atlantis by John Russell Fearn (January) *

Parasite Planet by John Russell Fearn (April) *

Earth Divided by John Russell Fearn (July) *

Zagribud by John Russell Fearn (August) *

Gareth Kavanagh

Vworp Vworp! Vol 3: *The Daleks*: 'Deadline to Doomsday' (story completed by Lee Sullivan (1 page colour) (March) *

2020

Book Palace

John Steel Special Agent (four stories reprinted from Super-Detective Library, b/w) *

Panini

The Daleks (all instalments, reprinted from TV Century 21) (colour) *

2021

Book Palace

Rick Random (four stories reprinted from Super-Detective Library, b/w) *

Wildside Press

The Stellar Legion by E C Tubb (September) *

The Warbirds by E C Tubb (September) *

Stellar Assignment by E C Tubb (September) *

Menace From the Past by E C Tubb (September) *

The Hell Planet by E C Tubb (September) *

2022

Profondo Rosso (Italy)

L'uomo dei Due Mondi (*Man of Two Worlds*) by Vargo Statten (back cover, colour) (June) *

Wildside Press

Starslave by E C Tubb (February) *

Planetoid Disposals Ltd by E C Tubb (May) *

Fifty Days to Doom by E C Tubb (November) *

2023

Wildside Press

Seetee Sun by John Glasby (May) *

The Crimson Sun by John Glasby (May) *

The Sun Movers by John Glasby (May) *

Primordial World by John Glasby (May) *

2024

Profondo Rosso (Italy)

Universo In Fiamme (*The Cosmic Flame*) by Vargo Statten (back cover, colour) (January) *

Wildside Press

Here and Now by John Russell Fearn (October) *

1,000-Year Voyage by John Russell Fearn (October) *

2025

Wildside Press

Secret of the Towers by E C Tubb (January) *

Painted in 1992, Turner's new cover for the 1953 novel *Dark Boundaries*, written by John Russell Fearn as Paul Lorraine.

ENVOI
by Philip Harbottle

The passing of John Lawrence is a devastating loss, not only to his family, to whom he was devoted, but to the wider community of science-fiction and comics fans, in which I include myself. John was my staunch friend and colleague for four decades, during which time, working together to promote Ron Turner's fantastic art, we also managed to resurrect and sustain the careers and standing of authors John Russell Fearn and E C Tubb, many of whose books have been graced by Turner covers. And John himself, an indomitable champion for Ron Turner, succeeded magnificently in reviving and sustaining Turner's own career as a science-fiction artist.

The Fantastic Art of Ron Turner, John's wonderful biography (which no one else could have written), admirably captures the peerless talent and spirit of the artist. It also reveals John as his utterly tireless and dedicated friend.

I am privileged to have been asked by John to help steer this book, completed shortly before his death, to its eventual publication. It was the least I could do to repay my immense debt to him for his help in making many of my own dreams come true. It will surely be enjoyed by Turner's – and John's – legion of fans. Hopefully its publication will also drive John's hope – and my own – to maintain Turner's marvellous legacy well into the future. There is still a wealth of material that needs to be collected in permanent form.

Ron Turner's best artwork – that produced when he had time to complete it to his satisfaction – is uniformly brilliant, and has a dynamic quality, full of movement, with his trademark cinematic panoramas showcasing wonderful machines and cityscapes. No mere 'talking heads' where Turner strips were concerned! And his early endeavours showed that he was always experimenting, trying new techniques to improve his work. Turner was unique in that he could draw anything, and make it look authentic. His alien fauna and flora always appeared convincing, because he had an understanding of biology. His architecture was always impressive, too, and his futuristic machinery always had a 'designer' look and seemed as if it would actually function.

His work is up there with that of the likes of Chesley Bonestell, Frank Hampson, Burne Hogarth and Alex Raymond. All of their influences can be clearly seen, but Ron had his own unique technique of lineless shadow/shading that marked him out as a true original. His 'party piece' was his astonishing ability to show vast vistas and huge machinery with tiny, dot-like human figures moving amidst them. His true genius lay in his storyboarding, his cinematic layouts and his astonishing changes in perspective and viewpoint. He was above all else a superb illustrator, with a fantastic colour sense.

Turner told me that his own favourites amongst all his works were the covers he produced for the John Russell Fearn science-fiction novels, on which he brilliantly captured the sense of wonder in the stories. One of the smartest things I ever did, after commissioning him to recreate my favourite vintage 'Vargo Statten' and 'Volsted Gridban' covers, was to carry that forward and have him produce new paintings for every other science-fiction novel Fearn ever wrote, where he had not done so first time around!

Whenever John interviewed Turner, it was fascinating to read his analysis of his own work. He came across as a really deep thinker, almost an intellectual, but with an innate modesty and down-to-earth quality that was immensely likeable.

Philip Harbottle, Cosmos Literary Agency, 2025

ABOUT THE AUTHOR

John Lawrence (10 September 1944 – 13 August 2023)

John Frederick Lawrence was born on 10 September 1944 at the Luton and Dunstable hospital to parents Gladys and John, and was the eldest of three sons. He met his wife, Rita, in 1964 and they went on to marry on 9 September 1967. They have two daughters, Julie and Angie.

John lived in Dunstable all his life, attending Northfields school before studying bookbinding at the London School of Printing and Graphic Arts. He began his career at Waterlows printers and engravers, before going on to work at another printing firm, De La Rue, where he remained for the rest of his working life, until he retired at age 60.

In the mid-1980s, he became Ron Turner's agent, securing for him almost all of the commissions he undertook in the latter years of his life.

John was a kind-hearted, caring family man, with a great sense of humour. From a young age, he was into art and science fiction, and during his retirement was able to fulfil his passion for these, including through his collaborations with Turner and with his friend Philip Harbottle. He wrote articles and comic-strips, and published numerous collections of Turner's work, becoming well known for these within the science-fiction community.

When he first met Turner, greeting him with the phrase, 'Are you Ron Turner, the artist?', Turner replied, 'Oh, you're *the* John Lawrence, are you?'

John sadly passed away on 13 August 2023.

Below: the covers of some of the Ron Turner comic-strip collections self-published by author John Lawrence.

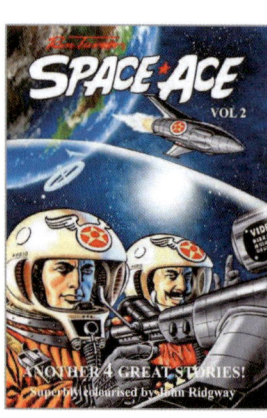

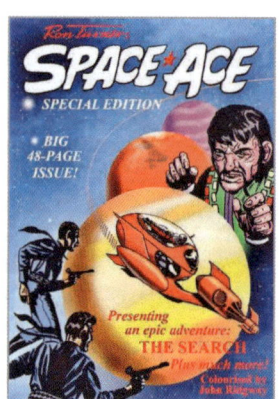

Printed in Dunstable, United Kingdom